Developmental Regionalism and Economic Transformation in Southern Africa

Interrogating the notion of developmental regionalism as applies to Southern Africa, this volume explores the policy options and interventions necessary to ensure a peaceful and stable regional development process.

With a focus on the Southern African Development Community (SADC), the contributions explore how regional institutions such as this can be drivers of developmental regionalism. Institutional architecture, along with key policy priorities, and implementation strategies in areas such as trade, industry, agriculture, private sector development and conflict management are analysed, and the ramifications of regional interventions for peace building and regional security in post-conflict Southern African countries are explored. Drawing on this analysis the book proffers key policy options and strategies for how developmental regionalism can be both consummated and sustained, ultimately driving economic transformation.

Illustrating to policymakers, scholars and development practitioners how regional institutions can be engines or facilitators of regional development, the book will be of interest to researchers in a broad range of areas including development studies, public policy and African studies.

Said Adejumobi is Director of the Strategy Planning, Oversight and Results Division of the United Nations Economic Commission for Africa (UNECA), Addis Ababa, Ethiopia, and formerly the Director of its Sub-Regional Office for Southern Africa, Lusaka, Zambia.

Cyril Obi is Director of the Africa Peacebuilding Network (APN) and Next Generation Social Sciences in Africa (Next Gen) programs of the Social Science Research Council (SSRC), New York, USA.

Routledge Studies in Peace, Conflict and Security in Africa
Edited by Cyril Obi
Social Science Research Council, New York, USA

The International Criminal Court and Peace Processes in Africa
Judicialising Peace
Line Engbo Gissel

The Unfinished Revolution in Nigeria's Niger Delta
Prospects for Socio-economic and Environmental Justice and Peace
Edited by Cyril Obi and Temitope B. Oriola

Developmental Regionalism and Economic Transformation in Southern Africa
Edited by Said Adejumobi and Cyril Obi

Developmental Regionalism and Economic Transformation in Southern Africa

Edited by
Said Adejumobi and Cyril Obi

Routledge
Taylor & Francis Group
LONDON AND NEW YORK

First published 2020
by Routledge
2 Park Square, Milton Park, Abingdon, Oxon OX14 4RN

and by Routledge
52 Vanderbilt Avenue, New York, NY 10017

Routledge is an imprint of the Taylor & Francis Group, an informa business

British Library Cataloguing-in-Publication Data
A catalogue record for this book is available from the British Library

Library of Congress Cataloging-in-Publication Data
A catalog record for this book has been requested

ISBN: 978-1-138-48387-3 (hbk)
ISBN: 978-1-351-05357-0 (ebk)

Typeset in Bembo
by Apex CoVantage, LLC

In Memory

Thandika Mkandawire (1940–2020)
Pan-African scholar
and rare intellectual asset

Contents

Illustrations

Tables

Figures

Boxes

Notes on contributors

Said Adejumobi (PhD) is currently Director of Strategic Planning, Oversight and Results Division of the United Nations Economic Commission for Africa (ECA), Addis Ababa, Ethiopia, and was formerly the Director of ECA Sub-Regional Office for Southern Africa, Lusaka, Zambia. Before that, he was also Director of the Governance and Public Administration Division at the ECA Headquarters in Addis Ababa, Ethiopia. He is a former university professor who taught for about two decades and won several academic awards and fellowships. These include post-doctoral fellowship, Social Science Research Council (SSRC) award; Norwegian Nobel Institute fellowship; and visiting scholar fellowship at Aalborg University, Denmark. He also served as Governance Adviser to the ECOWAS Commission, Abuja, Nigeria, before joining the UN. At the ECA, he coordinated the flagship *African Governance Report* (AGR), which is reputed to be the most comprehensive report on governance in Africa. He has researched and published extensively on issues of governance, democracy, citizenship, regional integration and development in Africa. He has edited/authored 11 books and contributed over 70 articles to international journals and as chapters in books. His recent edited books include *Voice and Power in Africa's Democracy: Institutions, Participation and Accountability* (New York and London: Routledge Publishers, 2018); *National Democratic Reforms in Africa: Changes and Challenges* (New York: Palgrave Macmillan, 2015), *Democratic Renewal in Africa: Trends and Discourses* (New York: Palgrave Macmillan, 2015), *State, Economy and Society in Post-Military Nigeria* (New York: Palgrave Macmillan, 2011) and *Governance and Democracy in Post-Military Nigeria: Changes and Challenges* (New York: Palgrave Macmillan, 2010). He serves on the editorial advisory board of several academic journals, including *Social Dynamics* and *African Journal of Democracy and Governance* and is currently the editor of the *Journal of African Transformation*.

Fantu Cheru (PhD) is Emeritus Professor of international relations, American University (Washington, DC) and a senior researcher at the African Studies Centre, Leiden University (The Netherlands). He was a research director at the Nordic Africa Institute in Uppsala, Sweden (2007–2012) and a member of UN Secretary-General Kofi Annan's Panel on Mobilizing International Support for the New Partnership for African Development. Professor Cheru's publication include *Oxford Handbook of the Ethiopian Economy* (with Chris Cramer and Arkebe Oqubay, 2018); *Agricultural Development and Food Security in Africa: The Impact of Chinese, Indian and Brazilian Investments* (2013); *Africa and International Relations in the 21st Century*,(with Scarlett Cornelissen and Timothy M. Shaw (2011); *The Rise of China and India in Africa* (2010). Dr. Cheru serves on the editorial board of several scholarly journals.

Annie Barbara Chikwanha (PhD) is Associate Professor at the Department of Political Science, University of Johannesburg, South Africa. Her broad research interests include democracy, governance, security sector governance, transitional justice and peace and conflict in the African region.

Peter Chikwekwete is an economist who has over 13 years of working experience in both the public and private sectors. His experience includes working as an economist and researcher at the Reserve Bank of Zimbabwe and lecturing at various universities. In 2015, Peter completed a one-year fellowship programme with the United Nations Economic Commission for Africa (UNECA), Southern Africa Office on issues of macroeconomic policy, regional integration, trade and development, data management, and governance, monitoring and tracking of economic and social conditions of member states in Southern Africa. Currently, Peter is working as a project manager for a research and consulting firm in South Africa whose vision is to provide solutions to socio-economic challenges which most developing countries are facing. Peter's research interests include trade, monetary and fiscal policy analysis, international trade policy, national and regional economic integration and policy analysis.

Brian Chisanga holds an MSc degree in agricultural economics. He has extensive research experience serving in various positions in Zambia and South Africa and has contributed to several publications. His main research area is the analysis of grain markets including maize, soya beans and wheat, focusing on trade policy, value chain analysis and market outlook. He has also previously researched the sugar and sugarcane industry in Zambia with emphasis on competitiveness, competition policy and farmer livelihoods.

Dauda Garuba (PhD) is a technical adviser to the executive secretary of the Nigeria Extractive Industries Transparency Initiative (NEITI) on Planning, Partnerships and Engagement under the DFID-funded Facility for Oil Sector Transformation (FOSTER 2) managed by the Oxford Policy Management (OPM). At NEITI, he also heads the Policy, Planning and Strategy Department. Prior to joining NEITI, Dauda was a pioneer as the Nigeria Programme Coordinator and Nigeria Officer at the Natural Resource Governance Institute headquartered in New York for nine years. Previously, he was Senior Program Officer on Governance, Security and Development at the Centre for Democracy and Development (CDD) where he coordinated the Peace and Security Programme for West Africa and represented the organization at the Africa Security Sector Network (ASSN). Dauda is widely published in local and international research outlets. He is co-editor of *ECOWAS and the Dynamics of Conflict and Peacebuilding* (CODESRIA, Dakar, 2011).

Zebulun Kreiter holds a Master of Arts degree in economics and is currently an Associate Economic Affairs Officer in the International Trade and Integration Division at the United Nations Economic Commission for Latin America and the Caribbean in Santiago, Chile. There, he works on trade policy issues with the aim to strengthen the region's participation in global trade and promote regional integration. Previously, he was an Associate Economic Affairs Officer at the United Nations Economic Commission for Africa, Southern Africa Office in Lusaka, Zambia, which he joined in 2014 as a member of the UN Secretariat's Young Professionals Programme. Prior to joining the UN, he worked in the private sector as an analytics consultant.

David Luke (PhD) is the coordinator of the African Trade Policy Centre at the United Nations Economic Commission for Africa. He is responsible for leading ECA's research, policy advisory services, training and capacity development on inclusive trade policies, in particular, boosting intra-African trade and the continental free trade area initiatives. His portfolio also includes WTO, EPAs, Brexit, AGOA, Africa's trade with emerging economies and trade and cross-cutting policy areas such as trade, industrialization and structural transformation, trade and gender, trade and public health and trade and climate change. Prior to joining ECA in 2014, he served as UNDP trade policy adviser in Southern Africa and Geneva and also as Senior Economist and Chief of Trade at the Organization for African Unity/African Union Commission, and as a post-doctoral fellow, assistant professor and associate professor at Dalhousie University in Halifax, Canada. He has published widely on trade and development issues.

Zodwa Mabuza is a trade and development economist currently working for the African Development Bank (AfDB) in the Regional Development and Regional Integration Department as Principal Regional Integration Officer. She holds a Master of Science degree in International Business from Lancaster University in the United Kingdom. Before joining the African Development Bank, Zodwa worked for COMESA Secretariat in Lusaka, Zambia, and was in charge of coordinating trade negotiations among the 29 member states of the Common Market for Eastern and Southern Africa (COMESA), East African Community (EAC) and the Southern African Development Community (SADC) within the context of the Tripartite Free Trade Area (TFTA) agreement. Prior to joining COMESA, she held various positions in Swaziland, including that of Chief Executive Officer for the Federation of Swaziland Employers and Chamber of Commerce, Strategic Planning Manager and Economist in the Government of Eswatini (Swaziland.)

André Mbata Mangu (PhD) is a research professor in the College of Law at the University of South Africa (UNISA), Pretoria. Professor Mangu has also taught at the University of Kinshasa (DR Congo), the University of the North, the University of Paris 13 and the University of Paris Sud (France). He is a member of the Executive Committee of the Council for the Development of Social Science Research in Africa (CODESRIA, Dakar, Senegal) and the Advisory Board of African Peacebuilding Network/Social Science Research Council (APN/SSRC, New York, US). He is the editor-in-chief of the *African Journal of Democracy and Governance* (AJDG; journals.co.za/content/journal/ajdg) and serves on the editorial boards of several other scientific journals. Professor Mangu is a pan-African constitutionalist and human rights law expert. His areas of expertise include constitutionalism, the rule of law, democracy, human rights, integration, migration, the fight against corruption and the law and practice of African Union Member States.

Mzwanele Mfunwa (PhD) is Economic Affairs Officer at the United Nations Economic Commission for Africa (UNECA), Sub-Regional Office for Southern Africa, Lusaka, Zambia. His research focuses on macroeconomic policy, private sector promotion, trade and economic governance.

Rhoda Mofya-Mukuka (PhD) is Senior Research Fellow and Head of Research on Agriculture, Food Security and Nutrition at the Indaba Agricultural Policy Research Institute (IAPRI), Zambia. She is a trained agricultural economist with more than 20 years of engagement in agriculture and rural development work in Zambia and in Southern Africa. Her current work includes analysis of agricultural policy and implications for agricultural growth, value chains, poverty reduction, food security and nutrition. She also serves as the Chairperson of Zambian Women in Agricultural Research and Development (ZaWARD).

Theresa Moyo (PhD) is a Professor at the Turfloop Graduate School of Leadership, University of Limpopo, South Africa. Since 2004, she has been lecturing on the Master of Development in Planning and Management Programme. Although she currently teaches research methodology and regional and local economic development, she has also taught development theory and practice and project planning and management for masters students. Professor Moyo also has ten years of experience lecturing about economics at the University of Zimbabwe, where she taught at both undergraduate and postgraduate levels. She has published mainly on issues of trade, industrialization and development, local economic development and gender and development. She has supervised many students at the master's level as well as a few PhD candidates.

Chrispin Mphuka (PhD) is the Head of the Department of Economics at the University of Zambia where he teaches econometrics and microeconomics. His current research interest is in applied microeconometrics with focus on small and medium enterprises in Africa and poverty.

Obrian Ndhlovu holds an MSc degree and is a lecturer in the Department of Economics at the University of Zambia. He has mainly been teaching quantitative courses and agricultural economics. His research interests encompass agricultural and economic development. He has co-authored two books, one on mathematics for economics and another on statistics. Before joining the University, Mr. Ndhlovu worked as a research officer at a local NGO Afya Mzuri.

Cyril Obi (PhD) is a programme director at the Social Science Research Council (SSRC), New York, US, and leads the African Peacebuilding Network (APN) and Next Generation Social Science in Africa programmes. He is also a Research Associate at the Department of Political Sciences, University of Pretoria.

Acknowledgements

Africa has adopted a regional strategy of development in which regional norms, standards, frameworks, protocols, conventions and treaties constitute the benchmark of socio-political conduct and the basis of accelerating economic growth, fast-tracking industrialisation and promoting sustainable development. The African Continental Free Trade Area (AfCFTA) is the latest of such regional initiatives aimed at creating a regional market, boosting production and breaking down barriers to trade, investments and business opportunities on the continent. It is a major step towards the realisation of an African Economic Community (AEC) as envisaged in the Abuja Treaty of 1991. But regionalism by itself cannot guarantee development especially of all the constituent units that make up the regional whole. Indeed, regionalism may accentuate poverty and inequality if not well consummated with clear focus, direction and strategic policies. The notion of developmental regionalism therefore fills the gap in ensuring that a regional integration project serves the fundamental objective of promoting even and accelerated development for all the member states involved. This book focuses on the attempt at promoting developmental regionalism in Southern Africa especially within the context of the Southern Africa Development Community (SADC) and the opportunities, challenges and policy options necessary for facilitating it. It also draws on comparative experiences from elsewhere in doing so.

The book interrogates the notion of developmental regionalism and its relevance to Southern Africa within the context of the SADC and reviews various sectoral agendas driving it. These include the areas of trade, monetary policy, industrialisation, agriculture, free movement of persons and goods and the ensuing xenophobia in some countries, women in the informal sector on cross-border trade and comparative experiences, especially from West Africa and the nascent BRICS experiment. The main conclusion is that developmental regionalism is never a finished project but one that requires continuous refinement, adjustment and reinvention anchored on strong institutional capacity of the regional organisation, in-ward looking strategy of development, greater domestic and regional financing and resource mobilisation mechanisms and a clear strategy of industrial growth and development. The principles of even development or at least complementary growth processes of all countries, and citizen inclusion in regional integration through the regional market and social space are core elements. Market expansion must be complemented by citizen mobility in the regional arena.

The chapters of this book include revised version of papers selected from a regional conference titled "*Developmental Regionalism, Peace and Economic Transformation in Southern Africa*" which took place in the Kingdom of Eswatini in September 2016, organised by the United Nations Economic Commission for Africa, Southern Africa Office and the African Peace Building Network of the Social Science Research Council (SSRC), New York, US, in collaboration with the SADC Secretariat. The Conference was hosted by the Government of the Kingdom of Eswatini. We would like to extend our sincere thanks and appreciation to the Government and people of the Kingdom of Eswatini for hosting the meeting and providing us a free and open environment for robust intellectual discussion on how regional institutions can be major catalysts of development in Southern Africa, and Africa in general. The Executive Secretary of SADC, Dr. Stergomena Lawrence-Tax also deserves our appreciation for her support of the meeting. We also thank the participants of the meeting, especially the discussants and reviewers of the papers, who provided insightful comments on improving the papers. To the chapter contributors, we are pleased that our collective efforts have finally borne fruit. The painstaking revision of the chapters based on reviewers' comments is highly commendable.

To colleagues at Routledge Publishers—Leanne Hinves, Leela Vathenen and Henry Strang—we are indeed very grateful for your patience and faith in us. Due to our very busy schedules, it took much longer than we had anticipated to submit the manuscript. Your cooperation and understanding are well appreciated.

As African leaders intensify their commitment towards regional integration, we hope this book will offer new perspectives, options and strategies on how developmental regionalism can be promoted necessary for building a stronger, more peaceful, prosperous and developed continent and, in particular, Southern Africa region.

Said Adejumobi and Cyril Obi
Lusaka and New York

Abbreviations

AAFC	Allied Armed Forces of the Community
ACP	African, Caribbean and Pacific
ACTESA	Alliance for Commodity Trade in Eastern and Southern Africa
AEC	African Economic Community
AfCFTA	African Continental Free Trade Area
AfDB	African Development Bank
AGOA	African Growth and Opportunity Act
AIDA	African Industrial Development Action
AMV	African Mining Vision
ANC	African National Congress
APEC	Asia-Pacific Economic Cooperation
APRM	Africa Peer Review Mechanism
ASEAN	Association of South East Asian Nations
ASM	Artisanal and Small-Scale Mining
ATPC	African Trade Policy Centre
AU	African Union
AUC	African Union Commission
AUC/PSD	African Union Commission Peace and Security Department
BDF	Botswana Defence Force
BRICS	Brazil, Russia, India, China and South Africa
CAADP	Comprehensive Africa Agriculture Development Programme
CCARDESA	Centre for Coordination of Agricultural Research and Development for Southern Africa
CCC	Community Computer Centre
CCCI	COMESA Climate Change Initiative
CCGB	Committee of the Central Bank Governors
CEDAW	Convention on the Elimination of All Forms of Discrimination Against Women
CEMAC	Central African Economic and Monetary Community
CEN-SAD	Community of Sahel Sub-Saharan States
CET	Common External Tariff

CFA	African Financial Community
CFTA	Continental Free Trade Area
CIP	Competitive Industrial Performance
CLEEN	Centre for Law Enforcement Education
CMA	Common Monetary Union
COMESA	Common Market for East and Southern Africa
CONCP	Conference on National Organisations in the Portuguese Colonies
CONSAS	Constellation of Southern African States
COSATU	Congress of South African Trade Unions
CPI	Consumer Price Index
CRA	Contingency Reserve Arrangement
CSOs	civil society organisations
CTPD	Centre for Trade Policy and Development
CU	customs union
DBSA	Development Bank of Southern Africa
DFID	Department for International Development
DoE	Department of Energy
DRC	Democratic Republic of the Congo
DTI	Department of Trade and Industry
EAC	East African Community
EAMU	East African Monetary Union
EBF	ECOWAS Business Forum
EBID	ECOWAS Bank for Investment and Development
ECCAS	Economic Community for Central African States
ECDPM	European Centre for Development Policy Management
ECOMOG	ECOWAS Monitoring Group
ECOWAP	ECOWAS Agricultural Policy
ECOWARN	ECOWAS Early Warning System
ECOWAS	Economic Community of West African States
EMCP	ECOWAS Monetary Cooperation Programme
EMU	European Monetary Union
EPAs	Economic Partnership Agreements
EPZs	Export Processing Zones
ESF	ECOWAS Standby Force
ETLS	ECOWAS Trade Liberalisation Scheme
EU	European Union
FANRPAN	Food, Agricultural and Natural Resources Policy Analysis
FDIs	Foreign Direct Investments
FLS	Frontline States
FNLA	National Front for the Liberation of Angola (Portuguese: Frente Nacional de Libertação de Angola)
FOCAC	China-Africa Forum
FRELIMO	The Mozambique Liberation Front
FTAs	Free Trade Agreements

FWACCI	Federation of West Africa Chambers of Commerce and Industry
GATT	General Agreement on Trade and Tariff
GCCASP	Gender, Climate Change and Agriculture Support Programme
GDI	Gender Development Index
GDP	Gross Domestic Product
GVCs	Global Value Chains
HSRC	Human Sciences Research Council
IAF	India-Africa Forum
IBSA	India, Brazil, South Africa
ICBT	Informal Cross Border Trading
ICT	Information Communication Technology
IDF	Industrial Development Forum
IDPF	Industrial Development Policy Framework
IDZs	Industrial Development Zones
IGAD	Intergovernmental Authority on Development
IMF	International Monetary Fund
IPAP	Industrial Policy Action Plan
ISID	Inclusive and Sustainable Industrial Development
MBGS	Mauritius Business Growth Scheme
MCAI	Multilateral Cooperation Agreement on Innovation
MDC	Maputo Development Corridor
MDC-T	Movement for Democratic Change—Tsvangirai
MIDP	Motor Industry Development Programme
MoU	memorandum of understanding
MPLA	People's Movement for the Liberation of Angola (Portuguese: Movimento Popular de Libertação de Angola
MPSU	Macroeconomic Performance Surveillance Unit
MU	monetary union
MSC	Mediation and Security Council
MVA	manufacturing value added
NAC	National Approval Committee
NAFTA	North American Free Trade Association
NANS	National Association of Nigerian Students
NEPAD	New Partnership for Africa's Development
NTBs	non-tariff barriers
OAU	Organisation of African Unity
OCA	Optimum Currency Areas
ODA	Official Development Assistance
OECD	Organisation for Economic Cooperation and Development
PAC	Pan-African Congress
PAIGC	The African Party for the Independence of Guinea and Cape Verde (Portuguese: Partido Africano para a Independência da Guiné e Cabo Verde)

PGN	practical gender needs
PPP	Purchasing Power Parity
PRSPs	Poverty Reduction Strategy Papers
RAP	Regional Agricultural Policy
R&D	research and development
RECs	regional economic communities
REIPP	Renewable Energy Independent Power Producer Scheme
ReNAPRI	Regional Network of Agricultural Policy Research
RESTRAP	Regional Strategy and Action Plan
RIDMP	Regional Infrastructure Development Master Plan
RISDP	Regional Indicative Strategic Development Plan
ROs	Regional Organisations
RoM	Republic of Mauritius
RTAs	regional trade agreements
RVCs	regional value chains
SACU	Southern African Customs Union
SADC	Southern Africa Development Community
SADCC	Southern Africa Development Coordination Conference
SADF	South African Defence Force
SAIIA	South Africa Institute for International Affairs
SAMP	Southern African Migration Programme
SAPs	structural adjustment programmes
SATCC	Southern Africa Transport and Communications Commission
SBC	SADC Business Council
SDGs	Sustainable Development Goals
SDI	Special Development Initiative
SDP	Spatial Development Programme
SGN	strategic gender needs
SIPO	Strategic Indicative Plan for the Organ
SIRESS	SADC Integrated Regional Electronic Settlement System
SIs	statutory instruments
SMEs	small and medium-sized enterprises
SSA	sub-Saharan Africa
STEM	science, technology, engineering and mathematics
STR	Simplified Trade Regime
SWANU	South West Africa National Union
SWAPO	South West Africa People's Organisation
TFTA	Tripartite Free Trade Area
TNCB	Trade Negotiation Capacity Building
TTNF	Tripartite Trade Negotiating Forum
UK	United Kingdom
UMA	Arab Maghreb Union
UNAMSIL	United Nations Mission in Sierra Leone
UNCTAD	United Nations Conference on Trade and Development

UNECA	United Nations Economic Commission for Africa
UNECOSOC	United Nations Economic and Social Council
UNESCO	United Nations Educational, Scientific and Cultural Organisation
UNHCR	United Nations High Commissioner for Refugees
UNIDO	United Nations Industrial Development Organisation
UNITA	Union for the Total Independence of Angola (Portuguese: União Nacional para a Independência Total de Angola)
UNMIL	United Nations Mission in Liberia
UNSC	United Nations Security Council
US	United States
USAID	United States Agency for International Development
VTE	vocational and technical education
WACIP	West African Common Industrial Policy
WACSOF	West Africa Civil Society Forum
WAEMU	West African Economic Monetary Union
WAGP	West Africa Gas Pipeline
WAHO	West Africa Health Organisation
WOA	world order approach
WTO	World Trade Organisation
ZANU	Zimbabwe African National Union
ZANU-PF	Zimbabwe African National Union-Patriotic Front
ZAPU	Zimbabwe African People's Union

1 A common history and shared future?

Southern Africa in the 21st century

Said Adejumobi

Introduction: *a common history?*

The history of Southern Africa, like that of the whole of the continent, is characterised by migration, settlements, intergroup relations and interactions, identity diffusion, conflicts and collaboration. In a sense therefore, it is a region with strong historical ties, yet with marked differences in terms of economic structures and stages of economic development in the modern state system. As Ndangwa Noyoo (2013: 100) rightly noted, Southern African countries "have a shared history as well as linguistic and cultural ties. Thus, it is not incidental that the present political economy of Southern Africa is linked to the historical trajectory of the area".

Early settlement in Southern Africa, especially of the San and Khoekhoe groups, saw the gradual emergence of pastoral and farming communities, which were complemented by migration from other parts of the continent especially Central Africa in creating new identity groups.[1] Issues of intergroup conflicts and conquests, trade, labour migration, and centralised colonial administration system fostered the growth of transboundary ethnic identities, which encouraged social cohesion and served as a foundation for regional cooperation and integration. For example, the Sotho speaking people criss-cross South Africa, Lesotho, Namibia and Zambia, while the vast majority of the Shona people can be found in Zimbabwe, but they are also present in South Africa, Botswana and Mozambique.[2]

The political economy of Southern Africa changed dramatically in the 19th century with the discovery of minerals and metals like gold, diamond and copper and the growth of large farms and plantation agriculture in the region. This had three profound effects. First, mineral sourcing and exploitation led to the inflow of capital from the West in the development of mines and in a sense facilitated the colonial enterprise in the region. Second, labour migration assumed a new but heightened phenomenon with labour flows from all parts of the region in search of employment. Wage labour, urbanisation and multiculturalism accompanied the process. Third, there was the growth of regional or transboundary infrastructure of roads, railways and the like to facilitate the export of minerals and goods across and beyond the region and transport labour as well. Kyu-Deug Hwang (2007: 56) captures this 19th-century trend in these telling terms:

> Since the discovery of diamonds (1867), and gold (1886) in South Africa, copper in Zambia, and coal in Zimbabwe, the regional setting of relations within and among nations have had a "long but infamous pedigree", even so much as to influence the current regional orders. Therefore, the present and the future scenario of regionalism in Southern Africa can be, to some extent, approached and understood in the context of the past.

The rise of intraregional labour migration and market facilitated greater cultural ties and identity diffusion in the region. Intraregional labour migration, as Jonathan Crush et al. (2005: 1) noted, was the "single most important factor tying together all of the various colonies and countries of the sub-continent into a single regional labour market during the twentieth century". The Kimberley diamond mines in South Africa attracted labour migrants from modern-day Lesotho, Zimbabwe and Mozambique, and the discovery of gold on the Witwatersrand brought a new dynamic to labour flows in the region during that period. Labour flows also tended towards countries like Zimbabwe, Namibia, Mauritius, Swaziland and Tanzania, where commercial agriculture and plantation farms existed. As Crush et al. (2005: 2) further noted, "by 1970, there were over 260,000 male labour migrants in the South African mines. Migrants came from as far north as Tanzania. Other mining centres in Zambia, Zimbabwe, Namibia and Tanzania also became magnets for labour migrants from other countries".

Colonial rule, in its efforts to rationalise administration, reduce cost, and ensure effective political control in Southern Africa, in some cases, opted for a transboundary governance system. For example, the federation of Nyasaland and Rhodesia consisting of present-day Malawi, Zambia and Zimbabwe was administered by the British through centralised administration from 1953–1963. This encouraged the free movement of people, goods and services amongst the three countries. Botswana, Lesotho and Swaziland were part of the British High Commission territories and shared many institutions that were run from South Africa, and Namibia was administered as part of South Africa after the end of World War I in 1918 (Mbuende, 2012: 41–42). As Kaire Mbuende rightly puts it, "the settler regimes created an environment that helped to solidify the affinities established among the peoples of the region" (Ibid: 42).

As such, transboundary human mobility, settlement and social acculturation produced accumulated social capital, while the construction of transboundary economic infrastructure of roads and railways, trade and the exchange of goods and services facilitated economic capital, all supportive of regional integration in the region. Hence, the incentive for economic cooperation was quite high. Thus, in 1910, the Southern Africa Customs Union (SACU) was negotiated including South Africa, Botswana, Lesotho and Swaziland to facilitate a meso-regional market and customs union in Southern Africa.

In this introductory chapter, we provide the historical context to the issue of regional integration in Southern Africa by mapping the socio-cultural affinities of the peoples of the region, their collective encounters in the struggle against colonial rule and the apartheid system, which further provided a bond of solidarity and a basis for regional cooperation and the metamorphosis of that process towards establishing regional integration arrangement. The chapter also captures the economic similarities and differences amongst countries of the region, which sometimes create tensions and contradictions for the regional integration project and the call for developmental regionalism that "leaves no nation or people" behind in the process and dividends of regional integration. Finally, the chapter previews the subsequent chapters of the book, outlining their main arguments and conclusions.

Cooperation through adversity: liberation struggles as a regional asset

The generic form of colonial rule, which manifested in settler colonialism and apartheid in Southern Africa, prompted an armed struggle approach to political liberation, unlike in many parts of the continent, where negotiated but peaceful political transition was the route to independence. Also, the fact that Southern Africa was relatively more developed than other parts of the continent with different stakes and interests in the region meant that the struggle for independence would be rough and tortuous. The liberation movements, in order to stabilise, grow and mobilise support, had to form both regional and international networks and solidarities. Thus, liberation movements developed organic solidarity across borders based on ideological, political and leadership linkages and provided support on logistical and tactical issues to each other. For example, as Timothy Shaw (1976: 11) noted, organisations like FRELIMO, MPLA and PAIGC were grouped in the Conference of National Organisations in the Portuguese Colonies (CONCP), while the ANC and ZAPU had military cooperation. Countries like Zambia and Tanzania also provided bases for military training, political shelter and diplomatic networking for many of the liberation movements in Southern Africa.

At the international level, countries like Cuba, the Soviet Union and China provided support largely based on ideological affinities, while the Scandinavian countries rooted in social democracy adopted a humanist and human rights approach in their support to the liberation movements. For example, the Soviet Union supported the ANC, MPLA, ZAPU, FRELIMO and SWAPO. While, China supported liberation movements like the PAC, FNLA/UNITA, ZANU, SWANU and FRELIMO (Shaw, 1976: 11).

But this is not to suggest that there was unity of purpose and collaboration amongst all liberation movements in national contexts. There were rivalries, tensions and contradictions in national jurisdictions. For example, the ANC and the PAC had their differences in South Africa in terms of approach, strategy and result, while the MPLA and UNITA were arch-enemies in the struggle for independence in Angola. The rivalries and differences continued after Angolan independence in 1975.

The highpoint of collaboration and collective solidarity amongst the liberation movements and Southern African countries generally in the struggle for independence was with the formation of the Frontline States (FLS) whose purpose was to ensure the total independence of the region. The signing of the Lusaka Manifesto of 1969 brought together a group of countries that came to be known as the "Frontline States" (Plaut et al., 1981: 44). At this point, Mozambique and Angola were still considered part of the Portuguese territory, Rhodesia was a British colony in rebellion, Namibia was still being firmly ruled from Pretoria and South Africa was in the clutches of apartheid in which the liberation movements had been driven underground (Plaut et al., 1981: 44). The expanding influence of apartheid in South Africa and its urge to subdue or even destabilise many of the countries in the region was a major rallying point in the formation of the FLS. By 1976, the members of the FLS were Angola, Botswana, Mozambique, Tanzania and Zambia, with Zimbabwe joining after independence in 1980. The FLS as Evans (1984: 5) noted, "represent a loose coalition bound by common perceptions and beliefs concerning regional liberation and Africanist ideology" and were committed to the liberation of Zimbabwe, Namibia and South Africa and protecting the newly independent states. The FLS was the subset of the OAU Liberation Committee in Southern Africa, which assumed the mantle of coordinating the struggle for political liberation in the region. The leadership of Julius Nyerere of both the OAU Liberation Committee and the FLS was central to ensuring cohesion, commitment and sacrifice in the work of the FLS. Nyerere displayed exemplary leadership and commitment in the work of the FLS. The flexibility of the organisation in terms of absence of a permanent Secretariat was also a major asset, which allowed meetings to be called at short notice and in different locations and prevented any form of attack or sabotage of its Secretariat by Pretoria. The approach to decisions by consensus also boded well for the group in which dissent or disagreements were not muzzled, but respected. Finally, the group did not discourage individual diplomatic initiatives or those that did not emerge from it as long as they supported the cause of political freedom in the region. Some of these included the 1982 Kaunda-Botha summit, the 1984 Lusaka Understanding and, most significantly, the Nkomati Accord of March 1984 (Evans, 1984: 5).

It was in the womb of the FLS that the Southern Africa Development Coordination Conference (SADCC) was born in 1980. Regional liberation cooperation served as a useful asset in promoting regional economic cooperation in Southern Africa. As Samora Machel observed, "the experience of unity and cohesion of the Frontline States in the political liberation struggle of the people should be extended to other majority ruled states and governments in Southern Africa in economic liberation" (cited in Plaut, 1981: 44).

However, there is a paradox in the urge for regional cooperation and integration in Southern Africa. Even the apartheid state desired regional cooperation and integration but for different reasons—to boost its sphere of influence and control, perpetuate dependence and thereby create acceptance and legitimacy for the apartheid system. The apartheid government initiated the "Constellation of Southern Africa States (CONSAS)" project in 1979, which was to provide regional security and economic cooperation in Southern Africa, beyond the market access opportunity that SACU provided. The regional bloc was to comprise between seven and ten states, including South Africa, the homeland "states" of Transkei, Bophuthatswana and Venda, Botswana, Lesotho and Swaziland, Malawi, Zimbabwe and possibly Mozambique (Evans, 1984: 2). The FLS vehemently opposed it, and to counter it, began preparatory work on the formation of the SADCC. The foreign ministers of the FLS met in Gaborone, Botswana, in May 1979 to examine the feasibility of and make a decision on the establishment of the SADCC. Another meeting was convened in July 1979 in Arusha, Tanzania, in which the Arusha Declaration was made reiterating the decision on the establishment of the organisation. However, it was not until 1 April 1980 when the Heads of State Summit of the FLS met in Lusaka, Zambia, that the organisation was formally established. The Lusaka Declaration was adopted with the theme "Southern Africa: Towards with Economic Liberation" with the objectives of promoting economic cooperation and development and reducing the dependence on apartheid South Africa by its member states.

Engineering regional integration: of the SADCC and SADC

The SADCC established in 1980 has been aptly described as "the epitome of the liberation based infrastructure for regionalism" (Khadiagala, 2012: 27). Its *modus operandi* was both economic and political—to forestall the Pretoria initiative of CONSAS, reduce the economic dependence on South Africa and mobilise the resources of member states for economic development through economic cooperation. The membership of the SADCC at its inception included nine countries: Angola, Botswana, Lesotho, Malawi, Mozambique, Swaziland, Tanzania, Zambia and Zimbabwe.

The SADCC was not a regional integration initiative; it was mainly an economic cooperation project, a step ahead of the FLS agenda. Mirrored in the light of FLS structure, the SADCC adopted an eclectic institutional arrangement with a lean Secretariat and the devolution of major cooperation facilitation to member states. It was a functional cooperation model of a sectoral approach in which each member state took the lead in a sectoral area and reports periodically on progress in conjunction with the Secretariat. As Chris Landsberg (2012: 63) noted, the "SADCC lacked a complex decision-making matrix or tapestry of structures and institutions. States gather together at regular intervals and decisions were taken and the Secretariat in Gaborone, Botswana was expected to help operationalise and coordinate such decisions".

In terms of sectoral responsibilities, Angola was in charge of energy coordination; Botswana, Secretariat, crop research and animal control; Lesotho, soil conservation and land utilisation; Malawi, fisheries, wildlife and forests; Mozambique, transport and communications; Swaziland, manpower; Tanzania, industrial development; Zambia, mining; and Zimbabwe, food security (Khadiagala, 2012: 30). This decentralised approach encouraged political commitment and active involvement by member states, but given the different capacities of member states, the results were uneven and the issue of policy harmonisation was virtually absent.

The SADCC had an eight-point programme of economic development. This included transport and communication, food security, agricultural research, industrial and energy cooperation, regional training facilities and regional development funds. The Southern Africa Transport and Communications Commission (SATCC) was established in Maputo, Mozambique, with emphasis on roads and ports infrastructure in order to reduce the dependence on South Africa on maritime and trans-border road network needs. The ports in Dar-es Salaam, Nacala, Beira and Maputo in Mozambique and Lobito and Benguela in Angola were given priority. No less than 95 projects were listed by the Commission costing about $1.9 billion.

The SADCC relied on and attracted heavy external funding for its projects and activities. In a sense, the infusion of external funding was a carry-over from the liberation efforts, in which partner nations saw in the SADCC a sort of a Marshall Plan to support the reconstruction and development of countries that were battered by long years of colonial rule, destabilisation and deprivation. By 1993, with the SADCC already replaced by the SADC, Kaire Mbuende (2012: 40) observed that there were no less than 464 projects which were mostly carry-overs from the SADCC requiring funding of $9 billion, mostly expected from external sources, and only 22 percent of those projects were truly regional.

As the region's geopolitical dynamics were altered from the 1990s—with the independence of Namibia in 1990 and the winding down of liberation struggles in South Africa with the release of Nelson Mandela and other political detainees and political negotiations in creating a democratic, non-racial South Africa in progress—it needed to shift its focus to a higher level of economic cooperation and accelerate the process of economic development through regional integration. In 1992, the Southern Africa Development Community (SADC) was established to replace the SADCC. The SADC has three major pillars—political cooperation, functional cooperation and market integration, and it fused both the goals of the FLS and SADCC into one. As Mbuende (2012: 42–43) poignantly puts it:

> The Southern Africa Development Coordination Conference (SADCC) of 1980 represented an agenda for economic cooperation, while the

> Frontline States of 1975 had a focus on political cooperation. The SADC Treaty brought this two elements of political and economic cooperation together under one roof, even though there had always been a dimension of political cooperation in the economic cooperation agenda, as well as economic cooperation within the political agenda. Yet, the short term objectives of both sides varied in terms of attaining certain economic and political goals.

The vision of the SADC, as earlier noted, is to create amongst all the "countries and peoples of Southern Africa, a vision of a shared future, a future within a regional community" (SADC, 1992: 5). The key objectives include to achieve development and economic growth, alleviate poverty, and enhance the standard of living and quality of life of the citizens of Southern Africa, and support the socially disadvantaged through regional integration; evolve common political values, systems and institutions; promote and defend peace and security; promote self-sustaining development on the basis of collective self-reliance; and achieve complementarity between national and regional strategies and programmes (SADC, 1992: 5). The strategy for the SADC in achieving this is to harmonise political and socio-economic policies and plans in deepening regional integration; develop policies aimed at the progressive elimination of obstacles to free movement of capital and labour, goods and services, and the people of the region, generally; improve economic management and performance through regional cooperation; secure international understanding, cooperation and support and mobilise the inflow of both public and private resources into the region (SADC, 1992: 6).

The two major anchors of the SADC's regional development agenda are the Regional Indicative Strategic Development Plan (RISDP) (2005–2015), adopted in 2003, and the Strategic Indicative Plan for the Organ on Politics, Defence and Security (SIPO). The former provides the strategic direction on socio-economic development and focus for all its programmes, activities, plans and initiatives in that respect, while the latter deals with the peace, security, human rights and governance issues of the SADC. The key priority areas of the RISDP include poverty eradication, trade and economic liberalisation, regional infrastructure and services development, sustainable food security, and social and human development, with cross-cutting issues of private sector development, gender equality and development, science and technology, HIV/AIDS, environment and sustainable development and statistics.

The SADC has developed elaborate plans and strategies through which it seeks to promote its sectoral priorities. This include the Industrial Development Policy Framework; the Industrialisation Strategy and Roadmap (2015–2063); the Regional Poverty Reduction Framework, 2008; the Regional Infrastructure Development Master Plan (RIDMP) of 2012; the Regional Agricultural Policy (RAP) and many others.

In terms of trade liberalisation, promoting intraregional trade and economic integration, the SADC, through the RISDP, set itself the goals of launching a free trade area by August 2008, a customs union by 2010, a common market in 2015, a monetary union in 2016, and a single currency in 2018. In the global economic arena, the SADC sought to achieve economic competitiveness by 2015 and diversification of production structure and exports by 2015. Regrettably, virtually all of these targets remain unmet. The deficits in this regard and in many other areas led to the revision of the RISDP, with an extension of five years—from 2015–2020 (Revised RISDP). The review of the RISDP in 2014, while noting that modest progress has been made in promoting intraregional trade, observed the constraints of weak productive capacity of member states, continuing trade barriers including non-tariff trade barriers, limited value addition and competitiveness. To address this, the issue of industrialisation was to take centre stage with modernisation of production, skills development, innovation, science and technology, financial deepening and the development of regional value chains. The new direction requires the mobilisation of state and non-state resources and capacity, both public and private, to unleash the productive potentials of the region.

In courting the private sector, the SADC Secretariat is facilitating the establishment of the SADC Business Council (SBC) through which it seeks to elicit the voices, views and inputs of the private sector in the regional integration project. It has also been working with the private sector in organising the *SADC Industrialization Week* on an annual basis.

One region, many shades

While Southern Africa is bound by common historical ties, cultural affinities and identities, and as it experiences the triple economic challenges of poverty, inequality, and unemployment, there are marked differences in the economic structures, sizes, capacities, and stages of economic development of its countries. In terms of demography, three countries—DRC (26.3 percent), South Africa (16.8 percent) and Tanzania (15.6 percent)—make up over 58 percent of the population of the SADC region in 2017. Countries like Seychelles (0.03 percent), Mauritius (0.4 percent), Botswana (0.7 percent), Lesotho (0.6 percent) and Eswatini (0.3 percent) combined make up less than 3 percent of the population of the SADC region. In terms of aggregate income levels, while Seychelles is ranked as a high-income country, South Africa, Botswana, Mauritius and Namibia are classified as upper-middle-income countries, and others like Angola, Lesotho, Eswatini and Zambia are ranked as lower-middle-income countries. The low-income countries of the region are Malawi, Democratic Republic of the Congo (DRC), Mozambique and Zimbabwe.

The economic performance of Southern African countries has also been quite uneven. While few countries like Tanzania have maintained a relatively stable GDP growth rate of about 6 percent on average since 2010, many have slumped in their growth trajectory. Table 1.1 depicts the trend.

South Africa is undoubtedly the regional hegemon in the economic equation of Southern Africa. South Africa constitutes about 55 percent of the

Table 1.1 Annual real GDP (at market price) growth rate in SADC (%) 2008–2017

SADC Member states	*2008*	*2009*	*2010*	*2011*	*2012*	*2013*	*2014*	*2015*	*2016*	*2017*
Angola	10.5	0.8	5.2	4.1	8.8	5.0	4.0	0.9	−2.6	−2.5
Botswana	6.2	−7.7	8.6	6.0	4.5	11.3	4.1	−1.7	4.3	2.4
DRC	6.2	2.9	7.1	6.9	13.4	2.4	7.2	7.7	2.4	3.7
Eswatini	0.8	1.6	3.8	2.2	4.7	6.4	1.9	0.4	1.4	1.9
Lesotho	6.7	2.2	6.2	7.0	5.9	2.2	2.3	5.6	3.3	2.7
Madagascar	7.1	−4.0	0.3	1.5	3.0	2.3	3.3	3.1	4.1	4.5
Malawi	7.8	7.5	6.8	3.5	2.1	6.3	6.2	3.3	2.7	5.1
Mauritius	5.4	3.3	4.4	4.1	3.5	3.4	3.7	3.6	3.8	3.8
Mozambique	6.9	6.4	6.7	7.1	7.2	7.1	7.4	6.6	3.8	3.7
Namibia	2.6	0.3	6.0	5.1	5.1	5.6	6.4	6.1	0.7	−0.8
Seychelles	−1.9	−0.2	6.5	4.0	3.7	6.0	4.5	4.9	4.5	6.3
South Africa	3.2	−1.5	3.0	3.3	2.2	2.5	1.8	1.3	0.6	1.3
Tanzania	5.6	5.4	6.4	7.9	5.1	7.3	7.0	7.0	7.0	7.1
Zambia	7.8	9.2	10.3	5.6	7.6	5.1	4.7	2.9	3.8	4.1
Zimbabwe	−2.8	12.6	12.6	15.4	14.8	5.5	2.1	1.7	0.6	0.8
SADC Total	5.1	0.2	4.3	4.2	4.7	3.9	3.4	2.3	1.1	1.4

Source: SADC, *SADC Selected Economic and Social Indicators, 2017*

region's GDP, down from 63 percent in 2010, which is followed by Angola with 13.6 percent, and countries like Lesotho and Seychelles with shares of regional GDP at 0.4 percent and 0.2 percent respectively (GIZ and SAIIA, 2014: 2). South Africa also dominates intraregional trade with regional exports at 68.1 percent followed by Angola with 8.5 percent, while countries like Lesotho, Madagascar, Malawi, Namibia, Seychelles and Swaziland each contribute less than 1 percent to intra-SADC exports (Ibid.: 22). South Africa also controls about 70 percent of intraregional investments. Hence, the South African government, as Saurombe Amos (2010: 126) noted, regards Southern Africa region as the most important priority of its foreign policy.

The structure of the economy in terms of the relative importance of sectors also differs across countries. The minerals and mining sector is dominant in countries like Angola and Botswana, and it contributes substantially to the GDP. But for countries like Malawi, Madagascar and Mozambique, the agricultural sector constitutes the mainstay of the economy, while in Seychelles, Mauritius and South Africa, the service sector is dominant. However, the region has seen a growing service sector, outperforming other sectors and contributing more to the GDP of the region. Agriculture has been on the decline, while the industrial sector is also witnessing a deceleration. Indeed, manufacturing's contribution to GDP has continued to shrink in the region, from 13.6 percent in 2007 to 10.6 percent in 2013, and down further to 10.9 percent in 2017, which suggests a trend towards deindustrialisation.

The SADC region has sought to revitalise industrialisation through the formulation of the SADC Industrialisation Strategy and Roadmap of 2015, and the "Action Plan" towards its implementation of 2017. The industrialisation

Table 1.2 Sectoral GDP shares in Southern Africa, 2000–2016 (%)

Sectors	*2000–2006*	*2007–2009*	*2010–2013*	*2014–2016*
Services	47.0	48.6	55.0	57.6
Industry	30.8	31.0	27.3	24.9
Agriculture	22.2	20.4	17.7	17.5

Source: African Development Bank, *Southern Africa Economic Outlook, 2018* (Abidjan: AfDB, 2018), p. 7

strategy sets very ambitious targets, which include a minimum of 7 percent GDP growth rate per year, to double the share of manufacturing value added in GDP to 30 percent by 2030 and to 40 percent by 2050 including the share of industry related services, and increase manufacturing exports to at least 50 percent of total exports by 2030 from less than 20 percent at present.[3] These goals, if achieved, will facilitate the economic transformation of Southern Africa. However, they remain largely unmet.

The SADC policy organs have been forward-looking and proactive on the industrialisation agenda by initiating policy conversation on the Fourth Industrial Revolution (FIR). A ministerial dialogue attended by ministers of education and training and science, technology and innovation from SADC member states was held in June 2018 in Durban, South Africa. The dialogue resolved that there is need to prioritise digitisation, innovation and technology in the industrial policies of member states, restructure the educational system to keep pace with the dynamics of a rapidly changing world, and promote the involvement of the private sector in digitisation. Again, the issue of the FIR was also one of the subjects of discussion at the Industrial Development Forum (IDF) of the SADC, which took place in Johannesburg, South Africa, in November 2018. Undoubtedly, the FIR will impact significantly on the mode and form of manufacturing and other related sectors as robotics and artificial intelligence will increasingly be deployed in the production of goods and services. Human labour will be increasingly challenged, and the pace and quality of production will change dramatically. As such, SADC countries have to grasp this dynamic and position the region very well in the global production value chain.

Southern Africa in its regional integration development project is confronted with several challenges: How does regional integration produce a win-win situation for all parties in the region in which there is no highly disproportionate gains and losses for member countries, small or big? In other words, how can the principle of even development be promoted through regional integration? How can the slow growth rate of the region accentuated by South Africa's sluggish economy which hovers between recession and less than 2 percent growth rate be addressed? The average growth rate of the SADC region in 2016 was 1.1 percent, and this increased marginally to 1.4 percent in 2017. This is a far cry from the 7 percent growth rate envisaged by SADC policy documents. The deceleration of manufacturing constitutes another major challenge. Although the service sector, especially the IT sector, has overtaken manufacturing as the leading wealth creator, the manufacturing sector remains the largest absorber of labour in the world. For countries saddled with high unemployment rates, the growth of the manufacturing sector is indispensable in the structural transformation of their economies. The triple challenges of high rates of poverty, inequality and unemployment, especially of the youth, that confronts the region can only be addressed if there is sustained growth of the economies and social policy that tackles the historical legacy of apartheid and settler colonial rule in the region.

The issue of regional identity premised on the free movement of persons remains a major challenge in Southern Africa. Regional citizenship that allows for the free movement of skills, and capacity with rights and obligations is essential for promoting developmental regionalism. Regrettably, xenophobia is an enduring part of the socio-political landscape in Southern Africa. Ultimately, regional development is not about economic artefacts, but people and citizens bound together by common hopes, aspirations and a vision of the future for the region. Xenophobia is antithetical to a regional development project.

The institutional and structural issues confronting the region includes what kind of regional integration do SADC member states want and what kind of institutional structure should be created to facilitate it. Are member states willing to cede some sovereignty and create a supranational institution in the SADC or just a regional cooperation architecture micromanaged by the member states? What kind of funding capacity do they want to give to it? How is the issue of overlapping membership in several regional economic communities to be handled—what is otherwise known as the "spaghetti bowl" challenge of regional integration in Africa? As Amos Saurombe (2009: 102) rightly observed, the multiplicity of regulations and duplication of procedures tend to create business uncertainties that hamper intraregional trade. How is the participation of the private sector, civil society and marginalised groups like women and youth to be enhanced in the regional integration agenda? And will regional integration be part and parcel of the national policy framework in member states, promoting commitment and adherence to regionally agreed principles, goals and policies?

This book engages the salient issues in promoting developmental regionalism in Southern Africa and comparative experiences from elsewhere. These include deconstructing the notion of developmental regionalism, its key elements and features especially as it relates to southern Africa, the issue of monetary union in the SADC region, its aspirations and prospects, creating an expanded free trade area through the Tripartite Free Trade Area (TFTA) agreement involving three regional economic communities, the SADC, COMESA and EAC, industrialization, agriculture and regional development, migration and xenophobia, gender and informal trade in the region, as well as the comparative experiences of ECOWAS and BRICS.

Summary of chapters

Chapter 2, "The theory and discourse of developmental regionalism", by Said Adejumobi and Zebulun Kreiter, interrogates the notion of developmental regionalism, its features and elements, and how it relates to the Southern Africa region. The notion of developmental regionalism provides an analytical tool for understanding and measuring the nature, quality and content of a regional integration project and its developmental possibilities and outcome. The chapter argues that the notion of developmental regionalism has witnessed twists and turns based on the changing dynamics of the global political economy and its dominant ideology. This has ranged from the structuralist to the neo-liberal orthodoxy and now to the post-neo-liberal era. Based on this, it provides a conceptual working definition of the concept of developmental regionalism that captures the development imperatives of a regional integration project, failure of which the project will wither away. The chapter reviews the benefits and arguments for developmental regionalism, its theoretical perspectives and identifies seven main features of developmental regionalism. These features may provide the parameters by which regional institutions may benchmark their progress and by which it promotes equitable regional development for the key institutional stakeholders involved in the integration project.

Chapter 3, "The Tripartite Free Trade Area and African Continental Free Trade Area: the case for consolidation", by David Luke and Zodwa Mabuza, discusses the two most ambitious attempts at creating free areas in Africa and perhaps in the world. These are the Tripartite Free Trade Area (TFTA) involving three regional economic communities—the SADC, COMESA and the EAC—with a population of 632 million and a combined GDP of US$1.3 trillion, and the African Continental Free Trade Area (AfCFTA) with a market of 1.2 billion people and a continental GDP of US$2.3 trillion. The former was signed in in June 2015 and the latter in March 2018. June 2015 marked two significant events in the economic integration of the African continent. The TFTA agreement, bringing together 26 member and partner states of the Common Market for Eastern and Southern Africa (COMESA), the East African Community (EAC) and the SADC, was signed by the Third Tripartite Summit on 10 June 2015 in the resort town of Sharm El Sheikh, Egypt. Five days after the signing of the TFTA, on 15 June 2015, the African Union (AU) Summit of Heads of State and Government launched negotiations for the Continental Free Trade Area (CFTA), subsequently renamed African Continental Free Trade Area, in Johannesburg, South Africa. These negotiations were to encompass 54 AU member states (this number became 55 after Morocco rejoined the AU in 2017) and it was launched and signed by 44 member states in March 2018 in Kigali, Rwanda. The chapter reviews the salient provisions in the TFTA and AfCFTA agreements and argues that quite a number of elements are duplicated in the two agreements and as such, a road map for an effective transition of all the FTAs on the continent into the AfCFTA is urgently required.

Chapter 4, "Monetary union in Southern Africa: is the SADC ready?", by Chrispin Mphuka, Mzwanele Mfunwa, Obrian Ndhlovu and Peter Chikwekwete, examines the feasibility of establishing a monetary union in the SADC region and the comparative experiences from elsewhere. Using macroeconomic data, the chapter runs some tests to ascertain whether SADC is ready for currency convertibility leading to a monetary union (MU). The SADC region has decided to move towards an MU after concluding that the net benefits of such a union will be positive and that this move will advance the continental economic integration agenda. However, the findings of the chapter indicate that an SADC MU is not feasible based on current timelines. First, the initial conditions supporting the MU do not exist. Second, the diverse nature of economies is such that the benefits and costs of an MU will not spread equitably among member states. The core-versus-periphery divide among the EU member countries is a telling example in this regard. Furthermore, the deep cleavage between the leadership utterances in support of the MU and the slow progress in the implementation of key protocols to advance the MU agenda points to deep political concerns about who will benefit and who will lose from such a union. The chapter counsels realism in moving forward, including setting more realistic timelines, striving to overcome the hurdles towards deeper intraregional trade and agreeing on economic targets and milestones that take into account the countries' state of development, affordability and capacity limitations. A revised MU agenda along these lines will be more politically suitable than is the case currently.

Chapter 5, "Industrialisation in Southern Africa: towards a developmental and strategic perspective", by Theresa Moyo, examines the priority strategies and actions that are necessary at both regional and country levels in order to achieve transformational, inclusive and sustainable industrialisation outcomes in Southern Africa. In line with the continental developmental agenda, industrialisation in Southern Africa is one of the priority issues which member states of the SADC are advancing. The SADC Industrialisation Strategy and Roadmap 2015–2063 is one of the indicators that the region is committed to that agenda. An action plan for the implementation of the roadmap has been developed and approved. Driven by concerns over low rates of economic growth, unemployment and poverty as well as the vulnerability of the region to external shocks, industrialisation is widely viewed as an important strategy which has a potential to achieve those developmental goals. Recognising that a lot of work has already been done in terms of developing the strategic framework for industrialisation, the chapter raises critical questions on how can the SADC's industrialisation process generate developmental outcomes? How can it accelerate the process of industrialization especially the promotion of manufacturing production and regional value chains in the region? What are the strategic priorities that should be focused upon? And how can the region's industrialisation agenda be a catalyst for its economic transformation?

Chapter 6, "Agriculture and developmental regionalism in Southern Africa", by Rhoda Mofya-Mukuka and Brian Chisanga, examines the contribution of agriculture to the promotion of developmental regionalism in Southern Africa, including its benefits and opportunities. The chapter also reviews regional policies and programmes aimed at developing the agricultural sector, their net results and outcomes. It also analyses whether agricultural development is in fact taking place in Southern Africa and identifies pathways for agricultural development in the SADC region. Agriculture contributes significantly to the economies of SADC member states. As such, enhanced trade in agricultural products potentially provides a tool for fighting poverty, promoting regional integration and increasing economic growth and welfare. Furthermore, agricultural exports are a major foreign exchange earner, contributing on average 13 percent to total export earnings. However, growth in the agricultural sector is constrained by low productivity in crops and livestock. Limited agricultural development entails a low production base in individual SADC countries that further limits the scope of developmental regionalism because essentially countries have inadequate outputs of commodities and lack the diversity necessary for trade and regionalism to flourish. Southern Africa has performed dismally in agricultural trade as shown by the low level of intraregional trade and deficit trade balance in agriculture. The Southern Africa region is a net importer of cereals and livestock products. Additionally agricultural trade in the region remains highly constrained by a number of factors such as low productivity, poor infrastructure, low investments in research and development and weak institutions, among others. As such, the region is performing far below its capacity and potentials in agricultural production. The chapter therefore makes key policy recommendations in upscaling agricultural productivity in the region.

Chapter 7, "Women in the informal sector in Southern Africa: towards a developmental perspective", by Annie Barbara Chikwanha examines women's economic encounters in cross-border trade, agriculture, artisanal mining and other sectors of economic life and the limited opportunities and inequity they experience in their daily lives. The questions posed by the chapter include, how can the region pursue developmental regionalism that is inclusive of women? Do COMESA and the SADC's poverty eradication strategies, trade and investment policies facilitate women's roles in the formal and informal sectors? Considering that informal traders and agriculturists are mostly women, are the region's overall development policies in these sectors gender sensitive and gender responsive? These questions can be answered partly by interrogating what is the current scope of regional integration in relation to women's needs and how can this be part of a coherent developmental regionalism agenda in Southern Africa. Overall, the entire African region possesses the institutional frameworks required for steering the shift towards a paradigm of developmental regionalism, but lacks clear strategies for implementation. The same can be said about initiatives to reduce the gender gap in all the countries; there are many provisions on gender parity yet most African countries struggle to translate these into action and empower women to contribute meaningfully to economic development. The chapter proffers key policy recommendations on how this issue can be addressed.

Chapter 8, "Immigration, xenophobia and developmental regionalism in Southern Africa: a South Africa case study", by André Mbata Mangu, reflects on the interface between immigration, xenophobia, and developmental regionalism in Southern African with a focus on South Africa, which is reportedly home to the largest number of migrants and where xenophobic sentiments appear to be stronger than in any other country in the region. It first revisits the concepts of regional integration and developmental regionalism. It then examines the Protocol on the Facilitation of Free Movement of Persons adopted by the Heads of State and Government of the SADC in 2005 as a legal framework to promote regional integration. Finally, it examines the myths or perceptions and realities of migration and xenophobia in South Africa. Regional integration, which requires the promotion of human rights such as the right to freedom of movement or establishment and is at the heart of developmental regionalism, is the primary aim of the African Union and its eight regional economic communities. It would be meaningless if it was not to achieve development as its ultimate objective. Unfortunately, regional integration has been moving at a slow pace and regionalism has so far gone without development in Africa in general, and in Southern Africa in particular. Among the main challenges confronting regional integration in Africa is the lack of a strong political will to promote freedom of movement and combat xenophobia, which is inimical to immigration since this hostility is directed at foreigners, whether voluntary or forced migrants like asylum seekers and refugees who are generally perceived as a danger or threat to the community rather than an asset, with opportunities of supporting the development of their host country. The chapter provides evidence that contrary to what its name presupposes, the SADC is still far from being a "community", let alone a "development community". It contends that the SADC would fail to achieve this objective of becoming an integrated region if the people cannot enjoy freedom of movement and are considered to be "foreigners" once they are outside their national borders in the region. Also, if countries continue to espouse anti-migration and xenophobic sentiments, then the objective of an integrated region will be elusive. More than a decade after its adoption, the SADC Protocol on the Facilitation of Free Movement has not as yet received the minimum number of ratifications required for it to come into operation. Regional integration or developmental regionalism requires all SADC member states to urgently ratify and implement the protocol on freedom of movement and enforce a zero tolerance policy on xenophobia. South Africa as a regional leader has an important role to play in the process of regional integration or developmental regionalism in Southern Africa and must not only accommodate but protect and encourage other regional citizens to live in the country.

Chapter 9, "ECOWAS's experience in developmental regionalism: a comparative perspective", by Dauda Garuba examines the comparative experience of ECOWAS in economic and political integration and its lessons for the SADC. The chapter argues that both institutions, though relatively different in their origin and evolution, have no less confronted similar challenges, which include that of peace and security, and also economic development. The challenge of conflict in Lesotho and DRC were litmus tests for the SADC, just like ECOWAS was confronted in the 1990s with the conflicts in Liberia and Sierra Leone and more recently in Mali and Côte d'Ivoire. While ECOWAS seems to have developed a very robust mechanism in handling those issues, and addressed the challenges of democracy and good governance in West Africa, especially issues around elections and political transition as demonstrated recently in The Gambia, the SADC has also performed fairly well in managing some of those conflicts in Southern Africa, although less successfully than ECOWAS. The two institutions have made very limited progress in terms of the economic development of their regions. The issues of meeting the economic convergence principles, creating regional value chains and promoting even economic development remains a mirage in the regional blocs. While ECOWAS has developed a very good inward looking funding formulae to run the organization through the community levy on all imports entering West Africa, the SADC is still not able to fund itself to a high degree and hence, a heavy reliance on donor funding to promote its activities. Institutional capacitation and self-reliant regional development cannot take place with a high dosage of external funding. A major lesson for the SADC therefore is about developing robust institutional structures and funding mechanisms for carrying out its activities and conducting its development agenda in a sustainable manner.

Chapter 10, "Harnessing south-south cooperation: a BRICS perspective on regional developmentalism", by Fantu Cheru reflects on the experience of BRICS countries in promoting south-south cooperation and facilitating developmental regionalism in Southern Africa. Over the past decade, African governments have scaled up their economic diplomacy towards the so-called BRICS countries in order to strengthen their economic ties and secure critical finance for regional infrastructure development. This is particularly true in Southern Africa where development corridors have been the centrepiece of the SADC. While BRICS countries can indeed play a role as a source of finance for regional development in infrastructure, this will all depend on the success of SADC member states individually and collectively in putting in place the necessary enabling policy conditions that will allow private flows from the BRICS countries. As BRICS countries move into the mainstream of international development cooperation, they are demanding the same policy conditions that the traditional Western donors impose in the conduct of international trade and investment. For Southern African countries to gain the most from their relationship with the BRICS, they must do their homework in order to negotiate from a position of strength. The chapter cautions against any misplaced optimism that the BRICS will be the catalyst for economic transformation in Southern Africa.

Chapter 11, "Towards sustainable developmental regionalism and peace in Southern Africa", by Cyril Obi provides a broad overview of the challenges of developmental regionalism and peace in Southern Africa. It offers a critical analysis of the complex dimensions of developmental regionalism and its connections to peacebuilding. This includes understanding how the nexus between state, politics and society has influenced evolving efforts towards regional development and its impact on peace. The chapter also identifies and engages in a critical examination of the major challenges facing the regional developmental project. This discussion of the challenges systematically identifies and critically examines the constraints confronting, as well as the opportunities presented by, developmental regionalism as a catalyst for economic and conflict transformation. In conclusion, the chapter underscores the importance of a heterodox approach to developmental regionalism where the states of the region need to reach a consensus on how best to pool their energies and resources as the most viable option for overcoming constraints and maximizing existing opportunities. It also draws upon some success stories and best practices within and outside Southern Africa. In addition, it notes that the prospects for success can be enhanced by a people-centred developmental regionalism and peacebuilding approach.

Concluding note

Southern Africa is a region with strong historical ties, cultural affinities and human migration, which provides a bond of organic solidarity and social capital and a good foundational base for promoting regional cooperation and integration. The liberation struggles cemented that relationship in fostering fraternal solidarity and camaraderie amongst the liberation movements in the region. It was in the womb of political struggles that economic cooperation and integration was conceived. However, as Kaire Mbuende (2012: 42), a former Executive Secretary of the SADC once noted, "history and geography are an advantage, but are not sufficient for the construction of a regional community. There must be favourable environment, but also political will and commitment to the project". The goal of regional integration in Southern Africa, more specifically, in promoting developmental regionalism—an agenda that facilitates inclusive spatial economic growth and benefit for all countries and peoples in the region and ensures sustainable development—has been quite challenging. Developmental regional economic integration, as James Hentz (2005: 24) noted, must promote greater regional interdependence and equitable regional development. The SADC, as the main regional economic community in Southern Africa, constitutes the major regional vehicle for transformation and socio-economic development in Southern Africa and, hence, is the primary focus of this book.

The 21st century provides new challenges and opportunities for the SADC and the region to reposition itself in the African and global landscape in maximising its developmental potentials and capacity. Rapid and sustained economic growth, economic diversification and structural change, increased production and enhanced intraregional trade, free and unhindered human mobility in the region, empowerment of women in both the economic and social spheres and addressing the triple but debilitating problems of poverty, inequality and unemployment (especially of the youth) are some of the critical challenges that the region has to face in the 21st century. This would require innovative and strategic thinking and informed policy choices in the region. This book offers some ideas, views and thoughts on how the goal of developmental regionalism can be achieved in Southern Africa.

Notes

1 For a narrative of the early settlements, see, McDonald, Jared, "Southern Africans and the Advent of Colonialism", in Adrian S. Wisnicki and Megan Ward, eds. *Southern Africans and the Advent of Colonialism, Livingstone Online*. www.livingstoneonline.org/life-and-times/southern-africans-and-the-advent-colonialism, accessed on 9 January 2019.
2 See, Owen Jarus, "Shona People: History and Culture", www.livescience.com/58039-shona-people.html accessed on 3 January 2019.
3 See, SADC, *SADC Industrialisation Strategy and Roadmap* (Gaborone: SADC, 2015a).

References

African Development Bank (2018), *Southern Africa Economic Outlook, 2018* (Abidjan: AfDB).
Crush, Jonathan, Williams, Vincent and Sally, Perberdy (September, 2005), "Migration in Southern Africa", *paper prepared for the Policy Analysis and Research Programme of the Global Commission on International Migration*, Switzerland.
Evans, Michael (1984), "The Frontline-States, South Africa and Southern African Security: Military Prospects and Perspectives", *Zambezia*, Vol. 5, No. 12, pp. 1–19.
GIZ and South African Institute of International Affairs (2014), *Regional Economic Integration in SADC: Current Status of Key Economic Indicators-Regional Trends*. Mimeo.
Hentz, James (2005), "South Africa and the Political Economy of Regional Economic Cooperation in Southern Africa", *Journal of Modern African Studies*, Vol. 43, No.1, pp. 21–51.
Hwang, Deug Kyu (2007), "The Historical Evolution of SADC(C) and Regionalism in Southern Africa", *International Area Review*, Vol. 10, No. 1, Spring, pp. 55–72.
Khadiagala, Gilbert (2012), "The SADCC and Its Approaches to African Regionalism", in Chris Saunders, Gwinyayi Ozinesa, and Dawn Nagar (Eds.), *Region-Building in Southern Africa: Progress, Problems and Prospects* (London and New York: Zed Books).
Landsberg, Chris (2012), "The Southern Africa Development Community Decision-Making Architecture", in Chris Saunders, Gwinyayi Dzinesa, and Dawn Nagar (Eds.), *Region-Building in Southern Africa: Progress, Problems and Prospects* (London and New York: Zed Books).
Mbuende Kaire (2012), "The SADC: Between Cooperation and Development: An Insider Perspective", in Chris Saunders, Gwinyayi Dzinesa, and Dawn Nagar (Eds.), *Region-Building in Southern Africa: Progress, Problems and Prospects* (London and New York: Zed Books).
Noyoo, Ndangwa (2013), "Bringing Social Cohesion into the Equation of Regional Integration: The Case of Southern Africa", *Regions and Cohesion*, Vol. 3, No.1, pp. 94–111.
Plaut, Martin, Unterhalter, Elaine and David Ward (1981), *The Struggle for Southern Africa: Can the Frontline States Escape Apartheid Stronghold?* (London: War and want and Liberation).
Saurombe, Amos (2009), "Regional Integration Agenda for SADC 'Caught in the Winds of Change': Problems and Prospects", *Journal of International Commercial Law and Technology*, Vol. 4, No. 2. pp. 100–106.

Saurombe, Amos (2010), "The Role of South Africa in the SADC Regional Integration: The Making or Breaking of an Organisation", *Journal of International Commercial Law and Technology*, Vol. 5, No. 3, pp. 124–131.

Shaw, Timothy (1976), "International Organisations and the Politics of Southern Africa: Towards Regional Integration or Liberation", *Journal of Southern African Studies*, Vol. 3, No. 1, pp. 1–19.

Southern Africa Development Community (SADC) (1992), *Declaration and Treaty* (Gaborone: SADC).

Southern Africa Development Community (SADC) (2003), *Regional Indicative Strategic Development Plan* (Gaborone: SADC).

Southern Africa Development Community (SADC) (2015a), *SADC Industrialisation Strategy and Roadmap* (Gaborone: SADC).

Southern Africa Development Community (SADC) (2015b), *SADC Revised Regional Indicative Strategic Development Plan, 2015–2020* (Gaborone: SADC).

Southern Africa Development Community (SADC) (2017), *SADC Selected Economic and Social Indicators, 2017*. Mimeo.

2 The theory and discourse of developmental regionalism

Said Adejumobi and Zebulun Kreiter

1. Introduction

The urge towards regional integration has assumed renewed momentum in Africa. Indeed, the vision of a united, integrated and prosperous continent as envisioned in Agenda 2063 and the African Union Strategic Plan suggest that African countries have opted for a regionalist approach towards economic transformation and development. For Africa, regionalism is not just a mere basis of interstate cooperation but a development strategy. This is true for the African Union (AU) as it is for all the regional economic communities (RECs). As Rok Ajulu (2008: 25) noted, "the continental experience is one of a continuous attempt to place regionalism at the centre of the transformative agenda". In his welcome remarks to the 36th session of the SADC Heads of State and Government Summit held in Swaziland on 30–31 August 2016, King Mswati III of the Kingdom of Swaziland noted:

> Regional integration is a goal we constantly discuss in our meetings and strive to meet through our numerous regional projects and programmes. It is expected that all these efforts should go towards enhancing development and economic growth of the SADC region which will include alleviation of poverty, improving health conditions, and uplifting the standard and quality of life of the people of Southern Africa.
>
> (*Southern Africa Times*, 26th August 2016, p. 1)

The issues of trade flows, capital and human mobility, and accelerated industrialisation are central to the developmental potentials of a regional integration project like the SADC. However, regionalism should not be taken for granted in terms of its developmental potentials and possibilities. The Brexit phenomenon that triggered the process of the exit of the United Kingdom from the European Union on 23 June 2016 through a national referendum clearly indicates that regionalism as a development strategy cannot be taken for granted. Regionalism must not only spur regional economic growth and relative even development for the member states but also ensure palpable benefits through the provision of regional public goods for the citizens of the region, which will invariably increase their sense of regional identity and commitment to the regional integration project. The EU which hitherto was a model of regional integration has been shaken to its very foundation by Brexit, questioning the essence and value of the EU project (Adejumobi, 2016). The important thing to note, however, is that regionalism is not an immutable project, and therefore is constantly a "work in progress". It can grow or decay, consolidate or regress depending on the circumstances, development impact and citizens' perception of their involvement in it. As Bjorn Hettne (2005: 548) rightly observed, since "regionalism is a political project, created by human actors, it may, just like a nation-state project, fail".

Efforts at regional integration in Southern Africa which started initially as essentially a form of defence and political cooperation mechanism through the Southern Africa Coordinating Conference (SADCC) in 1980 meant primarily to ward off the aggression of the apartheid regime, reduce economic dependence on it and facilitate political liberation for hitherto colonised countries in the region has since metamorphosed into a regional development project in the SADC[1] that seeks to promote economic development and transformation in Southern Africa. The revised Regional Indicative Strategic Development Plan (RISDP), the SADC Industrialisation Strategy and Roadmap 2015 and the SADC Infrastructure Master Plan are some of the main anchors for the economic transformation of the region by the SADC. However, there could be a wide gap between precepts and practices, formulated plans and actual implementation, which may leave a gaping hole in regional integration projects.

This chapter interrogates the notion of developmental regionalism, its features and elements and how such relate to the Southern Africa region. The chapter argues that the notion of developmental regionalism serves as the basic anchor and essence of regional institutions especially in developing countries, although its content and strategy have witnessed twists and turns based on the changing dynamics of the global political economy and its dominant ideology. This has ranged from the structuralist to the neo-liberal orthodoxy and now to the post-neo-liberal era. Essentially, how regional institutions will catalyse development in Africa in general, and in Southern Africa in particular, will depend on their developmental capacity, orientation, focus and drive.

2. Notion of developmental regionalism

Regionalism is a contested concept which has meant different things to different people, and approaches to studying it vary. It thus presents epistemological challenges on what it is and how it should be studied. However, its conceptualisation is central to the notion of developmental regionalism. Hettne (2005: 545) defines regionalism as "a tendency and a political commitment to organize the world in terms of regions; more narrowly, the concept refers to a specific regional project". Margaret Lee (2002) views regionalism as "efforts by a group of nations to enhance their economic, political, social and cultural interaction. Such efforts may take on different forms including regional cooperation, market integration, development integration, and regional integration". Anthony Payne and Andrew Gamble (1996: 2) argue that regionalism is a "state led or states-led project designed to reorganize a particular regional space along defined economic and political lines".

From a nuanced perspective, Christopher Dent and Peter Richter (2011: 31) contend that regionalism can be "understood as a multivariate process, involving various interrelated and multilevel economic, social, political and cultural factors". In a broad sense, it refers to the "structures, processes and arrangements that enhance greater coherence within a specific region in terms of economic, political, security, socio-cultural and other kinds of linkages". In creating taxonomy of regionalism, Hettne (2005: 548) makes a classification in terms of the level of development and hierarchy of regionness or regionalism. The five levels he identifies are a regional space, a trans-local social system, an international society, a regional community and a regionally institutionalised polity. In the hierarchy cadre, the three he identified are the core regions, the peripheral regions and, between them, the intermediate region. In hierarchy levels, the emphasis for him was on the relative position of the region or the states constituting it in the global development map. In terms of scale of the regional project, it is possible to identify three main types or levels of regionalism. These are the micro, meso and macro levels. "Growth triangles" for example like the Zambia-Malawi-Mozambique growth triangle or the Indonesia-Malaysia-Thailand growth triangle are meso forms of regionalism, while regional economic communities and continent-wide bodies are macro forms of regionalism.

Developmental regionalism can be viewed as an analytical tool for understanding the synergetic development processes and outcomes of regionalism. It underscores how regional integration institutions and initiatives promote collective development capacity and outcomes. Dent and Richter (2011: 34) put it succinctly:

> Developmental regionalism are those activities that are particularly oriented to enhancing the economic capacity and prospects of less developed countries with the view of strengthening their incorporation into the regional economy, and thereby bringing greater coherence to regional community building.

From a neo-liberal perspective, the United Nations Conference on Trade and Development (UNCTAD) Economic Development in Africa Report 2013, which looks at "Boosting Intra-African Trade in the Context of Developmental Regionalism", defines developmental regionalism as a "development-based integration agenda aimed at securing the traditional benefits of regional integration ensuring that such benefits flow to all member countries and seeking to enhance the integration of member countries into world market as a means of fostering sustainable development" (UNCTAD, 2013: 96–97).

In the same vein, Mathew Doidge (2007: 9) defines developmental regionalism in its current form as "a means of overcoming the negative effects on less developing countries of integration into the global economy as well as of promoting the liberalizing process".

These conceptions of developmental regionalism by UNCTAD and Doidge derive essentially from the neo-liberal context of the "new regionalism" in which emphasis is placed on globalisation and integration into the global economy as the most viable means of promoting economic transformation for less developed countries. As such, the primacy and strategy of regional institutions in promoting developmental regionalism is the extent to which they facilitate the regional block into the global economy through market, trade and investments. Put differently, it is a market driven paradigm of developmental regionalism.

In a post neo-liberal context, developmental regionalism can be viewed as a corollary of the developmental state project. It can be conceived of as how regional institutions and initiatives are drivers of collective and sustainable regional development through conscious and increasingly harmonised policies, processes, mechanisms and instruments with requisite institutional capacity and coherent regional-state interface and synergy in development priorities and agenda.

Development capacity, as Dent and Richter (2011) argue, is very central to promoting developmental regionalism. And the main features of development capacity include technocratic capacity, institutional capacity, industrial capacity, infrastructural capacity, human capacity and sustainable development capacity. All these in terms of capacity make up the stream of developmental regionalism.

The notion of developmental regionalism in terms of its object and strategy has changed in time and space based essentially on the dynamics of the global political economy, dominant development discourse and the ideology defining regionalism. From the 1960s to the 1980s, when the structuralist perspective dominated the development discourse, especially in less developed countries, regionalism was viewed as a strategy of creating a buffer zone against the encroaching forces of imperialism in the global economy by the less developed countries. As such, the issues of collective self-reliance, strong state and regional planning, intraregional trade, collective regional defence and security infrastructure were the main elements of developmental regionalism. This was more in the context of the cold war when ideological power blocs influenced regional settings.

In the 1980s, when the neo-liberal discourse assumed the orthodoxy of economic policy and practice, the concept of the "new regionalism" emerged. The emphasis moved from the regional to the global. Regionalism assumed only a grid in connecting the global network, and its failure or success depended on how far it facilitated integration into the global market economy. Global or international trade agreements like the WTO world trade agreements (Doha rounds) and EPAs have serious implications for intraregional trade and development agenda and compel regional institutions to respond to a global competitive dynamics rather than a regional one. As such, the extent to which regional institutions connect to global value chains in the trade and production networks will determine the extent of economic development capacity. Also, the neo-liberal perspective on regionalism broadens the emphasis beyond the state in regional relations. Non-state actors of the private sector, civil society networks and professional groups are conceived to be part of the maze of regionalism. This fits the "beyond the state" construction of the neo-liberal paradigm of development.

"New regionalism" emphasises open, competitive and dynamic interregional and global engagements in facilitating developmental regionalism. However, there are still differing interpretations of how developmental regionalism is to be consummated in the context of globalisation in the contemporary era. The neo-liberals argue that regional arrangements only have relevance when they promote trade and markets on a global scale and contend that unfettered free trade not only in regions, but across the world is the answer to creating global welfare. On the other hand, the political economy perspective contends that while globalisation is real, regionalism provides a means of negotiating the contours and travails of globalisation and ensuring that some evenness, equity and fairness prevail in the global order, hence, developmental regionalism has meaning within this reordered system of globalisation that gives space and support to the weaker countries through collective regional development. In other words, developmental regionalism must have interventionist impulses that allow it to promote the collective good in the regional space, and expand economic opportunities for the less developed countries. It cannot only be a market driven but must also be a strategic regional planning arrangement as well.

3. Benefits and arguments for developmental regionalism

The benefits of and arguments for developmental regionalism remain consistent with that of regional integration in which countries come together to pull resources and capacity for achieving better results at the regional level. Doidge (2007) identifies both economic and non-economic benefits accruing from developmental regionalism. The economic benefits include expanded markets from the national to the regional level, trade and increases in foreign direct investment as bigger market props investments, and better negotiating economic power with external actors—either regional or international. Some studies have suggested that joining a trade or regional block does in fact lead to higher FDIs (Lederman, 2003; World Bank, 2005). The non-economic benefits which assume social and political dimensions include the possibility of accelerating the process of poverty reduction, creation of a security community, ensuring relative political stability through regional efforts and promotion of common norms and collective identity, which may support the process of regional economic transformation. The orthodox narrative on the benefits of regional integration has however been severely questioned especially in the case of Africa. Some argue that challenges abound which distort and thwart efforts at realising the goal of developmental regionalism. Challenges identified include lack of comparative advantage and economies of scale, low production capacity that does not utilise the expanded markets created, huge disparity amongst countries, the uneven distribution of benefits especially to the bigger countries or regional hegemons, contradictory ideas on the philosophy and direction of regional development (mostly between liberalisation and the logic of self-reliance) and overlapping membership in several RECs resulting in contradictions in policy objectives, goals and priorities, lack of commitment to the goal of regionalism and dependence on external funders or donors to finance the regional project in Africa (Lee, 2002; Buzdugan, 2007). Indeed, Margret Lee (2002) argues that regional integration has assumed part of the problem of development in Africa, rather than the solution. While the challenges of regional integration are real, they are not unsurmountable. The issue of comparative advantage, for instance, is not a static phenomenon; it thus shifts as countries scale up capacity in different sectors and regional value chains are created. Strategy, political commitment and capacity are central in transforming the regional landscape for reaping the outlined benefits of developmental regionalism in Africa.

4. Theoretical perspectives on regionalism

The study of regionalism has taken many forms, often informed by the regional integration processes that took place in post-World War II Europe. Theories of regionalism have often looked primarily at interstate interaction as the basis of region building, in the tradition of the classical regional integration of the 1950s and 1960s in accordance with the bipolar Cold War structure (Söderbaum, 2013). Theories of regionalism have generally spanned two main variants: "rationalist" and "reflectivist" approaches.

Each general variant of regionalist theory has developed into many subsets of theoretical approaches. Among the rationalist approaches are neorealism, liberal institutionalism and market integration. Based on the underlying assumption that states are predisposed to competition and conflict, neorealist theories of regionalism look at how circumstances can lead to cooperation between states for geopolitical reasons (Gilpin, 1987; Buzan, 1991). An important neorealist argument is the role that a hegemonic power can play in fostering cooperation. In this view, hegemons play a stabilizing role, essentially underwriting regional cooperation when it serves their perceived unitary interests.

Liberal institutionalist theories of regionalism also assume actor rationalism, but stress the influence of institutional frameworks on state behavior. Neoliberal institutionalists argue that regionalism is primarily brought about by the need for public goods and the avoidance of the negative impacts of state interdependence. Functionalism and neofunctionalism, which fall under the purview of liberal institutionalist theories, stress that the provision of regional public goods can foster unity across national borders.

Market integration theories of regionalism take a linear approach to regional economic integration, which culminates in economic and monetary union and eventual complete economic integration. Their emphasis is on the welfare effects from greater economic integration without focusing on the political considerations that underlie such decisions (Balassa, 1962; Robson, 1993). Some regional organisations in Africa such as the Common Market for Eastern and Southern Africa (COMESA) implicitly follow this perspective in their approach to regional integration.

Development integration theory, an intellectual predecessor of developmental regionalism, was proposed as a response to the liberal market integration approach. The primary objectives of a development integration approach are a planned stimulation of productive capacities and investment by the state and a balanced distribution of the benefits of economic cooperation and integration (Haarløv, 1997). This theory arose as a structuralist-inspired response to the orthodox market integration approach.

In all of the rationalist theories, the rationale for regionalism is always to further the ends of the state. This state-centric view of regionalism is by extension Eurocentric in that it assumes the primacy of state institutions. In the context of Southern Africa, cross-border identities and partnerships through non-state structures such as civil society and the formal and informal private sector lessen, or even contradict, the role of the state as the primary actor in region formation, particularly in the context of weak post-colonial states.

The reflectivist approaches are generally newer, having stemmed from some of the perceived shortcomings of rationalist schools of thought. A few of the reflectivist approaches to understanding regionalism include the world order approach (WOA), the new regionalism approach (NRA), and the new regionalisms approach/weave-world.

The primary contribution of WOA theorists to the debate is the addition of ideational considerations to theories of regionalism. In particular, WOA scholars argue that regionalism emerges from policy-making elite discussions in key countries as a means to promote liberal democracy and free market economic principles. This critical assessment of regionalist projects suggests that regionalist projects will face difficulties if issues of inequality and uneven development are not appropriately addressed.

The NRA looks holistically not just at economic integration processes, but also at the social and cultural factors that underlie regionalism. This nuanced view of regions beyond state structures is a key departure from theories of regionalism that focus only on intergovernmental processes and ignore the plethora of regional dynamics that persist at the civil society and private sector levels.

A similar and related approach is the new regionalisms approach/weave-world, which argues that greater emphasis should be placed on the wide range of non-state actors and informal activities that cross national boundaries (Marchand et al., 1999; Shaw, 2000). These "informal regionalisms from below" are a crucial complement to intergovernmental processes that attempt to impact regions from the top down.

Rationalist and reflectivist theories of regionalism look at similar issues from different viewpoints. While some emphasise the role of the state, others emphasise the importance of transnational networks of non-state actors. It is evident that all of these processes are relevant. The developmental regionalist approach, which is outlined in greater detail in the subsequent section, aims to appreciate both the crucial role of the state and intergovernmental institutions while acknowledging that other sectors of society have an important role to play in making the developmental vision come to life.

5. Features of developmental regionalism

The key features of developmental regionalism are discussed in this section. These broadly include the seven following elements, which are elaborated upon in subsequent sections:

1. A strong institutional architecture and capacity to drive the regional integration agenda;
2. A clear articulation of goals, objectives, essence, nature and direction of the regional integration project, and the benefits of regional integration as mechanism for facilitating regional development;
3. Ensuring peace and security as a composite and foundation of a regional integration agenda;
4. Evolving complementary and symmetrical benefits for all member states involved in the regional development project;
5. Articulation of regional public goods and development priorities necessary for facilitating economic transformation in the region including on infrastructure, trade, agriculture and food security, private sector development and industrialisation;
6. Evolving a bond of common regional citizenship and identity necessary for regional human capital mobilisation; and
7. A regional development financing mechanism that is inward looking and self-sustaining.

1. Strong institutional architecture and capacity

A strong institutional architecture and capacity is central to facilitating developmental regionalism without which regional development plans, policies, and priorities cannot be effectively implemented. Institutional architecture requires an audit of the kind of structures and processes needed and the human and material capital required to drive the regional development agenda. This may include building a strong, effective and resilient bureaucracy to be recruited based on merit and results, taking cognizance of the issues of diversity and representation. The institutional architecture of regionalism may go beyond the formal interstate structures to include the non-state institutions like the business networks, civil society and different interest and coalition groups that may relate and interface with the regional body in advancing the development prospects of the region. The notion of "regionalism from below" is underscored by the capacity of regional institutions to tap into and make use of the vast array of regional resources, networks and capacity that may constitute part of the architecture of regional development.

Oftentimes, the strategic goal defined and the nature of the regional institution established (whether of interstate cooperation or supranational nature), which determines the kind of institutional architecture that is put in place. For mere interstate cooperation regional bodies, a more flexible institutional architecture may be considered, but for supranational institutions with the mandate to facilitate the building of a regional community and drivers of regional development, a more institutionalised architecture—both at a technical and political level—may be required. The former may demand a professional bureaucracy of a centralised organ or of decentralised agencies, but with the necessary relative autonomy, capacity and resources to undertake regional strategic planning, implementation of key projects and priorities and catalyse the process of regional development.

2. *Articulation of goals and objectives of regional integration for development*

Regional integration involves trade-offs between economic sectors, groups of citizens and short- and long-term benefits. The reasons for pursuing regional integration need to be clearly spelt out, given that regionalism may not necessarily be developmentalist and can be co-opted by interest groups for private ends or thwarted if not well defined. A fundamental principle of developmental regionalism is that the process should be oriented for the development of human and economic capacities for the widest possible societal benefits.

Therefore, the rationale for pursuing such an agenda should be made clear. The objectives, goals and priorities have to be clearly articulated. The strategic direction of the regional project must be well defined in the short, medium and long term, and a monitoring and evaluation system put in place to ensure the tracking of progress, challenges and prospects of future efforts.

The net benefits of regional integration are based on long-term improvements in welfare, however, there are short-term costs, making it politically difficult for governments to justify such policies. Acknowledging that reducing barriers to trade or taking a regional approach to supply chains could entail losses for certain domestic constituencies, governments may need to plan accordingly in addressing the concerns of those constituencies or supporting their efforts in other ways and also for the regional institution to have policy initiatives and interventions that will target those constituencies in mitigating their losses. A key component of this is conducting preliminary analyses that assess how developmental policies will impact various segments of society and the economy to determine natural partners and champions as well as to mitigate some of the negative impacts greater regional integration can have through compensatory policies.

3. *Ensuring peace and security as a composite and foundation of a regional integration agenda*

Peace and security are necessary conditions for facilitating sustained regional economic growth, industrialisation and broad-based development. Although regional integration may not necessarily be about political issues, for it to achieve its stated objectives, political and security considerations cannot be ignored. The issues of conflict, political bickering and tension amongst states or citizens may derail a regional development agenda. Developmental regionalism must therefore take a holistic approach to promoting development in which issues of political stability, peace and security form part of the corpus and features of the regional development agenda. Indeed, the democracy promotion theory argues that when countries are democracies, they rarely go to war with each other. There is a high possibility that conflicts will be settled amicably both within and between states and that democratic principles will be the guiding force of interstate development integration. While this may not be true in all cases, the truth is that common regional political norms or open systems of governance may support a regional development agenda. Hence, peace, security and democratic stability constitute a feature of developmental regionalism.

Security issues have frequently been the most reliable basis for regional cooperation in Southern Africa due to the tangible benefits of collaboration and the large risks for spillovers and escalation. Therefore, cooperation on peace and security issues could form a reliable entry point for confidence building and collaboration on a wider scale.

4. *Evolving complementary and symmetrical benefits for all member states involved in the regional development project*

Developmental regionalism must promote symmetrical benefits for all countries involved in it, especially the weak and relatively undeveloped ones. In other words, the incentives for integration must outweigh the costs for the parties engaged in it. As Lee (2002: 18) rightly noted, "if policies are not put in place for all member states to share in the benefits of market integration, there is the probability that they will either withdraw from the organisation or become non-active members". Regional integration projects in Africa have often been underwritten by a regional hegemon, for example by Nigeria in ECOWAS and South Africa in the SADC. Understanding the crucial roles of regional powers is essential since without their support, efforts at region building may not succeed. However, there must be an alignment of interests between all partners in regional development projects since any perception of uneven benefits may block cooperation. Ensuring that all parties to regional projects benefit in a symmetrical way can be brought about through appropriate policy measures. These may include promoting even processes of industrialisation through regional value chains that involve all countries in the development process, and compensatory mechanisms that are context specific. This can help alleviate the spread of uneven development, which has sometimes been a trigger of conflict and discontent in the politics of regional development.

5. Articulation of regional public goods and development priorities necessary for facilitating economic transformation in the region

An essential component of a developmental regionalist approach is the provision of regional public goods that can help foster greater investment in productive capacity. This includes public goods across a range of complementary and interconnected sectors, including transport and energy infrastructure, trade facilitation measures, agriculture and food security and investments that enhance private sector development. Before embarking on ambitious investments, an assessment of the supply-side constraints is necessary towards understanding what public goods are necessary for achieving the greatest developmental impact. It is impossible to know in advance which products and industries will ultimately succeed and fail, but thorough planning based on available capabilities, market conditions and other factors is essential to maximising the developmental potential of regional integration.

6. Evolving a bond of common regional citizenship and identity

Building a sense of common regional citizenship and identity must complement economic integration efforts for genuine regional integration to take place. Beyond simply ensuring the mobility of people across national borders, a shared sense of identity can forge a greater sense of purpose and unity. Greater economic integration may to some extent lead to greater regional identity, however, education and the early inculcation of regional identity may be as effective as the implementation of protocols on the free movement of persons. According to the African Development Bank (AfDB) and Africa Union, *Africa Visa Openness Report* (2018), Africans need visas to travel to 51 percent of other African countries, a slight improvement on the 2017 and 2016 figures of 54 percent and 55 percent respectively. Furthermore, Africans can get visas on arrival in 24 percent of other African countries, which was the same in 2017 (24 percent) and 25 percent in 2016. The road to free movement and constructing a sense of common regional identity remains long and arduous in Africa.

7. A regional development financing mechanism that is inward looking and self-sustaining

A regional integration project is vulnerable, weak and precarious if it depends largely on external of sources of financing for its institutional and developmental needs. The tendency is that the articulation of its vision, priorities and implementation processes will likely be compromised. External funds are usually not interest neutral; they are often targeted at strategic geopolitical or economic needs of the sources of those funds. It is the most effective way to leverage power and control over the process of regional development agenda. The notion of "mutual accountability", which has become a buzzword in global development financing circles, only serves to mediate the issue of power and control in the asymmetrical relationship between the donors and recipients, but does not obliterate it. He who controls the funds, ultimately controls the agenda. Hence, for regional development to be internally directed and owned by its members, its financing must be endogenous.

It is this reality that has increasingly challenged Africa's regional integration institutions to seek for inward-looking financing mechanisms especially in covering their institutional and programme costs. ECOWAS is the most successful in this regard, with a 0.5 percent levy on imports of goods into all member states in the region. The AU as part of its reform process has proposed a levy on air travels on the continent, which has provoked resistance from member states of the AU. The SADC, forits part, has established the *SADC Development Fund* through which it seeks to mobilise resources to finance its key development priorities and projects especially industrialisation projects, to complement the statutory contributions of member states to the organisation. Essentially, inward-looking and sustainable financing remains a major challenge for Africa's regional development institutions.

6. Harnessing the concept for regional development in Southern Africa

Based on the framework of developmental regionalism described in the previous section, we explore how such an approach can work in Southern Africa given the unique aspects of the region. Southern Africa is a heterogeneous region economically, politically, socially and culturally. However, there is a long history of regional cooperation and integration, albeit not always in a developmentalist sense. Based on each of the key features of the developmental regionalist approach discussed earlier, potential approaches and challenges are outlined in the following sections.

1. Strong institutional architecture and capacity

Successful regional integration, as the SADC Declaration and Treaty (1992: 9) noted, "will depend on the extent to which there exists national and regional institutions with adequate competence and capacity to stimulate and manage efficiently and effectively, the complex process of integration". As such, crafting a strong institutional architecture with requisite capacity is central to aligning and facilitating regional priorities towards a developmentalist agenda. This includes the political organs and the technical bureaucracy at the heart of formulating and implementing regional policies and projects. The key policy and political organs and institutions of SADC include the Summit of Heads of State and Government, the Council of Ministers, Commissions, the Organ for

Politics, Defence, and Security Cooperation, the Troika, Sectoral and Cluster Ministerial Committees, SADC National Committees, the SADC Secretariat and its other related technical institutions, such as the administrative and implementing bureaucracy.

The SADC has seen a transition in terms of the nature of its bureaucracy established to facilitate regional development. From the former practice of apportioning sectoral projects to member states to coordinate and drive, which was the initial approach of the SADCC, this has shifted to a more professional bureaucracy in the SADC Secretariat with the hitherto 21 sectors coordinated by the member states now clustered into four Directorates manned by professional technical cadres. The internal restructuring of the SADC bureaucracy is a "work in progress" meant to realign it with the new priority focus of the institution and make it more effective, responsive and results oriented.[2] This is also true for some of the specialised bodies like the SADC Tribunal. Some scholars have argued that institutional weakness constitutes a major constraint inhibiting the SADC from realizing its development capacity (Tjønneland, 2005). As Tjønneland (2005: 181) puts it, the SADC

> has progressed rapidly at the formal level of policies and agreements. However, its institutions are still weak and the organisation has not come far in the implementation of protocols and regional decisions. There is a major gap between what SADC wants to do, and actual developments and implementation on the ground.

The reluctance of countries to cede some level of sovereignty in creating a supranational organisation with adequate powers, capacity and authority on regional affairs in a relatively autonomous way without overt or substantial control from member states has implications for the nature of the institution and its capacity. The debate is on the nature of the institutional architecture to consummate regional integration—through either more interstate cooperation mechanisms or the creation of a supranational body with adequate powers and capacity. Evidently, issues around relative autonomy for the SADC Secretariat, building a stable professional core, adequate human capacity and financial resources are germane to its transformative potentials.

Institutional reforms are needed not only at the regional level, but also at the national level. Regional development can only be meaningful with adequate institutional capacity both at the national and regional levels, with clear understanding and support from the national stakeholders for the regional agenda.

Institutional mechanisms should incorporate needs-based flexibility that allows them to fulfil crucial functions in alignment with regional priorities. Organisational structures and protocols that follow an idealised notion of regional development objectives but do not work in reality only decrease the legitimacy of regional organisations when there are no consequences for noncompliance. As a result, institutional capacity building efforts should therefore focus on aligning incentives around specific achievable areas (ECDPM, 2016).

At the grassroots level, the transnational business, informal trading, and civil society networks that pervade Southern Africa need to participate and be incorporated into regional planning processes. Their perspectives and interests must be reflected in the developmental regionalist project for it to ultimately succeed. The objective of regional public goods and policies is to create the environment in which these different sectors can thrive. Without their input and articulation of their needs, regional public goods may not be used optimally and policies may remain unimplemented. While they have their own drawbacks in terms of both design and implementation, development corridor initiatives provide one example of flexible institutional design that leverages networks of business and civil society actors based on cross-border ties that complement formal state-driven structures.

Finally, recognition that countries use different regional fora for addressing different issues is crucial in terms of strengthening institutions. Rather than designing institutions that will attempt to address all types of regional issues, capacity-building efforts should focus on strengthening the ability of institutions to deal with their areas of strength so that different organisations and networks can complement each other to tackle the plethora of issues that affect Southern Africa.

2. *Articulation of goals and objectives of regional integration for development*

It is important that policymakers and political leaders at the national and regional levels clearly articulate the justification and end goals of undertaking regional initiatives that will transform the region's economic and social structures. This requires articulating the objectives, goals, priorities and strategic direction of regional integration projects. This also requires clear communication regarding the policy instruments and investments to be made, the targets of the programme and what should be expected.

The objectives and goals that the SADC seeks to achieve are clearly articulated in its major policy documents, namely the SADC Treaty and the RISDP. The SADC's vision is to build "a common future, a future in a regional community that will ensure economic wellbeing, improvement of the standards of living and quality of life, freedom and social justice and peace and security for all the peoples of Southern Africa" (SADC, 2001). Its main objective is to promote economic and social transformation in Southern Africa through sustained and equitable economic growth and development via effective production systems, deeper cooperation and integration, the alleviation of poverty, ensuring competitive economies and region, and promoting peace and political and democratic stability.

The SADC adopts a development integration approach that focuses on a comprehensive strategy for regional development including in the economic, social and political spheres, and recognising the disparities amongst countries in the region. The SADC, as Jakaya Kikwete (2016: 3–5) noted, is guided by two strategic plans. First is in the economic plan, which is driven by the revised RISDP, and second is the Strategic Indicative Plan for the Organ (SIPO). The objective of the latter (SIPO) is to create a peaceful, secure and stable political environment in the region promotive of economic development.

The SADC's strategic goals and key targets are further elaborated in its key sectoral plans, which include the SADC Industrialisation Strategy and Roadmap, the Regional Infrastructure Development Master Plan (RIDMP), and the Agriculture Development Policy. There appears to be clear objectives, goals and targets but a wide gap tends to exist between enunciated goals and implementation processes and capacity.

A major challenge is in the role of the private sector and civil society in formulating regional plans and strategies, which has been minimal in Southern Africa (Vanheukelom and Bertelsmann-Scott, 2016). The interests of the private sector and civil society are often diverse and sometimes in conflict. Finding areas of convergence, whether by sector or subregion, is a way to take advantage of areas where the interests of multiple actors—state, society and business—overlap. The East African Community (EAC) provides a useful example of how the convergence of interests of multiple actors across the region in specific sectors can contribute to regional integration. Rwanda and Uganda, which are landlocked, sought port access while the Kenyan private sector—the strongest in the region—desired new markets for its goods. As a result, the EAC Northern Corridor was fast-tracked as a regional priority (ECDPM, 2016).

There may not always be such a natural convergence of interests, in which case it is necessary to demonstrate the value of integration through evident progress in a relatively short time frame. Therefore, focusing on regional projects in areas that can demonstrate results and quick wins may be preferable than areas that are very contentious with serious divergences amongst the regional stakeholders. It is important to note that converging interests may be sector-specific and therefore it is important to focus on areas of cooperation where interests overlap rather than inflating the cooperation agenda to incorporate areas where stakeholders may be inclined to pursue different objectives. Finally, it is critical to consider national interests that feed into the regional project not simply in terms of the perceived interests of national governments, but also of the agendas of the private sector, civil society, trade unions and other segments of society.

3. Ensuring peace and security as a prerequisite and foundation of a regional integration agenda

Peace and security are prerequisites for any regional integration agenda. Without basic stability and mutual trust and confidence, it is impossible to establish a good environment for investment and trade facilitation necessary for regional economic integration. Some of the factors that can contribute to establishing a peaceful security environment in Southern Africa include ingraining a culture of democratic processes and practices and effective conflict resolution. The SADC has developed conflict management mechanisms and the promotion of democratic elections that are essential for ensuring peace and stability in the region. In spite of some conflict incidents, mostly of a political nature, the SADC region records appreciable levels of peace and stability, levels that are better than those of other regions of the continent.

In addition, addressing the problems of poverty, inequality and unemployment will help address grievances that have undergirded conflicts in the region. The Southern African regional development project should be based on the principle of equity, which will help ensure that the benefits of such an approach are shared widely.

Part of ensuring the equity of a regional approach to development involves visionary leadership that looks beyond the confines of the nation state and takes a regional perspective to policy-making. The issue of xenophobia which has reared its head in some countries recently in the region demands a pan-Southern Africa vision and leadership instrumental in promoting collective regional identity. Acknowledging that legitimate disputes will emerge between both state and non-state actors in Southern Africa, effective institutions and early warning systems should be developed at the local, national and regional levels (Kreiter, 2016).

Together, these measures can help ensure a basic level of peace and security that can provide a basis for greater regional integration.

4. *Evolving complementary and symmetrical benefits for all member states involved in the regional development project*

Sharing the gains of regional development among stakeholders is essential not only for the sake of equity but also for the legitimacy of a regional approach to development challenges in general. If projects labelled as regional are seen as benefitting only one nation or constituency, further cooperation may not be forthcoming. While resources are limited, ensuring complementarity and greater symmetry in the benefits of regional integration can be brought about in multiple ways. Compensatory mechanisms such as tax transfers, budgetary transfers, preferential tariffs and variable geometry are all ways that benefits can be more evenly spread across parties to regional development plans in a mutually beneficial way.

Tax transfers are a mechanism that can redistribute gains in some sectors to parts of society that stand to lose or not gain from the changes stemming from a regional development approach. The rationale is that the overall growth emanating from structural transformation should make everyone better off even if some dislocations are suffered by individual sectors. Progressive taxation schemes and other redistributive fiscal measures can help reallocate these gains so that no segments of society are left behind.

A major strategy in ensuring symmetrical gains from regional integration in Southern Africa addresses how to transform all countries in the region into production centres rather than consumption sites with a lopsided pattern of industrial production. In other words, how does the SADC consummate regional value chains that will bring all countries into the production network? The SADC Industrialisation Strategy and Roadmap provides a working document through which this could be realised. The strategy anchored on three key pillars provides an opportunity for this. These are industrialisation as a champion of economic and technological transformation, competiveness as an active process to move from comparative to competitive advantage and regional integration and geography as a context for industrial development and economic prosperity (SADC, 2015: 5).

Preferential tariffs are a tool of trade policy used to level the playing field for individual sectors or nations. Reducing tariffs on products that meet certain criteria can be an important strategy for developing specific industries or building trade ties with specific countries. Economic Partnership Agreements such as the African Growth and Opportunity Act (AGOA) with the United States, for instance, use preferential tariffs in specific sectors such as clothing and textiles to confer advantages on African manufacturers of these products in gaining access and market share. Within the SADC, the Free Trade Area grants preferential market access for other member states as a way to boost intraregional trade. As one of the primary objectives of the SADC Industrialisation Policy is building regional value chains, preferential tariffs will be a critical policy tool for encouraging the import of cheap inputs and locally produced manufactures within the region.

Variable geometry, an approach that has been adopted by the Tripartite Free Trade Agreement (TFTA) process, is another method by which countries at different levels of development can benefit reciprocally from the regional integration process. By giving countries at a lower level of development additional time to grant market access to other parties to the agreement, variable geometry ensures that all signatories benefit from greater integration. Given large disparities in income and levels of development in Southern Africa, variable geometry will continue to be crucial to ensure that regional integration is to the benefit of all.

5. Articulation of regional public goods and development priorities necessary for facilitating economic transformation in the region

Beyond an articulation of the goals and objectives of a regional development process, the specific instruments and priorities of such an approach are important in the current environment of dwindling development resources in providing regional public goods that could accelerate economic growth and development. Regional public goods in Southern Africa may include infrastructure of transnational roads, railways, air transportation, ICT networks, energy and water resources. The more regional public goods that countries share, the more interdependent and close-knit they are likely to become, and the greater the possibility of collective and even regional development.

Regional public goods may tap into the relative resource endowment of countries and the comparative advantage of countries in creating regional hubs of development priorities, goods and services which the entire region can benefit from. The SADC through its regional RIDMP has sought to provide regional public goods but leaves much to be desired at the level of project implementation of those regional services.

Also, regional industrial policies and strategies recently launched by the SADC and COMESA are important steps towards bringing about a regional approach to industrialisation and economic development. In order for these policies to achieve their objectives, a number of other modes of coordination are necessary. In particular, harmonised investment codes, affording investors a common framework, helps to reduce risk and simplify the procedures necessary for making complex investments that may span multiple legal jurisdictions.

Regional development banks, such as the Development Bank of South Africa, and the proposed SADC Development Fund, are highly important for securing financing for projects that many commercial banks and other investors would be unwilling to back. Given the long-term nature of many investments in plants and equipment, commercial banks are not willing to take on either the risk or duration of the investment necessary to bring them to fruition. Regional development banks serve a crucial role in terms of providing equity investment and guarantees that are often sufficient to bring other, otherwise hesitant, investors on board (African Banker Magazine, 2016).

In addition to the policy and institutional features described earlier, articulating the regional public goods necessary for implementing a developmental regionalist agenda are equally important. Southern Africa's infrastructure needs are immense, and thus prioritizing projects requires difficult trade-offs. The revised SADC RISDP is a good example of reassessing the region's priorities based on current needs and objectives.

6. Evolving a bond of common regional citizenship and identity

Over the longer term, a truly regional approach to development requires that the region's citizens share a common sense of citizenship and identity. Some of the recent economic difficulties that have faced the region have brought xenophobic and nationalistic sentiments to the surface, which threaten the regional integration project. While greater economic integration itself can help bring about a stronger regional identity, the formation of a Southern African or African identity that goes beyond local and national identities requires education from a young age.

Incorporating pan-African or pan-Southern Africa elements into school curricula can help educate citizens about cross-border identities. Greater information about the benefits of human mobility can also dispel some of the myths surrounding immigration and the role of migrant labour in contemporary Southern Africa. Issues of unhindered social mobility and education are central to creating a bond of common regional identity and citizenship. The initiative to establish the SADC University of Transformation announced by King Mswati III at the 36th session of the SADC Heads of State and Government as a major priority of his chairmanship of SADC is a major step in that direction. Such a university will not only address the skills deficit of the region in the areas of science, innovation and technology but also promote a sense of regional identity and citizenship as its students are to be drawn from all member countries on an equal basis of 20 per country for the inception group.

At the policy level, inculcating a shared Southern African identity starts with ratifying and implementing the protocol on the free movement of persons. While the right to travel freely within Southern Africa exists on paper, large implementation gaps remain, especially in terms of occupational mobility and settlement.

7. *A regional development financing mechanism*

The issue of a self-sustaining and inward looking financing strategy for the SADC is an ongoing discussion in its policy organs. A major outcome of this is the establishment of the SADC Development Fund. While this fund is still in its infancy, considerable efforts should be made to ensure that it is not a donor-dependent funding portfolio and that it generates enough resources to support its key development priorities and projects. There is an appreciable amount of dependence in the level of donor support for the SADC's programmes and activities, which overtime should be substantially reduced through an inward looking and sustainable funding strategy.

Evidence from other regions

While the Southern African context is unique, certain factors that led to the success of other regional development initiatives can be informative. A 2007 study on the design features of regional development programmes that contributed to successful outcomes by the World Bank (2007) identified strong country commitment, appropriate matching of objectives to national and regional capacities, clear delineation and coordination of the roles of national and regional institutions, accountable governance arrangements and planning for sustainability as most crucial.

In Southeast Asia, the Greater Mekong subregion economic cooperation programme is seen by some as a successful example of a developmental regionalist approach (UNCTAD, 2013). The critical success factors included the adoption of an activity-based and results-oriented approach to the design and implementation of sector-specific subregional projects that were completed within tight timeframes to achieve buy-in and build confidence. Flexibility to changes in development plans, participation by all stakeholders in the management and coordination of the programme, the ability to mobilise resources and the establishment of institutions to provide a simple and flexible framework for implementation also contributed to the programme's success. This shares some similarities with the Maputo Development Corridor, which also followed a lean approach to administration.

While the unique attributes of the Southern African context preclude a cut-and-paste approach based on what succeeded in other regions, some of the key lessons of other experiences can be applied to a developmental regionalist approach in the SADC. Most importantly, the need for flexibility, champions, effective institutions and quick wins can all be applied to the implementation of regional projects in Southern Africa.

7. Conclusion

This chapter elaborates a framework of developmental regionalism that can be applied to regional integration efforts in Southern Africa and elsewhere. The chapter begins by unpacking the notion of developmental regionalism, the development discourses that have shaped its understanding and dynamics, benefits and arguments for developmental regionalism, its features and elements and how such relates with the Southern Africa experience, especially in the SADC.

Undoubtedly, the approach of the SADC to regional integration is one of a developmentalist strategy and the institution has been quite responsive and dynamic in the face of the changing realities of its environment and the international system. But in spite of progress made, there are challenges to realising its full potential for developmental regionalism. For example, the planned process of transition from a free trade area to a custom union and market integration has been delayed or slow, and it still lags behind in the free trade zone. Also, economic growth has decelerated remarkably recently in the region; regional public goods remain largely elusive, while the notion of regional identity and citizenship are still being contested. Strong institutional capacity, effective implementation strategies of organizational programmes and projects, synergy between regional and national priorities, and strong political commitment are necessary for facilitating developmental regionalism in Southern Africa, as it is necessary elsewhere in Africa.

The literature on effective development approaches to promoting regional transformative agenda and programmes remains quite limited, hence the need for more analytical studies in this regard. As Southern Africa enters a new era in which regionalism becomes more relevant than ever, leaders in various sectors of the subregion will need to devise new ways to work together to achieve collective goals. To this end, a developmental regionalist approach, which incorporates private sector and civil society participation into development plans that are guided by the state but executed through a collective framework and builds on past successes and failures is necessary. Also, issues of equitable development amongst countries, and tangible benefits for the large majority of the citizens in the region are important, for the goal of development regionalism to be realized.

Notes

1 The SADCC was transformed into the SADC on 17 August 1992.
2 In August 2017, a new organisational structure was approved for the SADC Secretariat by the Council of Ministers. In the new structure, six new departments were approved that report to the Deputy Executive Secretary. These are policy planning and resource mobilization; industrial development and trade; finance, investments and customs; infrastructure; social and human development and food, agriculture and natural resources. Meanwhile, two other departments—HR and Administration and Finance—are under the Deputy Executive Secretary, Corporate Affairs.

References

Adejumobi, S. 2016. 'Brexit: When Democracy Fails?', *Guardian Newspaper* (Lagos, Nigeria), July 7th. See, http://m.guardian.ng/opinion/brexit-when-democracy-fails/

African Banker Magazine. March/April 2016.

African Development Bank and the African Union. 2018. *Africa Visa Openness Report, 2018*. Abidjan: Africa Development Bank.

Ajulu, Rok. 2008. 'Open versus Developmental Integration-What Options for SADC', Institute for Global Dialogue, *Revisiting Regionalism in Southern Africa: Proceedings on the Fourth South Africa Forum on Trade (SAFT)*, Pretoria, South Africa, 3–4 April. Pretoria: Institute for Global Dialogue and Friedrich Ebert Stifung.

Balassa, Bela. 1962. *The Theory of Economic Integration*. London: Allen & Unwin.

Buzan, Barry. 1991. *People, States and Fear: An Agenda for International Security Studies in the Post-Cold War Era*. Hemel Hempstead: Harvester Wheatsheaf.

Buzdugan, Stephen. 2007. 'A Critical Analysis of Regionalism as a Development Strategy in Southern Africa: Beyond Institutional Explanations of Failure of the Southern Africa Development Community (SADC)', *Paper prepared for the British International Studies Association Annual Conference*, University of Cambridge, Cambridge, December.

Combaz, Emilie. 2013. 'Regional Development Programmes and Poverty Reduction', *GSDRC Applied Knowledge Services Helpdesk Research Report*.

Dent, Christopher and Richter, Peter. 2011. 'Sub-Regional Cooperation and Developmental Regionalism: The Case for BIMP-EAGA', *Contemporary South East Asia*, 33 (1): 29–55.

Doidge, Mathew. 2007. 'From Developmental Regionalism to Developmental Inter-Regionalism: The European Union Approach', *NCRE Working Paper*, No. 07/01.

European Centre for Development Policy Management (ECDPM). 2016. *Political Economy Regional Integration in Africa Synthesis Report*.

Gilpin, Robert. 1987. *The Political Economy of International Relations*. Princeton: Princeton University Press.

Haarløv, Jens. 1997. *Regional Cooperation and Integration within Industry and Trade in Southern Africa*. Aldershot: Avebury.

Hettne, Bjorn. 2005. 'Beyond the "New Regionalism"', *New Political Economy*, 10(4), December: 543–571.

Kikwete, Jakaya. 2016. 'Regional Integration: Sacrifices Have to Be Made', *Lecture delivered at the University of Swaziland on 25th August 2016*, see, *Southern Times* (Windhoek, Namibia) 26th August, pp. 3–5.

Lederman, Daniel, Maloney, William, and Luis, Serven. 2003. *Lessons from NAFTA for Latin America and the Caribbean Countries: A Summary of Research Findings*. Washington, DC: World Bank.

Lee, Margret. 2002. 'Regionalism in Africa: A Part of the Problem or a Part of the Solution', *Polis*, 9 (Special Edition): 1–24.
Marchand, Marianne H., Bøås, Morten, and Shaw, Timothy M. 2003. 'The Weave-World: The Regional Interweaving of Economies, Ideas and Identities', in Fredrik Söderbaum and Timothy M. Shaw (eds.), *Theories of New Regionalism*. A Palgrave Reader. Basingstoke: Palgrave—Now Palgrave Macmillan.
Payne, Anthony and Gamble, Andrew (eds.). 1996. *Regionalism and World Order*. New York: Macmillan.
Robson, Peter. 1993. 'The New Regionalism and Developing Countries', *Journal of Common Market Studies*, 31 (3): 329–348.
Shaw, Timothy. 2000. 'New Regionalisms in Africa in the New Millennium: Comparative Perspectives on Renaissance, Realisms, and/or Regressions', *New Political Economy*, 5 (3): 399–414.
Söderbaum, Fredrik. 2004. *The Political Economy of Regionalism: The Case of Southern Africa*. New York: Palgrave Macmillan.
Söderbaum, Fredrik. 2016. 'Rethinking Regions and Regionalism', *Georgetown Journal of International Affairs*, Summer/Fall 2013, 9: 18.
Söderbaum, Fredrik and Brolin, Therese. 2016. Support to Regional Cooperation and Integration in Africa-What Works and Why? Rapport 2016:01. *Expertgruppen för biståndanalys (EBA)*.
Southern Africa Development Community (SADC). 1992. *SADC Declaration and Treaty*. Gaborone: SADC.
Southern Africa Development Community (SADC). 2001. *SADC Regional Indicative Strategic Development Plan (RISDP)*. Gaborone: SADC.
Southern Africa Development Community (SADC). 2015. *SADC Industrialization Strategy and Roadmap*. Gaborone: SADC.
The Southern Times (Windhoek, Namibia), 26th August 2016.
Tjønneland, Elling, N. 2005. 'Making SADC Work? Revisiting Institutional Reform', in W.B. Dirk Hansohm, Trudi Hartzenberg and Colin McCarthy (eds.), *Monitoring Regional Integration in Southern Africa Yearbook* (Vol. 5). Windhoek: Namibia Economic Research Unit.
UNCTAD. 2013. *Economic Development in Africa Report 2013: Intra-African Trade: Unlocking Private Sector Dynamism*. Geneva: UCTAD.
Vanheukelom, Jan and Bertelsmann-Scott, Talitha. 2016. *The Political Economy of Regionalism in Africa: The Southern African Development Community (SADC)*. Maastricht: ECDPM.
World Bank. 2005. *World Development Report, 2005: A Better Investment Climate for Everyone*. Oxford: Oxford University Press.
World Bank. 2007. *The Development Potential of Regional Programs: An evaluation of World Bank Support of Multicountry Operations*. Independent Evaluation Group. Washington, DC: World Bank.
Zebulun, Kreiter. 2016. 'Conflict, Peace and Regional Economic Integration in Southern Africa: Addressing the Policy Challenges', *APN Briefing Note*, 5, July.

3 The Tripartite Free Trade Area and African Continental Free Trade Area

The case for consolidation

David Luke and Zodwa Mabuza

Introduction

June 2015 marked two significant events in the economic integration of the African continent. The Tripartite Free Trade Area (TFTA) agreement, bringing together 26 member and partner states of the Common Market for Eastern and Southern Africa (COMESA), the East African Community (EAC) and the Southern African Development Community (SADC), was signed by the Third Tripartite Summit on 10 June 2015 in the resort town of Sharm El Sheikh, Egypt.

Five days after the signing of the TFTA, on 15 June 2015, the African Union (AU) Summit of Heads of State and Government launched negotiations for the Continental Free Trade Area (CFTA, subsequently renamed African Continental Free Trade Area, AfCFTA) negotiations in Johannesburg, South Africa. These negotiations were to encompass 54 AU member states (this number became 55 after Morocco rejoined the AU in 2017).

Both of these initiatives were aimed at rationalizing multiple memberships among African countries of economic integration schemes as well as consolidating market potential. In the case of the TFTA, this was to be achieved by creating a free trade area bringing COMESA, the EAC and the SADC together in a market with a population of 632 million and a combined GDP of US$1.3 trillion. In the case of the AfCFTA, it was to be achieved by creating a continent-wide market of 1.2 billion people and a continental GDP of US$2.3 trillion.

The proximity of the two events on 10 and 15 June 2015 highlighted a challenge for Africa's trade liberalization agenda. Rationalization of multiple memberships of trading arrangements was a key objective in both the TFTA and the AfCFTA. Indeed, the initial expectation was that the TFTA would be a "building block" of the AfCFTA. That is to say, the TFTA would be incorporated into the AfCFTA. There was a similar expectation that the existing free trade area (FTA) arrangements on the continent would similarly be incorporated into the AfCFTA. This has not happened. Instead, the AfCFTA has added a new layer to the other FTAs on the continent. It remains unclear how and when the other FTAs will be phased out to consolidate the African market in the AfCFTA. There is a case of course for deeper integration within the regional economic communities (RECs) including through customs union arrangements. But at the FTA level (or preferential trading partnerships),[1] rationalization requires consolidation in the AfCFTA.

This chapter reviews the salient provisions in the TFTA and AfCFTA agreements. It will become clear that a number of elements are duplicated in the two agreements. We argue that a road map for an effective transition of all the FTAs on the continent into the AfCFTA is urgently required. The chapter is divided into three sections. The first briefly revisits the decision of the AU Assembly to consolidate the FTAs into the AfCFTA. The second highlights a number of similarities in the legal structure of the TFTA and the AfCFTA agreements. The third concludes with the argument on the need for consolidation.

1. Rationalization as a key objective of the TFTA and AfCFTA

According to the "Declaration on Boosting Intra-African Trade and the Establishment of a Continental Free Trade Area (CFTA)" adopted by African Heads of State and Government at the 18th Ordinary Session of the African Union Assembly in January 2012, the following milestones and timelines were agreed upon:

> Finalization of the East African Community (EAC)-the Common Market for Eastern and Southern Africa (COMESA)-Southern African Development Community (SADC) Tripartite initiative by 2014;—Completion of FTA(s) by Non-Tripartite RECs, through parallel arrangement(s) similar to the EAC-COMESA-SADC Tripartite initiative or reflecting the preferences of their Member States, between 2012 and 2014;—Consolidation of the Tripartite and other regional FTAs into a Continental Free Trade Area (CFTA) initiative between 2015 and 2016; Establishment of the Continental Free Trade Area (CFTA) by 2017 with the option to review the target date according to progress made.
>
> (Extract from Assembly/AU/Decl.1(XVIII))

There was slippage from the timelines envisaged in 2012 by the AU Assembly as the Tripartite Agreement was signed in 2015. But more importantly, the TFTA and AfCFTA were negotiated as separate agreements, and indeed, other free trade agreements on the continent remain parallel arrangements to the AfCFTA. However, the AfCFTA is a comprehensive trade liberalization and partnership agreement encompassing 55 countries. It provides the most logical framework for conducting trade throughout the continent underpinned by the vision of the AU Assembly for one continent-wide arrangement. Article 19(1) of the Agreement Establishing the African Continental Free Trade Area provides that: "In the event of any conflict and inconsistency between this Agreement and any regional agreement, this Agreement shall prevail".

All tripartite member states either signed the Kigali Declaration for the Launch of the African Continental Free Trade Area or the AfCFTA agreement itself. This implies an uncontested acceptance of Article 19. However, a provision under this article allows for deeper integration in the RECs including through customs unions. It should be noted that within the three RECs in the tripartite arrangement, some countries are already operating as customs unions (EAC and Southern African Customs Union SACU subset within the SADC) while the rest aspire to become customs unions (COMESA and the SADC).

2. Similarities between the TFTA and AfCFTA provisions

The approach to the two negotiations and the substance of the agreements that were reached were remarkably similar. This begs the question, what is the point of having two agreements that are almost identical? The TFTA negotiations were to be conducted in two phases, the first covering trade in goods and a separate and parallel track on movement of businesspersons. In the second phase, negotiations were to cover trade in services, competition policy, intellectual property rights, cross-border investments and cooperation in trade and development. Other pillars of the TFTA include cooperation in industrial development and infrastructure development.

Similarly, the AfCFTA negotiations have been conducted in two phases, with the first phase covering trade in goods and trade in services. The second phase will cover competition policy, intellectual property rights, investment and possibly e-commerce. The AfCFTA is complemented by other continental initiatives, including the Protocol on Free Movement of Persons, Right to Residence and Right to Establishment, which is expected to promote free movement of people, and the Single African Air Transport Market (SAATM) which is expected to lead to improvement in continental air transportation and to contribute to increasing Africa's global share of the aviation industry.

Trade in goods

Both the TFTA and AfCFTA agreements on trade in goods follow WTO best practices. Both cover tariff liberalization, provisions on non-tariff barriers, rules of origin, trade remedies and provision for dispute settlement lie at the core of what was agreed. Other provisions include elimination of quantitative restrictions, customs cooperation, trade facilitation, transit trade, infant industries, balance of payments, and so on.

Tariff liberalization

As regards tariff liberalization, the ultimate aim of the TFTA is to liberalize 100 percent of tariff lines taking into account the usual general, specific and security exceptions. This is to be achieved by consolidating the tariff regimes of the EAC—which, as noted above, is a customs union and SACU subset of SADC member states—into the TFTA in line with the principle of building on the *acquis*[2] and subject to reciprocity. In addition to the ten EAC and SACU countries, ten COMESA countries participating in the COMESA FTA made TFTA tariff offers based on the COMESA acquis of 100 percent tariff liberalization on a reciprocal basis. It should be noted though that the modalities for tariff negotiations agreed among tripartite countries in 2013 are not ambitious. It was agreed that 60–85 percent of tariff lines will be liberalized upon entry into force of the agreement and the remaining 40–15 percent to be negotiated over a period of five to eight years. This presents a challenge for countries that have fairly liberalized trade regimes (with more than 80 percent of their tariff lines at 0 percent MFN) vis-à-vis the principle of building on the acquis.

Bilateral meetings on tariff exchanges began taking place between Egypt and EAC, EAC and SACU and Egypt and SACU between 2015 and 2018. The EAC/Egypt negotiations have been concluded whilst those between EAC/SACU and Egypt/SACU are at an advanced stage. The process of negotiating tariff offers took longer than anticipated.

In the case of the AfCFTA, the AU member states adopted modalities for the liberalization of trade in goods. This required the removal of 90 percent of tariffs on goods imported from other member states at the time of entry into force of the AfCFTA agreement. The remaining 10 percent of tariffs is to be distributed between sensitive and excluded products with varying timelines for progressive liberalization over a maximum of 15 years to reach a level of liberalization contained in a bracket of 90 to 100 percent. At the time of writing, it had not been fully clarified how the 10 percent is to be distributed between sensitive and excluded products and whether the 90 percent is of total tariff lines only or a combination of a minimum of 90 percent of total tariff lines and not less than 90 percent of total value of imports, also known as double qualification. Following the clarification of this issue, it is expected that the member states will notify and submit new tariff schedules to the AU Commission.

Non-tariff barriers

To address the challenges of non-tariff barriers (NTBs), the TFTA agreement provides for the harmonization of the COMESA, EAC and SADC NTB arrangements into a single mechanism and a process for identifying, categorizing, reporting, monitoring and resolving NTBs in the tripartite region. The institutional framework includes a tripartite subcommittee on NTBs as well as national monitoring committees and focal points.

The AfCFTA has similar provisions in the protocol on trade in goods. It also provides for a mechanism on NTBs based on arrangements at the REC level, including the COMESA, EAC, and SADC arrangements.

Rules of origin

The TFTA agreement sets out the criteria and conditions for goods to qualify for preferential treatment based on a list of product-specific rules of origin. Negotiations of product-specific rules is ongoing as part of the built-in agenda.

Interim arrangements on rules of origin were agreed to, pending negotiations of the product-specific rules. As of September 2018, more than 60 percent of tripartite product list rules had been agreed upon and the requisite instruments had been developed, such as certificates of origin, export and import declaration forms, among others.

The AfCFTA provisions on rules of origin follow a similar approach. It is based on a product list of rules with interim transition arrangements while product-specific rules are being negotiated. It is known that some AfCFTA negotiators hold the view that the non-contentious TFTA product rules should simply be incorporated into the AfCFTA in order to expedite the work on product list rules.

Trade remedies

The TFTA agreement provides for the application of anti-dumping, countervailing and safeguard measures to address dumping, subsidization, imports surges and so forth. There are accompanying guidelines on implementation of trade remedies.

The AfCFTA has similar provisions with accompanying guidelines.

Other provisions

Other provisions in both the TFTA and AfCFTA agreements include those on the elimination of quantitative restrictions, customs cooperation, trade facilitation and transit trade, infant industries, balance of payments, among others. These are generally consistent with obligations under the WTO and international best practices.

Trade in services

A Protocol on Trade in Services underpinned by agreed modalities for the liberalization of priority service sectors was concluded under the AfCFTA. Five priority sectors—transport, communication, tourism and financial and business services—were selected as the priority sectors with flexibility for market access requests to be made in other sectors. On entry into force of the AfCFTA agreement, each state party is required to provide a schedule of commitments including initial market access offers.

The second phase of tripartite negotiations which was to cover trade in services was put on hold in the light of the participation of its member states in the AfCFTA protocol on services.

Dispute settlement

The TFTA agreement provides for a Dispute Settlement Body and its powers include, among others, the establishment of panels and an appellate body, surveillance over the implementation of rulings and recommendations of panels and the appellate body.

The AfCFTA Protocol on Rules and Procedures on the Settlement of Disputes has almost the same provisions.

Institutional arrangements

The institutional arrangements for oversight and implementation of the agreements are almost exactly the same. In the case of the TFTA this includes, among other things, the Summit of Heads of State and Government, the Council of Ministers, the Tripartite Task Force (made up of the Secretariats of the three RECs), the Tripartite Sectoral Ministerial Committee, the Tripartite Committee of Senior Officials and the Tripartite Committee of Experts.

The AfCFTA has a similar institutional structure that cascades down from the AU Assembly, to the Council of Ministers and so forth, with provision for an autonomous Secretariat within the AU system responsible for coordinating and enforcing the provisions of the agreement.

Ratification and entry into force

The TFTA requires ratification by 14 of the 26 parties to the agreement for entry into force. At the time of writing, four countries had ratified the agreement. The AfCFTA requires 22 ratifications with 11 ratifications concluded by the time of writing. With half the required number of ratifications already attained, there appears to be stronger momentum behind the AfCFTA than behind the TFTA. It is interesting to note that three of the four countries that have ratified the TFTA have also ratified the AfCFTA.

Second phase negotiations

The second phase of tripartite negotiations on intellectual property rights, competition policy and cross-border investments have been put on hold. Lack of human and financial resources as well as evident duplication in the AfCFTA seem to have reduced the appetite to proceed.

The better-resourced AfCFTA is on track to launch negotiations on intellectual property rights, competition policy, investment and possibly e-commerce in early 2019.

3. Conclusion: the case for consolidation

A comparison of the TFTA and AfCFTA provisions demonstrates great convergence between the two agreements. A situation has been created whereby tripartite member states could opt to trade under either regime when trading among themselves. This duplication is not only unnecessary but also costly in maintaining parallel institutional support systems. The vision in the 2012

Declaration of the AU Assembly for the consolidation of the African market has not been realized. The coexistence of parallel regional FTAs with the AfCFTA not only challenges the integrity of the AfCFTA but also undermines the attractiveness of Africa as an investment destination. It further complicates the negotiation of trade deals with third parties such as the European Union that maintains the consistency of the AfCFTA. A peculiarity in both the TFTA and AfCFTA agreements requires the TFTA and AfCFTA member states to accord to each other on a reciprocal basis preferences that are no less favourable than those given to third parties under their respective most favoured nation state (MFN) provisions. This risks giving third parties the same preferential access that trade liberalization among African countries provides for the African market.

What is now needed is a roadmap for the phasing out of the regional FTAs, consolidation of the AfCFTA and an MFN provision that safeguards the African economic space. Such a road map should further clarify the relationship between the AfCFTA and customs unions at the REC level as well as the pathway for the AfCFTA itself to evolve into a continental customs union.

Notes

1 An FTA is typically a preferential trading agreement on goods. However, modern preferential trade agreements include services as well as provisions for regulatory convergence or cooperation in policy areas such as investment, competition policy, intellectual property etc.

2 Building on the acquis is one of the negotiation principles for the TFTA, which means building on what has been achieved or agreed.

4 Monetary union in Southern Africa

Is the SADC ready?

Chrispin Mphuka, Mzwanele Mfunwa, Obrian Ndhlovu and Peter Chikwekwete

Introduction

The Southern African Development Community (SADC), made up of 15 countries (Angola, Botswana, the Democratic Republic of the Congo (DRC), Lesotho, Madagascar, Malawi, Mauritius, Mozambique, Namibia, Seychelles, South Africa, Swaziland, Tanzania, Zambia and Zimbabwe), will soon search for mechanisms by which all the member states' currencies are made convertible to each other, as the community progresses on its monetary integration agenda to its ultimate objective of a single currency, slated for 2018. Towards this objective the SADC has agreed to pursue macroeconomic stability and harmonize monetary and financial policies. A regional central bank law has been finalized and is ready for mainstreaming into national laws. Plans for a single regional central bank are part of the monetary integration agenda.

The key question for the region is whether all or some of the SADC member states are ready for a full-fledged monetary integration. In addition, the chapter examines which SADC member states can kick-start the currency convertibility process as a step towards adoption of a single currency by the entire membership.

A monetary union refers to a group of economies that have decided to share a common currency and thus a common monetary union (Saka et al. 2015). It involves the irrevocable fixing of exchange rates and the abandonment of margins of fluctuations among a number of currencies with the implication that individual currencies are no longer distinguishable and a common currency may be substituted, individual central banks lose their autonomy and a common monetary policy is pursued in an environment where capital controls have been freed and financial markets are not segmented (Masson 1992).

There are several developments that work in SADC member states' favour in this regard. First, a number of them have been members of a Common Monetary Area (Lesotho, Namibia, South Africa and Swaziland). Second, 13 member countries are already participating in the SADC Integrated Regional Electronic Settlement System (SIRESS) where bulk intraregional payments are settled using the South African Rand as the currency of settlement. Third, there are already ongoing annual monitoring of macroeconomic convergence criteria which have been in place for over a decade, indicating intent to harmonize policies and thus easing adoption of a single currency later.

This chapter is divided into five sections. The first section examines the mandate and the rationale for the SADC's monetary integration objective. The second section reviews the relevant theoretical literature in order to give conceptual grounding to the discourse. The third section takes a parenthetical look at other regions that have adopted or planned to adopt a single currency. The fourth section examines the time series data and selected economic indicators for the 15 SADC member states and runs models in an attempt to ascertain, at least statistically, which countries within the SADC possess sufficient common economic features to warrant their being part of a common currency in the first stage. The fifth and final section concludes with key recommendations.

Background

SADC documents and protocols calling for monetary integration towards economic community

Monetary and economic integration in Africa traces its roots to the Organization of Africa Unity which was formed in 1963 and later transformed into the African Union in 2002 with one of its objectives being cooperation among African states (Adams 2005). The vision was reinvigorated by the Abuja Treaty which was signed in 1991 and launched in 1997. The Treaty set the stage for the establishment of the African Economic Community (AEC) which was to be turned into a monetary union and a currency union for Africa by 2028. The Treaty outlined a programme to drive economic integration with specific time frames. It outlined the implementation stages, which were to start with the creation of regional economic communities (RECs) by 1999, strengthening of intra-REC integration and harmonization of policies by 2007, establishing a free trade area and customs union within each block by 2017, the establishment of a continent-wide free trade area and custom union by 2019 and finally the establishment of a continent-wide African Common Market by 2023 (African Development Bank 2011).

To regionalize the continental vision to Southern Africa as enshrined by the Africa Union Commission (AUC) in the Abuja Treaty, the SADC launched a number of initiatives in order to move towards economic integration for the subregion. The region pursued a linear mode of economic integration which started with loose cooperation with deeper integration reserved for later stages. The SADC launched the Free Trade Area (FTA) in 2008 as a step towards economic integration. This was to be followed by the customs union in 2010, common market in 2015, monetary union in 2016 and a single currency in 2018. Regional integration for the SADC was driven by the desire to create a fully integrated and internationally competitive region and to ensure economic growth and eradicate poverty (African Development Bank 2011). In striving towards these goals, the region has encountered severe structural challenges, including weak productivity capacities, low value added in the production value chains, weak business environment and cumbersome regulatory frameworks, which have raised the costs of doing business (Zehirun et al. 2015).

The Revised Regional Indicative Strategy for Development Plan (RISDP)

RISDP is an SADC programme of action which provides a direction for the region's economic integration agenda, policies and programmes over the long term. It was adopted by member states as a plan for deepening regional integration by providing consistent and comprehensive programme for medium-term economic and social policies over a period of 15 years (2005–2020). The economic goals outlined in the revised RISDP are the creation of a Free Trade Area (FTA) by 2008, a customs union (CU) by 2010, a monetary union (MU) by 2016 and a single currency by 2018 (Southern African Development Community 2015).

An important part of RISDP is its programme to achieve macroeconomic convergence among member states as it recognizes that economic instability in any of the member states has contagion and negative spill over effects to the rest of the region. The ministers responsible for finance and investment in SADC member states signed a memorandum of understanding (MoU) in August 2002 committing their countries to work towards achieving and maintaining macroeconomic stability and to follow stability oriented economic policies. The MoU also established a procedure for monitoring member countries about achieving macroeconomic convergence measured against specific convergence criteria for primary indicators which are inflation, fiscal balance, public debt and current account balance as well as secondary indicators which are months of import cover and real economic growth rate. An agreement was also reached to establish a Macroeconomic Performance and Surveillance Unit (MPSU) within the SADC Secretariatwith an accompanying Peer Review Mechanism (PRM), whereby ministers of finance and investment and central bank governors would monitor the annual convergence programmes submitted by each member state. The actual monitoring and macroeconomic convergence activities are carried out by a subcommittee of the Committee of Central Bank Governors (CCGB). The CCBG is therefore central in the process of developing a harmonized policy framework, common currency and monetary union.

Tripartite Free Trade Area and its implications

The countries' membership to more than one regional community continues to pose challenges for RECs' attempts to integrate their economies. For example, the Democratic Republic of the Congo, Madagascar, Malawi, Mauritius, Seychelles, Swaziland, Zambia and Zimbabwe are members of both COMESA and the SADC, while Tanzania, Burundi and Rwanda are members of both the EAC and COMESA. This has divided their energies and resources as well as capacities to work for a common goal as different RECs have come up with different timetables for the harmonization of their trade policies to eliminate trade and non-trade barriers.

A TFTA arrangement for COMESA, the EAC and the SADC—the COMESA-EAC-SADC pact—launched on 10 June 2015 in Sharm El Sheik, Egypt, for the purposes of streamlining the system of the three RECs to reduce duplication of efforts and to remove the conflicting targets for policy harmonization of member countries. The objective of the pact was to remove some of the inconsistencies and costs in regional integration brought about through the overlapping of memberships and fast-tracking the attainment of the AEC.

Why should the SADC be an OCA? Some guiding theories

In deciding on currency convertibility and a monetary union, the SADC will have to decide the basis for such a decision. Since the pioneering work of Mundell (1961), theorists have developed several reasons why countries should join together in a monetary union in order to reap the related benefits. This section discusses a few of those theories. Initially, much work focused on initial conditions as a basis for Optimum Currency Areas (OCA). Later work argued that conditions can be met ex post facto too, even if they were not met ex ante (Broz 2005).

The theory of a single currency is borrowed from Robert Mundell's seminal work of 1961 (Mundell 1961) which sets the theory of OCAs. Mundell argued that a common currency would create savings on various types of transaction costs whilst it also brings in costs for a country which abandons its currency as it gives up the ability to use its national monetary policy to respond to asymmetric shocks. Mundell further argued that the costs of abandoning own currency could be minimized by greater flexibility of the economy through labour mobility, wage and price flexibility, and fiscal transfers. This point was emphasised in the work of Kenen (1969) about labour homogeneity and perfect occupational mobility (say, in the mining and medicine sectors), which the SADC has been working on under its skills upgrade and other higher education qualifications. The likelihood of a country experiencing asymmetric shocks depends on how similar its production and export structures are relative to its partners in the monetary union.

The second criterion the SADC can use to embark on OCA relates to the ratio of tradables and non-tradables between the countries (McKinnon 1963). When there is more openness in the economy, the likelihood that foreign prices of tradables will be transmitted to the domestic cost of living is higher, which may also affect non-tradables. This effect would cause the reduction of money illusion, so that wage contracts and prices will be highly influenced by the exchange rate. Simply put, with a common currency, consumers can compare the value and prices of goods traded, exposing local markets to competition that leads to adjustments that increase consumer welfare, increase productivity of local industries and create more innovation and new methods to reduce costs (Saka et al. 2015).

Of importance to the SADC's agenda on industrialization is the hypothesis advanced by Frankel and Rose (1997) that if there is a huge intercountry trade and/or a high intercountry income correlation, these countries might find it advantageous to form a currency union. In fact, currency union lowers barriers peculiar to national borders and this leads to improved trade and welfare. Investment flows would also increase due to exchange rate certainty. Increased trade in a common currency area can cause either increased industrial specialization between regions in the goods in which they have comparative advantage, or else increased trade may result in increased correlation between their business cycles if common demand shocks prevail or if intra-industry trade accounts for most of the trade.

The recent seeming end to the "commodity super cycle" is affecting virtually all SADC member states negatively, cutting growth and reintroducing macroeconomic instability as public deficits and debts rise and poverty intensifies. Since SADC countries' natural endowments and basic structures of economies are similar, external shocks such as those currently underway will continue hitting the region's countries in the same manner. On the other hand, financial and capital markets are at different levels of development with a few large ones such as that of South Africa linked to global markets while others are still in their infancy. According to Alesina et al. (2003), suffering from similar external financial shocks is a good enough justification to form an OCA. However, real shocks that may need fiscal adjustment including fiscal transfers from the relatively well-off members to the least well off may undermine efforts to form or enter an OCA since different countries may need to adjust exchange rates differently to cope with such shocks.

The final criterion is the political willingness and commitment to regional integration and to ceding certain powers to supranational institutions. Edwards (1996) argues that this commitment means government will not inflate to boost employment, thus instilling discipline. Collins (1996) also argues that a fixed exchange rate enhances transparency and honesty in that changes to boost growth or employment will be more visible and thus politically costlier. Therefore, sustainable but less popular measures to increase economic growth and employment will have to be implemented under a fixed exchange rate.

The cost associated with the loss of monetary independence depends upon how well the individual countries were conducting monetary policy prior to joining the currency union (Mandhur 2002; Rose et al. 2000). The currency union has been found to instil some discipline and commitment to member countries for implementation of sound macroeconomic policies which brings stability when compared to results of periods prior to joining the currency union.

The major benefit of a single currency in a currency union is its ability to facilitate trade and investment among countries of the union which increases income growth and improves the welfare within the union. Welfare gains are realized through the reduction of transaction costs which are associated with costs of exchange, exchange rate uncertainty and speculative attacks (Eudey

1998). When countries are trading, traders have to exchange their domestic currency for foreign exchange. These transactions take place in a banking system where service fees are charged. The European Commission (1990) estimated these fees to be around 0.4 percent of GDP of potential members of the European Monetary Union. Other studies (Frankel and Rose 1997; Rose et al. 2000) have shown a strong link between membership to a monetary union and economic growth.

Experiences from other regions: monetary integration in selected regions

This subsection discusses the criteria that the different regions used to enter or join a monetary union or integration. Indeed, political factors were an initial driving force in most of these regions; later attempts were made to calibrate economic conditions to suit the OCA. For example, the political decision in Europe to form a union was to avert future wars. In Africa, the colonial powers sought to serve as an anchor to colonies to facilitate trade and exert control over monetary developments in the colonies. The political decision at the African Union level seems to be driven by the desire to create a politically and economically united Africa.

African Financial Community (CFA) Franc Zone

The CFA Franc Zone is a monetary arrangement made up of 14 member states, all former French colonies except Equatorial Guinea and Guinea-Bissau, set up by France and composed of two monetary subunions (Qureshi and Tsangarides 2008). The subunions are the Western African Economic Monetary Union (WAEMU), consisting of Benin, Burkina Faso, Côte d'Ivoire, Guinea Bissau, Mali, Niger, Senegal and Togo, and the Central African Economic and Monetary Community (CEMAC), consisting of Cameroon, Central African Republic, Chad, Republic of Congo, Gabon and Equatorial Guinea.

West African Economic and Monetary Union (WAEMU)

WAEMU was formed in 1964 by eight Western African countries that share the same money, Western francs (CFA francs), have a supranational central bank, the BCEAO, which formulates and implements monetary policy and use French as their official language. The monetary union was formed with the objective of promoting regional economic integration and creating a common market. The WAEMU zone has strived to converge after suffering from economic instability which led to the establishment of WAEMU convergence criteria in October 1999 in the framework of the Pact of Convergence, Stability, Growth and Solidarity. The convergence criteria targeted inflation not exceeding 2 percent, civil service wages not exceeding 30 percent of government revenues, government revenues equal to at least 17 percent of GDP and government investment not lower than 25 percent of GDP. The criteria also called for member countries to target a balanced primary budget, zero new payment arrears, elimination of borrowing from the central bank, reduction in the current account deficit to 3 percent and a total external and domestic debt not exceeding 60 percent of GDP.

Lack of coordination between monetary and fiscal policies has led to situations where the central bank, such as in Côte d'Ivoire, has extended excessive credit to the government leading to the crowding out of the private sector and huge capital outflows. This eventually led to lower economic growth rates. As a result of these weaknesses, calls to strengthen the independence of central banks from the central government became louder. Borrowing of external loans by the governments also triggered the deviations from the convergence criteria as the foreign debts increased, leading to capital outflows in the repayment of these debts. The other cause of the instability in the CFA Franc was generated from the pegging of the CFA Franc to the French Franc which was exposed to domestic inflation and the appreciation of the French Franc against the dollar which rendered the exports of the WAEMU more expensive and less competitive whose result worsened the current account position and accumulation of further external debt.

Central African Economic and Monetary Community (CEMAC)

CEMAC was established in 1994 by leaders of Central African Economic and Customs Union (UDEAC). The objectives of CEMAC were to promote the process of subregional integration with the framework of an economic union and a monetary union. In 2001, CEMAC established four main surveillance criteria for the purposes of achieving convergence among member countries. The convergence criteria were based on attaining average annual inflation not exceeding 3 percent, domestic and external debt not exceeding 70 percent of GDP and eliminating all external payment arrears. These criteria were followed by secondary non-obligatory criteria in 2008 which required member countries to have net international reserves to monetary base ratio of at least 20 percent, non-negative primary fiscal balance to nominal GDP, non-oil fiscal revenue to nominal GDP of at least 17 percent, a share of the change in public wages of the total change in public revenues of less or equal to 1 percent and a non-negative current account balance net of grants as a ratio of GDP.

These criteria were set taking into account that the CEMAC countries have experienced volatile economic business cycles which were caused by shocks to terms of trade and real effective exchange rates. All CEMAC countries, except the Central African Republic, have experienced significant volatility in terms of trade where the standard deviation exceeded 10 percent, while the standard deviation in real exchange rate was 10 percent for all the member countries. The shocks to these variables led to volatility in their economic growth which hampered the attainment of the CEMAC convergence criteria.

Due to the large share of the public sector in the non-oil economies of CEMAC countries, Lossifov et al. (2009) propose that the counter-cyclical fiscal policies such as discretionary public spending increases and tax cuts could mitigate the impact of external shocks on CEMAC countries' business cycles. More specifically, there is a high degree of correlation between fiscal balance and external balance in all CEMAC countries which can be attributed to the correlation between oil revenue and oil exports. However, fiscal policy reaction to external shocks may be desirable in terms of stabilizing economic activity but counterproductive for external stability. Such a problem could be avoided by accumulating sufficient government foreign reserves at the regional central bank when external conditions are favourable to cover any sudden external shock.

ECOWAS Monetary Cooperation Programme

The Economic Community of West African States (ECOWAS) Monetary Cooperation Programme (EMCP) was established in 1987 to strengthen sub-regional payment systems under the West African Clearing House (now West African Monetary Agency; WAMA), introducing limited currency convertibility, establishing a single monetary zone, and eventually a common Central Bank and a single currency initially set for 2005. Lack of political will, probably stemming from consideration of who the winners and losers will be under the currency union, and commitment from the subregional leaders has been cited as some of the deficiencies which have stalled the implementation of the programme to realize the set goals. Non-uniformity in the adoption of the required framework and lack of policy coordination and harmonization between the Francophone West African countries under WAEMU and the Anglophone countries, except for the Republic of Guinea, are additional challenges faced. Other challenges include different levels of development and shocks, distrust and suspicion among member countries, problems in meeting the stringent convergence criteria, inadequate financial markets and infrastructure, problems of regulating and supervising the financial market integration and uncertainty on how to conduct effective monetary and fiscal policies (Saka et al. 2015). This partly resulted in low economic growth in ECOWAS and periods of macroeconomic instability.

The establishment of a single currency that was slated for 2020 has been postponed to a future date, pending the successful implementation of prior actions such as strong and harmonized financial systems among member states. To work towards the new target, notable achievements which have been made are that of harmonizing the regulatory and supervisory frameworks for banking and financial institutions, establishing a payment system infrastructure for cross-border transactions, completion of a payment system infrastructure in Guinea, The Gambia and Sierra Leone and the completion of the ongoing integration of the financial markets in the region.

East African Monetary Union (EAMU)

A treaty to form the East Africa Community was signed in 1967 during the colonial era by Kenya and Uganda and Tanzania. The countries jointly administered customs excise and income taxes and other services such as medical, industrial research, education, transport and communication and agriculture. Besides a common market and services, East African countries also belonged to a monetary union whose conditions exhibited a high degree of fiscal integration. The community had a currency board, East Africa Currency Board (EACB) which was responsible for issuing and redeeming local currency for sterling as the East African countries during that time belonged to the Sterling Exchange System. Monetary integration was high such that there were no restrictions on the movement of capital between countries (Mkenda 2001).

The treaty allowed for the creation of separate central banks which were required to harmonize their monetary policies for proper functioning of the common market. The governors of the respective central banks were required to meet regularly for the purposes of harmonizing their policies. Each country maintained its own currency but could be used in all member countries for transactions, notes could as well be exchanged freely whilst transfers between member countries were also completed with no difficulties. However, between 1967 and 1970, the union came under threat as result of unilateral decisions which were made in Tanzania and Uganda where all banks were nationalized and exchange controls imposed against other member countries. This led to retaliations from other members, as the currencies of these members could not be allowed to circulate freely. Because of exchange controls, some member countries pursued divergent policies regarding the pegging of their currencies and this led to the suspension of all transactions until it was agreed to that all currencies were to be pegged against the dollar. However, this did not last as the union was officially dissolved in 1977.

Mistrust among members was one of the reasons leading to the collapse of the EAC. Uganda and Tanzania felt that Kenya was accruing more benefits from the common market as it was more industrialized than other members. Uganda and Tanzania became the markets for Kenya's industrial output which resulted in trade imbalance in favour of Kenya. Differences in ideologies also played a part. Tanzania and Uganda pursued a socialist-oriented development path whilst Kenya pursued a capitalist path (Musonda et al. 1997; Mkenda 2001).

An agreement to revive the union was signed in 1999, seeking to establish a common market as well as cooperation in other areas such as fiscal and monetary policies, promotion of trade and investment in the region. Some of the achievements which have been made to date are the introduction of an East African passport to ease the movement of people, full convertibility of the three currencies and an agreement to liberalize the capital accounts, holding of pre- and post-budget consultations by Finance Ministers, synchronization of budget day and development of a macroeconomic framework for the region which guides the member countries towards economic convergence with the objective of strengthening and consolidating cooperation. Other achievements are harmonization of customs documentation and execution of a tripartite agreement to avoid double taxation aimed at achieving a single market.

The region's objective of forming a currency union is attainable given sufficient political will from all the three governments, the sharing of similar historical and cultural ties and a common language for ease of communication, and the support being received from the European Union. Furthermore, recent empirical works (Mkenda 2001) have produced results which affirm the economic optimality of such a union.

Association of South East Asian Nations (ASEAN)

The Association of South East Asian Nations, comprising Indonesia, Malaysia, Philippines, Singapore and Thailand, is using the EU model to form an economic union to create a common currency area which they believe could help to prevent a repeat of the financial crises they experienced in 1997 (Gharleghi et al. 2015). In 1997, the leaders of ASEAN countries agreed to the establishment of currency swaps and repurchase agreements as a credit line against future financial shocks. These countries considered the possibility of creating an ASEAN Economic Community by 2020, a time frame they later agreed to shorten to 2015. As result of the progress made on the initial plans, in 2005, ASEAN Members agreed to expand their network of bilateral currency swaps into multilateralization which eventually created a de-facto "Asian Monetary Fund". In addition, the Asian Bond Market Initiative created in 2003 is meant to ensure that Asia collects more of its own savings to channel into local investment. These steps are now providing a significant basis for regional integration with the possibility of a single common currency.

European Monetary Union

The European Monetary Union (EMU), consisting of Austria, Belgium, Cyprus, Estonia, Finland, France, Germany, Greece, Ireland, Italy, Latvia, Lithuania Luxembourg, Malta, the Netherlands, Portugal, Slovakia, Slovenia and Spain, is arguably one of the successful monetary unions created in recent years with a single currency replacing the member countries' individual national currencies. It was established in 1999 and came into full force in 2002. The EMU is a result of a European Community goal, under the Maastricht Treaty, to create a single market (Klein 1998). This was to deepen the community and move towards a monetary union to further strengthen economic integration and achieve a larger single market for the Western and Central European countries which use a single currency. The single currency was envisaged to reduce the transaction cost that come with trading in multiple currencies. It should also be noted that the EMU was also guided by the need to develop a political union bringing together the countries with rather stable democratic constitutions (Gonzalez and Launonen 2005).

Although the introduction of a single currency simplified trade between European countries, each country gave up its ability to use monetary policy to influence its economy leaving their respective central banks with no power to set interest rates. Furthermore, no country within the EMU was left with the ability to adjust its exchange rate vis-à-vis others. The extent of the loss of independent monetary and exchange rate management depends on the types of macroeconomic shocks that hit the economy and how well other adjustment mechanisms compensate for the lack of exchange rate flexibility. This depends on the level to which prices and wages adjust to accommodate those shocks, the degree to which labour can move across borders and the extent to which fiscal policy can be used to control the economy.

The EMU holds a lot of lessons for SADC and other regions that are aiming at currency and monetary union in their endeavours. Various member countries had differences in attitudes as far as the role of monetary policy in economic integration was concerned. The dispute was a conflict between "monetarists" and "economists". The monetarists believed that monetary integration had to start first with economic and political integration following whilst the "economists" believed that economic convergence between national economies must occur first before the national economies could move close to monetary integration and a monetary union.

Criteria for entering a currency union

The concept of convergence has been used as the criteria which represent the conditions of entry into a currency and monetary union (Gonzalez and Launonen 2005). The criteria are based on the theory of optimum currency area (OCA) which was pioneered by Robert Mundell in 1960s when he attempted to explain the appropriate domain of a currency area. He offered the first definition of the OCA through labour flexibility criteria where an OCA is an economic region where there is intraregional labour flexibility. However, this definition did not come without criticisms and modifications from a number of studies which followed. McKinnon (1963) widened the definition and pointed out that the degree of openness was an essential criterion for an OCA. Openness was regarded as the ratio of tradable to non-tradable goods and he concluded that smaller economies were set to benefit from entering an OCA. Kennen (1969) brought a new dimension which considered production diversification as a criterion to define an OCA. His argument was that a well-diversified economy was in a better position to absorb asymmetric shocks than an economy which depends on primary economic activities or relies heavily on the exports of raw commodities which are on the lower end of the global value chains.

In the case of the EMU, the criteria for entering the currency union were anchored on the Maastricht Treaty, signed in 1992. The Treaty became a strong political commitment in moving European economies towards the currency union and was supported by several policies which were implemented at the EU level. The Maastricht criteria were particularly concerned with the normal variables which were to form the basis of entering the currency union upon satisfying them. These variables were inflation rate, interest rate, budget deficit, public debt and nominal exchange rate (Elena 2010). The drive for convergence as a prerequisite for entrance into a currency union based on these variables in the Euro area became known as the nominal convergence. However, the Maastricht framework for convergence did not include product diversification, degree of openness of the economies, labour flexibility or financial integration which isreferred to as the real convergence which originates from the growth theory as the basis for the criteria to enter into the currency union. This could have been as a result of the fact that most economies in the developed world, Europe included, were already highly integrated compared to the other regions in the world.

The basis for the criteria of member countries to enter the currency union remains a challenge for SADC countries. It becomes an issue because not all countries have met all the primary and secondary goals. Some countries would meet primary goals at one point in time and fail the test of either primary or secondary goals in subsequent years or fail to sustain the goals which would have been met at a particular time. This has raised questions on whether SADC is ready for a currency union because of non-compliance with the set criteria by member countries. In a paper by Doré and Masson (2002) in which they assess the experience and convergence in WAEMU, they conclude that a true measure of progress towards convergence depends on the initial position from which the prospective member countries began their journey. Their view was that continued progress towards the convergence criteria by participating countries is probably a better indication of a commitment to unification, rather than actual compliance at any given point in time. In a study of macroeconomic convergence in SADC, Rossouw (2006) also weighed in and concluded that even if the convergence criteria has not been met it is still possible for a monetary union to be established as long as there is evidence that countries are moving towards permanent goals set out in the convergence criteria.

Even if all member countries have converged on key macroeconomic indicators, there could still be challenges in forming a currency and monetary union. Wang et al. (2010) assessed macroeconomic frameworks of the EMU and found that its member countries were exhibiting a high degree of dispersion on the main economic indicators of the Eurozone which points to the need for further convergence. He concluded that even though countries enter into a currency union, there is a need to continuously strengthen policy coordination among member countries to ensure a high degree of convergence on major economic indicators as a precondition for effective operation of the monetary policy. This is because the operating mechanism of the monetary policy becomes the deciding factor of a monetary union where the benefits of a single currency need to outweigh the opportunity cost. Consequently, the coordination between the central bank of a monetary union, whose goal is to ensure stability of the single currency policy, and member states, which maintain relatively independent fiscal policy, becomes one of the key factors of economic stability and development in the currency union.

Modelling currency union in the SADC

The economic theory of convergence implies that relatively similar economies would make better candidates for monetary integration. If economies diverge in their development levels and macroeconomic conditions, the costs of monetary integration and sustaining integration would be high. The recent events in the Euro area attest to this fact with Greece unable to adjust macroeconomic policy to mitigate the impact of economic shocks as much as Germany can, hence sustaining enormous costs in terms of economic growth, unemployment and fiscal deterioration.

A regional currency agreement is expected to provide stable intraregional exchange rates and maintain flexibility of the exchange rates against that of non-members. In this regard, it may be mentioned that changes will have to be made by some of the SADC countries. For example, Botswana will have to abandon its crawling peg exchange regime. This regional agreement is expected to deliver more benefits than costs to member states.

Several tests are needed to ascertain the suitability of SADC countries, or at least some of them, for a currency union. First, there is a need to test the income convergence hypothesis to see how much diversity in average growth rates and income levels across countries there are. In particular, is real per capita income among SADC countries or at least a certain number of them converging?

The second test is meant to see whether the SADC is a natural currency area based on historical patterns of international trade and of co-movements of prices and outputs. Indeed, the costs of adopting a single (or another country's) currency as an anchor will be lower if the countries have high co-movements of outputs and prices with potential anchors. Furthermore, countries that trade more with each other are found to benefit more from adopting the same currency under reasonable assumptions about elasticities of substitutions between goods (Alesina and Barro 2002).

The final test for assessing the state of readiness for countries intending to join a monetary union is the well-known convergence in development levels and macroeconomic conditions. As mentioned earlier, the SADC has been monitoring member states on economic indicators for inflation rates (in the range of 3–7 percent up to 2018), current account balance (percent of GDP), budget balance (3 percent of GDP within a band of 1 percent), public debt (less than 60 percent of GDP), months of import cover (not less than 6 months), and real economic growth (not less than 7 percent).

Income convergence hypothesis

To assess the convergence of income, a test based on the Solow-Swan model is employed as used in Saka et al. (2015). The theory holds that for economies to converge, poorer economies must grow faster than richer economies so that the former can catch up with the latter.

The Saka et al. model postulates that the poor economies tend to grow faster than rich economies so that, overtime, there is convergence in per capita income or level of production. In this chapter, we look at how economic growth, measured by growth in GDP per capita, relates to levels of per capita GDP. A strong negative relationship indicates that growth is slow for richer economies compared to the poor economies. This will be evidence of convergence in incomes of the concerned economies. If, however, the relationship is not negative, it means convergence would not occur. We therefore estimate

$$g_t = \alpha + \beta lny_{t-k} + \gamma X_i + u \qquad \text{Eqn. 1}$$

Where g is the growth rate in per capita income while y is the lagged level of per capita income measured by GDP per capita. The X is a vector of status variable. According to Saka et al., these will include time variants such as level of central bank financing, fiscal deficit, inflation rate, fixed capital formation and interest rates. In this chapter, we use the level of population as well a dummy variable separating landlocked to non-landlocked countries as control variables. The model will be run on a panel of all SADC countries and data ranging from the late 1960 to 2014. If the β is found to be significantly negative, we conclude that there is some convergence in per capita income among all countries in SADC. This is a precondition for convergence.

If, however the test on β fails, we will then isolate some "resembling" countries and test the same model. This is based on the understanding that even if conditions are not ripe for monetary union among all countries, the same may be ripe for a subgroup of countries. Therefore, a test based on a subgroup of SADC countries may be conducted depending on the outcome of the main test. In this regard, the chapter isolates the continental countries from non-continental SADC members.

The regression results are shown in Table 4.1.

In Table 4.1, the first three columns are OLS, fixed effects and random effects regressions respectively based on all SADC member countries. The last

Table 4.1 Income convergence test results

	All SADC			*Continental SADC*		
	OLS	*FE*	*RE*	*OLS*	*FE*	*RE*
VARIABLES	*gpc*	*gpc*	*gpc*	*gpc*	*gpc*	*gpc*
L.lgdppc	0.000590	−0.0167***	−0.00609*	−0.00161	−0.0184***	−0.00841**
	(0.00208)	(0.00509)	(0.00342)	(0.00232)	(0.00579)	(0.00399)
lpoplw	−0.00625***	0.00237	−0.00676**	−0.00980***	0.00199	−0.00677*
	(0.00140)	(0.00527)	(0.00266)	(0.00228)	(0.00594)	(0.00396)
landlocked	0.00683	0	0.000293	−0.00434	0	−0.00275
	(0.00454)	(0)	(0.0104)	(0.00661)	(0)	(0.0139)
Constant	0.101***	0.0976	0.158***	0.177***	0.110	0.177**
	(0.0317)	(0.0727)	(0.0527)	(0.0449)	(0.0830)	(0.0704)
Observations	662	662	662	516	516	516
R-squared	0.052	0.017	.	0.051	0.021	.
No of countries		14	14		11	11

***p<0.01,
**p<0.05,
*p<0.1

Standard errors in parentheses

three present regressions results based on continental SADC members only (this excludes Madagascar, Mauritius and Seychelles which are off the continent).

The results, though suggesting some convergence in the growth pattern, are less clear. The OLS result shows a β, which is not statistically significant. Nonetheless, in the other regression, there is consistence in the negative sign for the parameter, which is significantly negative in most regressions. This is evidence of some convergence in per capita incomes among SADC member countries. We can also infer from the results that the convergence is subtly stronger among continental members only.

Is the SADC a natural currency area?

Although a currency area can be imposed, it often comes with cost. The cost increases with the level of disparity among member countries. As a result, it is necessary to check whether a currency area exists naturally or not as this guarantees minimal costs from convergence of currency. A natural currency area is said to exist if there is co-movement in prices and outputs. In this subsection, therefore, we test for the co-movements in two variables: prices and output. The motivation to consider these two variables is that the paper deals with a monetary or currency problem. As such, prices always come into play. The effects of monetary policies often manifest through prices. Output is also an important end result of a monetary union. As such, co-movement in output, measured by GDP, is a good sign for a currency union.

The test for co-movement in variables is based on the model used by Alesina et al. (2003). According to the model, the co-movement or absence of it in a variable can be measured by examining the country pair-wise ratios as shown in

$$R_{it} = \frac{x_{it}}{x_{jt}} \qquad \text{Eqn. 2}$$

That is, if x_{it} and x_{jt} are values of the variable X for countries, i and j respectively in period t, then the ratio given in Eqn. 2 can be used to measure co-movement in the respective variable in the two countries. If the ratio is computed for each possible pair of fifteen (15) SADC member countries, there will be a total of 105[1] time series of ratios. In the analysis, we define an anchor country. This must be a country buoyant enough so comparison of country prices and outputs is made relative to this country. Considering the various level of development of SADC countries and their integration, South Africa is chosen as an anchor country. It will suffice to mention that South Africa is the biggest economy both in terms of GDP and population.[2] In addition, South Africa is a leading member of an already existing Southern African Customs Union (SACU). This effectively reduces the number of series to only 14.

Then an autoregressive model is run. In particular, Alesina et al. (ibid) run a second order autoregressive model. For each country, we examine the model

$$R_{it} = \alpha + \beta R_{i,t-1} + \gamma R_{i,t-2} + u_t \qquad \text{Eqn. 3}$$

As in all models of this nature, the u_t captures variations in the ratio that are not explained by the past values. Therefore, the mean squared error (MSE) is used to measure co-movements. That is, for country *i*

$$MSE = \frac{1}{T-3}\sum_{t=1}^{T} u_t^2 \qquad \text{Eqn. 4}$$

where T is the total time periods and the 3 represents the number of parameters in the AR(2) model. The higher MSE indicates a lot of variation not explained by past values and is therefore a pointer to absence of co-movement in the variable. Co-movement is considered higher the lower the MSE.

Co-movement in per capita GDP

In measuring co-movement in per capita GDP, this paper is influenced by the works of Saka et al. (2015), in particular, all country GDP per capita values are divided by the respective values for South Africa. Then second order autoregressive models are run on the generated countries time series. The results are shown in Table 4.2.

According to the results, countries with the highest co-movement to South Africa's path of development are Tanzania, Congo DR and Malawi. Seychelles, Botswana and Mauritius are on the other extreme side of the scale. Their respective GDP per capita had little or no co-movement with South Africa's, suffice to say that Botswana is actually in the SACU as mentioned earlier in the chapter.

Co-movement in prices

As discussed already, co-movement in prices is an indication of commonality in general prices. In this chapter, the CPI is used as a measure of general prices in the economy. This is a good proxy, though not devoid of limitations. The major limitation is that it is based on prices of consumer goods. Even if these goods form a bigger portion of tradable goods and widely used in the measurement of inflation, there are other important goods such as producer goods whose prices are not captured.

The CPI for each country is divided by the South African CPI for each year. Then a second order autoregressive model is run. The results are shown in Table 4.3.

In the table, the listing of countries is in the order of ascending magnitude of the root of the MSE (rmse). Countries closer to zero are considered to have a high level of co-movement with prices in South Africa. According to Table 4.3, countries that have the highest level of co-movement with South Africa are Namibia, Botswana, Swaziland and Zambia. As discussed in the earlier section, we are not surprised with the top three countries. Namibia

Table 4.2 Co-movement in per capita GDP

VARIABLES	*L.gdppc*	*L2.gdppc*	*Constant*	*Observations*	*rmse*	*R-squared*
South Africa	0	0	1	24	0	.
	(0)	(0)	(0)			
Tanzania	1.261***	−0.184	−0.00514	24	0.00137	0.972
	(0.188)	(0.200)	(0.00332)			
Congo DR	1.238***	−0.366**	0.00535***	24	0.00176	0.986
	(0.189)	(0.159)	(0.00156)			
Malawi	0.553**	0.0959	0.0153**	24	0.00222	0.443
	(0.218)	(0.200)	(0.00684)			
Mozambique	0.945***	0.0635	0.00174	24	0.00232	0.980
	(0.218)	(0.222)	(0.00193)			
Madagascar	0.606***	0.324	0.00266	24	0.00239	0.861
	(0.199)	(0.202)	(0.00452)			
Lesotho	1.320***	−0.350*	0.00554	24	0.00316	0.951
	(0.205)	(0.198)	(0.00635)			
Zambia	1.048***	0.0538	−0.0114	24	0.00490	0.917
	(0.217)	(0.251)	(0.0110)			
Swaziland	1.036***	−0.151	0.0496	24	0.00723	0.828
	(0.152)	(0.102)	(0.0381)			
Zimbabwe	1.407***	−0.452**	0.00340	24	0.00777	0.955
	(0.188)	(0.192)	(0.00548)			
Namibia	1.049***	−0.0866	0.0325	24	0.0197	0.844
	(0.225)	(0.230)	(0.0606)			
Mauritius	1.256***	−0.284	0.0412	24	0.0212	0.980
	(0.216)	(0.206)	(0.0302)			
Botswana	0.848***	0.0836	0.0845	24	0.0318	0.901
	(0.221)	(0.210)	(0.0647)			
Seychelles	1.274***	−0.473**	0.443*	24	0.0929	0.794
	(0.191)	(0.180)	(0.213)			

***p<0.01,
**p<0.05,
*p<0.1

Standard errors in parentheses

and Swaziland are already part of a Common Monetary Area (CMA) with South Africa while Botswana belongs to the SACU. Congo DR and Seychelles have the least co-movement with prices in South Africa. The former lies on the northern end of the SADC geography and is closer to other markets and regional blocs. Seychelles on the other hand is an oceanic country and more likely to be influenced by trans-regional markets.

The challenge with this method is the lack of benchmark; it is a comparative measure which cannot be benchmarked. That is, we cannot objectively distinguish countries that have co-movement from those that do not have co-movement. Instead, the measure relies on the strength of one country's co-movement relative to another's. In the results, the measure does not produce countries that have a high level of co-movement in both the GDP per capita and the CPI. No country makes it into the top four of each measure.

Table 4.3 Co-movement in prices

VARIABLES	*L.cpi*	*L2.cpi*	*Constant*	*Observations*	*R-squared*	*rmse*
Namibia	0.265	−0.192	0.926**	11	0.090	0.0112
	(0.329)	(0.289)	(0.339)			
Botswana	1.459***	−0.483**	0.0272	24	0.983	0.0180
	(0.203)	(0.212)	(0.0253)			
Swaziland	1.358***	−0.389*	0.0331	24	0.945	0.0215
	(0.203)	(0.214)	(0.0506)			
Zambia	1.633***	−0.648***	0.0239**	24	0.997	0.0216
	(0.157)	(0.157)	(0.0102)			
Mauritius	0.875***	−0.224	0.352***	24	0.780	0.0218
	(0.180)	(0.147)	(0.0783)			
Tanzania	1.553***	−0.600***	0.0518*	24	0.983	0.0295
	(0.170)	(0.162)	(0.0257)			
Angola	1.787***	−0.821***	0.0311*	18	0.994	0.0371
	(0.149)	(0.152)	(0.0161)			
Madagascar	1.304***	−0.347*	0.0495	24	0.967	0.0456
	(0.201)	(0.201)	(0.0295)			
Mozambique	1.321***	−0.390*	0.0682**	24	0.972	0.0488
	(0.198)	(0.189)	(0.0278)			
Malawi	1.809***	−0.786***	0.00772	24	0.989	0.0491
	(0.176)	(0.187)	(0.0189)			
Lesotho	0.598**	0.426*	−0.0122	20	0.981	0.0505
	(0.215)	(0.217)	(0.0425)			
Seychelles	1.140***	−0.327*	0.163**	24	0.907	0.0564
	(0.196)	(0.159)	(0.0575)			
Congo DR	1.344***	−0.367	0.0402	23	0.967	0.0892
	(0.214)	(0.221)	(0.0272)			

***p < 0.01,
**p < 0.05,
*p < 0.1

Standard errors in parentheses

Concluding remarks and recommendations

We have highlighted the comparative experiences of monetary unions across different regions to provide insights that could be useful for the SADC. Multiple analytical methods were used to arrive at different empirical conclusions about the state of readiness for a monetary union in the SADC. The SADC region has decided that the net benefits of a monetary union are positive, and taking this position as given, we suggest that if the region is committed to this policy it should consider deeply at least some of the issues in the next concluding paragraphs.

First, with the experiences of Europe and other regions as a lesson, the SADC should consider how it wants to approach a monetary union given the challenges in Europe that mirror those in the SADC. In particular, in Europe a single currency has led to greater fluctuations in output and employment, and a slower adjustment to declines in aggregate demand. When a country has its own monetary policy it can respond to a decline in demand by lowering interest rates; however, centralized monetary authorities make monetary policy based on the overall condition of all the countries in the monetary union leading to: (i) interest rates that are too high in those countries with rising unemployment and too low in those countries with rapidly rising wages; (ii) the tendency for the largest country in the bloc to have the strongest impact on monetary policy. In Southern Africa, this could lead to South Africa's economic priorities receiving a higher weight as is the case with Germany in Europe; and (iii) even taking Mundell's arguments on addressing the issue, still serious moral hazard issues that exist since ignoring "no bailout" clauses in treaties runs counter to the argument that monetary unions help enforce macroeconomic policy stability.

Second, unlike Europe, where there was a high degree of economic integration before the formation of a currency union, in the SADC, as earlier noted, intraregional trade is much lower. While a monetary union might be a way to increase intraregional trade through the reduction of transaction costs, the lower the creation of a monetary union is costlier for less integrated groups of countries. Indeed, as can be seen from the experience of the "peripheral" Euro countries in the ongoing debt crisis, a common monetary policy made macroeconomic adjustment much harder for them than it would have been with their own currencies. A similar thing could happen in an SADC monetary union with South Africa at its core and many smaller, less competitive countries at the periphery.

Third, the low intra-SADC trade comes from the lack of economic complementarity between countries, as countries possess similar production structures, which limits the amount of tradable goods between them. Beyond reducing trade barriers, increasing intraregional trade might require enhancing the productive structures of member states. A monetary union will not necessarily help with this.

A fourth consideration for SADC is that the slow pace of integration agenda is due to political factors. Primarily, the seeming "lack of political will" is underpinned by these considerations: (i) A regional integration agenda has both winners and losers and so it is important to understand who gains and who loses to understand who the champions for implementation would be; (ii) although the rhetoric at SADC summits is always in support of regional integration, lack of implementation of FTAs and other agreements show that it is not always in the interest of member states to open their economies; and (iii) as the chapter explained, the impetus for integration in Europe was political and so an understanding of the political factors that could help or hinder the regional integration agenda in Southern Africa would be helpful, beyond the African Union agenda of continental integration.

Finally, while the chapter gave a slightly favourable impression of a monetary union based just on convergence of macroeconomic indicators, more is needed to decide the issue. For example, the complementary policies that would be necessary for a monetary union to work (that is, actual implementation of protocols on freedom of movement, etc.) need practical expression. The number of SADC member states that have signed agreements is not as telling as the implementation of these agreements, which might reveal a different story about the current state of integration in Southern Africa and whether the region is ready for a common currency.

Notes

1 Using the formula for combination, there are 105 possible pairs from 15 members.
2 SADC Secretariat (2013) *SADC Selected Indicators—2013*, Gaborone.

References

Adams, Paul Duncan. 2005. *Optimal Currency Areas: Theory and Evidence for an African Single Currency*. Manchester: University of Manchester.

African Development Bank. 2011. "Eastern Africa Regional Integration Strategic Paper 2011–2015." Tunis.

Alesina, Alberto, and Robert J. Barro. 2002. "Currency Union." *Quarterly Journal of Economics* 117 (2): 404–436.

Alesina, Alberto, Robert J. Barro, and Silvana Tenreyro. 2003. "Optimal Currency Areas." *National Bureau of Economic Research* 17.

Broz, Tanja. 2005. "The Theory of Optimum Currency Areas: A Literature Review." *Privredna Kretanjaiekonomskapolitiksa* 104: 53–78.

Collins, Susan M. 1996. "On Becoming More Flexible: Exchange Rate Regimes in Latin America and the Caribbean." *Journal of Development Economics* 51 (1): 117–138.

COMESA, EAC, and SADC. 2015. "Communique of the Third COMESA-EAC-SADC Tripartite Summit." Sharm El Sheikh.

Doré, Ousmane, and Paul R. Masson. 2002. *Experience with Budgetary Convergency in the WAEMU*. Working Paper No. 02/108, IMF.

Edwards, Sebastian. 1996. "Exchange Rates and the Political Economy of Macroeconomic Discipline." *AEA Papers and Proceedings* 86 (2): 159–163.

Elena, Putinelu Alexandra. 2010. *The Nominal and Real Convergence of the Romanian Economy to the Euro Area*. Working Paper, Bucharest: The Academy of Economic Studies.

Eudey, Gwen. 1998. "Why Is Europe Forming a Monetary Union?" *Federal Reserve Bank of Philadelphia Business Review* 13–21.

European Commission. 1990. *One Market, One Money: An Evaluation of the Potential Benefits and Costs of Forming an Economic and Monetary Union*. European Union. New York: Oxford University Press.

Frankel, Jeffrey A., and Andrew K. Rose. 1997. "Is EMU More Justifiable Ex Post Than Ex Ante?" *European Economic Review* 41: 753–760.

Gharleghi, Behrooz, NajlaShafighi, and Benjamin Chan Yin Fah. 2015. "Financial Integration and Common Currency Area in ASEAN." *Journal of Economics, Business and Management* 3 (1): 111–114.

Gonzalez, Fernando, and Simo Launonen. 2005. *Towards European Monetary Integration: The Evolution of Currency Risk Premium as a Measure for Monetary Convergence Prior to the Implementation of Currency Unions*. Working Paper No. 569, European Central Bank.

Iossifov, Plamen K., Noriaki Kinoshita, Misa Takebe, Robert York, and Zaijin Zhan. 2009. Improving Surveillance Across the Cemac Region (November 2009). IMF Working Papers, Washington, DC, pp. 1–57.

Kenen, Peter B. 1969. "The Theory of Optimum Currency Areas: An Eclectic View." In *Monetary Problems in International Economy*, by A. Mundell and A. K. Swoboda, 41–60. Chicago: University of Chicago Press.

Klein, Michael W. 1998. "European Monetary Union," *New England Economic Review*, Federal Reserve Bank of Boston, March, pp. 3–12.

Mandhur, Srinivasa. 2002. *Costs and Benefits of a Common Currency for ASEAN*. Manila, Philippines: Asian Development Bank.

Masson, Paul R. 1992. "Exchange Rate Policy in a Monetary Union." In *Approaches to Exchange Rate Policy Choices and Transition Economics*, by R.C. Barth and W. Chong-Huey. Washington, DC: IMF Institute.

McKinnon, Ronald I. 1963. "Optimum Currency Area." *American Economic Review* 53 (4): 717–725.

Mkenda, Beatrice Kalinda. 2001. *Is East Africa an Optimum Currency Area?* Working Paper No. 41, Goteborg University.

Mundell, Robert A. 1961. "A Theory of Optimum Currency Areas." *American Economic Review* 51 (4): 657–665.

Musonda, M. Flora, Godwin Mjemaand, and Anders Danielson. 1997. *The Urge to Merge: The Revival of East African Co-Operation*. SIDA Macroeconomic Report 1997: 7, Stockholm.

Qureshi, Mahvash Saeed, and Charalambos G. Tsangarides. 2008. "Monetary Union Membership in West Africa: A Cluster Analysis." *World Development* 36 (7): 1261–1279.

Rose, Andrew K., Ben Lockwood, and Danny Quah. 2000. "One Money, One Market: The Effects of Common Currencies on Trade." *Economic Policy* 15 (30): 7–45.

Rossouw, Jannie. 2006. "South Africa's Role in Macroeconomic Convergence in SADC." *South Africa Reserve Bank Conference*, Pretoria.

Saka, Jimoh Olakunle, Ibiyemi Ajoke Onafowokan, and Adekunle Ademayowa Adebayo. 2015. "Analysis of Convergence Criteria in a Proposed Monetary Union: A Study of the Economic Community of West African States." *International Journal of Economics and Financial Issues* 5 (1): 230–239.

Southern African Development Community. 2015. *Regional Indicative Strategic Development Plan*. SADC: Gaborone.

Wang, Jian-Ye, IyaboMasha, Kazuko Shirono, and Leighton Harris. 2010. *The Common Monetary Area in Southern Africa: Shocks, Adjustment and Policy*. Working Paper No. 07/158, IMF.

Zehirun, Mulatu F., Marthinus C. Breitenbach, and Francis Kemegue. 2015. *Assessment of Monetary Union in SADC: Evidence from Cointegration and Panel Unit Root Tests*. Pretoria: University of Pretoria.

5 Industrialisation in Southern Africa

Towards a developmental and strategic perspective

Theresa Moyo

Introduction

In the last ten years, the industrialisation agenda has re-emerged as a priority issue both at continental and regional levels. The African Union Commission (AUC) has a new vision, commonly referred to as "Agenda 2063: The Africa We Want", for the development of the continent (African Union Commission, 2015: 11). The Sustainable Development Goals (SDGs) 2030 also include industrialisation as one of the means to achieve sustainable development. Although Southern Africa is richly endowed with natural resources in the form of vast arable land, mineral resources and abundant labour, industry is not developed in most of the countries with the exception of South Africa and Mauritius. The region continues to depend on the production and export of primary commodities. As demonstrated by the impact of the global and financial crisis in 2008/2009, such dependence makes them vulnerable to some of the negative effects of globalisation. The urgency for Southern Africa to industrialise, therefore, cannot be overemphasized. This has been highlighted in several publications and by the member states of the region themselves. The Southern African Development Community (SADC), a community of 14 member states in the region, has developed a long-term strategic framework for industrialisation. The SADC Industrialisation Strategy and Roadmap 2015–2063 was approved by the SADC Heads of State in 2015 (SADC, 2015). It is a comprehensive framework that was designed to guide member states in achieving inclusive, participatory and sustainable industrialisation in the region. The Roadmap was informed by the SADC Treaty, the SADC Regional Indicative and Strategic Development Plan (RISDP), the Industrial Development Policy Framework (IDPF) and Agenda 2063 which is Africa's continental industrialisation agenda. The Roadmap is also aligned to African Industrial Development Action (AIDA) Plan. Subsequent to the endorsement of the Roadmap, an Action Plan for its implementation was drafted and approved by the SADC Summit of head of States and Governments.

While countries such as South Africa and Mauritius are relatively more industrialised as compared to the rest of the region, overall, the region is still not industrialised. This is reflected in the low shares of manufacturing to gross domestic product (GDP), world manufacturing value added (MVA) and also the low values of their Competitive Industrial Performance (CIP) indices (UNIDO, 2013a). In addition, the historical patterns of industrialisation have tended to exclude women, a reflection of the gender inequality in terms of education particularly with respect to science, engineering and mathematics fields that are so critical in industry.

The chapter argues that whilst significant progress has been made in achieving regional consensus on the strategic framework for industrialisation, and even though there are efforts at national level to industrialise, more action is necessary in order to significantly increase MVA, increase GDP growth and raise the levels of human development. Some observers (for example, Out Law, 2016) point to the likely positive effects on Africa of the challenges facing the Chinese domestic economy, that is, that rising cost pressures facing China's light manufacturing sector may lead to their relocation to cheaper locations. Given China's growing role in Africa, albeit in the context of extraction of Africa's natural resources, it is possible that China's light manufacturing companies could chose to relocate to Africa (including, of course, Southern Africa). This is an opportunity which the region should seize on but do so in a manner which is mutually beneficial.

Given the limited capacity for industrialisation in most of the countries particularly due to limited access to technology and the inadequate pool of the kind of skills required for structural transformation, the SADC should prioritise the creation of partnerships with those countries and investors who can invest in the region. Foreign Direct Investment (FDI) has to play a very significant role because of the nature of the agenda at hand. The region should also prioritise the setting up of critical institutions that can ensure efficient and timely implementation of the Roadmap. The setting up of the SADC Regional Development Bank must be top priority because availability of long-term development funding for infrastructure and support to industry, will be crucial. The implementation of the SADC Regional Infrastructure Development Master Plan is another priority action. An intensive resource mobilisation effort must be made in order to link the region by roads and rail. Governments of member states need to adopt a developmental state approach so that they become pivotal to the design and implementation of an industrialisation strategy that harnesses the use of local resources, actively supports the participation of women and youth in the process because past efforts excluded them largely. Member states should integrate the SADC Industrialisation Roadmap into their national planning processes and allocate substantial resources towards the implementation thereof. They should also design more comprehensive industrial policies to promote the emergence and growth of industries. Another top priority action is the need to invest massive resources into the development of skills in the framework of science, technology, engineering and mathematics (STEM) education. That is because the industrialisation agenda critically depends on availability of such skills.

1. Theoretical perspectives on industrialisation

There is a consensus that Africa needs to industrialise because its continued dependence on primary production and commodity exports means that it is not optimising on the potential value-addition from its rich natural resource base (The United Nations Economic Commission for Africa (UNECA, 2015: xix). The Commission has emphasised that Africa's continued dependence on primary commodities will limit its growth and also increase its vulnerability due to global market changes.

One of the major priorities on the African development agenda is structural transformation, a strategy which is precisely designed to change this dominant pattern of production and exchange (UNECA, 2015: 4). The Commission defines structural transformation as a process which entails the allocation of resources—especially new investments—from low to high productivity activities within and across sectors, especially the agriculture, industry and services sectors. Structural transformation is characterised by a declining share of agriculture in gross domestic product and employment, rapid urbanisation, the rise of a modern industrial and service economy and a demographic transition from high to low rates of births and deaths

A leading proponent of industrialisation, Danny Rodrik, postulates that development is fundamentally about structural change (Rodrik, 2001). He explains structural change as a process which leads to an increase in the share of manufacturing in a country's GDP. Proponents of industrialisation argue that the emergence of a dynamic manufacturing sector has typically marked a country's transition from low to intermediate income levels. A strong industrial sector also generates employment and enhances the development of backward and forward linkages in the wider economy (Owusu and Samatar, 1997).

Another advantage of manufacturing relative to other sectors is that there are very strong linkage and spillover effects associated with manufacturing activities. For example, it is well known that manufacturing is a critical source of demand for other sectors. In particular, manufacturing firms are important consumers of banking, transport, insurance and communication services. Furthermore, manufacturing provides demand stimulus for growth of the agricultural sector. Consequently, manufacturing has high forward and backward linkages, thereby contributing to domestic investment, employment and output in the development process. Manufacturing is also said to have a higher potential for employment creation relative to agriculture and traditional services. In this regard, it has a potential to advance social development depending on the relative mix of factors that the industries adopt.

It is also argued that manufacturing has historically been the main source of innovation in modern economies. The research and development activities of manufacturing firms have been the key source of technological advances in the world economy and that manufacturing is a major conduit for diffusion of new technologies to other sectors of the economy. In particular, the existence of diminishing returns to scale in agriculture (due to fixed factors such as land) implies that the opportunities for employment growth in the sector are limited. Consequently, as a country's population grows and urbanisation takes place, there is the need for growth in manufacturing employment to absorb labour displaced from agriculture. United Nations Conference on Trade and Development (UNCTAD, 2011: 6).

This view is also supported by Marti and Ssenkubuge (2009) who argue that industrial production creates job opportunities at higher skill levels, facilitates denser links across the services and agricultural sectors, between rural and urban economies and between consumer, intermediate and capital goods industries. From a developmental perspective, they also explain how industrialisation is an important strategy for poverty eradication, employment generation and regional development policies. They also point out that prices of manufactured exports are less volatile and less susceptible to long-term deterioration than those of primary goods and thus, it is strategic for commodity dependent economies to shift their production pattern.

There are several other empirical studies that also argue for industrialisation as the main engine of growth in economic development. Based on econometric analysis of 90 countries over the period 1950–2005, one study confirmed that there was an *empirical correlation* between the degree of industrialisation and per capita income in developing countries (Szirmai, 2012). A strong manufacturing base enables a region to produce and add value to its natural resources. Export of manufactured goods increases value from exports and also cushions the region from the instability which is normally associated with commodity prices. The United Nations Economic and Social Council (UNECOSOC), Economic Commission for Africa (ECA) and the African Union (AU) caution against the dependence on primary commodity production and exports because:

> It exposes the continent to external demand shocks and leads to procyclical fiscal spending in many resource revenue-dependent countries. Equally important, the commodity driven feature of Africa's economy poses serious questions about its long-term sustainability, as agriculture is subject to diminishing returns to scale due to land constraint while exploitation of non-renewable natural resources is limited by available reserves.
>
> (United Nations Economic and Social Council Economic and Economic Commission for Africa, 2013)

Critics of RBI argue that it is a very expensive route for new industrialisers to adopt because in the context of many African countries, they do not have the technological capacity and skills-base that is required particularly in the Medium to High Technology Manufacturing. These arguments have been used for decades and are responsible for perpetuating the inequalities in global trade and income patterns. In the era of globalisation where there are basically unlimited opportunities for nations to collaborate in production, trade, distribution and investments, Southern African countries have the opportunity to industrialise even though currently, their capital, technology and skills base may be limited in terms of what is required for industrialisation.

There is an interesting perspective that postulates that globalisation also offers opportunities for developing nations to industrialise through a non-traditional route, namely, by participating into Global Value Chains (GVCs). Baldwin (2011) is one of the proponents of this approach. In his opinion, there have been revolutionary transformations of industry and trade from 1985 to the late-1990s where there has been a trend towards what he refers to as "regionalisation of supply chains". This differs from the pre 1985 era successful industrialisation involved building of domestic supply chains (Baldwin, 2011: 1).

He therefore argues that because trade and industry in the 21st century have radically transformed from what it was in the 20th century, a different approach to industrialisation is necessary. He suggests that new industrialisers should rather explore and participate in existing supply chains rather than building the whole chain because the latter is likely to be not only expensive but also to take a long time to achieve.

> Indeed, in some industries the concept of a one-nation supply chain has disappeared. No nation today produces all the parts and components necessary to make aircraft, cars, or electronics. Some nations are headquarter-economies, others are factory-economies, but no one has the whole value chain.
>
> (Baldwin, 2011: 10)

With respect to inclusivity and sustainability, past industrialisation efforts in Africa have had limited impact on social development even though they contributed to GDP growth. It also had negative environmental effects due to lack of regulations and effective enforcement mechanisms. But in recent years, more countries are integrating sustainability in industry and, indeed, all other sectors of the economy. Past experience shows that industrialisation does not automatically lead to social development. Additionally, unless there are effective mechanisms in place, it can continue to damage the environment and contribute to global warming. Naudé and Nagler (2015: 2) define socially inclusive industrialisation as a situation where all the people in a country have equal opportunities to share in industrial growth. UNIDO (2014: 4) advocates what they refer to as an "Inclusive and Sustainable Industrial Development" (ISID) approach, one that not only leads to an increase in the share of the contribution of industry to a country's GDP but is also inclusive and sustainable. The Lima Declaration of UNIDO calls member states to ensure that their industrialisation pathways are inclusive and sustainable. Inclusive in terms of ensuring equal opportunities and access to jobs, incomes, assets ownership in the industry sector, equality in terms of participation of women, youth and across race, ethnicity, among other categories. In essence, Africa's industrialisation agenda, and indeed, that of the SADC as well, should not just be about increasing economic growth through higher production and exports, but has to be inclusive and sustainable.

2. Industrialisation in Southern Africa: review of key issues

The industrialisation of Southern Africa is anchored within a continental developmental agenda which also includes industrialisation (African Union Commission, 2015). The Action Plan for the implementation of the SADC Industrialisation and Roadmap was approved by Summit in Lozitha, Swaziland on 18 March 2017 (SADC, 2017). It is now being implemented.

The continental approach to industrialisation is also evident in that not only is there a drive to industrialise Southern Africa, but other African regions are also embarking on a similar path. For example, according to UNECA (2016: 82), the East African Community (EAC) has introduced its Industrial Strategy (2012–2032) and the Industrial Policy (2012–2032). These are designed to promote structural change of the manufacturing sector through value addition and product diversification based on comparative and competitive advantages of the region. In 2010, the Economic Community of West African States (ECOWAS) launched the West African Common Industrial Policy (WACIP) whose vision is to "maintain a solid industrial structure which is globally competitive, environment-friendly and capable of significantly improving the living standard of the people by 2030". The policy is also designed to accelerate industrialisation by diversification of industrial productive capacity, promoting backward and forward linkages in the processing of natural resources and strengthening regional integration and expansion of manufactured goods.

Continental initiatives such as the Tripartite Alliance, an attempt to bring together the Common Market for Eastern and Southern Africa (COMESA), the EAC and the SADC, also provide an important platform for strengthening regional integration, expanding trade opportunities and also for joint design and implementation of regional industrial projects. The planned establishment of a Continental Free Trade Area (CFTA) should also create opportunities for trade-induced industrialisation. Thus, the industrialisation of Southern Africa is taking place not as an isolated regional agenda but as part of a continental process. This offers the region some opportunities for knowledge sharing, collaborative partnerships, networking, joint initiatives in the development of infrastructure, communications, services and other related fields, all of which should contribute significantly to the region's industrialisation drive. Although there are variations in the status of industry in the region, generally, as indicated by UNIDO (2013a), compared to the rest of the world, most economies in sub-Saharan Africa (SSA) have shown the least change in their manufacturing base in terms of technological complexity of products over 2002–2011. The report also indicates that in 2012, *resource-based manufacturing* accounted for about 49 percent of total manufacturing value added in the region, compared with 24.9 percent for low-technology manufacturing and 26.1 percent for medium- and high-technology manufacturing (UNIDO, 2013a). The share of low-tech and resource-based sectors combined accounted for about three-quarters of manufacturing value addition, compared to an average of about 50 percent for East Asia and Pacific (except China) for example. The picture is more skewed if South Africa is discounted. Indeed, only 8.3 percent of total value added was accounted for in the medium-to high-tech manufacturing sector in the rest of SSA, while the resources sector accounted for as much as 66.2 percent of manufacturing value added (Ramdoo, 2015).

Although Southern Africa is relatively more industrialised as compared to most other regions in Africa, it is still one of the most un-industrialised regions in the world. This is reflected in the low size of its manufacturing value added (MVA). Table 5.1 shows that most of the countries in the region, except for South Africa, Swaziland and Mauritius, have a low MVA/capita, an almost negligible share in World MVA and also relatively low shares of MVA in the medium to high technology category. China is included to show the wide gap in performance between the region and an industrialised country.

Another challenge is the low competitiveness of industry in the region. This is shown in Table 5.2 which compares the CIP for different countries.

The CIP measures a country's industrial competitiveness in terms of manufacturing development. The United Nations Industrial Development Organisation

Table 5.1 Indicators of industrial performance by economy

Economy	*MVA/Capita ($) (2005 prices)*		*Share of MVA GDP (%)*		*Share of World MVA (%)*		*Share of Medium and High Tech Activity (%)*	
	2006	*2011*	*2006*	*2011*	*2006*	*2011*	*2006*	*2011*
Botswana	19.5	230	3.45	3.75	0	0.01	21.59	21.53
Malawi	23	27	10.27	10.2	0	0	11.16	12.51
Mauritius	895	982	17.37	15.75	0.01	0.01	2.27	2.98
Mozambique	45	48	13.6	11.71	0.01	0.01	10.74	10.74
South Africa	897	897	16.62	15.19	0.55	0.52	23.47	21.24
Swaziland	720	727	30.15	29.88	0.01	0.01	0.01	0.01
Tanzania	31	40	8.08	8.71	0.02	0.02	1.18	1.18
Zambia	69	79	10.66	10.21	0.01	0.01	21.08	21.08
China	One 631	1063	32.62	34.15	10.44	16.42	41.29	40.7

Source: United Nations Industrial Organisation (UNIDO, 2013a: 196)

Table 5.2 Competitive Industrial Performance Index (CIP) for selected countries

CIP ranking 2 010	*CIP index 2010*	*Country*	*MVApc*	*MXpc*	*MHVAsh (%)*	*MVAsh (%)*	*MHXsh %*	*ImWMVA %*	*ImWMT (%)*	*CIP ranking 2010*
1	0.5409	Japan	7993.99	5521.02	53.70	20.39	79.75	91.62	14.126	6.532
2	0.5176	Germany	4666.91	13397.43	56.76	18.57	72.34	86.81	5.317	10.219
3	0.4822	US	5522.09	2736.13	51.52	14.85	64.74	76.76	24.036	7.974
4	0.4044	Republic of / Korea	4782.7	9280.33	53.41	29.09	75.85	96.85	3.220	4.183
5	0.3456	Singapore	8198.27	35709.08	73.41	24.47	68.99	89.76	0.521	1.519
6	0.0240	Mauritius	803.997	1103.53	2.98	15.63	2.93	95.59	0.014	0.013
7	0.0772	South Africa	567.274	991.15	21.24	14.93	45.66	68.32	0.387	0.452
8	0.0212	Swaziland	496.923	883.78	0.01	30.97	28.96	92.86	0.008	0.010
9	0.0206	Botswana	184.355	2252.13	21.59	4.28	4.84	93.70	0.005	0.041
10	0.0077	Zambia	44.2736	111.49	21.08	10.01	14.33	19.55	0.008	0.013
11	0.0034	Mozambique	47.6064	7.61	10.74	11.86	9.28	7.84	0.015	0.002
12	0.0031	Malawi	17.2107	19.57	12.51	9.48	14.64	27.64	0.004	0.003

Source: UNIDO 2013a. Competitive Industrial Performance Report 2012/2013 *The Industrial Competitiveness of Nations: Looking Back, Forging Ahead*, UNIDO, Vienna

(UNIDO, 2013a) defines industrial competitiveness as "the capacity of countries to increase their presence in international and domestic markets whilst developing industrial sectors and activities with higher value added and technological content". The CIP consists of three key dimensions:

Dimension 1

A country's capacity to produce and export manufactures. This is measured by the manufacturing value added per capita (MVApc) and Manufactured Exports per capita (MXpc).

Dimension 2

A country's level of technological deepening and upgrading. This is measured by two composite sub-indicators: (i) industrialisation intensity and (ii) export quality.

Industrialisation intensity is derived as a liner aggregation of the medium and high-tech manufacturing value added share in total manufacturing value added (MHVAsh) and manufacturing value added share in total GDP

- Countries' export quality is obtained as a linear aggregation of the medium- and high-tech manufactured.
- Exports share in total manufactured exports (MHXsh) and the Manufactured exports share in total exports (MXsh).
- Exports share in total manufactured exports (MHXsh) and the manufactured exports share in total exports (MXsh).

Dimension 3

- A country's impact on world manufacturing, proxied by value added share in world manufacturing value added (ImWMVA) and in world manufactures trade (IMWMT).
- The CIP index is a composite index obtained through a geometric aggregation of these.
- Six sub-indicators to which equal weights are assigned.

Whereas for the more industrialised countries like South Korea, Germany, Japan and the United States, the CIP is above 0.4, for most of the countries in Southern Africa, it is very low, ranging from 0.0031 for Malawi to 0.0240 for Mauritius. South Africa, Mauritius and Swaziland fare relatively better than most of the region even through globally, their performance is on the low side.

Evidence also shows that industry sectoral growth rates have declined on average from the period 2000–2013 to 1990–2013. For example, agriculture fell from 3.0 to 2.4 percent; industry, from 3.8 to 2.4 percent; manufacturing from 2.7 to 1.9 percent; and services from 4.9 to 3.6 percent over that period.

It should also be pointed out that even though South Africa is relatively more industrialised as compared to other countries in the region, industrialisation has had a limited developmental impact in terms of employment. As observed by Zalk (2014), South African manufacturing has been heavily dominated by resource processing sectors which are capital and energy-intensive. There is therefore a case for a structural shift towards higher growth in more value-adding and higher labour absorbing manufacturing sectors in order to create more jobs.

The region faces some challenges as it embarks on the industrialisation path. These include the regional and global context within which this is taking place. The rules of the game have changed over the years. A more restrictive framework in terms of the policy space, increased international competition from lower cost producers, limited access to technology and critical skills necessary for manufacturing processes and a history of poor resource mobilisation and financing to support the process. These challenges are briefly explained in the following section.

a. Industrialisation in the context of globalisation

Industrialisation in Southern Africa is not going to be an easy process because the global environment in which this is taking place is relatively much harsher than was the case when the current industrialised countries embarked on a similar path. They benefited from state support in the form of subsidies and protectionist industrial policies. Under the rules of the World Trade Organisation (WTO), some of these policies are no longer permitted. For example, signatories to the WTO agreements have to liberalise trade by reducing tariffs against imports. In Southern Africa, a number of countries have already been adversely affected through what some have called "premature" trade liberalisation, which is liberalisation taking place before local industry is strong enough to withstand external competition. There are also some restrictions on the use of industry policy. For example, that countries may not use export subsidies and also are not permitted to discriminate between local and foreign owned enterprises (the clause on differential treatment), a policy that previously would have favoured domestic over foreign firms.

Ibrahim (2013), writing on the impact of globalisation in Africa, argues that, while there have been both positive as well as negative effects, the net impact has been negative. Among the negative effects are what the author refers to as "the extinction of indigenous development of technology and distortions in the patterns of production in Africa" where the target of production shifted from meeting local consumption needs towards production of primary goods for export to foreign or external markets. Ibrahim also contends that globalisation has diminished the "human capacity of the state" for local development. This has been through the outward movement of both skilled and unskilled labour from Africa to the industrialised countries of the North. Southern African economies have been affected in the manner that Ibrahim describes, although part of the outward migration of labour from countries such as Zimbabwe to South Africa has largely resulted from the political and economic crisis that the country has experienced since 2006.

Based on their research on the Nigerian experience, Ogaboh and Odu (2013) also argue that globalisation also led to the destruction of indigenous industries in the country. They also point out that multinational companies entered the country as the economy was liberalised and because of their relative advantage in terms of ownership of extensive capital, technology and skills as compared to indigenous businesses. These companies displaced local industry which could not compete.

The challenge for Southern African states is how to access foreign investments without destroying indigenous business, knowledge and technological progress. It is also to ensure that industrialisation enables the region to shift from commodity production towards manufacturing and other methods of adding value to the region's rich resource base.

In Southern Africa, structural adjustment programmes (SAPs) had similarly negative effects on the economy of Zimbabwe where many companies closed down and retrenched workers because they could not compete with cheaper producers who had flooded the market. The textile and clothing sector in Zimbabwe, South Africa and Lesotho, were particularly hit hard by Chinese imports which were cheaper relative to locally produced goods. In South Africa, trade liberalisation led to the decline of the textile and clothing industry which saw production volumes and exports fall especially between 2008 and 2009. It also led to retrenchment of workers, most of whom were women (Moyo, 2013). After signing the WTO agreement, South Africa had drastically reduced its tariffs to levels well below what is was legally bound. That is one of the reasons there was a flooding of the market by cheaper goods from Asia. To deal with the problem, one of the strategies which the Department of Trade and Industry used was to raise the tariff levels but without exceeding the WTO bound levels. In that way, it could still provide some measure of protection for some industries (Moyo, ibid.).

Feenstra and Hanson (2001) argue that much of the growth in income inequality has arisen because of the process of global integration of manufacturing processes, in which much low-skilled production work, formerly undertaken in developed countries, has been outsourced to suppliers in less developed countries. The industrialisation of Mauritius, though widely cited as a success story in terms of diversification and to some extent, industrialisation, is not without controversy. One of the sectors that the government promoted under its early industrialisation strategy was the textile and clothing sector. The government set up Export Processing Zones (EPZs) in order to attract FDI (mostly from Asia). Even though the country benefited from FDI in terms of industrialisation, the conditions in the EPZs have been widely condemned for the low wages, long working hours and the casualisation of labour. South Africa's automobile assembly industry is dominated by multinational auto companies from the United States, Britain, Germany, Japan. But a highly regulated labour market has protected workers against exploitation through low wages. However, relatively speaking, these wages are lower than what the companies would pay in their home countries.

An important opportunity which globalisation offers relates to a region's participation in Global Value Chains (GVCs). These are production processes, networks and linkages involving the production of high value-manufactured goods and services. The Action Plan for the SADC Industrialisation Strategy and Roadmap had identified some GVCs in which member countries can implement. These include the following:

a Agro-processing covering sugar, meat products, soya, cassava, dairy, horticulture and food and drinks.
b Minerals (around iron and steel)-the value chains include ferrous metals, fertilizer, diamonds, platinum, cement, soda ash, mining, and small-scale mining.
c Pharmaceutical products which include manufacturing of anti-retroviral drugs, condoms, surgical equipment, and a number of other medicinal drugs.
d Manufacturingwith a focus on leather, leather goods and footwear and clothing and textiles.
e Services such as tourism and financial services and ICT.

(African Union Commission, p. 11)

Details on these value chains are presented in the Action Plan.

Globalisation also has opportunities to offer in terms of access to technological innovations and knowhow. Some industrialised countries are now in the industrialisation phase called "the fourth industrial revolution". That is characterised by adoption of digitalisation. Sweden's adoption of "smart industrialisation" is about digitalising industrial processes. Its advantages are well explained by the Ministry of Enterprises and Innovation of Sweden (2016) when it states that:

> Digitalisation is changing everything. Digitalisation is resulting in enormous opportunities to develop a new, smarter and more sustainable industrial sector. The sweeping changes that increasingly sophisticated digital technologies bring with them have given rise to the term, 'fourth industrial revolution'. In order to increase the competitiveness and attractiveness of the industrial sector, many companies are working on comprehensive solutions for increased productivity, flexibility and higher quality.
>
> (Ministry of Enterprises and Innovation, Government of Sweden, 2016)

The Ministry further argued that:

> Industries and individual companies that are able to supply goods and services on a large scale and doing so efficiently, with minimal damage to the

> environment, have a good chance of being winners in the future. By transitioning to business models based on a circular economy, in which principles are closing the flows of materials and resource efficiency throughout the entire production chain, and the product's lifecycle, Sweden's competitiveness can be improved.
>
> (Ministry of Enterprises and Innovation, Government of Sweden, 2016: 15)

Smart industrialisation is a strategy which can enable Southern African countries to find new competitive advantages on the basis upon which to specialise. That will also lower production costs and enhance the region's competitiveness. The big question or challenge though lies in the feasibility of adopting the smart industrialisation route. Constraints include the large cost of the technology, the scarcity of the kind of skills that are required to operate the technology and maybe even access to the technology itself. However, this is an issue that the SADC could explore further through research.

Although the environment is difficult, it is still possible for Southern African countries to industrialise. Success will critically depend on the ability of the governments to continue to lobby and negotiate for a global political and economic architecture that integrates development considerations in international agreements in order to enable those countries that are yet to industrialise, to do so. It is also about the region taking advantage of some provisions that are permitted, for example, certain types of subsides such as research and development and infrastructure development. Some sectors are not subject to liberalisation, for example, the WTO Agreement on Agriculture. This is why agro-based industrialisation is one of the possible paths that the region's industrialisation strategy could take.

Ethiopia provides a good example of the role of state intervention and a supportive industrial policy. One of the pillars under the country's Growth and Transformation Plan is the development of industrial parks and industrial zones across the country in order to accelerate economic transformation and create jobs. Consistent with the dominance of agriculture in the country's economy, these parks also include agro-industrial parks which aim to support the growth of agro-processing enterprises.

Ethiopia's industrialisation strategy integrates substantial roles for investors. According to the United Nations Industrial Development Organisation (UNIDO), the government has taken the initiative to invite the participation of investors from China, Turkey, Japan, India and other countries to come and develop Industrial Parks in Ethiopia (UNIDO, 2016). These investors are important because they can provide the much needed investment capital and technological capabilities. The government has created a number of incentives to induce these both foreign and domestic firms to export. Examples of such incentives are (i) subsidised land rent in industrial zones, (ii) generous credit schemes, (iii) 100 percent exemption from the payment of duties on import of all capital goods and raw materials that cannot be provided domestically but are necessary for the production of export goods; and (iv) five-year tax holidays on profits (UNECA, 2016: 102).

An important dimension of industrialisation in the context of globalisation is the question of multiple or overlapping membership of SADC countries in other regional trade agreements (RTAs). Multiple or overlapping membership of a country in multiple RTAs which may take the form of preferential trade agreements (PTAs) is motivated by the potential benefits offered by the larger markets that constitute such arrangements. Regional economic communities (RECs) such as the SADC and Common Market for Eastern and Southern Africa (COMESA) are an attempt to promote regional integration by reducing trade barriers among members. This is expected to create a larger economic space with enhanced opportunities for trade, economic growth and economic welfare for the populations of the members. Meyer et al. (2010: 4–7) observe that most SSA countries have multiple membership in various regional trade agreements (RTAs) and that on average, each African country belongs to at least four RTAs. These overlapping memberships are usually for strategic and political reasons. Figure 5.1 illustrates examples of overlapping RTAs.

RECs are basically structured as Preferential Trade Areas (PTAs) in that members agree on a regime of preferences (usually in the form of tariff levels). PTAs can be classified into a customs union (CU) or a Free Trade Area (FTA). A CU describes the case where members to a bloc liberalise internal trade (that is, among themselves) but apply a common external tariff or trade policy.

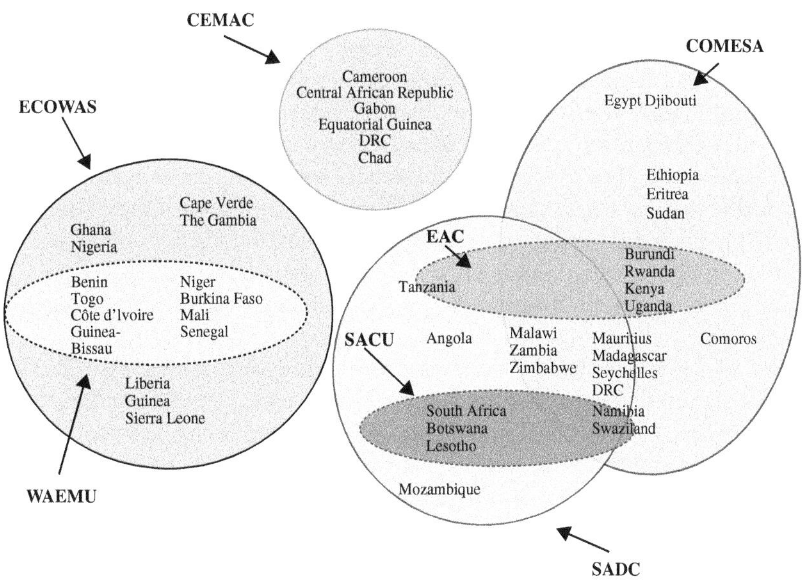

Figure 5.1 Multiple or overlapping memberships in regional trade agreements (RTAs)

Source: Fergin, E. 2011. p. 15

An FTA is different in that members to a bloc liberalise internal trade but each decides on their own external tariff regime. The CU is considered a deeper form of integration in comparison to a FTA.

Although there are diverse views on the effect of overlapping memberships on trade and regional integration, it appears that there is consensus that the benefits outweigh the disadvantages. In their research on COMESA and the SADC, the Development Policy Research Unit at the University of Cape Town (2001) argues that trade integration improves trade, industrial development and diversification. They also point out that the creation of a Free Trade Area (FTA) creates a larger market which presents opportunities for economies of scale for the members of a regional trading bloc. These arguments are also supported by Szepesi and Bilal (2003) and Khandelwa (2004: 6).

With specific reference to overlapping membership of SADC countries to the European Union (EU) Economic Partnership Agreement (EPA), Szepesi and Bilal (ibid.) point out that such arrangements can yield some benefits to the participating members. A notable advantage relates to technology transfers which may take place from the more industrialised EU region to the SADC members and this may contribute towards the development of new manufacturing and engineering industries.

Fergin (2011) applied an econometric model (gravity model) to analyse the impact of the "spaghetti bowl"—a term she uses to refer to overlapping preferential trade agreements phenomenon on 53 African countries. Her study concluded that there was no evidence of a negative effect of overlapping agreements on preferential integration and trade.

Meyer et al. (2010: 10) argue that however, "the complex patchwork resulting from the multiplicity and overlapping membership in regional economic communities raise considerable problems for policy and programme coordination and harmonisation". Some of the challenges include fragmented economic spaces and approaches to regional integration, increased cost of membership in regional economic communities, unhealthy rivalry for donor funds, contradictory obligations and loyalties for member countries, inconsistent objectives and conflicting operational mandates, duplicated efforts, and reduced ability for regional economic communities to pursue coherent and effective integration programmes

One of the major challenges of multiple memberships is that they are likely to limit the implementation of preferential integration and increase transaction costs in trade. Due to capacity limitations in implementing regional integration, African countries are likely to encounter more challenges as compared to the more industrialised countries where capacity is stronger. Capacity is an issue because multiple agreements exert more demands on a country in terms of administration of potentially conflicting sets of rules that regulate the different blocs to which a country is a member. Mengistu (2015) also highlights the challenges of overlapping memberships in regional agreements and these include duplication of effort, high costs of administration and the difficulties of achieving harmonisation.

Overlapping trade agreements also bring about administrative difficulties that may limit the trade effect of regional integration and partly explain the low performance of trade agreements in Africa. Bhagwati, Greenaway and Panagoriya (1998: 1129), who coined the term "spaghetti bowl" to describe these overlapping memberships, argues that such arrangements tend to complicate trade procedures because of the larger numbers of tariffs and rules of origin. Administration of complex procedures is likely to increase transaction costs which may then slow down the pace of regional integration and anticipated benefits thereof. Iringo (2005) gives an example of Kenya on the challenges the country faced as dual members of COMESA and EAC, and these include more onerous compliance and reporting responsibilities. Luis (2004) also adds voice to the challenges of such overlapping arrangements.

From the previous discussion, one concludes that although overlapping memberships to RTAs may have a positive impact on industrialisation as members gain access to larger markets and also may have enhanced access to technology and cheaper imports, it is also possible that negative effects may slow the pace. Increases in costs of administering relatively more complex RTAs, potential trade diversion and the possibility that increased competition could destroy domestic industries because of capacity constraints all suggest the need for SADC to assess, empirically, the impact of overlapping memberships on the integration of the region and on industrialisation.

b. Transformation and inclusivity

Transformation in the context of industrialisation has multiple dimensions. One is economic transformation which refers to the structural changes which occur in an economy as a result of improvements in productivity in sectors such as (but not exclusive to) agriculture. This leads to a shift or reallocation of resources to industry which facilitates the process of manufacturing and other value-addition activities. Structural transformation is indeed important for economic growth. However, that is not enough because growth alone is not a guarantee for human development. Mechanisms must be put in place to translate growth to development. The social and developmental dimension of transformative industrialisation therefore puts emphasis on strategies that ensure that the citizens of Southern Africa benefit from the process. The historical evolution of industrialisation in the region did not transform power and economic relations to benefit the majority of the region's population. While foreign capital dominated natural resources sectors such as mining and agriculture, benefits to the region's economies were limited. That explains why, for example, mineral-rich economies like South Africa and Zimbabwe, diamond-rich countries like Botswana, Namibia, the Democratic Republic of the Congo (DRC), oil-rich countries like Angola, copper-abundant countries like Zambia, among others, have continued to experience poverty and low rates of human development despite years of multinational corporate presence in their natural resource sectors. The industrialisation of the colonial (and apartheid in the case of South Africa and Namibia) and even post-independence eras in most of the region was not transformational to the extent that it was part of a capitalist political economy growth model in which state and markets colluded in advancing the interests of a minority ruling class. Industry was owned and controlled by and benefited that small elite. The role of most of the indigenous population was to supply cheap labour to agriculture, mining and manufacturing sectors. This history is well documented in the works of authors like Giovanni Arrighi, Dani Wadada Nabudere, Samir Amin and Thandika Mkandawire, to name a few.

A transformational industrialisation model therefore has to depart from the traditional and narrow conceptualisation of industrialisation only as a structural and strategic process that is designed to empower and enrich a narrow elite at the expense of millions of the region's population.

Another important dimension of transformation is the gender dimension

Castillo et al. (2014: 2) emphasise the importance of skills in the STEM fields in driving innovation and structural transformation of economies. Based on a review of evidence, argue that countries that have a higher proportion of engineering graduates tend to grow faster than those with less even though they may have relatively higher proportions in other disciples.

Despite the centrality of STEM in industrialisation, there are gender disparities in STEM education in Southern Africa. Inclusive industrialisation therefore requires more active participation of women because historically, industry has tended to be male dominated. One of the reasons which explain why women are underrepresented from labour force participation in manufacturing and other production-oriented industries relates to the disparities between boys and girls in terms of education in STEM areas. Masanja (2010: 1) argues that:

> Education statistics in sub-Saharan African (SSA) countries show that women continue to lag behind men in education in general and specifically in science, mathematics and technology (SMT) education. Also, education stereotyping continues, with women and girls tending to study programmes related to so-called 'women's occupations' such as nursing, secretarial jobs and social work. Programmes in engineering, physics and the so-called "hard sciences" continue to be dominated by men and boys.

Possible strategies to achieve gender equality and women's participation in the region's industrialisation activities include (i) Increasing investment in STEM education and ensuring equal participation of men and women, girls and boys at the different levels of STEM education (secondary schooling, tertiary education, vocational training, internships or attachments) and (ii) promoting gender parity by domesticating the African Action Plan for the implementation of the Second Decade of Education for Africa (2006–2015); Africa's Science and Technology Consolidated Plan of Action (ECOSOC and UNECA, 2011, para 4). These are the fields which produce the kind of skills required by industry.

Masanja (2010: 5) observes that many African States have developed national policies on SMT education. Common issues in these policies include demystifying science and technology, encouraging the enhancement of targeted funding to the sector, promoting female SMT education, building science and technology institutional and human capacity, protecting and promoting indigenous knowledge systems.

Consistent with the democratic and political transition (although incomplete), that independence has ushered in, a transformational industrialisation strategy must be a shift from the traditional/orthodox and historical model that has shaped most of the region, towards what the author boldly refers to as "a new generation industrialisation" framework to guide the region. Figure 5.2 illustrates some of the key constituent elements of such a framework.

The United Nations SDGs imply that, among other things, the industrialisation strategy of Southern African countries has to be sustainable, politically, economically, environmentally and socially. In political terms, the strategy should yield win-win solutions so that all countries benefit from regional efforts to industrialise. Essentially, this means that stronger economies should not dominate the less strong particularly when regional industry projects are selected. It should be possible for each country to have some competitive advantage

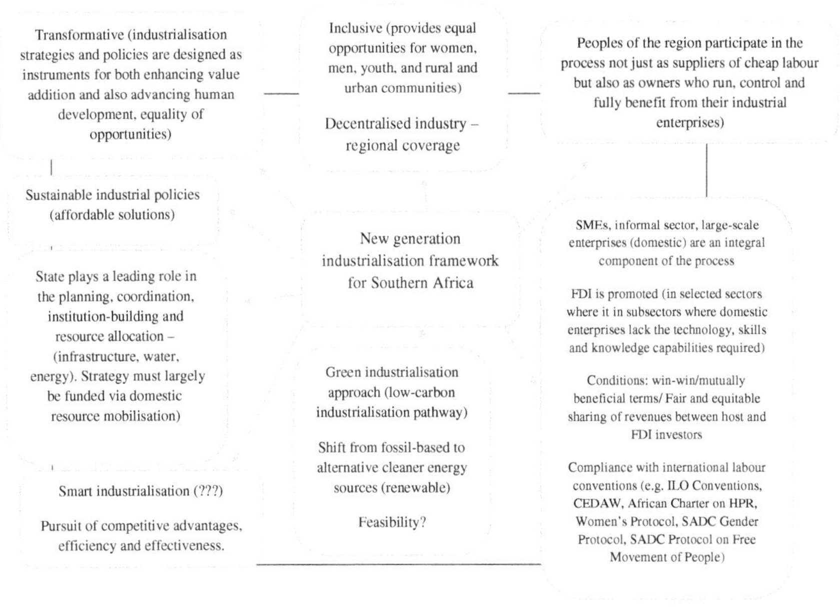

Figure 5.2 Elements of a "new generation industrialisation framework"

in some line of production so that all countries in the region can mutually benefit from industrialisation. However, this must be the subject of a comprehensive analysis to determine the competitive advantages of every country in the region, on the basis upon which, regional industrialisation projects or ventures can be established, nurtured and supported. Industrialisation will also have to be sustainable in economic terms. It therefore goes without saying that feasibility studies have to precede any decisions to initiate or establish industry whether at regional or national level before a thorough feasibility is carried out. That is to ensure that only bankable projects are selected.

This will also make it possible to source funding from agencies such as the African Development Bank, Development Bank of Southern Africa and other financiers.

At the social level, equity considerations have to be prioritised. The region should pursue an inclusive and transformative industrialisation agenda. This is clearly a departure from the past where the primary consideration in attracting FDI into industry was to tap on their capital, technology and skills even if this led to capital-intensive production methods as was the case in South Africa for example. Inclusivity calls for an industrialisation approach in which SMEs, informal sector businesses, women-owned enterprises, rural based small businesses, are supported so that they also participate in the backward and forward linkages that are created in sectors like agriculture and mining, for example. Transformation is about empowerment of local enterprises, large and small, so that they can grow into larger—scale manufactures in the long run. There are opportunities in agro-processing that SMEs can be involved in, in pharmaceuticals, in wood and furniture, to name a few. The region has to pursue a multipronged strategy where SMEs are nurtured to participate in certain sectors or activities in which their skills and competencies allow but also that their capacity to grow and participate in higher value activities will have to be supported. Because of gender biases in the education system where men tended to dominate science and maths and other technical fields and women located in fields such as nursing, teaching and humanities, women have been marginalised from industry through a gender hierarchy that characterises the patriarchal system which dominates most of Southern Africa, even though the picture is now changing.

Under its Industry and SME Development Strategy 2010–2013, the Republic of Mauritius (RoM) introduced several strategies to support the participation of the SME sector in industrial development. The SME strategies focused on the need to develop a salient, competitive and technologically strong SME sector capable of meeting global challenges'. Key pillars of the strategy include developing a salient, competitive and technologically strong SME sector capable of meeting global challenges and also strengthening the existing ongoing entrepreneurship and support programmes to stimulate the growth of new enterprises and equip existing SMEs with technical and innovative capabilities to raise productivity, efficiency and profitability (Republic of Mauritius, 2010).

Specific strategies included improving SME access to finance, upgrading their management capabilities, providing export assistance, establishing a Market Link Fund, a Technology Diffusion Scheme, implementation of the Mauritius Business Growth Scheme (MBGS).

A key pillar of the strategy was to establish greater collaboration between technology-based institutions and SMEs. This was to be achieved by setting up a Networking System which would link Technology providers, Research and Development Institutions and SMEs. Another strategy to develop the SMEs was to set up an Industrial Linkage Programme which was designed to develop linkages between small and larger enterprises (including Multinational Corporations). Within the Programme, an Enterprise Linkage Unit was to be set up in order to identify potential products, components and parts that the larger enterprises required and which the SMEs could supply. Government would then nurture the SMEs and build their capacity to supply, on a consistent basis, to the larger enterprises. Republic of Mauritius (2010). Another aspect of the strategy was the development of new growth poles for SMES. Through designated sector associations or agencies, the government planned to identify niche global markets that SMEs could participate in and then nurture them to enter those markets through building their technological and skills capacities. The government also planned to create industrial clusters specifically in furniture, light engineering, agro-processing, printing and plastic sectors in the existing and new SMEs industrial estates in order to assist them to reduce costs, increase competitiveness and promote greater business linkages.

According to a report by the Sandton Chronicle on March 30, 2015, the Minister of Trade and Industry, Mr Rob Davies, addressing a black industrialists indaba (gathering), announced that the Department of Trade and Industry had allocated R1 billion to support the Black Industrialists Development Programme. The Minister explained that:

> The programme is intended to promote the participation of black industrialists as manufacturers for the key sectors identified in the Industrial Policy Action Plan and other related sectors," said Davies. "The government is committed to de-racialise the economy through the accelerated development of black industrialists.
>
> (Sandton Chronicle, 2015)

Since the announcement, the Department has launched the Black Industrialists Development Programme, an initiative which seeks to create more than 100 black industrialists over the next three years. The intention is to put black industrialists at the forefront of South Africa's industrialisation efforts. The government will support them to participate in some of the priority sectors outlined in the country's Industrial Policy Action Plan (IPAP) which include agro-processing, mineral beneficiation, wood and furniture, food and beverages, metal fabrication and pharmaceuticals, among others. Some of the strategies to be used to achieve the goal of developing black industrialists include providing access to finance, access to markets, skills development, and standards, quality and productivity improvement. In terms of funding, the government expected that the R1 billion in funding was expected to attract an estimated R10 billion to R20 billion from other funders, such as the Industrial Development Corporation, the Development Bank of South Africa, the National Empowerment Fund and the Public Investment Corporation (Republic of South Africa, 2016).

Botswana's Industrial policy also integrated SME sector development. The government introduced loan guarantee funds to enable the enterprises to access affordable finance. It also set up a Citizen Empowerment Facility in which informal businesses, SMEs, women-owned enterprises, were supported through training, access to finance, participation in business incubation demonstrations.

Ultimately, a transformative industrialisation agenda is about using industrialisation not as an end in itself but rather, as a strategy for advancing human, political, economic, social and cultural rights of the peoples of the region, it is about using the profits from industry to enhance the quality of life through investing in education, housing, health, social security, safety and security.

c. Sectoral priorities

In terms of the priority sectors for industrialisation, much groundwork has been done to reflect on his at continental level and this has also guided the SADC to identify its priority sectors as the focus of an industrialisation programme. When AIDA was adopted in 2008, there was consensus that value addition and processing of Africa's agricultural and mineral resources is the quickest industrialisation path. It was also emphasised that the development of infrastructure was pivotal to the development of a sustainable and successful industrialisation. Investments in energy, communications, transport emphasises the improvement of human capital through health, education and training policies. Another important dimension is the need to improve competitiveness and productivity. This can be achieved through new technology developments, acquisition and upgrading of manufacturing infrastructure and systems and also by investing in research and development (R&D). AIDA also advocated strongly, the need to promote private sector development and that this should also include support for SMEs. All these features are evident in the SADC Strategic Industrialisation Strategy and Roadmap and its Action Plan A review of the SADC Industrialisation Strategy and Roadmap shows that it is quite comprehensive in terms of identifying the priority sectors, the strategic interventions and activities to implement the plan. In order to ensure that the Plan is actually implemented and that it achieves the transformational and developmental goals that are envisaged, some priority actions are emphasised here. Firstly, the Roadmap has to lead to transformation in terms of shifting the region from dependence on primary commodity production and export to becoming manufacturers that add value to the region's rich resource base. In other words, the agenda of structural transformation should be realised in all of the member states. Secondly, industrialisation should be seen, not as an end in itself, but rather an instrument to solve the problems of poverty and unemployment in the region. Therefore, the approach should be a mixed strategy which includes one the one hand, pursuit of resource-based and labour-intensive industries and on the other, implementation of medium to high technology industries. Agro-processing and mineral processing have many prospects for labour absorption and the possibility for the participation of SMEs. At the same time, some aspects of mineral processing will require the establishment of heavy industries that use medium to high technology and that will be another category of industries. The Roadmap must also ensure inclusivity with regard to promoting the participation of women and youth who have usually been marginalised from industry.

d. Greening industrialisation

UNIDO (2013b) describes a green economy as one that results in "improved human well-being and social equity, while significantly reducing environmental risks and ecological scarcities". In its comprehensive report on "Greening Industrialisation", The Action Plan has been approved by Summit in Lozitha, Swaziland on 18 March 2017 (SADC, 2017). The UNECA (2016) outlines the challenge of climate change—a phenomenon which is widely considered to be caused by carbon emissions. Industry has been identified as a heavy polluter in terms of emission of greenhouse gases. Even though Africa is amongst the lowest emitters (with exceptions like South Africa) because of its low industrial base, as the continent fast tracks its industrialisation, these emissions are likely to increase. For that reason, African states have to mainstream climate change in their industrialisation strategies. Strategies for greening industrialisation include a shift from using fossil-based energy sources (such as petroleum and coal) to cleaner energy sources such as renewable energies (for example, solar, wind, hydro and more controversially, biofuels). It also entails reducing to optimal levels, the water use and other resources that are used in production processes. While biofuels are an important renewable energy source, the diversion of vast tracks of arable land from production of food to growing of feed stocks that are used to produce these fuels, has led to protests in a number of African countries. The reason is that in many instances, land is "grabbed" from local communities. Countries like Mozambique and Zimbabwe and more recently, Tanzania, have increased their production of biofuels but that has been controversial because land that is used to produce the feedstocks for biofuels has often displaced local communities. Land grabs, as the phenomenon is widely referred to, has stirred controversy around the use of biofuels as an alternative clean energy source. Despite the losses of livelihood, governments have not adequately compensated them (Nhamo, 2013).

According to UNIDO (2013b), green structural change can also be achieved by shifting towards sectors and within them, activities that efficiently use not only capital and labour but also natural resources, in order to minimise environmental impact; making heavy public and private investments to improve resource productivity and reduce environmental impact (in one of the worst manifestations, pollution) and securing the associated benefits of improved competiveness, employment and environmental conservation.

The United Nations Economic Commission for Africa (UNECA, 2016), recommends the adoption of a Sustainable Development Framework which consists of a number of strategies such as:

- Provision for investments in cleaner energy technologies and innovations.
- Environmental standards for industry.
- Targets for increases in share of cleaner energies in a country's energy mix.
- Adequate budgetary allocations for clean energy, technology and skills development.
- National initiatives to shift from fossil-based to alternative renewable energy sources such as solar, wind and hydro as well as biofuels.

The challenge of adopting a low-carbon path include the high initial costs of investments in clean-energy sources, the high costs of the technologies associated with renewable energies, and the costly nature of adaptation measures. Southern African countries therefore need to integrate into their national and local planning processes, issues of sustainable development and to include within that, provisions for transitioning to a low-carbon growth path. Even though South Africa is still among the top 20 emitters of greenhouse gases, the government has taken some concrete measures to reduce emissions.

An example of what can be done to increase the use of clean energy is what the South African government has done through its Department of Energy (DoE). The Department has embarked on a major initiative, the Renewable Energy Independent Power Producer Programme (REIPP). According to Africa Report (2014), this is a public-private partnership that forms part of the drive to alter South Africa's "energy mix" under which Eskom, backed by the DoE, commits to buy electricity from private entities through power purchasing agreements. Under the REIPP, the government has succeeded in attracting investment of an estimated R150 billion ($14.3 billion) in its first three phases. The REIPP was launched in 2011, bringing a competitive bidding process for tariffs and 20-year contracts with government. The DoE is also promoting the development of solar energy in the Northern Cape, a province which experiences the highest intensity of the sun's rays relative to the rest of the country. The government has also integrated climate change in its National Development Plan, or Vision 2030.

e. Role of domestic and external capital

A pragmatic and innovative approach will be crucial in order to achieve industrialisation of the region. While the hostility to foreign investors is rooted in historical realities, SADC member states have to realise that they will need FDI particularly for developing their medium to high technology industries (minerals processing, oil refineries, iron and steel, metals and metal fabrication, among others). One of the factors behind China's industrialisation progress is Foreign Direct Investment. According to UNECA (2016), the government introduced in 1995, Provisional Regulations of Guidance on Foreign Direct Investment. These were later revised to provide detailed guidelines for high technology sectors where foreign investments were either encouraged, restricted or prohibited (UNECA, 2016: 66). China's experiences demonstrate that a strong and developmental government can exercise its power and discretion in determining the kind of FDI investments that it requires and in defining the conditions under which such investment will be accepted. The historical record of FDI in Southern Africa unfortunately created a negative view because of the limited gains that the region derived. But it is about how to engage FDI and to negotiate for terms and conditions which lead to mutual benefit. Increasingly in Africa, there is need for capacity building of government officials in order to strengthen their capacity to negotiate. The UNECA Capacity Development Division in Addis Ababa, runs training which can be tapped into to build such capacity.

f. Participation of industry and business

Fourthly, development of mechanisms to engage industry and business, both large and small, will be equally important because they are the players who will make or break the agenda. Finally, the Roadmap requires developmental states who will be able to integrate the framework into their national development and planning strategies, design and implement effective industrial policies, establish functional and effective institutions and embark on aggressive activities to build win-win partnerships with countries that have successfully industrialised in order facilitate the transfer of technology and special skills, massive investments in STEM education, and a more intensive resource mobilisation effort to fund investments for industry building. In his various works on industrialisation, As cited in Marti and Ssenkubuge (2009: 1), Chang (2002, 2005) emphasises the important role played by a developmental state in developing the industrial policies, support systems and incentives which led to the emergence and growth of industry in the Northern as well as Asian countries.

g. Pace of industrialisation: taking context into account

Important as the regional industrialisation framework maybe, it is important to emphasise the uniqueness of each member state. Thus, the country context has to be taken into account. Equally important to note is the value in adopting an incremental approach within a long-term planning horizon. This implies starting with light manufacturing and gradually moving to medium- to high-technology manufacturing. The timing and duration of phases is something that can be decided at country levels. It must also be emphasised through that the caution around rapid industrialisation must not become another reason for non-action. Southern Africa should be taking decisive steps to transform the region by implementing its regional industrialisation strategy. The continent stands to benefit from the research that the UNECA, UNIDO and UNCTAD, among other institutions, have already done particularly on the policies and strategies to foster industrialisation in Africa (UNIDO and UNCTAD, 2011).

3. Implications for industrialisation in Southern Africa

The author advocates a framework which consists of an innovative, transformational, multidimensional, multilevel, multisectoral and multistakeholder/actor approach which is both inclusive and sustainable. It is characterised by stronger integration of the SADC Industrialisation Framework in the national development and planning strategies of member states, introduction and implementation of effective industrial policies, the establishment of functional and effective institutions for industrial development both at regional and national levels, a more aggressive effort to build win-win partnerships with countries that have successfully industrialised in order facilitate the transfer of technology and special skills, massive investments in STEM education, and a more intensive resource mobilisation effort to fund investments for industry building.

The SADC has developed quite a comprehensive industrialisation framework. Some urgent steps are necessary in order to ensure that the Roadmap is implemented successfully. The following are considered as the critical pillars that will contribute to the successful implementation of the Roadmap.

a. Commitment of member states to the Roadmap

The commitment of SADC member states to the industrialisation agenda has already been demonstrated by their approval of the Roadmap for industrialisation. However, that commitment must be translated into concrete action, for example, member states take steps to integrate the SADC Industrialisation Roadmap into their national planning and implementation processes such as the design of comprehensive industrial policies to promote the emergence and growth of industries. Commitment should also be reflected in how much they are prepared to invest in the implementation of the agenda. Sustainability demands that at least the greater proportion of the funding requirements should be met by the member states. When the costing of the Action Plan for the implementation of the Roadmap is endorsed and adopted, member states should commit to fund at least 50 percent of the costs. This should make it feasible to mobilise funding from Official Development Assistance (ODA), FDI and development banks. One of the innovations taking place at the continental level was the plan muted by President Kagame of Rwanda, in his capacity as the then Chair of the African Union Commission (AUC), to develop a finance model where the Commission can fully fund its activities rather than depend on regional and international financiers. The Southern African region could also adopt a similar model. ECOWAS largely funds its activities through the contributions of member states.

b. A developmental approach to industrialisation

As explained in the literature review, industrialisation is not an end in itself but a means towards achieving, economic, social and human development objectives. That means that in its pursuit of the Roadmap, SADC member states should pursue a multipronged approach. In order to promote transformation, inclusivity and development, they should identify and support (on a large-scale), opportunities for a mix of labour-intensive, low technology industrialisation as well as capital-intensive, medium to high technology manufacturing to enhance efficiency and competitiveness. The pursuit of labour-intensive industry development should be within the framework of international, continental and regional human and labour rights frameworks.

Sectors like agro-processing and aspects of minerals processing, the services sector, among others, should be the focus of such a strategy. At the same time, there are sectors or levels of processing that will require medium to high technology and expertise, for example, heavy manufacturing industries. In order to build a robust industrial base, it will be necessary for the SADC to identify and support such sectors and provide the necessary financial and technical assistance.

c. Development of a diverse, efficient and effective institutional base

The implementation of the Roadmap will certainly be a mammoth task which cannot be effectively executed by the SADC Secretariat alone, even if their role would consist of coordinating the various implementation activities. At regional and national levels, it will therefore be critical to review the operations of existing institutions in order to determine their capacity to deliver the Action Plan once it is in place. If necessary, new institutions can then be set up in order to ensure full implementation of the Plan.

In terms of institutional development to support the industrialisation agenda, the following could be considered.

i. Establishment of Ministries of Industry and Trade (where they do not currently exist).

Creation of a Ministry of Industry (and Trade) in each country—where these do not exist) will provide a strong basis for design and implementation of country-adapted industrial policies and strategies. The Ministry will play a useful coordinating role in providing a regulatory framework that promotes the emergence and growth of industry.

Even in those countries where such a ministry exists, sometimes they are not adequately funded or resourced in terms of human resources. Member states should commit to providing adequate budget allocations to enable such a ministry to do their work more effectively.

ii. At a regional level, it is proposed that the SADC considers the need for or feasibility of establishing a SADC Industrial Development Agency as an implementation arm of the Community. This recommendation arises from concerns about the adequacy of capacity of the SADC Secretariat to coordinate the wide range of implementation activities that the Action Plan for the Roadmap might entail. However, indeed, the region should avoid creating unnecessary institutions if the task can be done with existing currently existing institutions. The author emphasises though that SADC needs to review the capacity of existing institutions regarding implementation and then make a determination regarding the setting up of an agency. Should it be deemed necessary, the agency has to be a semi-autonomous institution which reports to the SADC Summit but must have a degree of autonomy to do its work. It should have an adequate budget to execute its activities. The agency should be entirely funded by SADC. The United Nations Industrial Development Organisation (UNIDO) could provide technical assistance to the Agency particularly with respect to the harmonisation of industrial policies in order to ensure that they are compliant with WTO rules, since most SADC member states are members of the WTO.

Its key responsibilities should include, but not be limited to the following:

- While SADC has a regional industrial policy framework, its implementation is yet to be fully realised. Equally important is the need to ensure that national industrial policies are harmonised or aligned to the regional policy framework. Meetings to consult with national ministries of industry, planning and finance will therefore be necessary in order to harmonise regional industrial policy frameworks.
- Conduct research to identify regional industrial projects that can be executed at regional level.
- Facilitate the establishment of regional industry hubs that will be located in different countries based on agreement among the member states. Each hub should be the central point for manufacturing based on sourcing from the rest of the region. Identification and funding of national and regional industry hubs will have to be based on extensive feasibility studies and consultations with member states, the business community and funding agencies.

  However, it must be emphasised that in order to shift away from commodity-based to MVA-based economies, there has to be a policy shift from dependence on the Ricardian notion of comparative advantage (which is what led to the region's specialisation in commodity production and exports), towards building competitive advantages. By building its skills and technological base, the region can realise certain cost competitiveness that it did not have before and which could permit it to move towards light to medium-technology manufacturing.

The following MAY be potential hubs that could be established in the region (these are listed in the Roadmap) but further studies are necessary to establish their competitive advantages:

- SADC Mineral Beneficiation Hubs (for example, Iron and Steel Processing, Jewellery Manufacturing and Copper Processing)
- SADC Capital Goods Manufacturing Hub (Iron and Steel-related)
- SADC Auto-Assembly and Components Manufacturing Hubs
- SADC Chemical Manufacturing Hub (includes fertilisers)
- SADC Agricultural Equipment Hub (including irrigation equipment)
- Provide technical and other support to the member states who are tasked to coordinate the specific regional industrial projects

iii. Develop a regional framework for attracting Domestic and Foreign Direct Investment.

There are some industrial processes for which SADC does not have the technological or skills capability. It therefore makes sense for the region to mobilise both domestic as well as identify and attract FDI in the context of south-south cooperation but also explore opportunities with Northern corporations who can transfer technology and skills to the region and are prepared to enter into *win-win contracts*. The region should harness FDI sources from countries such as for example, Malaysia, Japan, India and Brazil. The United States, Europe and other regions should also be considered provided SADC can agree on mutually beneficial and win-win terms that maximise benefits to the region. SADC should build the capacity of member states to negotiate FDI agreements/deals that allow them to maximise returns from their natural and other assets and also protect people from exploitation through low wages, long working hours and other unfair labour practices. In industrialised countries such as Sweden, the government took a position that:

> Sweden cannot and must not compete using low wages. Instead, it will compete using digital and sustainable production advanced or new products. This is where the potential for a new industrialisation of Sweden lies.
> (Ministry of Enterprise and Innovation, Government of Sweden, 2016: 24)

FDI for regional projects requires skilled negotiators in order to obtain the most favourable terms to SADC. The experience of the few countries in the region that have achieved some measure of success in industrialisation show that FDI has facilitated their industrialisation, for example, South Africa, Botswana and Mauritius. In Botswana, the government formed a joint venture with De Beers

Pvt Ltd, a diamond mining company. Whereas for many years, the company extracted and exported raw diamonds, the government made new demands when a new contract was negotiated and to demand that the company's mining licence would be renewed on condition that the company would assist the government to establish a local diamond polishing and jewellery hub. This has been achieved and is an important lesson to the region in terms of how FDI can be used to promote industrialisation. South Africa's automobile industry is a product of the participation of FDI with vehicle manufacturers from Germany, Japan, United States and others, setting up shop to assemble motor vehicles and trucks. The government has used special incentives to nurture and grow the industry. The Motor Industry Development Programme (MIDP) is a massive scheme to support auto assemblers in the country. The industrialisation of Mauritius was largely achieved through aggressive strategies by the government to attract FDI, mostly from Asia. It also developed industrial policies and incentives to encourage such investments. Mauritius has been successful in diversifying its economy from that the depended on sugar exports for years to one in which it has established new industries, for example, garment manufacturing, ICT and the Seafood hub.

Export Processing Zones (EPZs) have been used to attract FDI in some light manufacturing industries. Mauritius has used EPZs to attract FDI into its textile and clothing manufacturing industry. South Africa has established Industrial Development Zones (IDZs) and is planning to set up Special Economic Zones in each of its nine provinces. China is planning to introduce special economic zones in countries such as Ethiopia, Mauritius, Zambia and Egypt. Anthony and Kim (2015). EPZs have been criticised for exploiting workers (mostly women) through payment of low-wages and other poor working conditions. Based on his research on Singapore, Yuen (1991) also recommends establishment of industrial estates. The challenge for the SADC is how to enter into FDI agreements which guarantee respect for and compliance with labour legislation in the host countries.

The Regional Industrial Development Agency or an existing institution, if it does exist, could be tasked with identifying and attracting FDI in the context of South-South Cooperation but also with exploring companies in Northern Countries who are prepared to enter into win-win contracts with provision for technology transfer and skills to the region. FDI sources could include Chinese, Malaysian, Japanese, Indian, Russian and Brazilian companies. Corporations from the United States, Europe and other regions should also be considered provided SADC can agree on terms that maximise benefits to the region. FDI for regional projects requires skilled negotiators in order to obtain the most favourable terms to SADC. As part of its industrialisation drive, SADC will need to attract significant foreign direct investment (FDI) and regional investment into manufacturing. A targeted regional investment promotion programme focusing on specific priority sectors, particularly agro-processing, mineral beneficiation, pharmaceuticals as well as green industries such as renewable energy and bio-fuel manufacturing, amongst others, has the potential of enhancing the region's productive base (SADC 2015: 19).

iv. Effective management of multiple or overlapping regional trade agreements (RTAs).

As argued earlier in this chapter, overlapping memberships of SADC countries in RTAs can complicate the process of regional integration and slowdown or even derail industrialisation. Greater efforts at harmonisation of policies related to the different trading blocs will be necessary to minimise any potential negative effects on SADC.

v. The role of the African Development Bank and the Development Bank of Southern Africa.

Although the full cost of implementing the SADC Industrialisation Roadmap may not yet be known, it is likely to be a very expensive exercise and it will therefore be important for SADC to establish a close partnership with the African Development Bank and the Development Bank of Southern Africa (DBSA) who have the resource base to fund long-term national and regional industry projects. One of the issues that multilateral funding agencies have raised, concerns the absence of what they consider to be bankable projects. SADC could therefore commission studies in order to identify such projects.

vi. SADC Regional Infrastructure Development Agency.

The SADC already has an RIDMP. The setting up an agency that is entirely devoted to the project should facilitate the implementation of the Master Plan. The Agency should be tasked with the responsibility to construct highways linking all the SADC countries, by road and rail; implementing regional telecommunications and water projects.

vii. Selective participation in Regional and Global Value Chains.

While acknowledging the concerns about the potential disadvantages of RVCs and GVCs, the idea that a country could produce, for example, auto components and supply to global markets, is an attractive one. This can stimulate enterprise development at national level, create jobs and increase incomes. While such chains offer opportunities to enhance value-addition from the region's natural resources, there is also a danger that task manufacturing may limit the development of industrial capability particularly with respect to medium to high technology manufacturing. But it appears that there is not much information around these chains to guide states in terms of how to proceed. Therefore, SADC should seriously consider carrying out a more comprehensive research study in order to identify opportunities for establishing regional value chains and also identifying opportunities for member states to participate in GVCs without undermining their own long-term prospects for industrialisation and growth as well as political, economic and social interests. The Economic Commission for Africa (ECA), through its Southern Africa Regional Office (SRO), is currently researching on potential Value Chains development in the context of the minerals sector. SADC could also invest in exploring possible agro-based value chain development.

viii. Active participation of SADC Regional Industry Associations and other relevant stakeholders.

The SADC will not be effective in implementing the Roadmap without the active participation or engagement of various industry stakeholders. Even though there is a Regional Business Forum, it has been observed that members do not officially participate at SADC summits or meetings. It is therefore recommended that the SADC should support the full participation of the industry associations (for example, in the manufacturing, agriculture and mining industries), in SADC regional meetings or engagements on matters related to industrialisation and regional integration. They will be particularly important in terms of identifying regional projects and also in determining the best or ideal locations for the regional industry hubs referred to earlier. Universities and Research Institutions should also be represented so that they can contribute in terms of research output that is relevant to the industrialisation process. In order to facilitate engagement with SMEs and to support them, some countries also encourage them to form associations. For example, in Malaysia, the government has announced plans to use performance-based incentives to support SMEs. The objective is to increase productivity and innovation in order to grow the sector. An SME Development Council has been set up in order to facilitate interaction between government and the sector.

d. Human resource development

Skills development which is specifically targeted to build the human resource base for industry is an important pillar for industrialisation. Most of the countries that have been successfully industrialising have done so due to, among other factors, investing substantially in technical, science and engineering fields. Singapore used a private sector model to develop vocational and technical education (VTE). Representatives of industry and labour organisations constituted a significant part of the coordinating body. The system offers training programmes for key industries such as aircraft maintenance and ship manufacturing. The partnership between industry and education centres was formalised through agreements for technology and knowledge transfer and that ensured that education centres were kept up to date with industry developments. The bulk of the curriculum consists of practical work (UNIDO, 2013b:

154). India's Skills Development Initiative, which aims to provide 1 million workers with employable skills over five years with an additional million workers each year after that, is a public-private partnership (UNIDO, 2013b: 154).

Extensive investments in regional training centres will be important. For instance, for each of the areas identified as possible industrial hubs, a regional training institute could be set up in the country or countries where the hub or hubs are located.

i. SADC Regional Training Institute for Mineral Processing and Development (Beneficiation)

ii. SADC Regional Training Institute for Auto Assembly and Components Manufacturing

iii. SADC Regional Training Institute in Industrial and Chemical Engineering

iv. SADC Regional Centre for STEM Education

The regional institutes should serve the entire region and since they are likely to be expensive to set up and run, this regional arrangement should be more cost effective than for each member state to set up its own institutes. SADC will need to mobilise resources to finance such institutes. Member states could commit an agreed percentage of their resource rents towards financing of these initiatives.

At national level, member states should strengthen the capacity of existing colleges, universities and other training institutions in order to increase their capacity to provide STEM education and training. These are but a few examples. Member States should be in a position to identify those institutes that they consider to be priority in order to achieve their goal for industrialisation.

Member states should also ensure gender balance in the development of human capacity in STEM education. That is because due to gender bias, stereotyping and some cultural attitudes, women and girls have not equally accessed opportunities to acquire the education. However, most countries now have legislation and policies in place to create equal opportunities between men, women, girls and boys. More effort is required in terms of implementation.

4. Conclusion

The industrialisation of Southern Africa is no longer a debatable issue. The push for industrialisation is now a continental agenda which has been endorsed within the framework of Agenda 2063, the African Industrialisation Development Action Plan and the SDGs Agenda 2030. The SADC has developed an Industrialisation Strategy and Roadmap which is aligned to the continental industrial development agendas and developed an Action Plan which is being elaborated for implementation. Clearly, there is a clear Roadmap to guide the industrialisation of the region. While the chapter acknowledges the importance of the Roadmap, it is concerned about the rather limited institutional structure that is required for effective implementation of the strategy. It therefore strongly recommends a number of measures. Firstly, SADC member states demonstrate their commitment by pledging to finance at least 50 percent of the budget for the Action Plan. Member states can also show their commitment by integrating into their national development planning processes and budgets, the strategic and policy issues from the Roadmap. Secondly, it is recommended that the SADC and member states establish strong and effective institutions to support the industrialisation process both at regional as well as national levels. Each member state should at least have a Ministry of Industry (and Trade) (or similar configuration) that is adequately resourced in terms of human, technical and financial skills. Though the Department of Industry and Trade (DTI), South Africa has been effective in providing incentives and promoting investments into the manufacturing sector (Wentzel and Steyn, 2014).

At regional level, it will be important to establish a Regional Industrial Development Agency which shall be responsible for coordinating most of the implementation activities for the Action Plan. A range of other relevant institutions that must be top priority include a regional infrastructure development agency, a regional development bank, national development banks, national level SME Development Funds, strengthening or introduction of additional vocational and training institutions. Thirdly, mobilisation of FDI as well as domestic investment will also be critical because the SADC does not have all the technology and expertise particularly for high technology industries in mining and agriculture for example. Fourthly, each of the member states should also consider developing a comprehensive industrial policy framework which is aligned to the Roadmap. Fifthly, and as Wood (1994) notes, this can change the fortunes of the region. SADC member states should set up and support skills development initiatives particularly in the fields of STEM. They can invest in the expansion of the capacity of existing colleges and universities and where necessary, establish more institutions.

Finally, the SADC should consider developing a more inclusive industrialisation in terms of gender and participation of youth, rural communities and other marginalised groups. The Action Plan should have explicit activities which are adequately funded in order to integrate the participation of women and the youth into the different types of industries to be established at regional as well as national levels.

References

Adelman, I., Bourniaux, J.-M., and Waelbroeck, J. 1989. "Agricultural Development-Led Industrialization in a Global Perspective." In J. G. Williamson and V. R. Panchamukhi (eds.), *The Balance between Industry and Agriculture in Economic Development: Volume 2, Sector Proportions*, Houndmills and London: MacMillan Press, pp. 320–339.

African Union Commission. 2015. *Agenda 20163: The Africa We Want: First Ten-Year Implementation Plan 2014–2–23*, Addis Ababa: African Union.

Anthony, R. and Kim, Y. 2015."Chinese Industrialisation in Africa." *Opinion*. 30 November.

Baldwin, R. 2011. "Trade and Industrialization after Globalization's Second Unbundling: How Building and Joining a Supply Chain Are Different and Why It Matters." National Bureau of Research. Working Paper 17716. Available at http://www.nber.org/papers/17716. Accessed on 1 June 2020.

Castillo, R., Grazzi, M., and Tacsir, E. 2014."Women in Science and Technology: What Does the Literature Say?" *Inter-American Development Bank*. https://publications.iadb.org/bitstream/handle. Accessed on 19 October 2018.

Chang, H. J. 2002. *Kicking Away the Ladder: Development Strategy in Historical Perspective*, London: Anthem Press.

Chang, H. J. 2005. *Why Developing Countries Need Tariffs? How WTO NAMA Negotiations Could Deny Developing Countries' Right to a Future. South Perspectives*, Geneva: South Centre.

Deloitte Frontier Advisory. 2015. "Structural Transformation: Is China Bad for Africa's Industrialisation?" *Economic Perspectives*, Vol. 12, No. 4, pp. 31–50.

Development Policy Research Unit. 2001. "COMESA and SADC: What the Literature Says about the Current Situation." DPRU Policy Brief No. 01/P15. August. Industrial Strategy Project regional integration. Cape Town. University of Cape Town.

ECOSOC and UNECA. 2011."Mainstreaming Gender, Science, Technology and Innovation Systems in the East African Community." Second Session of the Committee on Development Information, Science and Technology (CODIST-II) 2 to 5 May.

European Centre for Development Policy Management. 2015. "Resource-Based Industrialisation in Africa: Optimising Linkages." *Discussion Paper No 179*.

Feenstra, R. C., and Hanson, G. H. 2001. *Global Production Sharing and Rising Inequality: A Survey of Trade and Wages*. Working Paper 8372. National Bureau of Economic Research, Cambridge. https://nber.org/papers/w8372/. Accessed on 30 April 2020.

Fergin, E. 2011."Tangled Up in a Spaghetti Bowl-Trade Effects of Overlapping Preferential Trade Agreements in Africa." Bachelor Thesis in Economics. Fall. Lund University. School of Economics and Management, Lund, Sweden.

Ibrahim, A.A. 2013."The Impact of Globalisation on Africa." *International Journal of Human and Social Sciences*, Vol. 3, No. 15, pp. 85–98.

Iringo, E.M. 2005. "Regional Economic Integration: The Challenge of Dual Membership to Kenya- with Special Reference to EAC and COMESA." Project Paper for Masters in International Studies. Institute of Diplomacy and International Studies, University of Nairobi.

Khandelwa, P.2004. "COMESA and SADC: Prospects and Challenges for Regional Trade Integration." *IMF Working Paper* WP/04/227.

Luis, M.A. 2004. "Swimming in the Spaghetti Bowl: Challenges for Developing Countries under the New Regionalism." In *Policy Issues in International Trade and Commodities Study Series*, no 27, Geneva: United Nations Conference on Trade and Development (UNCTAD).

Marti, D. and Ssenkubuge, I. 2009. "Industrialisation and Industrial Policy in Africa: Is It a Policy Priority?" Feasibility Studies Have to Precede Any Decisions to Initiate or Establish Industry Whether at Regional\or National Level before a thorough Feasibility Is Carried Out: That Is to Ensure That Only Bankable Projects Are Selected. This South Centre, Geneva.

Masanja, V. G. 2010."Increasing Women's Participation in Science, Mathematics and Technology Education and Employment in Africa." United Nations Division for the Advancement of Women. United Nations Educational, Scientific and Cultural Organization (UNESCO). Expert group meeting. Gender, science and technology, Paris, France, 28 September–1 October.

Mengistu, M.M. 2015. Multiplicity of African Regional Economic Communities and Overlapping Memberships: A Challenge for African Integration. International Journal of Economics, Finance and Management. Vol. 3, Issue 5, pp. 417–425. doi: 10.11648/j.ijefm.20150305.12

Meyer, N., Fenyes, T., Breitenbach, M., and Idsardi, E. 2010. "Bilateral and Regional Trade Agreements and Technical Barriers to Trade: An African Perspective." *OECD Trade Policy Working Papers*, No. 96.

Ministry of Enterprise and Innovation. 2016. "A Strategy for New Industrialisation for Sweden." Government of Sweden. Article no N2016.06. Printed by Elanders.

Moyo, T. 2013."Public Policy Responses to the Global Financial and Economic Crisis: Lessons from South Africa." *Africa Insight*, Vol. 43, No. 3 (Dec.), pp. 29–42.

Naudé, W. and Nagler, P. 2015."Industrialisation, Innovation, Inclusion", UNIDO/UNU-MERIT Background papers for the UNIDO, Industrial Development Report 2016: IDR 2016WP7.

Nhamo, G. 2013."Green Economy Readiness in South Africa: A Focus on the National Sphere of Government." *International Journal of African Renaissance Studies: Multi-, Inter- and Transdisciplinarity*, Vol. 8, No. 1, pp. 115–142.

Ogaboh, A. A. M. and Odu, E. 2013. "Globalisation and the Challenge of Industrialization in Developing Nations: The Nigerian Experience." *International Journal of Human and Social Sciences*, Vol. 12, No. 4 (Jul.–Aug.), pp. 41–47.

Out Law. 2016. China Boosts Investments in Namibia as Part of Growing African Presence for Chinese Firms. www.out-law.com/ Accessed on 11 September 2016.

Owusu, F. and Samatar, A. I. 1997. Industrial Strategies and the African State: The Botswana Experience. www.public,iastate.edu Accessed on 24 July 2014.

Ramdoo, I. 2015. Resource-Based Industrialisation in Africa: Optimizing Linkages and Value Chains in the Extractive Sector. Discussion paper, 179, European Centre for Development Management (ECDM), Maastricht.

Republic of South Africa (RSA). www.southafrica.info/business/economy/black-industrialist/ Accessed on 29 October 2016.

Rodrik, D. 2001. *Development Strategies for the Next Century*, Harvard: Harvard University.

Sandton Chronicle. 2015. R 1 Billion for Black Industrialists Programme. https://sandtonchronicle.co.za/114568/r1-billion-for-black-industrialists-programme Accessed on 30 April 2020.

Southern Africa Development Community (SADC). 2015. Communique of the Extraordinary Meeting of the SADC Summit of Heads of State and Government, Harare, Zimbabwe. http://sadc.int/ Accessed on 29 April 2015.

Southern Africa Development Community (SADC). 2017. 37th Summit of Heads of State and Government OR Tambo Building, Department of International Relations and Cooperation (DIRCO), SADC, Pretoria.

Szepesi, S. and Bilal, S. 2003. "EPA Impact Studies SADC and the Regional Coherence." EACDM in Brief, 2B. September.

Szirmai, A. 2012"Industrialisation as an Engine of Growth in Developing Countries, 1950–2005." *Structural Change and Economic Dynamics*, Vol. 23, pp. 406–420.

UNECA. 2015. *Economic Report on Africa 2015: Industrializing Through Trade*, Addis Ababa: UN Economic Commission for Africa.

UNECA. 2016. *Transformative Industrial Policy for Africa*, Addis Ababa: UN Economic Commission for Africa.

UNIDO. 2013a. "The Industrial Competitiveness of Nations: Back, Forging Ahead." Competitive Industrial Performance Report 2012/2013UNIDO, Vienna.

UNIDO. 2013b. *Industrial Development Report: Sustaining Employment Growth: The Role of Manufacturing and Structural Change*, Vienna: UNIDO.

UNIDO. 2014. *Inclusive and Sustainable Industrial Development: Creating Shared Prosperity: Safeguarding the Environment*, Vienna: UNIDO.

UNIDO and UNCTAD. 2011. *Economic Development Report: Fostering Industrial Development in Africa in the New Global Environment*, Vienna: UNIDO.

United Nations Conference on Trade and Development (UNCTAD). 2011. *Fostering Industrial Development in African in the New Global Environment*. Geneva: UNCTAD.

United Nations Economic and Social Council Economic Commission for Africa. 2013. "Industrialization for an Emerging Africa." Issues paper. Sixth Joint Annual Meetings of the ECA Conference of African Ministers of Finance, Planning and Economic Development and AU Conference of Ministers of Economy and Finance Abidjan, Côte d'Ivoire, 25 and 26 March.

United Nations Economic Commission for Africa (UNECA). 2016. Economic Report on Africa. Greening Africa's Industrialization.

United Nations Industrial Development Organisation (UNIDO). 2016. Ethiopia's Industrialization Drive Sets Example for Africa.6 February. www.ena.gov.et/en/ Accessed on 9 November 2016.

Wentzel, M. S. I. and Steyn, M. 2014."Investment Promotion in the South African Manufacturing Industry: Incentive Comparisons with Malaysia and Singapore." *South African Journal of Economic Management*, Vol. 17. No 3 (Jul.).

Wood, A. 1994. *North-South Trade, Employment and Inequality: Changing Fortunes in Skill Driven World*, Oxford: Oxford University Press.

Yuen, B. 1991. "Planning and Development of Industrial Estates in Singapore." *Third World Planning Review*, Vol. 13, No. 1, pp. 47–68.

Zalk, N. 2014. What Is the Role of Manufacturing in Boosting Economic Growth and Employment in South Africa? 11 February. www.econ3x3.org/article/ Accessed on 8 September 2016.

6 Agriculture and developmental regionalism in Southern Africa

Rhoda Mofya-Mukuka and Brian Chisanga

1. Introduction

It is a well-established fact that regional integration plays an important role in national and regional development. Central to the achievement of the aforementioned is a concept that has gained prominence in the trade discourse: "developmental regionalism". Developmental regionalism is defined as "development-based integration agenda aimed at securing the traditional benefits of regional integration ensuring that such benefits flow to all member countries and seeking to enhance the integration of member countries into world markets as a means of fostering sustainable development" (UNCTAD, 2011).

The current emphasis on developmental regionalism stems from the fact that since independence, regional economic communities (RECs) have laid emphasis on a linear process of attaining market integration, in which groups of countries move progressively from a free trade area to a customs union, a common market, an economic union and eventually a political union, by reducing barriers to economic and non-economic transactions amongst participating countries. This process has largely failed to uplift the economies of member countries (UNCTAD, 2013). The developmental regionalism paradigm, therefore, goes beyond the domain of trade by including cooperation in other, more ambitious areas, such as industrial policy, investment in strategic areas such as infrastructure, promotion of research and development and building the domestic productive capacities of both the private sector and state-owned enterprises, among other things (UNCTAD, 2013).

Agriculture contributes significantly to the economies of SADC member states. As such, enhanced trade in agricultural products potentially provides a tool for fighting poverty, promoting regional integration and increasing economic growth and welfare. Agriculture's contribution to the national GDP ranges from 3 percent (Botswana, South Africa) to 10–25 percent (Angola, Namibia, Zimbabwe, Zambia, Mozambique and Madagascar) up to 25–50 percent (DRC, Malawi, Tanzania). Furthermore, agricultural exports are a major foreign exchange earner, contributing on average 13 percent to total export earnings (UNECA Southern Africa, 2013). Given the importance of the agricultural sector in SADC countries, developmental regionalism is an important avenue for realising the full benefits for the SADC member states as well as the region as a whole. However, growth in the agricultural sector is constrained by low productivity in crops and livestock which limits agricultural development. Limited agricultural development entails a low production base in individual SADC countries that further limits the scope of developmental regionalism because essentially countries have inadequate outputs of commodities and lack the diversity necessary for trade and regionalism to flourish.

Given the foregoing, the key objectives of this chapter are 1) to identify the benefits of agricultural development and how that promotes developmental regionalism in Southern Africa, 2) discuss whether and how agricultural development in the SADC region is taking place, 3) review regional policies that favour agricultural development and 4) identify pathways for agricultural development in the SADC region.

The chapter is organised into ten sections. The first section is the introduction. The second discusses the importance of agricultural development in Southern Africa. The third section shows the challenges of agricultural trade in the region. The fourth section briefly highlights the status of agricultural production in Southern Africa. The fifth section analyses agricultural trade within and outside the SADC region, while the sixth section reviews the main trade policies, agriculture and their linkages with developmental regionalism. The seventh section examines the importance and evidence of regional collaboration in agriculture and the implications for agro-processing and the development of regional value chains in the region, and the eighth section closes the chapter with conclusions and recommendations.

2. The importance of agriculture in developmental regionalism

In general, developmental regionalism is important for national and regional development. One of the well-known benefits of openness to regional trade is that members can have access to expanded market for products and it offers consumers access to a wide range of products and services. In this regard, market integration initiatives are often aimed at reducing tariffs and non-tariff barriers. Another strand of the benefit of regional integration is the increase of Foreign Direct Investments (FDI) arising from the membership of regional blocs. Being part of regional trading blocs increases FDI (Lederman et al., 2005, p. 128). Regionalism also increases the regional bargaining power in trade negotiations. Developmental regionalism is necessary for developing states wishing to have their voices heard in the global system. Regionalism can also bring about other benefits such as the maintenance of peace and reducing political conflicts through increased regional trade arising from the creation of Free Trade Agreements (FTAs) (Mansfield & Pevehouse, 2000).

From an agricultural standpoint, developmental regionalism has the ability to increase the overall supply of food available in a country through a combination of domestic production and imports. Baldwin (1997) explain that this relationship is premised on the assumption that countries will specialise in the production of those food items over which they have a comparative advantage and import those food supplies that can be produced more cheaply by other regional member states

Developmental regionalism entails opening up to international trade which has a number of advantages for the region's consumers and producers. Open borders offer a financially inexpensive means of reducing the domestic price volatility of staple foods. Among smallholder farmers, many of who are net buyers of food, reliable food supplies and reduced price volatility permit them to diversify into higher-value production, thus opening new pathways out of poverty. Failure to allow regional trade in food staples could stall production growth and private investment in agriculture. With regional integration, food supplies flow from regions where they are in excess supply to areas where there is excess demand, thereby achieving parity and stability in price (Quigley, 2008).

3. The challenges of agricultural trade in the region

Rakotoarisoa et al. (2011) notes that Africa has become a net importer of food as a result of several factors including population growth, low and stagnating agricultural productivity, policy distortions, weak institutions and poor infrastructure. The challenges of agricultural trade within Southern Africa mainly hinge on low agricultural productivity and poor infrastructure. In turn, these challenges militate against developmental regionalism in several ways. First and foremost, the region does not have adequate production capacity to generate exportable surpluses of commodities.

Secondly, lack of infrastructure presents a major constraint. According to Platteau (2000), inadequate infrastructural development has long been identified as an important impediment to agricultural productivity in many African countries. Roads, transportation services and telecommunication networks are relatively undeveloped in several agricultural hinterlands, thereby restricting farmers' access to critical farm inputs. In some remote areas, poor transportation systems adversely affect the marketing of outputs, a problem that discourages farmers' efforts to increase productivity. A number of African countries also have limited irrigation systems, thus compelling farmers to depend almost exclusively on rain fed farming systems. Within the whole of sub-Saharan Africa, total investment in irrigation is 4 percent of crop area, a figure far below that found in other world regions. These infrastructural problems are well noted in the World Development Report (2008) which emphasises that sub-Saharan Africa is massively disadvantaged in infrastructure, increasing transaction costs and market risks. In part due to low population densities, there are fewer and less developed roads in sub-Saharan Africa than there were in Asia at the time of the green revolution. Sub-Saharan countries are small, many of them landlocked, and barriers to trade are relatively high because of high transport costs (Calderón & Servén, 2008).

Thirdly, low investment in research and development constitutes another critical constraint to raising agricultural productivity in Africa (Challinor et al., 2007). Even where innovative farming practices have been developed by research institutions, there are significant challenges in scaling up these successes. Oftentimes, these challenges result because the innovations either are not developed with farmers or do not fit their context-specific circumstances.

The other factor contributing to low intraregional trade are policies that restrict trade among countries within the SADC region such as non-tariff barriers and export/import bans. These are discussed in section six. Lastly, the region is also largely constrained by institutional deficiencies, insecurity and conflicts

4. Agricultural production in the SADC region

The SADC region has a diversity of agricultural products that are produced in different countries. Figure 6.1 shows the production and deficit/surplus position of maize in the region while Figure 6.2 shows the deficit/surplus position of other cereals. As the main cereal, maize is produced by most of the countries in the SADC region. However, in the 2015/16 agricultural season, most of the countries found themselves in a deficit position, due to the El Nino weather situation, which necessitated imports. Tanzania and Zambia were the only countries in the region able to supply to the region with maize.

The region is deficit in other cereals such as wheat and rice although it is surplus in cereals such as sorghum, millet and cassava. The major deficit countries

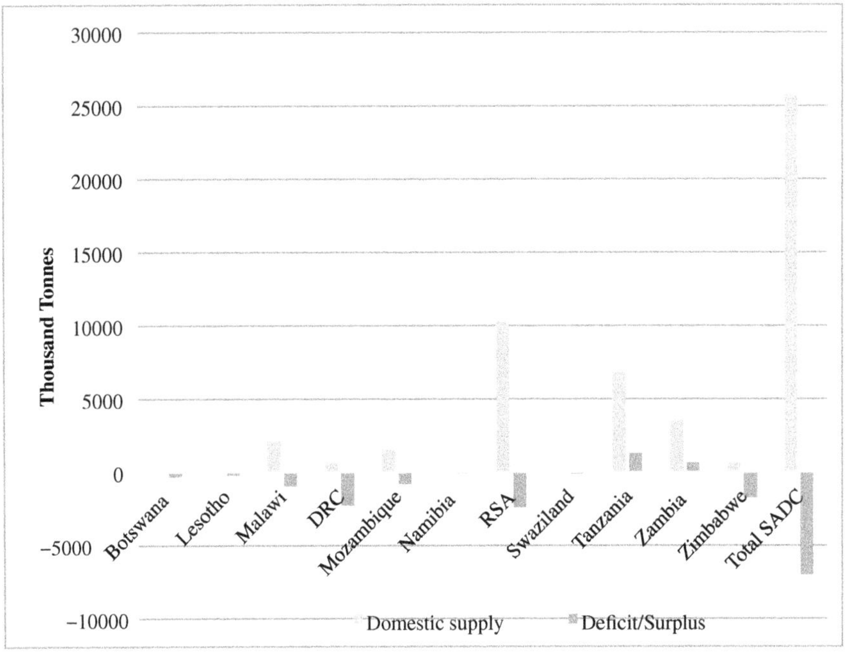

Figure 6.1 Domestic supply, deficit/surplus of maize in the SADC region: 2015/16 season

Source: FEWSNet, 2016

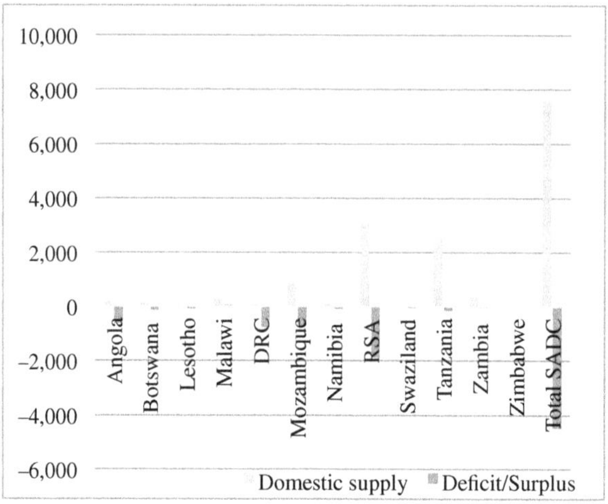

Figure 6.2 Domestic Supply, Deficit/Surplus of other cereals in the SADC region: 2014/15 season

Source: SADC, 2015

Note: No data for other cereals for 2014/15 except for maize

are South Africa, Angola, DRC and Mozambique. The major surplus country in rice is Tanzania, which also exports to other countries in the region, while Zambia and Malawi are self-sufficient in wheat.

Malawi seems to be a self-sufficient country in maize production but nearly self-sufficient in wheat and rice. Tanzania is self-sufficient in the production of maize and the largest surplus producer of rice in the SADC region. Zimbabwe is a major maize deficit country whose deficit averages around 600,000 to 800,000 MT per year although in the 2014/15 season it produced a surplus. Other structurally deficit countries in cereal include DRC, which is deficit in all cereal crops, Botswana, Lesotho, Namibia and Swaziland, which are structurally dependent on South Africa for all their cereal requirements. The situation in question highlights the great need for the SADC region to trade with each other, at least in cereal products, as there are variations in factor endowment in the production of various products.

5. Agricultural trade within and outside the SADC region

5.1 Formal trade

We briefly look at trade in selected products within the SADC region, with the rest of Africa and with the rest of the world. Table 6.1 shows the value of trade in cereals within the SADC region, between the SADC region and the

Table 6.1 SADC trade value of cereals: 2005 and 2015

	SADC Partner in Cereal Trade	*Export Value (USD '000)*		*Import Value (USD '000)*		*Trade Balance (USD '000)*	
		2005	*2015*	*2005*	*2015*	*2005*	*2015*
1	SADC	244,323	553,344	264,319	614,674	−19,990	−61,330
2	Africa (Outside SADC)	33,156	25,888	25,890	12,914	7,266	12,974
3	Rest of the World	58,690	41,809	1,002,962	2,301,431	−944,272	−2,259,622
	Total	**336,169**	**621,041**	**1,293,171**	**2,929,019**	**−956,996**	**−2,307,978**

Source: Authors' calculations of data from ITC Trade Map, 2016

rest of Africa and between the SADC region and the rest of the World in 2005 and 2015.

The value of cereal trade within the SADC region in 2015 was USD$614 million. This shows an increase from USD$264 Million in 2005. Trade in cereals within the SADC region was higher than trade with other African countries outside the SADC region. Furthermore, the SADC region exported more cereals to other African countries than it imported. However, when it came to trade with the rest of the world, the SADC region imported more cereals from the countries outside Africa than it exported outside Africa. The larger value of cereals imports from overseas markets puts the SADC region in trade deficit position for cereals. The trade deficit with the rest of the world also increased significantly between 2005 and 2015.

South Africa and Zambia were the largest exporters of cereals within the SADC region while Zimbabwe and Botswana were the highest importers of cereals within the SADC region. South Africa, Zambia and Tanzania were the countries that exported the largest value to countries in Africa but outside the SADC region as well as outside the African continent. South Africa, Zimbabwe and Mozambique were the largest importers of cereals from outside the African continent. South Africa was the highest cereal importer from overseas markets mainly (rice and wheat) from Thailand, Russia, India and Argentina. After South Africa, Zimbabwe also imported significant values of cereals from Thailand, Pakistan and United Arab Emirates. This analysis underscores the fact that the SADC region is trading more with countries outside the SADC region especially overseas markets outside the African continent.

Tables 6.2 shows SADC trade in livestock and livestock products within then SADC region, with African countries outside the SADC region and with overseas markets.

We note again that the value of trade in livestock and livestock products within the SADC region is larger than with other Africa countries outside the SADC region and that the SADC region exports more to African countries outside the SADC region than it imports from those countries. Similar to what was observed for cereals, the SADC region is in trade deficit for livestock and

Table 6.2 SADC trade of livestock and livestock product in 2015

	SADC Partner in	*Export Value (USD '000)*		*Import Value (USD '000)*		*Trade Balance (USD '000)*	
		2005	*2015*	*2005*	*2015*	*2005*	*2015*
1	SADC	293,585	416,740	107,033	378,451	186,552	38,289
2	Africa (Outside SADC)	4,816	16,520	5,753	4,149	−937	12,371
3	Rest of the World	114,354	314,660	600,432	121,6479	−486,078	−901,819
	Total	**414,760**	**747,920**	**715,223**	**1,599,079**	**−298,458**	**−851,159**

Source: Authors' calculations of data from ITC Trade Map, 2016

livestock products because the region imports more of those products from overseas markets than it exports. Between 2005 and 2015, this deficit has also increased significantly similar to the trend in cereals. These findings are in tandem with FAO's observation on agricultural trade in Africa. Using data from 1960 to 2007 the FAO noted that Africa has become a net importer of food and of agricultural products in the last three decades, which is puzzling given its vast agricultural potential. African food imports are composed mainly of cereals and livestock products. The main reasons cited for the rising trade deficit in the region and the continent at large are population growth, low and stagnating agricultural productivity, policy distortions, weak institutions and poor infrastructure (Rakotoarisoa et al., 2011).

Namibia and South Africa are the largest exporters of live animals in the region, while South Africa, Namibia and Botswana are the main exporters of meat within the SADC region. South Africa, Angola and the Democratic Republic of the Congo (DRC) are the main importers of meat from overseas markets. The main countries outside the African continent supplying the SADC region with meat include Brazil, Netherlands, Belgium, India and the United States.

This analysis demonstrates that the SADC region is a net importer of cereals as well as livestock and livestock products. This is mainly because SADC imports more cereals and livestock products from developed countries than it exports to those countries. When we look at cash crops such as sugar, tobacco and cotton, the SADC region exports more of those commodities outside the region. Thus, it is worth noting that SADC countries trade more with countries outside the region than within itself. On the basis of the data on trade in the main agricultural commodities, it can be concluded that SADC region is lagging behind in promoting the logic of developmental regionalism in the agricultural sector.

5.2 Informal cross-border trade in Southern Africa

Agricultural trade in Southern Africa consists of a large part of the informal economy and thus informal cross-border trade occurs to a large extent among traders across neighbouring countries. The challenge with informal trade is that it is not captured in the statistics and hence difficult for governments and their planning agencies to ascertain the size of this trade. According to the Africa Development Bank (2012) informal cross-border trade can have positive macroeconomic and social ramifications such as food security and income creation particularly for rural populations who would otherwise suffer from social exclusion. Most traders have no education and raise capital from their own resources or through loans from friends and relatives. Cross-border businesses are generally not bankable nor do they have assets that banks would accept as collateral (Afrika & Ajumbo, 2012).

Historically, the African continent inherited political borders that separated people from the same ethnic groups and even families. The current political borders vastly complicate current efforts to accelerate agricultural growth and reduce hunger. These borders often separate food surplus areas from the food deficit areas (Haggblade, 2013). Inevitably cross-border trade has to happen among these countries. An example is Zambia and the DRC, particularly the Katanga region which is famously referred to as Zambia's 11th Province. Zambia has to feed more than 13 million people in the Katanga region and most of the trade taking place between these countries is informal cross-border trade. Similarly, Northern Mozambique and Southern Malawi also illustrate the problems of political borders as well as the limitations of an individual-country focus for ensuring food security. Northern Mozambique, has fertile land and low population density of less than 30 people per square kilometre

Table 6.3 Cross-border trade in maize, rice and beans in Southern Africa

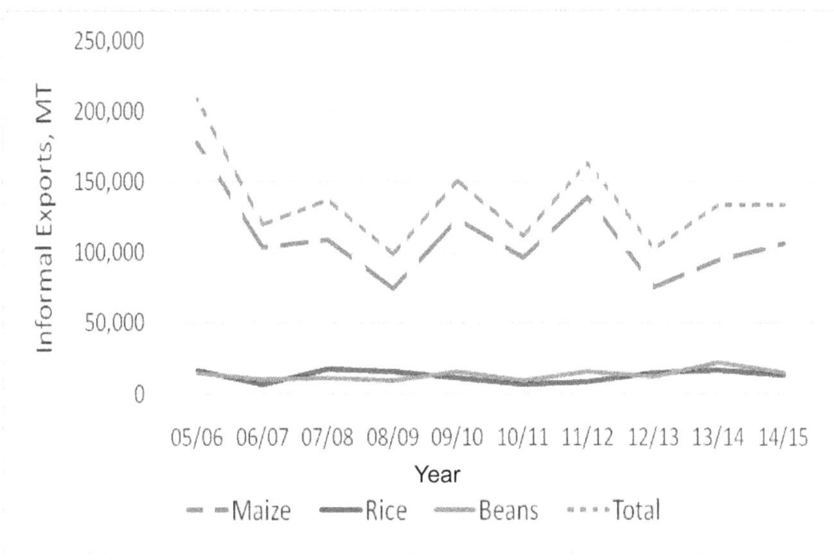

Source: FEWSNET, ICBT in Southern Africa, 2015.

and produces reliable surpluses of both maize and cassava. Across the border is the intermittently deficit Malawi, with a higher population density of 130 people per square kilometre crowded together on land holdings averaging one hectare per household. Inevitably, Malawian cross-border traders circumvent border authorities into Northern Mozambique to informally import maize and cassava (Haggblade, 2013). Examples of this nature abound in the Southern Africa region.

Despite efforts to control the borders and the many trade bans that have been instituted in the region before, informal cross-border trade continues to flourish. This is exacerbated by the poor border infrastructure, which makes borders extremely porous. In the SADC region, the value of informal cross-border trade is estimated to be $17.6 billion per year (Afrika & Ajumbo, 2012). The items mainly trades are foodstuff such as maize, rice and beans although additional products such as handicrafts and minerals are also commonly traded in the region. Table 6.2 shows volumes of maize, beans and rice traded within the SADC region. The data shows that informal cross-border trade in food represents a significant flow of commodities and that it contributes to food security through trade. Therefore, developmental regionalism entails harnessing informal trade by formalising it to the benefit of the region. Food security can no longer be viewed at a national level but at a regional level.

6. Trade policies, agriculture and developmental regionalism

Promoting developmental regionalism in agricultural sector is greatly affected by trade policies at the level of SADC as well as domestic trade policies. The SADC region has made tremendous progress towards reducing tariff levels. However, non-tariff barriers have replaced tariffs and these non-tariff barriers continue to stifle agricultural trade, negating efforts towards achieving developmental regionalism. Agricultural trade within the region is governed by the SADC Protocol on Trade of 1996. It sets the rules and regulations for regional trade in agricultural commodities. The objective of trade integration within SADC is to liberalize intraregional trade, thus creating mutual benefits arising from access to neighbouring markets by removing all barriers to trade. In August 2008, the SADC Free Trade Area (FTA) came into effect, but the implementation of it remains poor. The process is foreseen to lead to a customs union and a common market, leading to a monetary union in 2018. Agricultural trade is also affected by NTMs of non-agricultural products. Part of the reason is that the WTO allows countries to adopt appropriate protection for human, plant and animals under the SPS and TBT agreements. Members are even allowed to set more stringent measures if there is scientific evidence for such threats and risks (Kalaba & Kirsten, 2012). Member states of SADC tend to utilise these provisions to prohibit trade in agriculture rather than for the intended purposes. While there was a reduction in the tariffs within the SADC region of about 85 percent, there has been an increase in the Non-Tariff Measures.

For example in the year 2000, Mozambique, Malawi and Zambia had a total of 400 NTMs but by 2010 these had increase to about 1,400 NTMs (Kalaba, 2013). The increase in NTMS is a major threat to agricultural development in the SADC region.

Examples on the escalation of NTMs in Southern Africa include Botswana imposing a 25-percent import duty on flour in response to alleged 'dumping' from South Africa during the first three years of the protocol coming into being. Namibia, too, replaced its local-purchase requirement with a ban on flour imports. Swaziland requires a permit to be granted by its National Agricultural Marketing Board, which restricts the number of permits being granted. Mauritius controls all flour imports through its State Trading Corporation. South Africa made it a requirement that all domestically sold wheat flour be enriched with vitamins. Zambia imposed substantial cash-deposit requirements on wheat flour in transit from South Africa to the Democratic Republic of the Congo (DRC) (Kalenga, 2004).

While Zambia has become a surplus producer of maize in recent years, demand for its maize has increased tremendously. However, due to the fears of food insecurity, the Zambian government has issued a number of statutory instruments (SIs) banning the exportation of maize and related products. "The Controlled Goods Act" to effect export/import bans despite being a signatory to the SADC trade protocol (Government of Zambia, 2011). Notably, the government banned exports in December 2012 and September 2013. The export ban was later lifted in April 2014, when the government committed itself to maintain an open border policy towards maize exports (Centre for Trade Policy and Development (CTPD), 2014). In May 2016, the Zambian government banned the exportation of maize and related products again at the back of high regional demand for Zambia's maize due to the poor harvests resulting from dry weather patterns caused by the El Nino. The ban is meant to be temporal as it was lifted in September 2016 after securing sufficient stocks for local consumption. The government has allowed exports by the private sector for contracts from the previous season's harvests (Bloomberg, 2016).

The Zambian government also restricts the importation of wheat in order to protect the domestic industry from cheap imports and to hasten the country becoming wheat self-sufficient. In this regard, wheat imports have been banned in the country since June 2009 (Chapoto, 2012). Another commodity that is restricted by the Zambian government is sugar. Following a surge of imports of sugar from Malawi prior to the year 2000, the Zambian government instituted a law that required all sugar meant for domestic consumption to be fortified with Vitamin A. Few countries in the region have such as law. In effect, sugar imports have ceased (Chisanga et al., 2015).

Despite being a deficit maize producer, the Zimbabwean government imposed a maize import ban on maize and related products in the year 2014. This was done as a way of maintaining a high domestic price for maize in order to protect the local farmers. The ban was later abandoned in 2015 when it became eminent that there would be serious shortages of maize in the country (All Africa, 2014).

6.1 SADC policies on agricultural development

The trade policies highlighted earlier have had a profound impact on agricultural trade and therefore, affect the attainment of developmental regionalism. Within the SADC region, there has been consented effort aimed at agricultural development for the whole region. The Regional Agricultural Policy (RAP) has been in existence since 2014 when it was endorsed by the SADC Council of Ministers. The purpose of the RAP is to define common agreed objectives and measures to guide, promote and support actions at regional and national levels in the agricultural sector of the SADC Member States in contribution to regional integration and the attainment of the SADC Common Agenda (SADC, 2014). In 2003 the SADC Regional Indicative Strategic Plan (RISDP) was formulated. The RISDP suggested a roadmap for the agriculture sector that emphasised focus on improved food availability; access to food and improved nutritional value of food while minimising food losses, improving forecasting, prevention, mitigation and recovery from adverse effects of natural disasters; and improving the institutional framework (SADC, 2011). The revised RISDP covering the period 2015 to 2015 has among its objectives to Increase production, productivity and competitiveness of crops, livestock, forestry, fisheries and wildlife to support trade, industry and food security in the region. It further seeks to Increase market access for agricultural products (crops, livestock and natural resources) (SADC, 2017). Since the Maputo declaration of 2003, which urged African Governments to invest 10 percent of their budgets to the agricultural sectors and to attain a minimum of 6 percent agricultural growth there has been commitment by SADC countries to the CAADP guiding principles. The Malabo declaration of 2014 established a set of concrete agriculture goals to be attained by 2025. However, the attainment of the commitments has been varied. Most countries have not been consistently meeting the 10 percent investment while those that have attained the requirement do so because of investments in input subsidies and not necessarily in the key drivers of agricultural development such as research, extension, irrigation and infrastructure.

7. Agricultural development, poverty and gender

Agricultural development holds prospects of lifting the many poor farmers and traders involved in the movement of commodities. The structure of agriculture in the SADC region is dominated by smallholder production. About 70 percent of the population directly depends on the agricultural sector and these are characterised by cultivating small parcels of land and using poor technologies. For countries such as South Africa the sector is dualistic in nature, with commercial farmers playing a major role and existing together with smallholder farmers. In countries such as Zambia, large commercial farmers play a significant role in crops such as wheat, which are grown under irrigation while smallholders dominate in other staples. Due to the fact that agriculture production in the region is dominated by poor small-scale farmers, the majority of whom are women, this brings in the aspect of gender. Agricultural development is one of the most effective tool for reducing national poverty levels and addressing gender inequalities in effect making it possible to attain Developmental Regionalism within the SADC region.

Earnings from regional trade could benefit mostly women, given that the majority of the informal cross-border traders are women. This means, policies that restrict agricultural regional trade could adversely affect the women and the rural poor in general. Small-scale traders and farmers often lack the capacity to participate in regional trade and they remain uninformed about the opportunities and benefits of free trade.

8. Regional collaboration in agriculture

Another imperative of developmental regionalism is to foster regional cooperation. Some of the agricultural problems that each country in Southern Africa tries to deal with require regional rather than individual country solutions. For example, similar agro-ecological zones cut across different countries. Agricultural initiatives or technologies spread slowly across agro-ecological zones partitioned into multiple small countries with differing languages, phytosanitary controls and seed-certification processes. Indeed agricultural pests and diseases—such as cassava mealy bug, trypanosomiasis and foot and mouth disease—adversely affect agricultural productivity. Because these can easily transit the political borders that partition agro-ecological zones, individual countries face chronic difficulties in raising farm productivity in the absence of effective regional collaboration (Haggblade, 2013).

There are a number of regional efforts in Southern Africa that promote co-operation. One of the regional initiatives in agriculture is the harmonisation of seed policies in the region. The availability of quality seed affect crop productivity and food security. However, there are diverse national regulatory systems and national standard in SPS, seed certification and quality assurance. Facilitation of seed trade, would therefore positively impact on regional seed security. The SADC Harmonized Seed Regulatory System is currently undertaking regional initiatives in SADC member states to address these challenges. These include common variety testing and release, common seed certification and quality, common sanitary and phytosanitary and new plant variety protection (PBR) (Kawonga, n.d.). In this way there is increased access to improved seed varieties among farmers across the region through trade by avoiding the multiplicity of variety testing once seed varieties have been approved in one of the SADC countries.

COMESA is also undertaking a similar initiative through its specialised agency-Alliance for Commodity Trade in Eastern and Southern Africa (ACTESA). As a result of COMESA's seed trade harmonisation regulation, the region is now producing 500,000 MT of quality improved seed and exporting not less than 50,000 to other regions in Africa (Mukuka, 2014)

Another avenue for regional agricultural co-operation is the sharing of information and data on agricultural policies. In this vein, the Food Agricultural and Natural Resources Policy Analysis Network (FANRPAN) was formed to foster co-operation in policies on Food and Natural Resources in the SADC region. Other institutions conducting agricultural research for the region include the Centre for Coordination of Agricultural Research and Development for Southern Africa (CCARDESA) and the Regional Network of Agricultural Policy Research Institutes (ReNAPRI).

Although not restricted to agriculture, cooperation in infrastructure is one of the most powerful tools to realise the potential for developmental regionalism. The region is not well integrated in terms of infrastructure as most of the infrastructure is configured towards trading outside the continent. Development of key corridors within the region is an important strategic priority for the SADC, which will further the realisation of developmental regionalism in the agricultural sector.

9. Agro-processing and the development of regional value chains

Agro-processing is necessary in adding value to primary agricultural products. However, agro-processing by countries should not develop in isolation. Thus the concept of regional value chains holds more prospects for achieving greater competitiveness and moving towards agricultural transformation in Southern Africa.

A report by the World Bank suggests that if Southern African countries can take advantage of their collective capabilities to build competitive regional value chains that could feed into global value chains, it could spark economic growth, create high-quality jobs and reduce poverty. In this way the region could attract more investment and increase jobs not only in industry and agribusiness as well as other sectors (World Bank, 2016).

Development of regional value chains is important in that individual countries do not need to produce everything needed in the value chains but through regional trade, competitiveness can be achieved as countries trade at various stages of the value chain depending on factor endowment. South Africa has the most sophisticated industrial capacity in Southern Africa. Through regional value chains, South Africa can rely on its neighbours to supply primary agricultural products, which it cannot produce competitively and add value through processing. Alternatively South Africa can invest in the processing capacities of other Southern African countries through Foreign Direct Investments. Regional Value Chains in Southern Africa remain underdeveloped as each country tries to pursue their own industrial development in isolation—including in areas where they have low comparative advantage. Coupled with restrictive trade policies, this has muted the growth of the regional value chains.

South Africa's investments in the region from primary agricultural production to processing provides prospects for growth in regional value chains. However, this will only become viable if there is open trade in the SADC region.

10. Conclusions and recommendations

10.1 Conclusions

The notion that the phasing down of tariffs and creation of FTAs is a panacea for regional integration has been dispelled and instead the focus on developmental regionalism as a holistic approach is gaining more ground. The regional integration agenda in Southern Africa has focused disproportionately on reduction of tariffs and the creation of the FTA. Meanwhile trade restrictions in the name of no-tariff measures and export ban/imports have been on the rise in agricultural trade. As such, Southern Africa has performed dismally in agricultural trade as shown by the low level of intraregional trade and deficit trade balance in agriculture. The Southern Africa region is a net importer of cereals and livestock products. Additionally agricultural trade in the region remains highly constrained by a number of factors such as low productivity, poor infrastructure, low investments in research and development, weak institutions among others.

There is a large proportion of informal cross-border trade in agriculture in Southern Africa, which largely remains unaccounted for. This is largely because the region is characterised by areas of deficit and surplus, which do not necessarily follow the political borders. The most informally traded commodities in Southern Africa are maize, beans and rice. By implication, the proliferation of trade restriction is Southern Africa by no means limits trade flows. This means that food security can no longer be viewed at national level since commodities still move across borders.

Developmental regionalism also entails fostering co-operation among member states. The challenges that constrain agriculture in the region are similar across member states. Regional co-operation initiatives in agriculture include seed policy harmonisation, regional policy research and sharing of agricultural information and infrastructural development such as development of roads and rail.

Agro-processing or value addition enhances competitiveness. At a regional level there exist capacities and factor endowments that could benefit the region as a whole and enhance each member's capacity in their production and productivity. This entails the development of regional value chains as a means to attain regional competitiveness.

10.2 Recommendations

The chapter makes the following recommendations:

- Member states should remove unnecessary non-tariff measures in agricultural trade and should stop restricting trade through export/import bans.

Member states should start to view the issue of food security as a regional rather than a national issues.

- Attempts should be made at national and regional level to simplify cross-border trade. Similar to what has been done in COMESA, a Simplified Trade Regime could benefit the majority of informal cross-border traders.
- Increasing the capacity of farmers and traders to access the opportunities arising in trade in agriculture including targeting them with information
- Increased collaboration in agricultural development on matters of policy, harmonisation of standards and infrastructure.
- Development of regional value chains for commodities will increase agricultural trade and competitiveness and FDI.
- Policies that promote production and trade in agricultural sector need to be more gender sensitive taking into account that agricultural production and cross board trade is mostly by women.

References

Afrika, J.G. and Ajumbo, G., 2012. Informal cross-border trade in Africa: Implications and policy recommendations. *Africa Economic Brief, 3*(10), pp. 1–13.

All Africa, 2014. Zimbabwe: Shortages Feared As Zim Bans Maize Imports. Online accessed form: http://allafrica.com/stories/201407072063.html. Accessed on 30 June 2016.

Baldwin, R.E., 1997. Review of theoretical developments on regional integration. In *Regional Integration and Trade Liberalization in Sub-Saharan Africa: Framework, Issues and Methodological Perspectives*, edited by A. Oyejide, I. Elbadawi and P. Collier, 24–88. London: Macmillan Press Ltd.

Bloomberg, 2016. Zambia Suspends Corn Exports While Honoring Existing Contracts. Online accessed from: www.bloomberg.com/news/articles/2016-05-10/zambia-suspends-corn-exports-while-honoring-existing-contracts. Accessed on 30 June 2016.

Calderón, C. and Servén, L., 2008. Infrastructure and economic development in Sub-Saharan Africa. *World Bank Policy Research Working Paper Series, Vol.*

Challinor, A., Wheeler, T., Garforth, C., Craufurd, P. and Kassam, A., 2007. Assessing the vulnerability of food crop systems in Africa to climate change. *Climatic Change, 83*(3), pp. 381–399.

Chapoto, A., 2012. *The political economy of food price policy: The case of Zambia* (No. UNU-WIDER Research Paper WP2012/100).

Chisanga, B., Meyer, F.H., Winter-Nelson, A. and Sitko, N.J., 2015. Does the Current Sugar Market Structure Benefit Consumers and Sugarcane Growers? Indaba Agricultural Policy Research Institute Working Paper No.89. Lusaka, Zambia: IAPRI.

CTPD, 2014. *Scoping Study on Regulations in the Zambian Maize Market*. Lusaka: CTPD.

FEWSNET (Famine Early Warning Systems Network). June, 2010. *Informal Cross Border Food Trade in Southern Africa*. Issues paper 60. Pretoria, South Africa.

FEWSNET (Famine Early Warning Systems Network). 2016. *Domestic Supply, Deficit/Surplus of Maize in the SADC Region*. Pretoria, South Africa.

Government of Zambia, 2011. The Control of Good (Imports and Exports) (Agriculture) Prohibition of Importation. Statutory Instrument No.40 of 2011.

Haggblade, S., 2013. Unscrambling Africa: Regional requirements for achieving food security. *Development Policy Review, 31*(2), pp. 149–176.

Kalaba, M., 2013. *Non-tariff measures along the Beira Corridor: Impact on cross-border trade, in Barriers to agriculture and trade*. USAID and NEPAD Business Foundation, 2 (5). Pretoria, USAID.

Kalaba, M. and Kirsten, J., 2012. *Estimating the Quantity Effects of Non-Tariff Measures on SADC Meat and Milk Trade*. Paper presented at the Second International Conference of International Trade and Investment: Financial Crisis and Trade and Investment in Developing Countries, 24–26 October 2012, Mauritius.

Kalenga, P., 2004. Implementation of the SADC Trade Protocol: A preliminary review. In *Editors: Dirk Hansohm Willie Breytenbach Trudi Hartzenberg Colin McCarthy*, Namibian Economic Policy Research Unit (NEPRU), p. 17.

Kawonga, K.C., n.d. *Implementation of the SADC Harmonized Seed Regulatory System: Progress and Future Prospects: SADC Seed*. Gaborone: SADC.

Land Rights, Policy and Tenure in Africa. London: DFID/IIED/NRI.

Lederman, D., Maloney, W.F., Maloney, W.F. and Serven, L., 2005. *Lessons from NAFTA for Latin America and the Caribbean*. Washington, DC: Stanford University Press and the World Bank.

Mansfield, E.D. and Pevehouse, J.C., 2000. Trade blocs, trade flows, and international conflict. *International organization*, *54*(4), pp. 775–808.

Mukuka, J., 2014. Domestication of the COMESA Seed Trade Harmonisation Regulations in the Eastern and Southern Africa (ESA) region. Progress Report.

Platteau, J.-P., 2000. Does Africa need land reform? In *Evolving Private Sector Dynamism*, edited by C. Toulmin and J. Quan. Report No. UNCTAD/ALDC/AFRICA/2013. Geneva: UNCTAD.

Quigley, J.M., 2008. Urbanization, agglomeration, and economic development. *Urbanization and Growth*, p. 115.

Rakotoarisoa, M., Iafrate, M. and Paschali, M., 2011. *Why Has Africa Become a Net Food Importer?* Rome, Italy: FAO.

SADC, 2011. *Regional Agricultural Policy: Country Summary Agricultural Policy Review Reports*. Gaborone, Botwsana: SADC.

SADC, 2014. *Regional Agricultural Policy (RAP)*. Gaborone, Botwsana: SADC.

SADC, 2015. *SADC Food Balance Sheet, 2014–15*. Gaborone: SADC.

SADC, 2017. *Summary of the SADC Revised Regional Indicative Strategic Development Plan 2015–2020*. Gaborone, Botwsana: SADC.

UNCTAD, 2011. The Least Developed Countries Report 2011. The Potential Role of South–South Cooperation for Inclusive and Sustainable Development. United Nations publication. Sales No. E.11.II.D.5. New York and Geneva.

UNCTAD, 2013. Economic Development in Africa Intra-African Trade: Unlocking Private Sector Dynamism. Report No. UNCTAD/ALDC/AFRICA/2013. Geneva: UNCTAD.

UNECA Southern Africa, 2013. *Intra-Regional Agricultural Trade in Southern Africa: Trends, Issues and Challenges*. Lusaka: UNECA.

World Bank, 2016. *Factory Southern Africa? SACU in Global Value Chains*. Washington, DC: World Bank.

7 Women in the informal sector in Southern Africa

Towards a developmental perspective

Annie Barbara Chikwanha

Introduction

For inclusive and sustainable development to take root in the Southern Africa region, it is imperative for the region's member states to embrace developmental regionalism that is both gender sensitive and gender responsive.[1] Gender responsiveness is an essential element of inclusive governance that is central to the achievement of the Sustainable Development Goals (SDGs), yet it has not received much attention from regional policy makers. Bloom et al. (2001) define gender responsiveness as a "creating an environment . . . that reflects an understanding of the realities of women's lives and addresses their issues".[2] Emphasis is always placed on gender sensitiveness and gender responsiveness in government budgets and regional policies and institutions. Adopting a "developmental regionalism" approach, in which existing regional institutions' gender policies can be utilized to achieve broad development, holds much more promise for Africa. Addressing the key challenges of gender inclusiveness and equity that are key ingredients for economic transformation clearly requires the participation of women. Through the Southern African Development Community (SADC) and the Common Market for Eastern and Southern Africa's (COMESA) protocols on gender, the southern African region has the required policy and institutional frameworks in place to close the gender development gap.

What then would be the basic tenets for promoting gender empowerment within the framework of developmental regionalism in Southern Africa? How can the region pursue developmental regionalism that is inclusive of women? Do COMESA and the SADC's poverty eradication strategies, trade and investment policies, facilitate women's roles in the formal and informal sectors? Considering that informal traders and agriculturists are mostly women, are the region's overall development policies in these sectors gender sensitive and gender responsive? These questions can be answered partly by posing the question: What is the current scope of regional integration in relation to women's needs and how can this be part of a coherent developmental regionalism agenda in Southern Africa? Overall, the entire African region has the institutional frameworks required for steering the shift towards a paradigm of developmental regionalism but lacks clear strategies for implementation (UNCTAD 2013).

The same can be said about initiatives to reduce the gender gap in all the countries; there are many provisions on gender parity yet most African countries struggle to translate these into action.

The plethora of regional integration initiatives across different development sectors presents opportunities for the empowerment of women but member states' action on the recommended actions remains wanting. The failure of almost all the governments to implement many of the gender protocols partly explains the lip service paid to gender responsive and gender sensitive regional integration in African. Individual countries have the responsibility for translating the many protocols into concrete activities that heads of states commit themselves to. This chapter analyses SADC women's roles in the informal development sectors: mining, trading and agriculture. The intention is to find entry points for designing an approach that leads to developmental regionalism that is anchored on gender responsiveness.

Development as a woman's right: defining key gender concepts

Gender remains a contested topic and many of the concepts used in reference to the theme are often used interchangeably. For instance, gender equity is often used to refer to gender equality; hence a distinction has to be drawn between these two concepts. This is important for reflecting on divergent understandings of gender differences and formulating appropriate strategies to address them. Reeves and Baden (2000) point out that gender equality denotes women having the same opportunities in life as men, including the ability to participate in the public sphere, while gender equity denotes the equivalence in life outcomes for women and men, recognising their different needs and interests, and requiring a redistribution of power and resources. Gender equity goes beyond equality of opportunity by requiring transformative change. This brings it closer to the concept of gender responsiveness as it recognizes that women and men have different needs, preferences, and interests and that equality of outcomes may necessitate different treatment of men and women (Bloom and Covington 2001). This conceptualisation brings out the distinction between gender equity and gender equality with gender bias, which refers to the displays of favoritism to a specific gender resulting in unfair treatment. Belknap et al. (1997) make this distinction clear: "equality does not mean "sameness". Equality is about providing opportunities that mean the same to each gender and takes cognisance of needs beyond women's control in this case. For instance, cross-border trading support programmes for men are more likely to be successful when they focus on rules, and ways to advance within a highly regulated and structured environment. For women, trading ventures are more likely to be successful when emphasis is on relationships with others, strong networking systems, and flexible systems to manage their personal lives while keeping both elements balanced (Bossuroy et al. 2014). Designing such responsive systems levels the trading arena for women to participate.

Gender responsiveness is thus a woman's human right and is designed to ensure equality of treatment within regional and national development institutions. This implies mainstreaming women's needs across the different development sectors. A gender responsive developmental approach is important for creating an environment that supports and enables women to realize their full potential. A good example is the South African government's National Export Development Programme, implemented by the Department of Trade and industry since 2013, that recognizes the need to support women's exports by creating an enabling environment for Black, African, and female-owned businesses to access international markets (Bossuroy et al. 2014). The programme has measures for supporting all exporters but places more and specific emphasis on women's needs during the process.

The acute gender gap across all sectors, regional[3] activities and transactions in Africa, necessitates the collection of massive information on female participation to ascertain their participation in regional developmental initiatives. Regional economic communities (RECS) such as SADC, the Economic Community for West African States (ECOWAS), the Economic Community for Central African States (ECCAs), and the East African Community (EAC), have not compiled such extensive data bases on the development gender gap that could be useful for both tracking implementation, and identifying the specific sector gender needs and challenges (Ndomo 2009). Incorporating gender into the current regional frameworks implies factoring in gender responsive policies into the burgeoning developmental regionalism agenda to guarantee equitable development outcomes.

Defining developmental regionalism

This chapter uses Hettne and Söderbaum's (1998: 559) definition of developmental regionalism as "concerted efforts from a group of countries within a geographical region to enhance the economic complementarity of the constituent political units and capacity of the total regional economy". This definition transcends trade relations; it is an extensive concept and extends to a wider range of areas such as investment, research and development, regional industrial development and regional infrastructure provision (Ndomo 2009). Many other scholars continue to emphasize a narrower approach to developmental regionalism by focusing on the economy only. Nesadurai (2003) views it as "encapsulating the developmental state idea of state intervention in markets to promote national development agendas. . . . (as) an approach to regionalism through which to nurture emerging domestic firms to eventually become internationally competitive". Either way, inclusivity is paramount for spurring development.

Up to now, SADC has acknowledged economic globalization as a major force of regionalism with mostly the roles of nation-states clearly spelt out leaving civil society organisations (CSOs) constantly fighting for inclusion

(Mittelman 2000). This rigid approach by governments fails to take into account that developmental regionalism is clearly not only state-centric, but embraces all activities that take place within a region's social and cultural sectors (Hettne and Söderbaum 1998). Gamble and Payne (1996) concur with Hettne when they argue that there is close interdependence between politically negotiated, institutionalized, states-led, states-driven regionalization and spontaneous, 'natural' society and market-induced regionalization that works parallel to the inseparable relationship between state and civil society/market at the national level.

For the SADC, there is a noticeable sequencing of regional integration that switches between trade and security that recognizes the vulnerability of women in some of the policies, with other actors (women, civil society and the private sector) mostly pushing for inclusion for all the sectors.

What would gender sensitivity and gender responsiveness look like in developmental regionalism?

The inclusion of women in all spheres of life and development is hampered by the failure to act on the practical and strategic needs and priorities of women and men. The following two categories of needs define what gender responsiveness is about. Practical gender needs (PGNs) are the needs women identify in their socially accepted roles in society (Bloom and Covington 2001). PGNs do not challenge, although they arise out of, gender division of labour and women's subordinate position in society (Reeves and Baden 2000). PGNs are a response to immediate and perceived necessity that is identified within a specific context; they are practical in nature and usually concern inadequacies in living conditions such as water provision, health care and employment. In the case of regional interaction, these would be for instance; appropriate ablution facilities for women at the border posts, secure accommodation at the border posts, transparent tariffs and customs rates, trading facilities and inter country income generating activities that take into account women's unpaid care work (Bibler and Elaine Zuckerman 2013). Strategic gender needs (SGNs) are defined by women's subordinate position in society and these vary according to particular contexts (Bloom and Covington 2001). They are related to gender divisions of labour, power and control, and may include issues such as legal rights, domestic violence, equal wages and women's control over their bodies (ibid). These are all barriers that merit attention at a regional level to allow women to achieve greater equality and change existing roles.

Gender gaps favouring males in education, entrepreneurship-business ownership, trade and agriculture are prevalent throughout Africa (Jayachandran 2014). These arenas are not designed in a gender sensitive and gender responsive manner and this affects women's upward and physical mobility in all spheres. A gender responsive approach would incorporate the design of institutions, systems and facilities to challenge forms of gender inequalities and unequal power relations, while improving women's lack of control over resources. The need to view the design of regional development initiatives using a gender lens is based on the fact that the largest number of cross-border traders in Africa are women; most agriculture small-scale producers and subsistence farmers are women (UNCTAD 2016); and provision of infrastructural developments like water and communication enable women more to partake in other activities outside the domestic zone. All these are issues at the core of women enjoying their rights. The World Survey Report on the Role of Women in Development 2014 (UNWOMEN 2014)[4] that was conducted to input the development of the SDG asserts the central role of gender equality in development.

Gender responsiveness in regional policies would compel RECs to shoulder some responsibility in protecting, promoting and fulfilling the rights of all to safety, security, freedom and access to all services. It would compel governments to be accountable in protecting, promoting and fulfilling the rights of women to safety, security, freedom and access to public services. The institutionalisation of systems and mechanism to prevent and punish the violation of women and girls rights as well as the adoption of redistributive policies and mobilising resources to achieve equitable development requires the promotion of the voice and representation of women in decision-making (Pillar et al. 2015), energy, transport, business and agriculture. Women's participation is a key ingredient for a successful gender responsive developmental regionalism strategy. Table 7.1 depicts the limitedness of gender responsiveness in some of the major regional policies and institutions.

Table 7.1 Gender responsiveness in regional institutions

Regional level protocols	*Gender sensitivity*	*Gender responsiveness*
The Abuja Treaty or African Economic Community (AEC) Treaty (Organisation of African Union in 1991)	Acknowledges the need to address women's development	Does not specify the specific needs of women
New Partnership for Africa's Development (NEPAD) 2002[5]	Acknowledges the need to address women's development	Does not identify the specific needs of women
African Development Bank	African Gender institution and research-Gender equality index	Identifies each sector's specific needs—a move to responsiveness
Africa Agriculture Development Programme (CAADP)	Five-year programme-Gender, Climate Change and Agriculture Support Programme (GCCASP)	Piloted gender responsive policy in five countries

The SADC gender gap

There are potential entry points and strategies for shaping a women-friendly developmental regionalism, that is, infusing gender responsiveness across the entire range of regional initiatives in trade, agriculture, infrastructure and social services. Globally, there isn't a single country that has successfully closed the gender gap[6] though a few have managed to creep closer to that goal. According to the Global Gender Gap 2014 Report, which measures relative gaps between women and men, only South Africa in the SADC region is in the global top 20 countries that have made some significant strides in narrowing gender inequalities across select indicators and at the tail end of the rankings in the SADC region, is Angola at 120/145.[7]

The Gender Development Index (GDI),[8] also designed to measure gender equality by comparing female and male HDI values, gives another indication of the SADC gender gap in Table 7.3. According to the UNDP, the GDI enhances the understanding of the real gender gap in human development achievements and is useful for navigating policies to close the gap.[9] Within the SADC region, seven of the countries fall into the low to medium human development category. The gender gap is clearly very wide in the countries with the higher levels of gross national per capita income. However, the GDI does not take into account all socio-economic aspects that affect the gender gap hence it should be interpreted cautiously and supported by other indices for better informed policy-making.

Table 7.2 SADC: the regional gender gap

Country	*Inequality—*		*Literacy-rank*		*Women in lower house of*	
	Rank	*Score*	*Male*	*Female*	*Parliament & Cabinet*	
Angola	—	—	80	60.7	38.2	22.2
Botswana	98	0.434	88	88.9	9.5	15.8
Lesotho	135	0.544	70.1	88.3	25	18.2
Madagascar	—	—	66.7	62.6	19.2	17.9
Malawi	148	0.619	73	58.6	16.7	22.2
Mauritius	84	0.373	92.9	88.5	11.6	10
Mozambique	138	0.552	73.3	45.4	39.6	23.8
Namibia	115	0.472	79.2	84.5	41.3	24
Swaziland	—		—	—	6.2	26.3
Tanzania	130	0.537	84.8	75.9	36.4	20
South Africa	90	0.389	95.5	93.1	42	41.7
Zambia	125	0.517	70.9	56	18	33.3
Zimbabwe	128	0.534	88.5	84.6	32.6	16.1

Source: The rankings and scores are computed from various sources: the Inter-Parliamentary Union Women in Politics 2017 data on elections/appointments up to 1 Jan 2017; and the United Nations Educational, Scientific and Cultural Organization (UNESCO) Institute for Statistics Education indicators database, 2017

Table 7.3 The Gender Development Index (GDI)

	Country	*Gender Development Index -2017 value*	*Estimated gross national income per capita (2011 PPP $) 2014*	
			Female	*Male*
63	Mauritius	0.968	12,588	27,986
64	Seychelles	—	—	—
106	Botswana	0.976	12,613	18,521
116	South Africa	0.984	9,060	14,894
126	Namibia	1.014	8,895	9,907
139	Zambia	0.941	2,986	4,138
149	Angola	—	5,063	6,546
150	Swaziland	—		—
151	Tanzania (United Republic of)	0.928	2,282	3,037
154	Madagascar	0.962	1,173	1,544
155	Zimbabwe	0.924	1,173	1,544
161	Lesotho	1.004	2,608	3,940
173	Malawi	0.936	897	1,235
176	Democratic Republic of the Congo	0.852	703	889
180	Mozambique	0.904	1,052	1,135

Source: UNDP, The Gender Development Index 2017, Human Development Report, http://hdr.undp.org/en/composite/GDI

Despite the crafting of gender protocols and policies, progress on implementation is largely noted in celebratory mode[10] as illustrated by the African Union Commission Peace and Security Department (AUC/PSD), and COMESA's Trading for Peace: Promoting cross-border trade for women's civic, political and economic empowerment and sustainable peace initiative celebration in 2014. Whilst this is valuable, it leads to glossing over women's needs.

The SADC experience

The SADC does have extensive frameworks and institutions in place to advance the developmental regionalism approach to integration in a gender inclusive manner. The scattered gender advancement policies cover most development sectors: agriculture, energy, the environment, human resource development, telecommunications, transport and tourism. The SADC Protocol on Gender and Development was designed to facilitate integration through the mainstreaming of gender issues across the SADC Programme of Action and Community Building (www.sadc.int/issues/gender/gender-mainstreaming/),[11] and it operationalizes to some extent, the regional and international protocols. As a protocol to aid the inclusive and sustainable development of the SADC region, it provides a framework for the empowerment of women, elimination of discrimination and the use of gender responsive legislation, policies

Table 7.4 Regional protocols and plans on gender

AUC Agenda 2063
Convention on the Elimination of All Forms of Discrimination against Women (CEDAW), adopted in 1979
Gender Policy Action Plan (AU Policy) in 2008
Social Summit for Sustainable Development
The AU Solemn Declaration on Gender Equality in Africa
The African and Beijing Platforms for Action
The African Charter on Human and Peoples' Rights on the Rights of Women in Africa (2003)

and programmes and projects to achieve gender equality. The challenge is that other SADC protocols remain disconnected from the gender protocol though this has been acknowledged in different communiqués after summits.

The SADC Protocol on Politics, Defence and Security (2001) adopted the SADC Gender Protocol as a separate document to be used for mainstreaming; but reference to gender still has to be sought in the plans of specific organs.[12] The revised edition (2010), of the SADC's Harmonised Strategic Indicative Plan for the Organ on Politics, Defence and Security Cooperation, makes reference to women's security in the physical sense only: promote gender equity in the deployment of peace support operations and combat and preventing rape/statutory rape, abuse and violence against women and children. The Regional Indicative Strategic Development Plan (RISDP)[13] recognizes the crosscutting nature of gender and stresses the inclusivity of women in a more coherent way. At the same time, it admits that at the regional level, most of the core areas of regional interventions have not yet materialized despite the frequent policy and plan updates as reflected in the organisation's strategic priorities. Gender has been mainstreamed into the regional organs and not necessarily into sectoral policies, strategies and programmes (e.g. in trade, mining, agriculture). Obstacles exist in that the Gender and Development Declaration and its Addendum do not have the same legally binding effect as Protocols, which are SADC's primary documents of cooperation and integration.[14] Member States undermine regional policy efforts when they fail to incorporate the provisions of regional instruments into domestic laws and policies. Vanheukelom and Bertelsmann-Scott (2016) also noted these challenges, "While donors provide support for both SADC gender related projects and institution building, these initiatives are insufficiently translated into action on the ground by state and non-state actors or gender champions on the ground".

Table 7.5 shows the status of gender sensitivity/responsiveness in some RECs.

Streamlining gender sensitization is clearly a challenge for many of the RECS. COMESA is clearly aware of the duplications and overlaps in its strategy for engendering overall development, agriculture and climate change. For instance, its economic development aims state that it seeks to: Develop and

Table 7.5 Gender sensitivity/responsiveness in select RECs

Subregional level-REC	*Gender policy*
Common Market for Eastern and Southern Africa (COMESA, 19 countries)	May 2002, adopted the COMESA Gender Policy and the Addis Ababa Declaration on Gender. COMESA Gender, Climate Change and Agriculture Strategy, designed to ensure that the region is globally competitive. COMESA Climate Change Initiative (CCCI) yet to engender their policies
Southern African Customs Union (SACU-4 countries)	No reference to gender
SADC (14 countries)	SADC Protocol on Gender and Development 2008—*Post 2015 Agenda* (enforceable September 2012)—10 thematic areas: Constitutional and Legal Rights; Governance; Education and Training; Productive Resources and Employment, Economic Empowerment; Gender Based Violence; Health; HIV and AIDS; Peace Building and Conflict Resolution; Media, Information and Communication; Implementation of 50/50 parity by 2015
2001 Protocol on Politics, Defence, and Security Cooperation	Reference to gender is on peacekeeping and protection of women from violence only.

Support access to economic instruments; Promote technology transfer and skills development; Provide a framework for crediting and financing strategies for agriculture and climate change programme and Facilitate development of trade related capacities[15] through a specific strategy, the Regional Strategy and Action Plan (RESTRAP) for mainstreaming Gender into COMESA's Agriculture and Climate Change programmes. While this framework makes reference to gender differences, it is difficult to ascertain how women's programmes will be operationalized in this rather complex terminology. Most of the regional protocols take cognizance of gender differences but fall short of addressing gender responsiveness. Many institutions become in-ward servicing and address gender parity issues in their internal organs only. The likely impingement is the perpetual institution building that takes place in the region when there is a developmental challenge meriting attention. This fixation with procedural issues makes it impossible to address the substantive issues.

A cursory glance at most regional integration programmes reveals that they mention gender mainstreaming but do not address gender responsiveness. This is quite evident in all the social and economic policies, trade/economic liberalization and development, infrastructure support for regional integration, poverty eradication; science and technology; information and communication technologies; environment and sustainable development. In most cases, gender-related issues are addressed through the principle of non-discrimination stipulated in regional protocols.[16] A piecemeal and fragmented approach to addressing gender at a regional level stalls connected progress for women. This is evidenced by the way select regional initiatives address gender. Collective action by CSOs and other stakeholders to influence and monitor the development of inclusive approaches to regional development is paramount in this current paradigm of extensive economic liberalisation.

Women's contribution to development

A number of studies have demonstrated Southern African women's significant contribution to agriculture, artisanal mining, the formal employment sector in both the service and manufacturing industries, and their being the largest group in the informal sector especially in cross-border trade (Damon and Jeuring 2009). The SADC region has an average of 35 percent females engaged in artisanal mining and in some countries like Zimbabwe, it is over 40 percent (Hinton et al. 2003). In South Africa, the number of artisanal miners involved in small-scale mining is estimated to be in excess of 30,000, and a substantial proportion of these are females (Hoadley and Limpitlaw 2004). The relatively high representation of women in this marginalised economic sector has implications for the developmental potential of artisanal mining. The contribution of women artisanal miners to both a higher Gross Domestic Product, and improved livelihoods, can be achieved partly through making the 2013 African Union African Mining Vision (AMV) gender responsive.

The AMV evolved out of the Yaoundé Vision on Artisanal Small Scale Mining (2002) that drew attention to the role the small-scale miners in Africa can contribute to poverty alleviation. The Yaounde Vision adopted in Cameroon, in November 2002, under the theme "Artisanal and Small-Scale Mining in Africa: Identifying Best Practices and Building Sustainable Livelihoods of Communities", which recommended that artisanal and small-scale miners should be integrated in the Poverty Reduction Strategy Papers (PRSPs) of African governments and identified the goals, challenges facing Artisanal and Small-Scale Mining (ASM) sub-sector and actionable measures to be supported by national governments and development partners (Hayes 2008). The Yaounde Vision aimed to "Contribute to sustainably reduce poverty and improve livelihoods in African Artisanal and Small-scale Mining (ASM) communities by the year 2015, in line with the Millennium Development Goals" (ibid: 23).

The AMV can provide guidance on the legal and institutional frameworks essential for making indigenous women miners more productive. National mining policies and strategies would have to be crafted in a way that promotes overall greater relevant support and meaningful participation of women. Women miners experience challenges throughout the entire mining value chain since the business is generally conducted on rough sites with male employees who are often difficult to handle during extraction processes; and they generally tend to challenge the women's instructions.[17] The security threats in the gold mining sector in particular, deter many women from being actively involved in all the mining activities, hence the costs they incur in hiring a male middleman affects their economic empowerment.[18] Most SADC countries are signatories to the Elimination of All Forms of Discrimination Against Women

(CEDAW); members of the SADC Women in Mining Trust and some have national Women in Mining Associations. These efforts remain disconnected and this frustrates the women's efforts in the sector. Unless they own the mines, women are usually labourers in the ASM sector (e.g. panners, ore carriers and processors), providers of goods and services (e.g. cooks, shopkeepers) and are often solely responsible for domestic chores (Hinton et al. 2003).

In addition to physical and social security in productive ventures, women need economic freedom that is supported by political stability, which guarantees protection of their basic human rights. Social security in particular allows women to engage in productive activities, to develop and utilize their talents, be paid for the work they perform, and participation in the management of their societies as intellectuals, policy makers, producers and consumers (Meena 1992). Most regional integration processes, plans and national policies of African states are still "gender blind."[19] The regional planning and policy-making processes have failed to appreciate the fact that women and men have different needs and constraints that require specific attention. Socially structured subordination of women to men occurs at all levels from the unequal division of labour, legal discrimination against women to the abuse of women's basic human rights (Bhasin 2006). Regional policy makers have largely ignored the role of women in mining in regional development and implementation of gender strategies has been relegated to the background whilst paying lip service to the alleviation and elimination of sexual discrimination mostly in policy announcements and the establishment of gender departments that remain inward servicing as they tend to achieve gender targets within the regional organisations. While SADC continues to look to the mining sector as the main catalyst for economic growth, women empowerment does not seem to be on the table.[20] Officials are positive of the envisioned growth of the sector and forecasts remain high for all minerals despite the attendant economic problems such as the regional water and power supply shortages. Problems besetting the mining sector remain largely a function of the archaic and confusing legislation and policy frameworks that govern access, exploitation and management of the resource for the small-scale miners with women paying the highest costs (ibid).

Gender and trade

Informal trade has already demonstrated that it has a significant gender impact on the economic, social and political conditions that shape the ability of women to participate in overall development activities. Many studies concur that

> Trade policies and practices . . . have different effects on men and women, particularly in the African economies, because of the differences in the roles, responsibilities, rights and opportunities that society assigns to men and women. It makes economic sense therefore to pay attention to these gender differences in order to maximize the effectiveness of trade.
>
> (Ragodoo 2011)

In the African region, most cross-border trade takes place informally and is undocumented. Official sources report that in SADC, informal trade contributes an average US17.6 billion annually and Informal Cross Border Trading makes up 30–40 percent of intra SADC trade, with women making up 70 percent of the ICBTs.[21] It also makes about 40 percent of COMESA's trade (Muquyi 2015) yet the region is experiencing increasing protectionist tendencies by some of the countries. Despite this, the informal sector thrives and makes significant contributions to the GDP defying that "universal, open, rules based, predictable and non-discriminatory" (Doidge 2007). For Doidge, international trade is what defines development especially for women who are more vulnerable. For example, the SADC Protocol on Trade also remains gender blind (Shayo 2012), which undermines the fulfilment of the SADC Gender protocol and raises question on the commitment to the SADC Gender Strategy and the efficacy of the SADC Gender Unit. Shayo observed that informal traders, both men and women, spend a lot of their energy avoiding customs and dealing with other immigration and security challenges. Despite this group's valuable contribution, regional trading agreements and protocols remain indifferent to informal cross-border traders and this is noticeable in restrictions against trade in agricultural foods (UNWOMEN 2010). Services and resources remain limited to support the traders' efforts: lack of storage facilities, childcare facilities and lack of information on trade rules and market information (ibid). Women have taken the initiative to establish regional organisations to advocate for the engendering of trade policies. The Regional Export Promotion Women's Trust in Zimbabwe is one organization attempting to mainstream gender into trade policy at a national level with the aim of influencing regional policies since 2011.[22] The larger Southern Africa Cross-Border Trade Association emerged from these efforts but still, SADC has not adopted a Simplified Trade Regime (STR)[23] similar to COMESA's that was introduced in 2010, which is women friendly and stipulates the use of a simpler customs form for goods valued at less than USD1000 making the Free Trade Area as a progressive tool for addressing poverty.

Gender responsive agricultural systems

Women in Africa contribute significantly to agriculture as smallholders' subsistence farmers (50 percent according to UNWOMEN 2010). Informal women traders trade in foodstuffs such as maize and beans. A good example is Malawi where women contribute about 70 percent of the country's agricultural labour force, produce 70 percent of household food and perform between 50–70 percent of all agricultural tasks.[24] Food security in the region relies heavily on women yet gender barriers to small-scale farming schemes for women in rural areas continue to be influenced by socio-cultural and administrative settings that are exacerbated by the officialdom of supporting institutions. This goes on despite women having equal rights with men with respect to use, transfer, administration and control of land.

A Gender, Climate Change and Agriculture Support Programme was designed in 2014 within the already existing Comprehensive Africa Agriculture Development Programme (CAADP), which is Africa's policy framework for achieving an effective and more equitable participation of African women smallholder farmers, youth and other vulnerable groups in development planning and decision making through policy changes and access to climate-smart agricultural technologies (NEPAD 2014).[25] Launching this as a separate programme implies the failure to mainstream gender issues across all CADAAP systems. Agricultural value chain support systems have high potential to transform the lives of women yet regional emphasis is also on the already endowed large-scale commercial farming or men smallholder farmers with better asset holdings and so likely to adopt technologies.

SADC regional trade, just like international trade, is based on the neo-liberal macroeconomic assumption that liberalized world trade will result in equal benefits for all. In January 2008, 12 SADC member states signed the Free Trade Agreement, reducing tariffs on 85 percent of intraregional imports.[26] In 2012, SADC reiterated its commitment to liberalization when it expressed that it would 'increasingly support free trade as part of its agenda to eradicate poverty in Southern Africa'. The African Union (AU), for example, asserted in a Declaration of 5th July 2005 that the poverty reduction target and other Millennium Development Goals would only be achieved through, inter alia, the establishment of "a fair and equitable trading system and . . . facilitation of Africa's access to their [Developed Countries'] markets" (AU 2005, Decl.1, s.8). These gender-neutral types of trade liberalisation exacerbate existing gender inequalities and can leave women more vulnerable than before (Machacha 2015).

Gender and security

Economic upliftment is inextricably linked to regional and national stability and SADC lives up to the suggestion that "Free Trade Areas may also be concluded in an effort to stabilize potentially antagonistic relations" (Doidge 2007). RECs and all member states are clearly aware that promoting gender equality and empowerment of women benefits the economy and the region at large. In many African countries, gender inequalities and gender-based discriminations are perpetuated by customary practices,[27] and these inequalities are replayed at the regional level when women venture across borders in pursuit of livelihood means. How then have the regional authorities tackled the general environment of discrimination, which leads to violence against women, generally of a sexual nature, perpetrated by state officials, by the community and by those we trust the most even in the private sphere? This general discriminatory environment, which affects women from a very young age, is reflected in customary law rules that must be brought into compliance with regional protocols, administrative rules and national constitutions and institutions (Duarte 2008). These rules legitimate and perpetuate the subordination of women in all their endeavours. Defective law enforcement agencies in the region perpetuate these customs hindering gender responsive justice systems.

Gender responsive industrial development

Spurring diversification of the member states' economies, employment creation, poverty reduction and sustainable growth through industrial development is clearly at the core of SADC's regional development plans as outlined by the Industrial Development Policy Framework (IDPF) and the Industrialisation Strategy and Roadmap adopted by the SADC Heads of State (April 2015). The differences in the member states' levels of industrialization and managing gender sensitivities and responsiveness clearly present a challenge to this strategy. The failure to emphasise the needs of women coupled with the absence of strong private sector (indigenous) entities in most of the countries will likely make the efforts not very inclusive as the dominant informal sector is not emphasized. Vanheukelom and Bertelsmann-Scott (2016)[28] note that the regional industrial policy will take a more vertical approach or attempts to 'pick winners' resulting in the creation of clearly defined competitive dynamics between sectors (and even within sectors in some instances). This implies the increased marginalization of women since member states make different interpretations of industrialization and prioritizes their own agenda. Such a scenario makes it difficult to address gender inequalities in access to credit, capital, land and other means of economic empowerment as specified in the SADC Gender Protocol and Policy.[29]

Challenges

A major challenge for all RECs in Africa is that multiple institutions, policies and regulations within the same organization encumber them and slow down the operationalization of the many gender agreements. This rampant duplication in policies exists at all levels across all sectors and this takes away the focus on gender inclusivity and complicates the tedious task of making institutions and policies gender responsive.

Still, political will remains a big obstacle to harmonized gender responsive developmental regionalism. The SADC region has initiated trade liberalisation schemes with some countries selecting which country to grant freedom of movement for a limited period and in principle, the allowance of unprocessed goods; with traditional handicrafts, free from all duties and taxes (Markus 2012). This move is supposed to benefit women mostly but male traders tend to have the upper hand in moving crafts across borders for trade. Still, the region is still far from eliminating duties and taxes on industrial products originating in the subregion which affects virtually all women informal cross-border traders. These obstacles and many others such as those listed in Table 7.6 are prevalent across all the sectors.

Table 7.6 Some of the obstacles in enhancing women's development

Obstacles to accessing economic opportunities[30]	*Obstacles to accessing peace and justice*
Limited access to necessary technologies due to lack of information and know-how, and high cost of information-Customs departments rarely publicise any tariff related information in user friendly formats	**Limited access to legal support due to lack of knowledge** [high illiteracy rates] **and affordability**
Lack of skills for product diversification and value addition skills	**Lack of adequate skills to build capacity in articulating issues of injustice**
Inadequate skills in the fields of production, business management and marketing	**Lack of skills in articulating SGBV problems, cultural inhibitions and fear of stigma and shame**
Difficulties in finding appropriate production sites at competitive prices	**Difficulty in finding and understanding law enforcement agents**
Inadequate infrastructure and utilities, especially transport facilities in rural areas and insufficient power supplies	**Inadequate policing structures especially in peri-urban, low income urban suburbs and rural areas**
Limited access to finance	**Lack of money and access to information on accessing just**
A lack of both horizontal and vertical organization networking, among women in different sectors, and between women and existing business associations and support institutions.	**Lack of complementary networking amongst supporting women's groups and victim groups**

Source: Compiled with guide from Sultan Rehman Sherief & Asmahani Aswassalai, "Bottlenecks To Women's Economic Empowerment In Africa, Management and Science University, Shah Alam, Selangor, Malaysia, 2008

Conclusion

The constraints women face as equal drivers and actors in developmental regionalism are deeply rooted and can only be tackled first, at the national level, through the implementation of gender sensitive policies and developing relevant frameworks that would support gender responsiveness across different sectors. Information on how each development sector can be made gender responsive has to be collected from studies on what women identify as being essential for the full enjoyment of their rights as equal citizens. Women's organisations and human rights oriented CSOs can monitor the integration and development processes by documenting how the different sectors successfully meet gender-equitable targets, and if they are meeting the "needs" of women. Different national strategies, which remain important for successful regional development, ought to be analysed in order to identify and eliminate gaps in economic opportunities, and overall women's contribution at the regional level. Gender inclusiveness, gender responsive and women's participation are all imperative for balanced regional development and integration.

Notes

1 Whereas gender refers to the relations between men and women, this paper focuses on women only though the concept gender is used throughout to highlight the impact on women of regional initiatives.

2 Comprehensive gender responsive studies in the justice sector have been conducted by Bloom et al.; see working papers online Bloom, B.E. & S. Covington, "Effective Gender-Responsive Interventions in Juvenile Justice: Addressing the Lives of Delinquent Girls". 2001, www.centerforgenderandjustice.org/pdf/7.pdf and Bloom, B., Owen, B., & Covington, S. *Gender-responsive strategies: Research, practice, and guiding principles for women offenders*, Washington, DC: National Institute of Corrections. 2003.

3 Region is used interchangeably to refer to the African region and the subregion level—the RECS.

4 UN Women, The World Survey on the role of women in development 2014: Gender equality and sustainable development—See more at: www.unwomen.org/en/digital-library/publications/2014/10/world-survey-2014.

5 NEPAD- a holistic, comprehensive and integrated sustainable development initiative for the revival of Africa that has human security at its core.

6 A number of analysts amongst them George Arnett, noted in his commentary on the "Gender equality report: not one country has fully closed the gap yet", on Tuesday, 28 October 2014, www.theguardian.com/news/datablog/2014/oct/28/not-one-country-has-fully-closed-gender-gap-yet-report-shows.

7 See World Economic Forum latest report, The Global Gender Gap Report, 2016. www.weforum.org/reports/the-global-gender-gap-report-2016/.

8 It is important to recognise the limitations of the GDI; it measures development in terms of three dimensions only: life expectancy, education and income.

9 UNDP defines the GDI as a "distribution-sensitive" measure that accounts for the human development impact of existing gender gaps in the three components of the HDI. Distribution sensitive means that the GDI takes into account not only the average or general level of well-being and wealth within a given country, but focuses also on how this wealth and well-being is distributed between different groups within society. See UNDP, Human Development Reports,

10 See report of the event on www.peaceau.org/en/article/trading-for-peace-promoting-cross-border-trade-for-women-s-civic-political-and-economic-empowerment-and-sustainable-peace#sthash.ZQRu2vIF.dpuf.

11 See SADC guidelines on www.sadc.int/issues/gender/gender-mainstreaming/

12 SADC Protocol on Politics, Defense and Security Cooperation, 28th June 1996 www.sadc.int/files/3613/5292/8367/Protocol_on_Politics_Defence_and_Security 20001.pdf.

13 The Regional Indicative Strategic Development Plan of SADC is a comprehensive 15—year strategic roadmap, which provides the strategic direction for achieving SADC's long term social and economic goals.

14 See outline of the SADC Protocol on Gender and Development 2009, www.lawschool.cornell.edu/womenandjustice/upload/SADC-Protocol-on-Gender-and-Develop ment.pdf.

15 This is outlined in COMESA's Regional Strategy for Mainstreaming Gender In Agriculture and Climate Change, Strategic Framework 2011–2015.

16 Akina Mama wa Afrika hosted an event themed "The Power of Women's Leadership and Movement Building: Gender Based Violence and Sexual and Reproductive Rights in Conflict and Post Conflict Africa" Regional Consultative Meeting. 28th—29th April 2009, Munyonyo Commonwealth Speke Resort Hotel, Kampala, Uganda.www.akina mamawaafrika.org/index.php/publications/awli . . . /file

17 This is based on evidence from empirical research conducted in Zimbabwe by Chikwanha Annie Barbara, in the article "The Bricoleur Economy – Indigenous Gold Mining in Zimbabwe", forthcoming.
18 Ibid.
19 AUC African Union Gender Policy, www.un.org/en/africa/osaa/pdf/au/gender_policy_2009.pdf
20 This journal series was dedicated to South Africa's future mining prospects: Journal of the Southern African Institute of Mining and Metallurgy (SAIIM), "Future of the South African mining industry and the roles of the SAIMM" and the Universities, Vol.111 No.9, Johannesburg, September 2011.www.scielo.org.za/scielo.php?script=sci_arttext&pid=S0038-223X2011000900001.
21 UN Women, Unleashing the potential of women Informal Cross Border Traders to Transform Intra-African Trade, www.cpahq.org.
22 See the Trust's home page- http://regionalexportpromowomenstrust.blogspot.co.za/
23 Investigative journalists revealed these hurdles informal traders experience in the article "Cross Border traders still stuck in web of Corruption, 22 Oct 10–12 Nov 10, http://bordr.org/wp-content/uploads/2010/09/thebigissue-1.pdf.
24 This information is from a NEPAD, Gender, Climate Change and Agriculture Support Programme (GCCASP) programme proposal, October 2014
25 ibid. NEPAD, Gender, Climate Change and Agriculture Support Programme (GCCASP): a programme proposal, October 2014.
26 The sluggish pace of implementation is noted in the Southern Africa Trade Hub consultancy technical report by AECOM International Development on the "2011 Audit of the Implementation of the SADC Protocol on Trade", SADC Secretariat USAID/Southern Africa, https://tis.sadc.int/files/2513/3095/9663/CMT-23-7.4_2011_SADC_Trade_Audit_Final_-_Nov_2011.pdf.
27 These customary problems that hinder women's development have been documented worldwide and can be viewed on the www.genderindex.org/sites/default/files/docs/Brochure_SIGI_SSA_web.pdf.
28 Vanheukelom, J. & Bertelsmann-Scott, T., "The political economy of regional integration in Africa: The Southern African Development Community (SADC) Report", ECDPM, Brussels. 2016.http://ecdpm.org/peria/sadc.
29 SADC Industrialisation Strategy and Roadmap 2015–2063.
30 See Rehman Sherief, S. & Aswassalai, A., "Bottlenecks To Women's Economic Empowerment In Africa, Management and Science University, Shah Alam, Selangor, Malaysia. 2008.

References

AECOM International Development, "Audit of the Implementation of the SADC Protocol on Trade", SADC USAID/Southern Africa, 2011, https://tis.sadc.int/files/2513/3095/9663/CMT-23-7.4_2011_SADC_Trade_Audit_Final_-_Nov_2011.pdf

African Union Commission, African Union Gender Policy, www.un.org/en/africa/osaa/pdf/au/gender_policy_2009.pdf

Akina Mama wa Afrika, "The Power of Women's Leadership and Movement Building: Gender Based Violence and Sexual and Reproductive Rights in Conflict and Post Conflict Africa", Regional Consultative Meeting held from 28th–29th April, Munyonyo Commonwealth Speke Resort Hotel, Kampala, Uganda, 2009. www.akinamamawaafrika.org/index.php/publications/awli.../file

Arnett, George, "Gender Equality Report: Not One Country Has Fully Closed the Gap Yet", Tuesday, 28 October 2014. www.theguardian.com/news/datablog/2014/oct/28/not-one-country-has-fully-closed-gender-gap-yet-report-shows

Belknap, Joanne, Kristi Holsinger, and Melissa Dunn, "Understanding Incarcerated Girls: The Results of a Focus Group Study", *Prison Journal*, 77(4): 381–404. 1997.

Bhasin, Kamla, *What Is Patriarchy?* New Delhi: Women Unlimited. 2001.

Bibler, Sarah, and Elaine Zuckerman, "The Care Connection: The World Bank and Women's Unpaid Care Work in Select Sub-Saharan African Countries'", UN University, WIDER Working Paper No. 2013/131, November 2013.

Bloom, Barbara and Stephanie Covington, "Effective Gender-Responsive Interventions in Juvenile Justice: Addressing the Lives of Delinquent Girls", 2001. www.centerforgenderandjustice.org/pdf/7.pdf

Bloom, Barbara, Barbara Owen, and Stephanie Covington, *Gender-Responsive Strategies: Research, Practice, and Guiding Principles for Women Offenders*. Washington, DC: National Institute of Corrections. 2003.

Bossuroy, Thomas, Francisco Campos, Aidan Coville, Markus Goldstein, Gareth Roberts, and Sandra Sequeira, "Shape Up and Ship Out? Gender Constraints to Growth and Exporting in South Africa", in *Women and Trade in Africa: Realizing the Potential*, eds. Brenton Paul, Elisa Gamberoni and Catherine Sear. The World Bank. 2014. https://openknowledge.worldBank.org/bitstream/handle/10986/16629/825200WP0Women00Box379865B00PUBLIC0.pdf

Chikwanha, Annie Barbara, "The Bricoleur Economy – Indigenous Gold Mining in Zimbabwe", forthcoming.

Comesa's Regional Strategy for Mainstreaming Gender in Agriculture and Climate Change, Strategic Framework. 2011–2015. http://programmes.comesa.int/attachments/article/82/Regional%20Strategy%20on%20Mainstreaming%20Gender%20in%20Agriculture%20and%20Climate%20Change_RESTRAP.pdf

Damon, Malcolm, and Jeuring, Kristel, "Informal Cross-Border Trade as an Instrument in Alleviating Poverty", OSISA. 2009. www.osisa.org/resources/docs/PDFs/OpenSpaceMay2009/2_4_economic_i. Accessed 16 October 2016.

Doidge, Matthew, "From Developmental Regionalism to Developmental Interregionalism: The European Union Approach", NCRE Working Paper no 7/01 p. 14. 2007.

Duarte, Mariana, "African Women's Day: Violence against Women in Africa: From Discrimination to Impunity: A Call for Ratification and Implementation of the Maputo Protocol", World Organisation Against Torture (OMCT), 2008. www.omct.org/index.php?id=&lang=eng&articleId=7950. Accessed 20 August 2016.

Farell, Mary, Bjorn Hettne, and Luk Van Langenhoven, *Global Politics of Regionalism: Theory and Practice, Kindle Edition*. London: Pluto Press. 2005.

Gamble, Andrew, and Payne, Anthony, *Regionalism and World Order*. New York: St. Martin's Press. 1996.

Hayes, Karen, Common Fund for Commodities, PACT and the World Bank. 2008. http://common-fund.org/fileadmin/user_upload/Repository_docs/CFC_Report_Mining_2008_final_2_.pdf

Hettne, Björn, and Fredrik Söderbaum, 1998. The New Regionalism Approach, *Politeia*, 17(3).

Hinton, Jennifer J., Marcello M. Veiga, and Christian Beinhoff, "Women and Artisanal Mining: Gender Roles and the Road Ahead", in *The Socio-Economic Impacts of Artisanal and Small-Scale Mining in Developing Countries*, ed. G. Hilson. Netherlands: Swets Publishers. 2003. http://siteresources.worldbank.org

Hoadley, Marie, and Daniel Limpitlaw, *The Artisanal and Small Scale Mining Sector & Sustainable Livelihoods, School of Mining Engineering*. Johannesburg, South Africa: University of the Witwatersrand. 2004. http://regionalexportpromowomenstrust.blogspot.co.za/

Jayachandran, Seema, "The Roots of Gender Inequality in Developing Countries", *Annual Review of Economics*, 7. 2014. 115404. http://faculty.wcas.northwestern.edu/~sjv340/roots_of_gender_inequality.pdf
Mittelman, James H., *The Globalization Syndrome: Transformation and Resistance*. Princeton: Princeton University Press. 2000.
Journal of the Southern African Institute of Mining and Metallurgy (SAIIM), Future of the South African mining industry and the roles of the SAIMM and the Universities, vol. 111, n. 9, Johannesburg, September 2011. www.scielo.org.za/scielo.php?script=sci_arttext&pid=S0038-223X2011000900001
Machacha, Mandipa, An Examination of the Gender Implications of Trade Liberalisation in Southern Africa. 2015. www.osisa.org
Markus, Jelitto, "Trade in services liberalisation in SADC: Vehicle without a driver, or just getting into gear?" International Centre for Trade and Sustainable Development, SADC, BRIDGES AFRICA, vol. 1 no. 4, 2012. www.ictsd.org/bridges-news/bridges-africa/news/trade-in-services-liberalisation-in-sadc-vehicle-without-a-driver
Meena, Ruth, "Women and Sustainable Development", *Equal Opportunities International*, 11(6): 7–11. 1992.
Muqayi, Solomon, "The Relevance of the Simplified Trade Regime in Addressing State Protectionism: Addressing Small-Scale Traders at Chirundu One Stop Border Post", *Pakistani Journal of Social Sciences*, 12(4): 10–17. 2015.
Ndomo, Atieno, "Regional Economic Communities in Africa A Progress Overview", GTZ. 2009. www.g20dwg.org/documents/pdf/view/113/
NEPAD, Gender, Climate Change and Agriculture Support Programme (GCCASP). October 2014. www.google.com/search?client=safari&rls=en&q=NEPAD,+Gender,+Climate+Change+and+Agriculture+Support+Programme+(GCCASP)-,&ie=UTF-8&oe=UTF-8
Nesadurai, Helene E. S., "Attempting Developmental Regionalism through AFTA: The Domestic Sources of Regional Governance", *Third World Quarterly*, 24(2): 235–253.2003.
Pillar, Domingo, Rebecca Holmes, Tam O'Neal, Kate Bird, Anna Lawson, Elizabeth Presler-Marshall, and Valters Nicola Jones, "Women's Voice and Leadership in Decision making-Assessing the Evidence", ODI Report.2015. www.odi.org/sites/odi.org.uk/files/odi-assets/publications-opinion-files/9627.pdf
Ragodoo, Nicholas, "Raising the Role of Women in International Trade: A Developing Country's Perspective", Faculty of Social Studies and Humanities University of Mauritius, ICITI. 2011. http://sites.uom.ac.mu/wtochair/Conference%20Proceedings/57.pdf
Reeves, Hazel, and Sally Baden, "Gender and Development: Concepts and Definitions", Institute of Development Studies, Report no. 55, BRIDGE. 2000. www.bridge.ids.ac.uk/sites/bridge.ids.ac.uk/files/reports/re55.pdf
SADC Industrialisation Strategy and Roadmap 2015–2063. https://sadc-eu.sardc.net/sadc-industrialization-strategy-roadmap-2015–2063/
SADC Protocol on Gender and Development 2008. www.lawschool.cornell.edu/womenandjustice/upload/SADC-Protocol-on-Gender-and-Development.pdf
SADC, SADC Protocol on Politics, Defense and Security Cooperation. 28th June 1996. www.sadc.int/files/3613/5292/8367/Protocol_on_Politics_Defence_and_Security20001.pdf
Shayo, Rose, "Assessment of Gender Impacts of SADC Trade Protocol in Selected Countries", African Trade Policy Centre, Work in Progress No. 88, Economic Commission for Africa. 2012. www.uneca.org/sites/default/files/PublicationFiles/atpcworkinprogress88.pdf
Söderbaum, Fredrik, "Regionalisation and Civil Society: The Case of Southern Africa", *New Political Economy*, 12(3): 319–37. September 2007.

Sultan, Rehman Sherief, and Asmahani Aswassalai, "Bottlenecks to Women's Economic Empowerment in Africa", Management and Science University, Shah Alam, Selangor, Malaysia. 2008.

United Nations Conference on Trade and Development, "Economic Development in Africa Report: Intra-African Trade: Unlocking Private Sector Dynamism", 2013. http://unctad.org/en/pages/PublicationWebflyer.aspx?publicationid=604

United Nations Conference on Trade and Development, "Trade as a Tool for the Economic Empowerment of Women", Trade and Development Commission Expert Meeting on Trade as a Tool for the Economic Empowerment of Women, Geneva, 23–24 May 2016. http://unctad14.org/Documents/ciem8d2_en.pdf

UNDP, The Gender Development Index 2017, Human Development Report, http://hdr.undp.org/en/composite/GDI

UNWOMEN, "Unleashing the Potential of Women Informal Cross-Border Traders to Transform Intra-African Trade, Factsheet", 2010. www.unwomen.org/en/digital-library/publications/2010/3/unleashing-the-potential-of-women-informal-cross-border-traders-to-transform-intra-african-trade

UNWOMEN, "The World Survey on the Role of Women in Development 2014: Gender Equality and Sustainable Development." 2014. www.unwomen.org/en/digital-library/publications/2014/10/world-survey-2014

Vanheukelom, Jan, and Talitha Bertelsmann-Scott, "The Political Economy of Regional Integration in Africa: The Southern African Development Community (SADC) Report", ECDPM, Brussels. 2016. http://ecdpm.org/peria/sadc

World Economic Forum, "The Global Gender Gap Report", 2016. www.weforum.org/reports/the-global-gender-gap-report-2016/

www.peaceau.org/en/article/trading-for-peace-promoting-cross-border-trade-for-women-s-civic-political-and-economic-empowerment-and-sustainable-peace#sthash.ZQRu2vIF.dpuf

www.sadc.int/issues/gender/gender-mainstreaming/

8 Immigration, xenophobia and developmental regionalism in Southern Africa

A South Africa case study

André Mbata Mangu

Introduction

On 7 July 2000, African heads of state and government met in Lomé, Togo, and adopted the Constitutive Act of the African Union (AU) to replace the Organisation of African Unity (OAU), which was established in 25 May 1963. The AU became reality when its Constitutive Act entered into force on 26 May 2001.

The first aim of the AU is "to achieve greater unity and solidarity between the African countries and the peoples of Africa" (AU Constitutive Act, Article 3 (a)) through "regional integration" (Article 3 (c)–(j)), including "political, and socio-economic integration" (Article 3 (c). To achieve this aim, the AU should "coordinate and harmonize the policies between the existing and future regional economic communities (RECs) (Article 3 (l)).

To date, the eight RECs recognised by the AU are the *Communautééconomique des Etats de l'Afrique de l'Ouest*—Economic Community of Western African States (CEDEAO—ECOWAS), the *Communautééconomique des Etats de l'AfriqueCentrale*—Economic Community of Central African States (CEEAC—ECCAS), the Common Market for Eastern and Southern Africa (COMESA), the East African Community (EAC), the *Union du Maghreb Arab*—Arab Maghreb Union (UMA—AMU), the Intergovernmental Authority on Development (IGAD), the Community of Sahel Sub-Saharan States (CEN-SAD), and the Southern African Development Community (SADC). Regional integration as envisaged through these RECs is mainly "economic integration".

RECs are considered "imperative platforms for grouping individual countries together within different subregions for the specific objectives of attaining greater socio-economic unification". They are "building blocks" of regional integration although some scholars tend to consider them "an obstacle to the integration of Africa" (Olutayo & Adeniran 2015: 1, 3; Yaya 2011: 7, 19–20; Dzinesa, Nagar & Saunders 2012: 2–4) as some countries belong to several RECs at once. For instance, Kenya and Uganda are both members of EAC and COMESA, Tanzania is a member of EAC and the SADC and the Democratic Republic of the Congo (DRC) is also a member state of ECCAS, COMESA and the SADC. According to Olutayo and Adeniran, "such multiple and confusing membership creates unnecessary duplication and dims the light on what ought to be priority" (Olutayo & Adeniran 2015: 2–3, 13–15).

Regional integration is present in virtually all the discourses of African politicians and policy makers. Countries such as the Central African Republic and Senegal have even established ministries of African integration. Regional integration presupposes that people are able to move across the region freely. It also requires peace and development.

This chapter reflects on the interface between immigration, xenophobia and developmental regionalism in the SADC region, which consists of 15 Member States, namely Angola, Botswana, DRC, Lesotho, Madagascar, Malawi, Mauritius, Mozambique, Namibia, Seychelles, South Africa, Swaziland, Tanzania, Zambia, and Zimbabwe. It is therefore confined to the SADC and focuses on the dynamics in South Africa, which is reportedly home to the largest number of migrants in Southern Africa. On the other hand, xenophobic sentiments appear to be stronger in South Africa than in any other country of the region (Gonzalez-Gracia et al. 2016: 1–4). These two reasons explain why South Africa has been selected as a case study.

Migration is generally defined as a movement of one person or a group of persons from one region or one country to another. It can be individual, collective, internal, cross-border or international. Ever since immemorial times, migration has been part of human life. People are continuously on the move. Human beings have migrated throughout history to such an extent that we are all migrants or descendants of migrants. Migration has become a global, developmental, security, social, economic, and political issue (Mangu 2013: 281). People migrate for different reasons. They move out of necessity to escape violence or persecution. They move for joyful purposes and to change environment. They migrate in search for new adventures, to meet other people, and to improve their economic conditions and chances in life. Voluntary migrants need visas to enter foreign countries, unless they are exempted in terms of a bilateral or multilateral agreement.

People may also be forced to migrate by economic, historical, socio-cultural, climatic, geographical and political factors. This is the case of asylum seekers and refugees who are also international migrants unlike displaced persons who remain in the country (Mangu 2013: 281). Migration can be legal or illegal, regular or irregular, lawful or unlawful depending whether it complies with the immigration law of a particular country or not. From the perspective of the country of origin of migrants (sending country) or their country of destination (receiving country), the persons who migrate are emigrants or immigrants. Immigration and emigration are the two sides of the same coin of migration (Mangu 2013: 281).

According to Moser, Nyamnjoh and Mususa, there is a connection between migration and xenophobia (Moser 2016: 2; Nyamnjoh & Mususa 2012: 215). Xenophobia is defined as the intense dislike or fear of strangers or people from other countries, an attitudinal orientation of hostility against non-natives in a given population. It describes attitudes, prejudices and behaviour that reject, exclude and often vilify persons, based on the perception that they are outsiders or foreigners to the community, society or national identity (Neocosmos 2015: 30–32; Nyamnjoh 2015a: 28, 2015b: 34). Xenophobia is only directed at foreigners or migrants and would not therefore exist without migration. It also impacts negatively on migration trends since people would hardly migrate to countries or regions where their safety would be endangered by repeated xenophobic attacks.

By discouraging the peoples from moving freely and establishing in the region, xenophobia also constitutes a serious threat to regional integration since as Oucho remarked, international migration lies at the core of regional integration in all African RECs and its importance to the SADC cannot be overemphasised (Oucho 2007: 1). Regional integration cannot be achieved if people are prevented from moving and establishing freely and if xenophobia prevails across their region. Things even get worse when state's officials, intellectuals, community leaders, opinion-makers and the media who should play an important role in promoting migration and integration become themselves involved in the anti-migration campaign.

In Southern Africa, regionalism has gone without development and peaceful and unhindered movement of people across national borders. Moreover, the region is characterised by inequalities while its economies inherited from colonialism and apartheid have not been substantially transformed and social peace remains elusive. Accordingly, regionalism, peace and economic transformation in Africa should not be seen as a fact, but rather an ideal pursued by the states of the region and a process.

This chapter, which is based on a desktop study, aims to contribute to the literature on immigration, xenophobia and regional integration in Southern Africa. It may also contribute to improving legislation and policies that can advance regional integration by promoting migration and combating xenophobia. Nevertheless, as for any study significantly relying on desktop review, the chapter is limited in terms of its research methodology. This imposes inevitable constraints with respect to data and information, their sources and reliability (AUC & IOM 2018: 18).

The chapter is divided into several sections. The first section reflects on the concepts of regional integration and "developmental regionalism" in Southern Africa. The second section examines the SADC Protocol on the Facilitation of Free Movement of Persons as a legal framework to promote migration and regional integration in Southern Africa. The African people and the people of the rest of the world expected the Republic of South Africa being the second African country to be named after the continent like the Central African Republic, her policies and practices would be infused with pan-Africanism. Therefore, regime change and the advent of the first black government in South Africa raised expectations among the African people since their "countries had linked their fate to that of the blacks in South Africa, supported their liberation struggle and engaged in an armed struggle against apartheid.

It was hoped that democratic South Africa would acknowledge the contribution made by the Southern African region" (Modi 2003: 1759; Moser 2016: 1–2). Accordingly, the third section provides a background to migration from historical and contemporary perspectives with disaggregated data of African migrants in South Africa. The fourth section underscores the dynamics of the migration politics in South Africa. The fifth section revisits the discourses on migration and xenophobia in South Africa. The sixth section explains how popular and organised interest groups like the Confederation of South African Trade Unions (COSATU) and political parties have reacted and how the migrants, the governments of their home countries and SADC have responded to the discourses on migration and xenophobia which mainly amounts to *Afrophobia* as most victims are nationals from other African countries. The seventh section stresses the linkage between migration and xenophobiaon the one hand and South Africa's rhetoric of pan-Africanism couched in the African renaissance discourse on the other hand. The last section considers the role that the SADC and the AU have played or should play in addressing the problem. The chapter ends with a brief conclusion.

Regional integration and developmental regionalism

Regional integration and developmental regionalism are the key concepts of the study alongside migration and xenophobia, which have been already defined. Yet, social sciences' concepts are generally polemic, contested, controversial and complex. Even when there is no total disagreement among authors, each tends to adopt his or her own reading and there is always room for nuances which may be dictated by the background. Accordingly, it is worth revisiting the concepts of regional integration and "developmental regionalism" briefly in order to give them a concrete meaning and avoid that they remain meaningless abstractions.

"Regional integration" and "regionalism" are sometimes used interchangeably. Yet, regional integration can be considered the *terminus ad quem* of a process and an embodiment of the theory of regionalism (Dzinesa, Nagar & Saunders 2012: 2–4; Khadiagala 2012: 25–38). As an approach to regional integration, the concept of "developmental regionalism" is a bit controversial as development is the underlying aim of any regionalism.

In the case of Southern Africa, the idea of regional integration has to do with a desire to rebel against a global order designed to oppress, exploit and subjugate the periphery. It is as a result infused with the logic of self-reliance, solidarity, developmentalism, and anti-imperialism to give rise to what has been called "regional developmental integration". It is closely related to the idea of developmental regionalism, as encompassing cooperation among countries in a broader range of areas than just trade and trade facilitation, to include investment, research and development, as well as policies aimed at accelerating regional industrial development and regional infrastructure provision, such as the building of better networks of roads and railways. It is an approach underpinned by the paradigm of economic development as distinct from the dominant economic growth mantra promoted by neo-liberal institutions. This paradigm means sustained, inclusive, concerted and comprehensive efforts to bring about qualitative and quantifiable improvement in the well-being of the people.

Economic development is based on the acceptance that growth is insufficient to improve living standards of human beings, but it must be part of a combination of human, social, educational and technological, cultural and spiritual development. It is then extended to regional integration as a call to go beyond the classical economistic integration approaches that presuppose that economic growth stimulating progress in trade and investment amounts to regional integration. The orthodox idea therefore demands a linear process starting with a Free Trade Area to customs union, common market, and ultimately a monetary union.

In pursuit of this, the SADC placed poverty eradication at the apex of its regional priorities, thus forcing it to make well-being a central concern of integration.

It was expected that through policy harmonization, coordination of policy action and alignment of SADC institutions regional integration would be developmental rather than merely economic and aspirational. Economic development gives prominence to actions relating to trade and investment, financial integration, human development (especially education and health), infrastructure related issues of water, energy and communications.

Right from its inception at the inaugural Summit in Mbabane, Swaziland, in 1993, the SADC expressed the wish to have a people-based integration process and that for this reason it was in SADC's interest to deepen democratic governance in the region. It committed to use "common action" to ensure progress and well-being of the peoples of the region (SADC Treaty). In 1993, the very same year that South Africa assented to the SADC Treaty, in a speech to the Council of Foreign Relations in the US, Nelson Mandela committed the new South Africa to pursuing regional integration and cooperation designed to "restructure regional economic relations" forged in the colonial/apartheid period (Mandela 1993).

In terms of the SADC Treaty, the key pillars of regional integration consist of the following:

- Regional infrastructure;
- Regional resource development;
- Boost intraregional trade including by opening the South African market for regional goods;
- Regional water and environmentally friendly energy development;
- Regional crisis prevention and management/ending conflict and violence; and
- Regional institution building and consolidation.

The SADC Treaty ignored the free movement of people as one of the key pillars of regional integration. It is clear that SADC countries were primarily interested in trade and economic integration than in people.

Integration was to be measured in terms of movement of goods, services, and labour within a region more than the quality of lives peoples in the region. Developmental regional integration was meant to promote a balance between short-term economic reforms and long-term structural transformation of conditions that perpetuate underdevelopment, fragmentation, jobless growth and so forth and to contribute concretely to transforming and improving economic development and transforming lives (Mulaudzi 2006).

Unfortunately, genuine and sustainable regional integration should take people seriously. It entails focus on people and requires freedom of movement. Southern Africa has sought to pursue a particular type of regional integration, which since the 1990s has been termed "developmental integration" to underline the fact that it seeks to transform the structure of the inherited economy in order to eradicate poverty. Premised on the idea of cooperation beyond trade and investment, this approach is positioned as an alternative to the dominant liberal paradigm that places emphasis on market integration through free movement of goods and labour. Market integration would simply maintain the inegalitarian structure of the economy inherited from colonialism and apartheid. With the manufacturing sector as the main engine of economic growth, it resulted in huge socio-economic inequalities, worsening age-old inequalities that have been characteristic of colonial economic patterns in the region.

The concept of "developmental regional integration" is closely related to and entails "economic transformation". Whether economic transformation has been achieved and developmental states developed in Southern Africa is a different issue. Arguably, Southern Africa is still far away from economic transformation.

As stressed earlier, Southern African countries have not played an important role in the process of transforming economies inherited from colonialism and apartheid. They have not shown the courage required for the achievement of the ideal of the developmental regional integration and have failed to accelerate developmental regional integration. Economic structures as inherited from colonialism or apartheid remain almost the same and the poverty of the masses of the peoples has been increasing instead of being eradicated.

Clearly, as an approach to regional integration, developmental regional integration presupposes that nation states in southern Africa have capable and developmental governments in place to carry out the grandiose vision. It was thought these states were capable of transforming the regional institution into a vehicle for developmental regional integration. This approach to integration assumes the existence of developmental states at national level, that is, states that are organized and efficient enough to stimulate economic development through high-impact policy interventions combining guidance and incentives to industry and government's social expenditure. Indeed, many member states looked to the successful South-East Asian state model at least in talk, but failed to take concomitant action to strengthen the ability of the state to lead economic development, forge effective social partnerships and leverage international relations for economic development.

Speaking at the 2004 SADC Summit in Mauritius, the then SADC chairperson, President Benjamin Mkapa held that lack of policy coherence and political will among SADC member states was a function of narrow nationalism (or the narrow focus on national priorities (SADC 2004). He urged member states to lift their vision and focus from national to regional level because only through collective action could regional economic development and political stability be achieved for the benefit of nation-states. He warned member states against thinking about what they could achieve nationally individually, thus losing sight of what greater benefits could be derived through accelerated regional integration. There was therefore lack of courage to improve political will needed for regional integration. This lack of political will resulted in the deficit of ownership of the regional integration that was manifest in the fact that the bulk of the programmatic budget for SADC was funded by external donors without any due regard to what the donors' own strategic orientation towards developmental regional integration was.

Developmental regional integration should go beyond economic and political integration to include the integration of the peoples that would require the suppression of the borders inherited from colonialisation, freedom of movement and establishment of the peoples across the region, and the eradication of xenophobia as a consequence of the market regional integration. This was the main objective of the SADC Protocol on the Facilitation of Free Movement of Persons which is based on the assumption that freedom of movement is critical for regional integration.

The SADC Protocol on the facilitation of free movement of persons and regional integration in Southern Africa

Integration at the regional and subregional levels is generally based on different legal instruments. From a legal perspective, some of these instruments are binding and some are not. Non-binding instruments include resolutions, declarations or memoranda of understanding. Unless provided otherwise, they are not directly binding on states although the latter cannot ignore them. They may be considered "soft law" while "hard law" as compared to by binding instruments like treaties and protocols. With regard to regional integration and freedom of movement which entails migration, the relevant SADC instruments include the SADC Declaration, the SADC Treaty and the SADC Protocol on the Facilitation of Movement of Persons.

The first two instruments were adopted by the Heads of State and Government of the Southern African Development Coordination Conference (SADCC) on 17 July 1992 when they met in Windhoek, Namibia, and established the SADC, which replaced the SADCC.

In the Preamble to the SADC Declaration, which is not directly binding, Heads of State and Government of the SADCC committed themselves to the establishment of SADC as a "vehicle for the development and integration of the region" (SADC Declaration 1992, Preamble, Paragraph 3). They also called upon their peoples to make the same commitment and to participate fully in the process towards "regional integration". The terms "integration", "regional integration", or "integration" of the region" abound in the Declaration as "the challenging mission of SADC" and its contribution to regional efforts towards the continental or regional community (SADC Declaration).

Unlike the SADC Declaration, the SADC Treaty is binding on state parties. As a treaty, it is subject to the 1969 Vienna on the Law of Treaties, which governs the treaties concluded by states. It provides that the primary objective of SADC is to "achieve development and economic growth, alleviate poverty, enhance the standard and quality of life of the peoples of Southern Africa and support the socially disadvantaged through regional integration (Article 5(1) (a)).

One of the principles of the SADC Treaty (Article 4 (b)) is "solidarity, peace and security". SADC also aims to "strengthen and consolidate the longstanding historical, social and cultural affinities, and links among the people of the Region" (Article 5(a) (h)). However, how could one promote "solidarity" and "strengthen and consolidate the longstanding historical, social and cultural affinities and links among the people of the Region" without allowing the same people to migrate or freely move from one country to another in the same Region? To achieve regional integration, Member States have to "develop policies aimed at the progressive elimination of obstacles to the free movement of capital and labour, goods and services, and of the peoples of the region generally, among Member States" (Article 5 (2) (d)).

The SADC Protocol on the Facilitation of Movement of Persons was signed in Gaborone, Botswana, on 18 August 2005. In the Protocol, the Heads of State and Government of SADC Member States recalled that they were mindful of their "duty under the SADC Treaty to promote the inter-dependence and integration of their national economies" (SADC Protocol, Preamble, Paragraph 1).

They also recognised that full popular participation in the process of integration or community building process was "only possible where the Citizens of the Community enjoy freedom of movement of persons, namely, visa-free entry, residence and establishment in the territories of Member States" (SADC Protocol, Preamble, Paragraph 2).

The overall objective of the Protocol (Article 2) "to develop policies aimed at the progressive elimination of obstacles to the movement of persons of the Region generally into and within the territories of State Parties".

The Treaty provides that the specific objectives in relation to every citizen of a state party are to facilitate:

(a) entry, for a lawful purpose and without a visa, into the territory of another state party for a maximum period of ninety (90) days per year for bona fide visit and in accordance with the laws of the state party concerned;
(b) permanent and temporary residence in the territory of another state party; and

(c) establishment of oneself and working in the territory of another state party (Article 3).

The Protocol constitutes a way forward in the process of regional integration. However, it raises a number of questions with regard to its relation to the funding instrument, the SADC Treaty. First, it refers to the "facilitation of movement" while the SADC Treaty (Article 2) clearly stresses "free movement" and aims to achieve "the progressive elimination of obstacles to the free movement". Second, the Protocol contains some claw back clauses, taking away what was already granted to citizens of state parties. This is the case when it provides for "entry, for a lawful purpose and without a visa into the territory of another State for a maximum period of ninety (90) days per year for bona fide visit" and "in accordance with the laws of the State Party concerned". State parties should ensure that their legislation is in line with the Protocol instead of being required to "promote legislative, judicial, administrative and other measures necessary for co-operation in the implementation and effective achievement of the objectives of the Protocol" (Article 10).

In terms of the Protocol, state parties should, *inter alia*:

- take common action in implementing the Protocol (Article 6);
- ensure that all relevant national laws, statutory rules and regulations are in harmony and promotive of the objectives of the Protocol (Article 7);
- establish and maintain a population register from which the status of citizens and permanent residents can be determined accurately (Article 9);
- increase co-operation and mutual assistance to implement the protocol, including the training of competent authorities and educating communities regionally and nationally on the protocol (Article 11);
- harmonise their laws and administrative practices so that citizens of state parties are able to enter the territory of another state party for a maximum period of ninety (90) days over year for *bona fide* visits (Article 13 (a), (c), (f));
- establish a separate SADC DESK at each port of entry between state parties (Article 13 (c));
- abolish visa requirements where they still exist, provided that where visas are regarded as necessary they shall be issued gratis at the port of entry (Article 13 (f));
- grant visa-free admission to citizens of other state parties (Articles 3 (a) & 14)).

The entry into force of the Protocol is subject to its ratification (Article 35) and the Deposit of the instruments of ratification by two-thirds of SADC Member States (Article 36). Out of the 15 SADC Member States, it has only been ratified by four Member States, namely Botswana, Mozambique, South Africa, and Swaziland.

The fact that SADC Member States have already wasted so much time and still unable to bring the Protocol into force is clear evidence that SADC Member States are not really committed to free movement or regional integration and there is little political will to promote freedom of movements of peoples and accelerate regional integration in Southern Africa. Arguably, apart from Central Africa, Southern Africa is the region where it is more difficult for African citizens to migrate from one country to another and also the less integrated on the continent. This also contributes to fostering xenophobic sentiments in Southern Africa.

Background to migration from historical and contemporary perspectives and African migrants in South Africa

Arguably, South Africa as always been a land of migration, whether voluntary or forced migration. Few are people that can be considered natives of South Africa. The Bushmen in the Kalahari Deserthave been in the country for centuries and can qualify as the only native people of South Africa. Other black people who joined and fought them over land ownership are said to have migrated from the North of Limpopo.

The European migration started in the 17th century and intensified in the 18th and 19th centuries. It involved the British colonizers and the Boers (farmers, in Afrikaans) who were descendants of Dutch, German and French Huguenot settlers who arrived in the Transvaal and Orange Free State. British and Boers had to fight against themselves over land and gold prior to turning on the Black people who occupied the territory. The Anglo-Boer wars were won by the British and ended when the Union of South Africa was established at the beginning of the 20th century. In 1948 when the National Party took power in 1948 and established a system of institutionalised racial segregation known as apartheid that was only dismantled in the early 1990s.

Unlike in other African colonies, the white colonisers in South Africa and other Southern African countries like Zimbabwe and Namibia were there to stay as they came to consider themselves the natives while the Black people became foreigners on the land of their ancestors. The country was divided into areas for the white and non-white people respectively. The Black people had to carry on permits or passes in the urban areas reserved for the White while the Black were confined to rural areas or to the "townships". Inside the country, migration of the non-white and predominantly black people was carefully controlled. The apartheid government favoured a "temporary oscillatory migrant system" that saw labour migrants return to their country of origin after their contract in the farms or mining industry had expired (Adepoju 2006: 40; Moser 2016: 6).

The much-celebrated "Rainbow Nation", a multicolour, multi-ethnic, multinational, multi-religious nation constituted of people from around the world was developing. The apartheid policies favoured international migration as long as it benefitted South Africa. The minority government perceived the need to enforce such policies because during this time the proportion of white South Africans with regard to the overall population was shrinking. These policies turned out to be successful when in the late 1960s more and more immigrants from Europe and North America settled in South Africa (Anderson 2006: 99–102; Moser 2016: 6–7). Throughout the 20th century, the government actively sought white settlers but in turn rigorously limited Africans to only temporary forms of legal entry in accordance with the migrant labour system. Therefore, South Africa was the only country in the region to pursue a proactive immigration policy up until the 1990s, albeit with a heavily racial undertone (Klotz 2010: 831).

The demise of apartheid in the early 1990s constituted a turning point. For a few years under the Mandela's presidency and thanks to the leadership of the man whose liberation after 27 years of imprisonment was made possible by the solidarity of the people of the world in general and the rest of the continent in particular, South Africa continued its selective open-door immigration policy under a schizophrenic foreign policy. While claiming its strong solidarity with the rest of Africa, endorsing the rhetoric of an African renaissance and promoting African integration and succeeding in becoming the first country to host a summit of the AU that replaced the AU and later African institutions such as the Pan-African Parliament and the Secretariat of the New Partnership for Africa's Development (NEPAD), the new South Africa was more and more closing its borders to Africans from the rest of the continent. Her laws and policies made it more and more difficult for them to enter the country to work, study, reside or even as tourists and asylum seekers. African migrants were no longer welcome. Robin Ephraim Moser reflected on migration policies and xenophobia and stressed the linkage between migration and xenophobia in post-apartheid South Africa (Moser 2016: 2–16).

Our once beloved "African brothers and sisters" turned into enemies of the Nation and were made responsible for all the ills suffered by the new South Africa: HIV/Aids, high unemployment, economic recession, drug abuses, murders and other crimes. Draconian migration legislation and policies were adopted that made it difficult for foreigners to obtain or renew tourist, study, work, residence, asylum seekers' or refugees' permits. The government and law enforcement agencies also actively participated in the fabrication or making of more "illegal migrants" by not responding or renewing in time the permits of those who were once legal in the country.

Worse, at some academic institutions, foreigners who had been naturalised were unfairly discriminated against as they could not be appointed or promoted like South Africans by birth or descent. A distinction was being made between native South Africa citizens or those who were naturalised sometime after apartheid and are considered second-zone South African citizens.

Since the late 1990s, post-apartheid South Africa that already excelled in Rugby seems to have invented a "new sport" as every year unwanted African black migrants are burnt to death, murdered, illegally dispossessed, arrested, detained and deported while non-African (European, American and Asian) migrants are welcome as tourists and investors coming to create jobs in the country.

Draconian migration legislation, xenophobic policies and practices do not seem to have discouraged African migrants who can also take advantage of corruption that is rampant in the public sphere to enter and independently work in South Africa. Even though their number has been grossly exaggerated by the media and some interest groups who referred to "human tsunami", African migrants continue to migrate to South Africa.

Discourses on migration and xenophobia in South Africa: myths and realities

Southern Africa is made of a number of countries. As pointed out earlier, the selection of South Africa as a case study is justified by the fact that South Africa is the main destination of migrants in the region but also because xenophobic sentiments appear to be the strongest in this country (Gonzalez-Gracia et al 2016: 1–4).

According to Crush, Williams and Peberdy, Southern Africa has a long history of intraregional migration dating back to the mid-19th century. Migration was probably the single most important factor tying together all of the various colonies and countries of the sub-continent into a single regional labour market during the 20th century (Crush, Williams & Peberdy 2005: 1–2).

The end of apartheid, the ensuing integration of South Africa within SADC, growing rural and urban poverty and employment, the impact of the Mozambican and Angolan civil wars, and recurrent civil strife and human rights violations in the rest of Africa resulting in mass refugee movements have contributed to exacerbating migration and xenophobia in Southern Africa.

As Robin Ephraim Moser pointed out, "migration to and xenophobia in South Africa are closely intertwine phenomena" (Moser 2016: 2). Several discourses were developed on migration and xenophobia and need to be assessed to differentiate between myths or perceptions and reality.

Myths on migration and xenophobia

Migrants are increasingly viewed negatively in South Africa; xenophobia and intolerance of migrant workers have increased in the past two decades. The prevalent anti-immigrant attitudes have, at times, manifested in violence. In May 2008, there were a series of attacks in which immigrants from Mozambique, Malawi and Zimbabwe were attacked; at least 60 people were killed, hundreds were injured, and even more were displaced.

Sources blame a wide variety of factors for the increase in intolerance, such as anti-immigrant media coverage and policy-making, as well as a range of factors including high unemployment, porous borders, one of the world's highest crime rates, poverty, police and government corruption, ineffective service delivery, and an inept foreign policy (Neocosmos 2015: 32; Thrane 2013).

With regard to immigration, the general view of government, the wider public and the media is that there is a "tsunami", a "deluge of immigrants" in South Africa. According to some research, the numbers of immigrants in South Africa have been conflated, and this has been used by officials to push for "better management"—in order words, greater control of immigration in the country (Nyamnjoh & Mususa 2012: 216). The popular perception even made this worse when the people tend to consider South Africa "a nation over-run", "overwhelmed", "swamped" or "bombarded" with foreigners (Neocosmos 2010: 141; Nyamnjoh 2012: 216). This perception is also shared in Southern Africa countries such as Botswana, Namibia and even Angola.

In line with the perception that there are too many immigrants, most migrants are also considered "illegal". In South Africa, for instance, as far back as 1998, the Department of Home Affairs claimed there were up to five million illegal immigrants in South Africa. This figure reigned supreme for years, quoted liberally by politicians, and grossly exaggerated by the publicly funded Human Sciences Research Council (HSRC), which claimed that there were between four to eight million undocumented migrants and recommended that South Africa should close its borders to new immigrants (Nyamnjoh & Mususa 2012: 216). The Council, under the spotlight, withdrew its figure.

On the other hand, the popular sentiment is that because of the nature of illegal immigration, emboldened foreign nationals commit crimes and cannot be traced because they just do not have a return address. In South Africa, this sentiment is reinforced by some populist officials in the government, the South African Police Service, intellectuals, and the media who hold foreigners responsible or blame rising levels of immigration for violent crime or the rise in crime in South Africa (Nyamnjoh & Mususa 2012: 216).

In 1998, Buthelezi made quite some notoriety for his infamous xenophobic statements, which included *inter alia* the suggestion that all Nigerian immigrants were criminals and drug traffickers (Harris 2001: 74; Neocosmos 2010: 85, 124). In 2002, the Director General of Home Affairs reportedly remarked that "approximately 90 percent of foreign persons in South Africa with fraudulent documents were involved in other crimes (Neocosmos 2010: 85).

Also, in his 100-days-in-office speech delivered on 1 December 2016, Johannesburg Mayor Herman Mashaba described migrants as criminals occupying abandoned and derelict buildings in the inner city, and accused them of using their rundown shelters to hide from police who were too scared to go inside. He came under fire by foreign migrants who demonstrated against him and requested an apology while the ANC took the case to the South African Human Rights Commission (Pather 2016). Another perception holds that migrants compete with locals for scarce resources, "steal" jobs of citizens, contribute to high unemployment rate and impede development progress. It is generally held that foreign nationals take up scarce jobs, amenities and business opportunities in the country with an official 24 percent unemployment rate, and twice that for the younger population. With the high percentage of unemployment for nationals, migrants are accused of stealing jobs of citizens and competing with locals for scarce resources and contributing to high unemployment. The overwhelming perception is that of foreigners as "takers" and not "contributors" (Neocosmos 2010: 108). There is also a perception that the majority of foreigners in the country are here to stay. They will never return home but end up becoming residents or citizens. The situation would worsen if South Africa does not reinforce borders control. It is the negative bias against immigration that has led to xenophobia. Nyamnjoh and Mususa endorsed the finding in a 2008 Southern African Migration Project (SAMP) that South Africa had the highest ratings for anti-foreigner views in Southern Africa (Nyamnjoh & Mususa 2012: 217–219).

Xenophobia is based on several misconceptions and on "denialism". Denialists first argue that xenophobia does not exist in South Africa. Second, when they admit that it exists, they hold that xenophobia is recent and only a small minority of South Africans are xenophobic while poverty is the main cause of xenophobia. The underlying claim is that being poor predisposes one to violence. Poverty of the majority of South Africans tends to feed the anti-foreigner sentiment and xenophobic violence in South Africa. The May 2008 report of the Human Sciences Research Council xenophobic attacks (HSRC 2008: 48–49) also linked xenophobia to poverty (Neocosmos 2010: 129).

Realities of migration and xenophobia

As anywhere in the world, myths on migration and xenophobia in Southern Africa have proved unfounded (Neocosmos 2010: 2). The reality is that migration of SADC citizens has increased in the region. So has xenophobia.

Reality of migration

With three million people out of a population of 55, 91 million according to a census made in 2016 (Stats SA 2016a), migrants constitute less than 5 percent of the South African population. On the other hand, as illustrated by the Refugee Trends revealed by the United Nations High Commissioner for Refugees (UNHCR) in 2016 (UNHCR 2018: 23), South Africa does not feature among the top 10 receiver countries of refugees in Africa, which include Ethiopia, Kenya, Uganda, Democratic Republic of the Congo, Chad, Cameroon, Sudan, South Sudan, Tanzania and Niger.

African migrants contribute to creating jobs which benefit nationals instead of stealing the jobs reserved for South African citizens.

Therefore, they also contribute to economy and bring jobs. On the other hand, most people who commit crimes or transmit diseases are South African citizens themselves. The perception that most migrants are criminals or commit crimes is an anecdotal belief as there are no data to support such a contention (Harris 2001: 76; Neocosmos 2010: 85, 141; Nyamnjoh 2012: 216).

According to Neocosmos (2010: 129), the evidence also suggests that most foreign nationals see themselves as only temporary residents. They do not intend settling permanently in South Africa and end up returning home once the situation improves.

The following tables provide data on international migration in South Africa with an emphasis on African migration.

Table 8.1 Number of tourists per region from 2015 to 2016 (Stats SA 2016a: 12)

	Region	*Numbers in 2015*	*Numbers in 2016*
Overseas		**184,864**	**214,930**
	Europe	127,260	144,130
	North America	24,219	26,962
	Central & South America	4,914	5,332
	Asia	17,168	25,002
	Australia & New Zealand	8,650	10,011
	Middle East	2,653	3,466
Africa		**692,035**	**797,050**
	SADC	**678,068**	**782,002**
	East & Central Africa	5,750	5,812
	North Africa	1,343	1,378
	West Africa	6,874	7,849
	Other Africans	13,967	15,048
	Unspecified	813	688
TOTAL		**877,712**	**1,012,641**

Table 8.2 Number of tourists per African country from the SADC region from 2015 to 2016 (Stats SA 2016a: 13)

		Numbers in 2015	*Numbers in 2016*
SADC		**678,068**	**782,002**
Countries	Zimbabwe	220,583	250,514
	Lesotho	156,571	209,403
	Mozambique	136,272	145,775
	Swaziland	71,376	75,176
	Botswana	36,141	44,458
	Namibia	16,352	17,033
	Zambia	12,334	13,758
	Malawi	14,519	12,282
	Angola	6,292	5,565
	Tanzania	2,513	2,493

2016 census showed a decline of the number of foreign and African migrants in South Africa.

Accordingly, it is unsettling that South African political leaders and policy makers are not doing enough to encourage South Africans to disabuse themselves of the illusion that their problems can be solved through the logic of exclusion and scapegoating of certain types of foreigners that has pervaded, paradoxically, since the dawn of democracy in 1994. This explains why the "monster" (of xenophobia) reawakened in Durban and KwaZulu-Natal in 2015 although it was thought to be buried for good after the xenophobic violence of 2008 (Nyamnjoh 2015a: 28).

Table 8.3 Number of tourists from 10 top African countries outside SADC from 2015 to 2016 (Stats SA 2016a: 13–14)

		Numbers in 2015	*Numbers in 2016*
Countries			
	Nigeria	**4,322**	**5,381**
	Kenya	2,109	2,097
	Ghana	1,515	1,398
	Uganda	1,107	1,147
	Gabon	646	780
	Egypt	661	779
	Cameroon	651	632
	Ethiopia	470	450
	Congo	404	317
	Côte d'Ivoire	181	230

Table 8.4 Top ten African sending countries (Stats SA 2016b: 48–49)

No	*SADC Country*	*Number of Migrants*
01	Zimbabwe	547,047
02	Mozambique	293,405
03	Lesotho	160,749
04	Malawi	78,795
05	Swaziland	38,038
06	Democratic Republic of Congo	31,504
07	Namibia	30,701
08	Nigeria	30,314
09	Ethiopia	22,148
10	Zambia	19,119
	Total	1,278,820

Reality of xenophobia

Despite denials, xenophobia exists in South Africa as in other countries of the region. In the South African case, Neocosmos has demonstrated that xenophobia is endemic, widespread across all the sections of the South African society and aggravated by politicians, state officials or institutions, and the press (Neocosmos 2010: 1–2, 119, 124–125; 2015: 30–32). Crush and Pendleton found in a study undertaken in 2004 that xenophobia was not a preserve for a small minority of people. It cuts across age, race, income level and gender. Negative attitudes are so pervasive and widespread that it is actually impossible to identify any kind of "xenophobe profile".

In other words, the poor and the rich, the employed and the unemployed, the male and the female, the black and the white, the conservative and the radical, all express remarkably similar attitudes. This poses a significant problem of explanation because it runs counter to the more general belief that certain groups in a population (usually those who are or who perceive themselves to be threatened by outsiders) are more prone to xenophobic attitudes than others (Crush & Pendleton 2004: 2). As Achille Mbembe correctly put it, "the cancer [of xenophobia] has metastized" and is widely prevalent in society as well as within state institutions (Mbembe 2015: 29; Neocosmos 2015: 30).

A study carried out by the Southern African Migration Programme (SAMP) following the 2008 xenophobic attacks found that "South Africa exhibits levels of intolerance and hostility to outsiders unlike virtually anything seen in other parts of the world" and South Africa had the highest ratings for anti-foreigner views in Southern Africa. According to the study, South Africa was a prominent case of xenophobia and had overtaken Botswana and Namibia as the leading "rogue State" with regard to xenophobia in the SADC region (Nyamnjoh & Mususa 2012: 219–220).

Xenophobia is definitely an obstacle to regional integration and "developmental regionalism" in Southern Africa. It is nurtured by lack of economic transformation despite the demise of colonialism and apartheid as the majority of the local population feel excluded and poverty among them has been increasing instead of being eradicated.

Migration, xenophobia and South Africa's rhetoric of pan-Africanism in the African renaissance discourse

During the Mandela's era, South Africa that used to be a pariah state because of apartheid reconciled with the African continent by wasting no time to join the OAU and taking the lead in the creation of the AU that superseded the OAU. South Africa strongly reaffirmed its belonging to the continent with South Africans seeing themselves as Africans.

As Wayne Visser put it, "I am an African", "not because I was born there", "not because my skin is black", "not because I live on its soil", but "because my heart beats with Africa's", "my mind is engaged by Africa", "my soul is at home in Africa" (Visser 2016: 1–3). A decade earlier, Thabo Mbeki published his *Africa, the Time has Come* (Mbeki 1998) which contains his numerous speeches, including his famous "I Am an African" speech the then South Africa's deputy president pronounced on behalf of the African National Congress in Cape Town on 8 May 1996 on the occasion of the passing of the new Constitution of South Africa. This speech unequivocally expressed South Africa's commitment to Africa. Mbeki held that

> I am born of the peoples from the continent of Africa.
>
> The pain of the violent conflict that the peoples of Liberia, Somalia, the Sudan, Burundi and Algeria, is a pain I also bear.
>
> The dismal shame of poverty, suffering and human degradation of my continent is a blight that we share.
>
> (Mbeki 1998: 35)

The sentiment of African belonging is also captured in Nkosi Sikelel' iAfrika (Lord Bless Africa). "Nkosi Sikelel' iAfrika" (Xhosa pronunciation: [ŋk'ɔsisik'ɛlɛl‿iafrik'a]), an original song composed in 1897 by Enoch Sontonga, a Xhosa clergyman at a Methodist mission school near Johannesburg, which became the national anthem of the Republic of South Africa.

Since the late 1990s, South Africa has regularly been the theatre of xenophobic violence against African migrants to make then understand that they should not feel at home and do not belong to the country as the pejorative names given to them clearly indicate.

Strict migration policies and practices and xenophobic violence against African migrants contradict South Africa's rhetoric of pan-Africanism as couched on the African renaissance discourse. South Africa has also failed to ratify the SADC Protocol on the Facilitation of Free Movement to accelerate the process of entry into force. Yet, one cannot claim to be an African and yet develop *Afrophobia* or hatred against other Africans. On the other hand, a country cannot claim its commitment to African union, developmental regionalism and African integration by closing its doors or its borders and making it more and more difficult for other African people to enter and reside on its territory.

Migration and xenophobia in South Africa seen by organised interest groups like COSATU and political parties, migrants, their governments and SADC

Migration and xenophobia in South Africa are seen differently by South African organised interest groups like COSATU, political parties and by the migrants themselves, their governments and the SADC. The discourses on migration and xenophobia as examined earlier summarised the perceptions of the majority of the South African people. Organised interest groups like COSATU and political parties share the same view. Migration is seen as a threat to domestic labour as migrants are unjustly accused of taking up jobs reserved for Black South Africans. The same goes for other trade unions and civil society organisations.

On the other hand, political parties are known as organisations competing for power through elections. They must please and seduce people to win during elections. They are generally demagogic and tend to espouse the perceptions of the people in their constituencies. They are the ones which draft tough migration policy, adopt and implement them through Parliament, the Cabinet and law enforcement agencies. They also directly or indirectly support xenophobia when they do not condone xenophobic violence as African migrants are used as scapegoats for their inability to deliver.

On the other hand, diplomatic protection is used by the States to assist their nationals abroad or champion their rights and interests. No Western or even Eastern government would ever remain indifferent when their nationals are victims of violence or when their rights are infringed by the government or the people in foreign countries. It does not matter whether they are legal in those countries or not. The United States and European countries like France, Britain and Germany are known for being active in this regard. They can even threaten foreign state with sanctions and even war to protect the rights and interests of their nationals abroad. They can also take retaliatory measures.

African countries whose nationals were victims of xenophobic violence or whose rights and interests were infringed in South Africa were therefore expected to intervene in order to defend or protect them. Since these migrants mainly came from the SADC region and the rest of the African continent, SADC and the AU were also expected to respond.

Mozambique, Nigeria and Malawi were among the few countries that reacted on diplomatic front and condemned South Africa for the 2015 xenophobic attacks. Two Mozambicans were killed, 500–1000 were displaced and some of them were living in camps waiting to go back home. At the Vilankulo plant of Sasol, a South African state company, Mozambican workers went on strike and forced the expulsion of up to 250 South African workers. At the coalmines in Tete, Kentz Engineering, a South African company which serviced machinery for the mining companies, hired two aircraft to fly 433 South Africa workers back to South Africa, disrupting the mines. Mozambicans stoned South African registered trucks and buses on the road to the Ressano Garcia border post and also barricaded the main N4 road near the border post (Mozambique News 2015).

Nigerians in South Africa lost an estimated R21 million in the spate of attacks. Members of Parliament in Nigeria's lower house put forward a motion to sever diplomatic ties with South Africa, which was defeated. But a motion to recall Nigeria's high commissioner from South Africa for consultations was passed. Mass protests against South African xenophobia took place in several Nigerian cities. The South African High Commissioner in Abuja Lulu Mguni was summoned by the Nigerian government, which sought to express its displeasure. Nigerians under the One Africa Initiative threatened to unleash their anger on South African investments, and led protests to the offices of MTN, Shoprite, and Pick n Pay. Youths under the aegis of "The Flagship" also threatened to shut down South African firms, especially MTN, a mobile company with twice as many subscribers in Nigeria than in South Africa and which was growing in Nigeria while its South African business was stagnating (Ebrahim 2015).

In Malawi, around 2,000 Malawians protested outside the South African high commission in Lilongwe, giving an ultimatum to the South African government to respond to their petition and get Zulu King Goodwill Zwelithini to apologise for his remarks supporting xenophobic attacks, or face a boycott of South African goods (Ebrahim 2015).

The executive director of the Consumers Association of Malawi, John Kapito, called for a boycott of all South African goods and services, giving South African businesses one week to close their shops (Ebrahim 2015).

Although no Zambian national had been a victim of xenophobic attacks, but Zambia's biggest private radio station indefinitely blocked the playing of South

African music in protest against the xenophobic attacks against foreign nationals (Times Reporter 2015).

In response to fury over xenophobic attacks on African migrants in April 2015, the then South African President Jacob Zuma who had lived in Mozambique during the struggle against the South African apartheid regime, until its independence in 1994, travelled to Mozambique to apologize to the Mozambican government and people (Premium Times 2015). However, he did not apologize to Nigeria or any other African nation. The National Association of Nigerian Students (NANS) reacted by calling on President to stay away from the presidential inauguration of Gen. Muhammadu Buhari on 29 May 2015 (Daniel 2015).

Other countries of origin of the victims of xenophobic violence like the Democratic Republic of the Congo (DRC) did not react or simply condoned South Africa. This was not surprising since the DRC Government was unpopular among the Congolese people in the Diaspora. President Mugabe's government also took long before expressing shock, disgust at "horrible" xenophobic attacks as Mugabe thought most Zimbabweans in South Africa were MDC-T (Movement for Democratic Change—Tsvangirai, main opposition party) and would rise against him if they went back to Zimbabwe (News24 2015). However, how did the SADC and AU react to xenophobic violence in South Africa, especially that which took place in April 2015?

Malawian President Peter Mutharika urged Zimbabwean President Robert Mugabe—as the chairman of the SADC—to ensure the xenophobic attacks in South Africa were addressed (Ebrahim 2015). In his double capacity as the chair of SADC and AU, President Mugabe indicated that such attacks "should never happen again in South Africa or any other country" (News24 2015). But in the main, their responses to xenophobic attacks against African migrants proved that SADC and AU had not much changed and remained "clubs of African leaders supporting one another". At the end of their meeting that took place in Harare, Zimbabwe, shortly after the xenophobic attacks in South Africa, SADC leaders went on to applaud the South African government for measures they put in place to deal with the attacks on foreign nationals.

Instead of firmly condemning South Africa, President Mugabe even took the blame on South Africa's neighbours by suggesting that they should do what they could to prevent more people going into South Africa or try to get those in South Africa back home (Mugabe 2015). This could not promote developmental regionalism and African integration.

On the other hand, while calling for an immediate halt to the attacks and finding it "unacceptable" as Africans were about to remember the founding of OAU (on 25 May 2015), which played such a critical role in mobilising international solidarity for the end of apartheid, AU Commission Chairperson Dr. Dlamini-Zuma welcomed interventions by the South African government, including the deployment of an Inter-Ministerial committee to KwaZulu-Natal to engage with those affected, and with local communities, as well as the deployment of more police details to provide protection and maintain law and order (Mataire & 2015).

Yet, SADC and AU should play a more positive role to address the twin problems of migration and xenophobia not only in South Africa, but also on the rest of the African continent. Xenophobia, anti-migration legislation, policies, practices and discourses are inimical to the seven aspirations of "Africa We Want", namely (1) a prosperous Africa based on inclusive growth and sustainable development, (2) an integrated continent, politically united and based on the ideals of pan-Africanism and the vision of Africa's Renaissance, (3) an Africa of good governance, democracy, respect for human rights, justice and the rule of law, (4) a peaceful and secure Africa, (5) an Africa with a strong cultural identity, common heritage, shared values and ethics, (6) an Africa whose development is people-driven, relying on the potential of African people, especially its women and youth, and caring for children, and (7) Africa as a strong, united and influential global player and partner (AUC 2015).

Conclusion

The road to regional integration in Africa can be traced back to the early 1960s when most African countries acceded to independence. They then founded the OAU, which was replaced with the AU in 2000. RECs were established as building blocks for regional integration. They therefore became the embodiments of developmental regionalism or regional integration to promote peace and economic transformation. In Southern Africa, the SADC became the ideal framework to pursue developmental regionalism, peace and economic transformation.

The chapter argued that "developmental regionalism" as the engine of regional integration remains high on the agenda of this regional body. However, in Southern Africa, as in other parts of the continent, "developmental regionalism" has been elusive and regional integration has failed to achieve peace and economic transformation and to eradicate poverty among the overwhelming majority of the population. The SADC is still lagging behind other African subregions in terms of regional integration, including economic integration and integration of people. The Protocol on the Facilitation of Free Movement of Persons that would have encouraged migration and contributed to reducing xenophobia has not come into operation as yet. Governments adopted immigration laws and policies that do not favour regional integration and encourage xenophobia.

Vigneswaran (2007: 4), Crush and Pendleton (2004: 2), and Nyamnjoh and Mususa (2012: 215) deplore the fact that, despite the narrative of a better-integrated regional bloc and the neo-liberal idea of free movement of capital and labour, the SADC countries are moving towards tighter controls on the movement of people. They have not shown the political will to accelerate regional integration by allowing their people to freely move across the region.

On the other hand, xenophobic sentiments and attacks have increased over the past years. Ordinary people are not to blame exclusively for xenophobia; blame also falls on state officials who are responsible for the enactment of laws and the passing and enforcing of policies. Exacerbated by lack of economic transformation resulting in the increase of poverty, xenophobia also stands as a major obstacle to regional integration.

To achieve sustainable peace, economic transformation and regional integration, Southern Africa needs states which are not just developmental, but also democratic. Effective regional integration in Africa requires political and visionary leadership committed to the ideal of pan-Africanism that would ensure that national policies are aligned with regional agendas (Dzinesa, Nagar & Saunders 2012: 6). Lack of such a responsible, courageous, democratic and pan-African leadership is probably the main obstacle to effective regional integration, peace and economic transformation in Southern Africa.

President Mugabe's statement when he was the chair of SADC and AU that "Other African nations should stop their citizens from migrating to South Africa to prevent violence against foreigners" (Mugabe 2015) just meant that the AU, the SADC and their individual member states had failed to promote the right to freedom of movement of their people that is still so essential to regional integration.

As an influential SADC and AU member state, South Africa also failed to play the role of a catalyst of regional integration (Neocosmos 2010: 143; Nyamnjoh 2015a: 28) like Nigeria did in West Africa and France and Germany in Western Europe (Amos 2010). On the other hand, South African leaders have done little to fight xenophobia, which is both "a political discourse and practice" (Neocosmos 2015: 31).

According to Nyamnjoh, "The immigration policies and practices of the South African state, as well as the xenophobic attitudes of some South Africans, contradict the rhetoric and ties to the rest of Africa that proliferate in official pronouncements and civic society discourses"(Nyamnjoh 2015a: 28). The enforcement of the new draconian immigration measures only breed xenophobia that is directed at foreign migrants, more especially Black or African migrants, including and even mainly those from other SADC countries (Mbembe 2015: 29), who are labelled *Makwerekwere* (Nyamnjoh 2015b: 34). Neocosmos also deplored that neither the ideals of the African Renaissance nor those of Ubuntu (togetherness) have been taken beyond the stage of being simply state slogans to take roots in the population at large (Neocosmos 2010: 143). In his view, there is a "state construction of xenophobia" as xenophobic discourses mainly emanate from state officials (Neocosmos 2010: 2, 3).

The "normalisation" of the xenophobic and anti-migration discourse that results from the myth of "South African exceptionalism" (Neocosmos 2010: 142) and gives rise to the sentiment of South Africa being a besieged "fortress" does not contribute to regional integration and to the consolidation of the longstanding historical, social and cultural affinities and links among the

African peoples. As Oucho (2007: 9) pointed out, "Regional integration is meaningless unless people within a defined area of jurisdiction share experiences, exchange interests and move with their products". Successful regional integration therefore requires that Africans be entitled to move and establish freely as "citizens of Africa" and no African should be dealt with as a foreigner or a migrant on the African continent (Mbembe 2015: 30).

Despite repeated denials, xenophobia exists in South Africa. It is even systemic and has for long been nurtured by political, opinion leaders, law enforcement officials and the media through immigration laws, policies, practices, and popular discourses, and narratives.

More than two decades after apartheid, South African and other African leaders who committed themselves to working for a "greater unity and solidarity" within the AU and SADC, which has not unfortunately made significant progress with regional integration like other RECs, especially ECOWAS and the EAC, should do more to promote free movement of persons, combat xenophobia, which exists in all the compartments of the South African society, including the public and private sectors, trade unions, political parties, civil society organisations, and stop sanctifying the artificial colonial borders inherited from colonisation which continue to hinder the free movement of people in certain countries in Africa (Oluwashola 2013; AUC & IOM 2018: 11).

Arguably, as the largest economy, South Africa is poised to be the main beneficiary of regional integration in the SADC region. South Africa should therefore adopt immigration laws and policies aligned with the key objective of regional integration. It should play an important role in the coming into force of the SADC Protocol of the Facilitation of Free Movement of the Persons and comply with it fully. Finally, denying its existence is not the best way to combat xenophobia. South African leaders should avoid populist attitudes but adopt effective measures to combat xenophobia. They should also contribute to educating the South African people on the benefit of regional integration and freedom of movement and establishment for the development of the region and the well-being of their people.

As demonstrated in a study conducted by the AU Commission and the International Organisation of Migration despite economic, social-political, security and health-related challenges which will need to be addressed, freedom of movement of persons offers many benefits to Africa and its people (AUC & IOM 2018: 31–52). At the study pointed out,

> The future of Africa lies with its people. The people, however, will not contribute effectively to this future if they cannot move and explore the vast opportunities that the continent holds. Africa's modest contribution to aggregate global output, the impact of the 2014–2016 commodity price collapse on African economies, the continent's vulnerability to global economic downturns, and China's economic rebalancing, all suggest that Africa's future prosperity increasingly relies on closer regional connectedness and integration, underpinned by more intra-African circulation of

> productive factors such as labour, technology, skills and capital. As Africa seeks to catch up with the higher income nations, facilitating free intracontinental movement of persons will be an essential and key strategy in realizing the goals of the African Union's Agenda 2063. General freedom of movement is also the concrete expression of pan-Africanism. In a competitive, globalized world economy, it can foster universal equity across the continent in terms of African entrepreneurs being able to leverage opportunities and resources—land, mineral, human resources and other non-physical endowments—dispersed throughout the continent.
>
> (AUC & IOM 2018: 12)

The adoption of the Protocol on Free Movement of Persons in Africa by AU Member States at the January 2018 Summit in Addis Ababa, Ethiopia, constitutes a turning-point in the process of regional integration. The Protocol reflects the commitment of AU Member States to promoting economic, social and cultural development, and the integration of African economies through migration. However, this is not enough. Africa's post-colonial history is replete with conventions which took decades to enter into force or were never implemented fully. This is the case of the 1991 Treaty Establishing the African Economic Community (AEC) (Abuja Treaty) at the continental level and the SADC Protocol of the Facilitation of Free Movement which all aimed at promoting free movement.

AU aims to achieve regional integration and union of African people, not just their leaders. Such objective cannot be achieved through the adoption of bilateral conventions on visa exemptions and the institution of a common passport that only benefit officials of AU Member States, but also the African people who should be able to move and establish freely on the continent. Achieving free movement and combatting xenophobia is required to achieve "greater unity and solidarity between the African countries and the people of Africa" embodied in the AU Constitutive Act (Article 3(a)) as one of the key objectives of the African body. An Africa of free movement of persons and solidarity between its peoples, which excludes xenophobia, is definitely the "Africa we want" (AUC 2015).

References

AUC. 2015. Africa Agenda 2063. The Africa We Want. https://www.un.org/en/africa/osaa/pdf/au/agenda2063-first10 yearimplementation.pdf (accessed on 31 October 2018).

AUC & IOM. 2018. *Study on the Benefits and the Challenges of Free Movement of Persons in Africa*. African Union Commission (AUC) and the International Organization for Migration (IOM), IOM Geneva. https://ethiopia.iom.int/sites/default/files/document/IOM%20free%20movement%20africa%207sept2018.pdf (accessed on 31 October 2018).

Adepoju, A. 2006."Internal and international migration within Africa." In Kok, P. et al. (eds.). *Migration in South and Southern Africa: Dynamics and Determinants*. Cape Town: HSRC Press.

Amos, S. 2010. "The role of South Africa in SADC regional integration: The making or breaking of the organization." *Journal of International Commercial Law and Technology*, Vol. 5, No. 3, 124. www.jiclt.com/index.php/jiclt/article/view/109/107 (accessed on 20 June 2016).

Anderson, B.A. 2006. "Migration in South Africa in comparative perspective." In Kok, P. et al. (eds.). *Migration in South and Southern Africa: Dynamics and determinants*. Cape Town: HSRC Press.

Crush, J. & Pendleton, W. 2004. "Regionalising Xenophobia? Citizen attitudes to immigration and refugee policy in Southern Africa." *SAMP: Migration Policy Series No 30*. www.queensu.ca/samp (accessed on 20 June 2016).

Crush, J., Williams, V. & Peberdy, S. 2005. *Migration in Southern Africa*. A Paper prepared for the Policy Analysis and Research Programme of the Global Commission in International Migration. https://womin.org.za/images/impact-of-extractive-industries/migrancy-and-extractivism/Crush%20%20Williams%20and%20Peberdy%20-%20Migration%20in%20Southern%20Africa.pdf (accessed on 31 August 2018).

Daniel. 2015. Xenophobic Attacks: Jacob Zuma Not Welcome At Presidential Inauguration – NANS. https://www.informationng.com/2015/05/xenophobic-attacks-jacob-zuma-not-welcome-at-presidential-inauguration-nans.html (accessed on 31 October 2018).

Dzinesa, G.A., Nagar, D. & Saunders, C. 2012."Introduction." In Saunders, C., Dzinesa, G.A. & Nagar, D. (eds.). *Region-building Southern Africa: Progress, Problems and Prospects*. London and New York: Zed Books.

Ebrahim, S. 2015. African Fury Over Xenophobia Attacks. https://www.iol.co.za/news/africa/african-fury-over-xenophobia-attacks-1849398 (accessed on 30 July 2018).

Gonzalez-Gracia et al. 2016. Sub-Saharan African Migration. Patterns and Spillovers. Washington, DC.: IMF, DOI: http://dx.doi.org/10.5089/9781475546668.062

Harris, B. 2001. "A foreign experience: Violence, crime and Xenophobia during South Africa's transition." *Centre for the Study of Violence and Reconciliation, Violence and Transition Series*, Vol. 5, August. www.csvr.org.za/papers/papvtp5.htm.

Human Sciences Research Council (HSRC). 2008. *Citizenship, Violence and Xenophobia in South Africa: Perceptions from South African Communities*. Democracy and Governance Research Programme, HSRC, June. http://www.hsrc.ac.za/en/research-outputs/view/3853 (accessed on 31 August 2018).

Khadiagala, G.M. 2012. "The SADCC and its approaches to African regionalism." In Saunders, C., Dzinesa, G.A. & Nagar, D. (eds.). *Region-Building Southern Africa: Progress, Problems and Prospects*. London and New York: Zed Books.

Klotz, A. 2010. "Migration after apartheid: Deracialising South African foreign policy." *Third World Quarterly*, Vol. 21.

Mandela, N. 1993."South Africa's future foreign policy." *Foreign Affairs*, Vol. 72, No. 5. www.anc.org (accessed on 5 April 2016).

Mangu, A.M.B. 2013. "Protection of asylum seekers and refugees' rights under the African human rights system and the South African law: A comparative perspective." In Azoulay, G. et al. (eds.). *Mobilites et migrations: figures et enjeux contemporains*. Paris: L'Harmattan.

Mataire L & N Kakore. 2015. "SA xenophobia: AU speaks out". https://www.herald.co.zw/sa-xenophobia-au-speaks-out (accessed on 31 October 2018).

Mbeki, T. 1998. *Africa, the Time Has Come: Selected Speeches*, 1st edition. Cape Town & Johannesburg: Tafelberg Publishers Ltd & Mafube Publishing (Pty).

Mbembe, A. 2015."'Afrophobia'? 'Xenophobia'? Black on black racism? in South Africa." *CODESRIA Bulletin*, Nos. 1 & 2, 29.

Modi, R. 2003. "Migration to democratic South Africa." *Economic and Political Weekly*, Vol. 38.

Moser, R.E. 2016. *South African Migration Policies and Xenophobia after the Cold War: The Rising Anti-Foreigner Sentiment and Apartheid's Inherited Policy Framework, 1994–2008*. www.globalhistories.com/index.php/GHSJ/article/view/59 http://dx.doi.org/10.17169/GHSJ.2016.59 (accessed on 30 July 2018).

Mozambique News Reports & Clippings. 2015. "Mozambicans react to South African xenophobia". https://www.open.ac.uk/technology/mozambique/sites/www.open.ac.uk.technology.mozambique/files/files/Mozambique_285-20April15_xenophobia_IMF-and-education.pdf (accessed on 31 October 2018).

Mugabe. 2015. "Resist entering South African borders." www.enca.com/africa/southern-africa/mugabe-says-neighbours-should-stop-flow-migrants-south-africa (accessed on 20 June 2016).

Mulaudzi, C. 2006. *The Politics of Regionalism in Southern Africa*. Institute for Global Dialogue, Occasional Paper No 51.

Neocosmos, M. 2008. "The politics of fear and the fear of politics: Reflections on xenophobic violence in South Africa." *Journal of Asian and African Studies*, Vol. 43, No. 6, December.

Neocosmos, M. 2010. *From 'Foreign Natives' to 'Native Foreigners': Explaining Xenophobia on Post-Apartheid South Africa*. Dakar: CODESRIA.

Neocosmos, M. 2015. "From 'foreign natives' to 'native foreigners': Explaining Xenophobiain post-apartheid South Africa: Citizenship and nationalism, identity and politics." *CODESRIA Bulletin*, Nos. 1 & 2, 30–32.

News24. 2015. Mugabe Expresses Shock, Disgust at "horrible" Xenophobic Attacks. https://www.news24.com/Africa/Zimbabwe/Mugabe-expresses-shock-disgust-at-horrible-xenophobic-attacks-20150418 (accessed on 31 October 2018)

Nyamnjoh, F. 2015a. "Xenophobia at odds with South Africa's rhetoric of inclusivity and human rights." *CODESRIA Bulletin*, Nos. 1 & 2, 28.

Nyamnjoh, F. 2015b. "Xenophobia in South Africa: The personal account of a sweet-footed African." *CODESRIA Bulletin*, Nos. 1 & 2, 34.

Nyamnjoh, F. & Mususa, P. 2012. "Migration and xenophobia." In Saunders, C., Dzinesa, G.A. & Nagar, D. (eds.). *Region-Building Southern Africa: Progress, Problems and Prospects*. London and New York: Zed Books.

Olutayo, A.O. & Adeniran, A.I. 2015."Introduction." In Olutayo, A.O. & Adeniran, A.I. (eds.). *Regional Economic Communities: Exploring the Process If Socio-Economic Integration in Africa*. Dakar: CODESRIA.

Oluwashola, J.M. 2013. *Contemporary Discourses and Contestations around Sovereignty, Supra-Nationalism and the Future of African Regional Integration*. African Economic Conference. www.afdb.org/uploads/tx_llafdbpapers/Paper_Presentation_AEC.pdf (accessed on 20 April 2018).

Oucho, J.O. 2007. *Migration in Southern Africa: Migration Management Initiatives for SADC Member States*. ISS Paper 157, December.

Pather, R. 2016. Herman Mashaba defends his comments stating "illegal" immigrants are criminals. https://mg.co.za/article/2016-12-07-herman-mashaba-defends-his-comments-that-illegal-immigrants-are-criminals (accessed on 31 October 2018).

Premium Times. 2015. South Africa apologises to Mozambique for xenophobic attacks. https://www.premiumtimesng.com/foreign/183417-south-africa-apologises-to-mozambique-for-xenophobic-attacks.html (accessed on 31 October 2018).

SADC.2004. *Communiqué of the Summit of Heads of State and Government of the Southern African Development Community* (SADC). Grand Baie, Mauritius, August 16–17. http://www.dirco.gov.za/docs/2004/sadc0825.htm (accessed on 30 June 2018).

SADC Declaration. 1992. *Towards the Creation of the Southern African Development Community: A Declaration of Heads of State or Government of Southern African States of 17 August 1992.* www.sadc.int/files/8613/5292/8378/Declaration__Treaty_of_SADC.pdf (accessed on 30 June 2018).

SAMP.2008. *The Perfect Storm: The Realities of Xenophobia in Contemporary South Africa.* Migration Policy Series No, 50. SAMP, Cape Town.

Stats SA. 2016a. Tourism and Migration 2016. http://www.statssa.gov.za/publications/P0351/P0351January2016.pdf (accessed on 31 August 2018).

Stats SA. 2016b. Community Survey 2016 in Brief. http://cs2016.statssa.gov.za/wp-content/uploads/2017/07/CS-in-brief-14-07-2017-with-cover_1.pdf (accessed on 31 August 2016).

Thrane, A, 2013, "New Trends in Migration: South African Case Study". https://globalprosperity.wordpress.com/2013/10/04/new-trends-in-migration-south-african-case-study (accessed on 20 May 2018).

Times Reporter. 2015. International Uproar Over Xenophobia as S. AFRICA regrets "Insensitive" Attacks. https://www.newtimes.co.rw/section/read/188121 (accessed on 31 October 2015).

UNHCR. 2018. Global Trends. Forced Displacement in 2018. https://www.unhcr.org/5d08d7ee7.pdf (accessed on 30 December 2018).

Vigneswaran, D. 2007. *Free Movement and the Movement's Forgotten Freedoms: South African Representation of Undocumented Migrants.* Working Paper No 41. Oxford: Refugee Studies Centre.

Visser, W. 2016. *I am an African.* www.waynevisser.com/wp-content/uploads/2009/11/i-am-an-african-5th.pdf (accessed on 30 July 2018).

Yaya, B.H. 2011."Inter-regionalism as a mechanism, for the harmonization of Africa's regional integration projects." In Olutayo, A.O. & Adeniran, A.I. (eds.). *Regional Economic Communities: Exploring the Process If Socio-Economic Integration in Africa.* Dakar: CODESRIA.

9 ECOWAS's experience in developmental regionalism

A comparative perspective

Dauda Garuba

Introduction

Deriving from the realization at independence that they needed to collectivise their efforts to withstand the highly vicious threats posed by the advanced capitalist economies, many African states saw pragmatism in pooling resources together to stabilize themselves. The establishment of the Economic Commission of Africa (ECA) in 1958 by the United Nations assisted in spearheading the formation of regional economic groupings in Africa. The East African Community (EAC) was first to blaze the trail for subregional economic integration in 1967, after which the Economic Community of West African States (ECOWAS) followed with the signing of the Treaty of Lagos on 28 May, 1975. A preferential trade area established for Eastern and Southern Africa in 1981 got replaced by the Common Market for Eastern and Southern Africa (COMESA) in 1993, while Central African countries formed the Economic Community of Central African States (ECCAS) through an approved treaty in 1983. Even though the idea of an economic union of the Maghreb had lived in North Africa with the independence of Tunisia and Morocco in 1956, it was only in 1988 that the five states in the region (Algeria, Libya, Mauritania, Morocco and Tunisia) met at a summit in Marrakech, Morocco, to form the Arab Maghreb Union (AMU) in February 1989.

Beyond the specific peculiarities that they represent, the RECs seek to promote congruence of a common market where member states enjoy comparative advantage, import substitution and economy of scale (Kufour, 2006: xii; Fayomi & Adeola, 2015: 29) within a broader political umbrella represented by the Africa Union (formerly the Organisation of African Unity). Indeed, Article 6 of the treaty that gave force to the African Economic Community (AEC) provides for the establishment of the continental economic community whose building blocks shall be the RECs and their associated ingredients of free trade areas, custom unions, continental common markets and economic/monetary unions. This aligns with the commitment expressed in the 1980 Lagos Plan of Action and the Final Act of Lagos as well as the recent AU's Agenda 2063 all of which emphasised the realization of an African Continental Free Trade Area (AfCFTA) (Fajana, 2018: 1). To the extent to which they are accepted as the building blocks for regional integration, eight RECs across the continent are recognised by the AU, the remaining three being the Southern Africa Development Commission (SADC), the Community of Sahara-Sahelo States (CSS) and the Intergovernmental Authority for Development (IGAD) (Mangeni, 2014: 1; Chinyama & Tanoe, 2015: 1).

The emergence of ECOWAS followed such common colonial roots and legacies defined by the idea of West African Currency, West African Airways and a CFA zone common currency in eight West African Economic and Monetary Union (WAEMU/UEMOA) member states comprising Benin, Burkina Faso, Côte d'Ivoire, Guinea-Bissau, Mali, Niger, Senegal and Togo. The pattern underscores the argument by Bach (2016a, 2016b) that colonial rule "was as much about partition as about region-building". The very prominent bifurcation at independence comprised the radical left-oriented Casablanca bloc made up of Guinea, Ghana and Mali, and the bigger and relatively conservative Monrovia bloc composed of 24 countries led by Nigeria and Liberia. Commitment to a stronger and more effective African voice that could deliver better cooperation and coordination in matters of common interest resulted in self-dismantling of these two diametrically opposed blocs for the formation of the OAU—the precursor to the AU—in May 1963.

A common principle that underpinned these regional and subregional blocs up to the end of the Cold War was Keynesianism—an economic idea anchored on the belief that "government interference to allocate resources was a better option" in the midst of unfettered markets that favoured industrialised countries over newly independent countries of Africa (Kufour, 2006: xiii). As a platform for regional integration, ECOWAS sought to "foster the ideal of collective self-sufficiency for its member states . . . to create a single, large trading bloc through economic cooperation" (ECOWAS, 2016a). It was a response to a first wave of regionalism which Bach (2016b) argues anchored on the realities of post-World War II, and was shaped by the Cold War and the desire for "developmental policy template in developing world". The fundamental restructuring induced by post-Cold War conflicts which extended to West African states of Liberia, Sierra Leone, Guinea, Guinea Bissau, Côte d'Ivoire and Mali, prompted the collocation of international boundaries to the extent that facilitated the speedy flow of capital, goods and services across borders. The situation also facilitated move by advanced capitalist countries to collectivise their response through regional economic bodies (e.g. transition from the EEC to the EU) such that redefined integration in the sense of 'new regionalism.'

In Africa, the situation precipitated an expansion of the roles of regional organisations to include responsibility for peacebuilding and conflict management (Adetula, Bereketeab & Jaiyebo, 2016: 7). ECOWAS responded to this need in a Revised Treaty adopted by the Assembly of Heads of State and Government in Abuja in 1993. Within the context of a globalized world, developmental regionalism in the context of post-Cold War ECOWAS, SADC and other continental RECs, is reflective of a world in which capital, state and international institutions serve as driving forces to roll back Keynesianism for a more "allocative" and deepening function of the market. It reinforces the hegemony and self-confidence of capitalism and redefines power relations in a world supposedly replete with unprecedented differentials in terms of capacity to globalize.

This chapter examines ECOWAS contributions to developmental regionalism, peace and economic transformation in West Africa with a view to drawing comparative analyses and useful lessons for SADC. The chapter is divided into five sections. Following this introduction is a review of the foundations of ECOWAS regional integration and economic development, while section three examines how the regional body navigated the post-Cold War challenges and adjusted itself to the situation with the adoption of the Revised ECOWAS Treaty of 1993 with far-reaching components and the achievements and challenges of the process. The fourth section attempts a comparison of ECOWAS and SADC approaches to developmental regionalism, peace and security, and economic transformation, while section five summarises the key messages and lessons for Africa Union's dream that RECs will become its building blocks for delivering development in the continent.

Foundations of ECOWAS regional integration and economic development

ECOWAS is one of the biggest RECs in Africa, by virtue of its size, land area and strength of its membership. It comprises 15 countries occupying a land area of over five million square miles and a population estimated at 377 million. The fifteen founding members of ECOWAS (Benin, Burkina Faso, Côte d'Ivoire, The Gambia, Ghana, Guinea, Guinea Bissau, Liberia, Mali, Mauritania, Niger, Nigeria, Senegal, Sierra Leone and Togo) were soon joined by Cape Verde as a 16th member, while Mauritania relinquished its membership in 2002. Table 9.1 shows the basic statistics of ECOWAS member states with Nigeria representing the biggest economy with an estimated population of 195 million, while Cape Verde, Guinea Bissau and The Gambia are the smallest economies. The statistics shows that Nigeria has the highest GDP of US$349 billion to occupy the first place in Africa and 33rd in the world in 2017. Ghana is the closest to Nigeria with a nominal GDP of US$40 billion to occupy 11th position in Africa and 87th in the world; while The Gambia is at the bottom of the ladder with US$1 billion to place 52 in Africa and 178 in the world.

The idea of a West African regional integration driven by ECOWAS derived from crisis in international economic relations in which majority of citizens of the countries in the subregion experienced declining standards of living. The overdependence of these countries on advanced capitalist economies for survival at independence left many of them with limited space for manoeuvrability. Constrained by a paradox of sovereign equality of states with disproportionate capacities to act individually, ECOWAS emerged as an attempt by countries in the subregion to forge a collective self-response to global economic realities defined by the Cold War (Jaye, Garuba & Amadi, 2011: 1). Realising

Table 9.1 ECOWAS country by Area (2014), population (2018) and GDP (2017)

Country	*Area (Sq. km)*	*Population*	*Rank (Population)*		*GDP (US$)*	*Rank (GDP)*	
			Africa	*World*		*Africa*	*World*
Benin	112,622	11,485,674	31	81	9.238	32	139
Burkina Faso	274,200	19,751,651	19	59	12.569	26	128
Cape Verde	4,033	553,335	54	172	1.741	49	170
Côte d'Ivoire	322,463	24,905,843	16	53	40.360	13	92
The Gambia	11,295	2,163,765	44	146	1.009	52	178
Ghana	238,533	29,463,643	14	49	47.032	11	87
Guinea	245,857	13,052,608	27	75	9.721	31	138
Guinea Bissau	36,125	1,907,268	46	151	1.350	51	175
Liberia	111,369	4,853,516	38	123	3.285	44	162
Mali	1,240,192	19,107,706	21	62	15.318	22	119
Niger	1,284,000	22,311,375	18	57	8.253	35	143
Nigeria	923,768	195,875,237	1	7	349.299	1	31
Senegal	196,722	16,294,270	24	71	16.463	21	118
Sierra Leone	71,740	7,719,729	34	103	3.641	42	158
Togo	56,785	7,990,926	33	102	4.767	40	154
TOTAL	**5,129,704**	**377,436,546**			**US$524**		

Source: Compiled from *Statistics Times*. Available at: https://statisticstimes.com

that political freedom alone "had little meaning and even less substance in the absence of effective control over their economic destinies" (Gowon, 1984: 27), the second generation of West African leaders (largely of military orientation) made ECOWAS happened through closer collaboration with others in the league of first generation. Its emergence was an ingenious way of instrumentalizing and transforming politically and economically fragmented boundary lines into a comparative advantage (Bach, 1999: 48). For a member state such as Nigeria, It was a proactive response to its isolation during its 30 months' civil war that lasted from July 1967 to January 1970.

The ECOWAS vision is associated with Adebayo Adedeji—widely regarded as the "Father of ECOWAS" (*pére da la CEDEAO*)—who in a journal article published in 1970 identified six priority areas for West African integration. The areas were: building a regional road network, creating a regional airline, establishing regional infrastructure to facilitate trade and investment, facilitating the free movement of persons, goods and services, establishing a clearing and payment union, and abolishing foreign exchange controls (Adedeji, 1970: 213–231; Adebajo, 2014: 20). Adedeji's appointment as Federal Commissioner (Minister) into the cabinet of General Yakubu in Nigeria to oversee post-war Economic Development and Reconstruction a year after provided him a platform to praticalize his thesis about regional integration. This culminated in the establishment of ECOWAS, after a series of negotiations that lasted over three years with countries in the subregion whose colonial experiences were divided along Anglophone, Francophone and Lusophone influences. General Gowon was to acknowledge Adedeji's contribution to the creation of ECOWAS when he wrote that:

> Adedeji brought with him a new zeal and dynamism and a wealth of new ideas, determined as he was to succeed both as Commissioner of Economic Development and as leader of the Nigerian delegation at the joint Togo-Nigeria Ministerial Committee on ECOWAS. He was at once extremely popular with the Nigerian and Togolese delegations, and soon proved a capable leader.
>
> (Gowon, 1984: 209)

The ECOWAS agenda sought to promote market integration through policy harmonisation and coordination in the development of requisite physical infrastructure such as roads, telecoms and energy. It was founded on the recognition of the diverse opportunities available to its members to leverage their comparative advantages to facilitate intraregional trade for rapid socio-economic and political development.

Deriving from the reality of instability spewed by post-colonial coups and economic challenges, ECOWAS sought to mitigate the various contradictions that resulted from colonialism and independence, ideological warfare between democratic capitalism and communism, as well as internal and external tensions associated with relations between civilian and military leaders in the subregion. Prominent among the raving tensions in West Africa prior to the formation of the regional body was the rivalries around the economic strength of Côte d'Ivoire as the then leader of Francophone bloc and the sheer size and prowess of Nigeria as an Anglophone force.

Nevertheless, ECOWAS was born through the inspiration of subregional leaders, particularly Nigeria's Yakubu Gowon with invaluable assistance of Togolese President Gnassingbe Eyadema and other two successive Liberian presidents William Tubman and William Tolbert (Gowon, 1984: 109). It sought "the unity of countries of West Africa" through the elimination of all forms of obstacles to "free movement of goods, capital and persons" with a view to raising "the living standards of its people, ensuring economic growth, fostering relations among member states and contributing to the progress and development of the African continent" (ECOWAS, 1975). Its strategy for achieving these are located in policy coordination and harmonization, promotion of integration, establishment of a common market and joint enterprises, strengthening and creation of a single monetary zone, and promotion of free information flow among governments, peoples, media and business organisations, and labour unions.

Structurally, ECOWAS functioned under a largely prescriptive and loose self-governance system up to 1993 when a revised treaty was adopted and signed. The pre-1993 ECOWAS governance approach was only sufficient to the extent to which it met the limited regional economic integration and development goals espoused by the leadership of its founding countries. Besides the Secretariat in Abuja which handled the day-to-day implementation of programmes, the ECOWAS Assembly of Heads of State and Government and the Council of Ministers were the most visible political authorities that formulated and approved policies and programmes of the regional body. While the Assembly of Heads of State and Government remained the highest decision-making body, the Council of Ministers oversaw regulations and governance of ECOWAS through assistance from the Executive Secretariat which acted as the principal executive arm and coordinator of the Authority and Council of Ministers; the Tribunal which settled disputes among member states; and the Fund for Corporation, Compensation and Development which financed and compensated member states that suffered trade liberalization. A few commissions, namely, Administration and Finance; Defence, Social and Cultural Affairs; Transport, Communication and Energy; Agriculture, Industry and Natural Resources; and Trade, Customs, Immigration, Monetary and Payments were created with the responsibility of preparing and submitting reports with recommendations on a timely basis to the Council of Minister and performing such other functions as may be imposed under the treaty (Zagaris, 1978: 102).

Generally, this governance arrangement was both minimalist and self-selected to maintain a loose ECOWAS in early post-colonial period. Indeed, it is largely for this reason that its operations were bedevilled with "loopholes, ambiguities and room for each members state to interpret its responsibilities to the larger body, while maintaining focus on achieving internal (superseding) goals" (Goodridge, 2006: 39). This was the state of affairs until the end of the Cold War when security regionalism added to the core concerns and programmatic mandate of the regional body.

Post-Cold War realities and ECOWAS's responses to the challenges of peace and economic transformation

The demise of the Cold War in 1989 heralded a global wave of state collapse and state failure resulting in the relocation of sites of conflicts away from international to national arenas. In Africa, this manifested as one of crises, characterized by breakdown of structures, authorities, legitimate power, laws and political order. Many unpopular governments that had survived under the patronage of the Cold War soon became prey for ambitious usurpers of political power (Turner, 1998: 227). The situation gave rise to open expressions of historically rooted contradictions, many of which pointed to political and socio-economic factors of hegemony and exclusion. It also increased the audacity and tendency by non-state actors to freely challenge the monopoly of the state over the use of violence (Ibeanu & Garuba, 2009; Garuba, 2015).

As citizens navigated the cross-current of change precipitated by post-Cold War realities to challenge failing states in Africa, the demand for large army and weapon acquisition by leaders of these states to repress people took a heavy toll on the continent, thereby exacerbating the inability of many countries to meet the basic needs of their citizens (Garuba, 1996: 38–39). The insurrection derived thence made West Africa one of the most conflict-ridden subregions and theatres of some of the most atrocious post-independence brutalities ever witnessed in Africa. Interestingly too, the subregion became probably the only place in Africa where the most ambitious and the most determined internal efforts to find collective, regional solutions to conflicts have been deployed through the efforts of ECOWAS. Olonisakin (2011: 12) aptly captures ECOWAS foray into peacekeeping in Africa when she asserted that the subregional body "scored a number of continental 'firsts'", including deployment of troops in Liberia in 1990, collaboration with the United Nations to address complex emergency challenges after the Cold War, and development of a workable security management mechanism.

The lead role of the ECOWAS Monitoring Group (ECOMOG)—now West African Standby Force—in search for peaceful solutions to civil wars in Liberia, Sierra Leone, Guinea, Guinea-Bissau, Côte d'Ivoire and Mali has yielded a mix of successes in some cases, failures and ineptitude in others, and aggravation or new tensions in yet other cases (Garuba, 2015). Even at that, it is important to underscore the fact that ECOWAS intervention in these conflicts which started with Liberia was never an entirely easy task, especially as non-intervention in the internal affairs of member states was fundamental to its operational policies. Articles 1 and 2 of the ECOWAS Protocol on Non-Aggression (1978) encouraged and enjoined Member States to refrain from threats, use of force or aggression as well as the encouragement and conduct of "acts of subversion, hostility or aggression against the territorial integrity and political independence of other Member States." Indeed, these provisions underscored ECOWAS concerns and the division among leaders of its member states at the time (Aning & Atuobi, 2012: 218) of the Liberian civil war.

Arising from long-drawn divisions and clashes between two broad-base groups defined by Africo-Liberians[1] and Americo-Liberians,[2] the Liberian crisis escalated from an internally skewed political turmoil in the 1980s into one of subregional concern in the 1990s when the National Patriotic Front of Liberia (NPFL) led by Charles Taylor trained cadets in Libya, stationed a post in Burkina Faso and established conduit for supplies and trans-border facilities through Côte d'Ivoire (Akpomera, 1994: 63).

The goal of achieving peace in Liberia was high, but that was not without enormous challenges, complicated by the different positions of ECOWAS member states on the legality and otherwise of the regional body's direct intervention. Some leaders of countries in the subregion were up in support of armed intervention in Liberia to ward off the threats it posed to subregional security and integration. The then Executive Secretary of ECOWAS, Abass Bundu, aggregated the views of these leaders when he argued that:

> You cannot talk meaningfully about economic cooperation and integration by itself without also relating to the underpinning of political stability within the sub-region. The two are inseparable and therefore have to be

> discussed inter alia. It is clear . . . that regional solidarity and commitment to integration will be considerably enhanced where political stability becomes a common identity and is also perceived as a shared responsibility.
> (West Africa, 1991: 1085, as cited in Garuba, 1996)

Contrary to this position was the view expressed by leaders of all the Francophone countries—except Guinea—that the direct involvement of ECOWAS in Liberia would be contrary to the principle of non-intervention in the internal affairs of member states. Apparently, the leading exponent of voices in this camp was then Burkinabe ruler, Blaise Campaore, who challenged the legality of ECOWAS armed intervention in Liberia without the expressed authority of the Assembly of Heads of State and Government as provided for in Article 4 of the ECOWAS Protocol on Mutual Assistance on Defence signed in Freetown, Sierra Leone, in 1981. He noted:

> We learnt from the international media the momentous decision by some member states of ECOWAS to send a supposedly reconciliatory force to Liberia, and without first fully briefing other countries on the exact assignment of the force. As far as we (Francophone states) are concerned, the mediation committee of ECOWAS is not competent to intervene in a member state internal conflict.
> (as quoted in *Newswatch* [Lagos], 1990: 16, as cited in Garuba, 1996)

As opposing as were these two positions, ECOWAS foray and involvement with security regionalism, starting with the Liberian civil war, found instructive certain provisions in its earlier instruments—specifically Articles 2 and 4 of the Protocol on Non-Aggression signed in Lagos on 22 April, 1978 and the Protocol on Mutual Assistance on Defence signed in Freetown, Sierra Leone, on 29 May 1981. Both instruments, though fell short of the challenges that Liberian conflict and other subsequent ones that emerged thereafter posed, they "constituted the beginning of the realisation by West African leaders that security was linked with economic integration" (Jaye, Garuba & Amadi, 2011: 2).

Article 2 of the ECOWAS Protocol on Non-Aggression read that "any armed threat or aggression directed against any Member State shall constitute a threat or aggression against the entire Community", while Article 4 stated that "each member state shall undertake to prevent non-resident foreigners from using its territory as a base for committing the acts referred to in Article 2 above against the sovereignty and territorial integrity of member states." Also, Article 4 (b) of the Protocol on Mutual Assistance on Defence (1981) provided for Member States to take appropriate measures:

> In case of internal armed conflict within any Member State engineered and supported actively from outside likely to endanger the security and peace in the entire community. In this case the Authority shall appreciate

> and decide on this situation in full collaboration with the Authority of the Member State or States concerned.

As instructive as was this recognition of the interaction between ECOWAS's economic integration and security regionalism, it did not reflect the necessary requirements for dealing with the challenges of the regional body which, in the face of post-Cold War realities, had transcended the original economic cooperation. For instance, Article 6 of the ECOWAS protocol for Mutual Assistance on Defence (1981) states that ECOWAS Authority "shall decide on the expediency of military action and entrust its execution to the Force Commander of the Allied Armed Forces of the Community (AAFC)". The details on its nature and composition as enunciated in Articles 13 and 14 were, in the context of peacekeeping focus, insufficient for the new security challenges. Thus, ECOMOG became the appropriate response to the failure to an AAFC that was not empowered to function beyond peacekeeping to enforce peace agreements (Omede, 2012: 4) signed by the different warring parties. The then Liberian President, Samuel Doe, requested for the troop deployment in Liberia through a letter dated 14 July 1990:

> Assist in finding a constitutional and reasonable resolution of the crisis in our country (Liberia) . . . it would seem expedient at this time to introduce an ECOWAS peacekeeping force into Liberia to forestall increasing terror and tension and to assure a peaceful transition environment.
>
> (Bundu, 1997 as cited in Omede, 2012: 5)

Notwithstanding ECOWAS's response to this request, it took the adoption of a Revised Treaty signed in Cotonou, Republic of Benin, on 24 July 1993 for it to square up to the new realities depicted by demands for democratization, good governance, human rights and solutions to the internal convolutions escalated by the Liberian civil war and other protracted conflicts in Sierra Leone, Guinea, Guinea-Bissau, Côte d'Ivoire and Mali. The revised treaty increased the number of articles from 65 across 14 chapters to 93 articles across 22 chapters with "far more details in all aspects of its operations and clearly defined powers and rules for its officials" (Goodridge, 2006: 41). It re-enacted ECOWAS fundamental goal of "extended economic and political cooperation among members, and designated the achievement of a common market and a single currency as economic objective" (Essien, 2013: 2). In specific terms, Article 3 of the Revised Treaty sought "the removal of trade barriers and the harmonization of trade policies for the establishment of a Free Trade Area, a Customs Union, a Common Market and eventual culmination into a Monetary and Economic Union" (Fajana, 2018: 3).

On the political front, the regime sets out a governance structure comprising the Executive, the legislature and the judiciary. The Executive is headed by a Chairman elected from among the members of the Authority of Heads of State and Government who take policy decisions that are in turn implemented by the President (formerly Executive Secretary) of a new ECOWAS Commission, in close collaboration with a vice president and 13 commissioners, each of whom is a representative of a member country. The ECOWAS minister from the member state where the chairman hails from serves as the chair of the council of ministers.

On the legislative end, the new treaty provided for the establishment of a West African Parliament vested with the powers to create, initiate and modify institutions and strategies that seek to accelerate cooperation and integration as well as promote and ensure democratization and respect for human and people's rights. The ECOWAS parliament is the symbol of the legislature and its 115 members are seconded from national parliaments of member countries. It is led by a Speaker with full assistance by a Secretary General who serves as administrative head. Representation at the Parliament is based on the population of member countries with Nigeria occupying the highest number of seats (35), while Benin, Cape Verde, The Gambia, Guinea, Liberia, Sierra Leone and Togo allocated five seats apiece. Burkina Faso, Guinea, Mali, Niger and Senegal are allocated six seats each, while Côte d'Ivoire and Ghana hold seven and eight seats respectively. The Parliament has provided opportunities for the harmonization of regional legislations and delivery of landmark judgements by the Community Court.

The Community Court, or ECOWAS Court, as it is also called, is the symbol of the ECOWAS judicial arm of governance. It is saddled with the responsibility of interpretation and application of laws, protocols and conventions. The presiding justices of the court are usually seconded by the authorities of the supreme courts of member states. The Community Court of Justice has replaced the Tribunal earlier entrusted with the mandate to hear complaints against member states and enforce Community decisions (Essien, 2013: 2; Goodridge, 2006: 42).

The new treaty prioritizes market integration via liberalization policies defined under a common customs union, external tariff and intracommunity trade. The protocol on free movement of goods, services and persons and the introduction of regimes of ECOWAS e-passport and travellers' cheque have aided this process. It is to the glory of the free movement protocol that about five major trade corridors or transnational highways have continued to thrive in West Africa. The corridors are Lagos-Cotonou-Lome-Accra-Abidjan, Cotonou-Niamey, Lome-Ouagadougou, Tema-Ouagadougou-Bamako and Bamako-Ougadougou-Niamey-Jibia.

The treaty also made provisions for an Economic and Social Council that plays an advisory role to the Council of Ministers. This has helped to expand the civic space and private sector engagement through the facilitation of the formation of the West Africa Civil Society Forum (WACSOF) and the ECOWAS Business Forum (EBF) with a view to complementing advocacy for and monitoring of the implementation of the ECOWAS Common External Tariff (CET) and its precursor ECOWAS Trade Liberalisation Scheme (ETLS) for maximum benefits.

The ETLS was initiated to promote and liberalize intraregional trade through abolition of custom duties and non-tariff measures. After it recorded limited successes between 1990 when it entered into force and 2000 when it was anticipated to achieve "zero rate of duty and tariff in all member states", ECOWAS initiated the concept of National Approval Committee (NAC) that transferred the approval of ETLS products from regional to national level, and thus created opportunity for intense negotiations and lessons learned that delivered the ECOWAS Common External Tariff (CET) in October 2013 (Karaki & Verhaeghe, 2017: 6). It is important to stress that despite the disappointing results of ETLS, its sphere of influence has transcended "agricultural, artisanal handicraft and unprocessed goods to cover industrial goods", even though the latter are expected "to comply with the draft Supplementary Act on Community Rules of Origin and Procedures negotiated and approved by ECOWAS Ministers of Finance in November 2018. Statistics of ECOWAS intraregional trade indicates that Nigeria accounted for 40 percent of ECOWAS's agricultural imports in 2009 and 79 percent in 2011, while its industrial imports represented 79 percent and 65 percent of those of ECOWAS in 2009 and 2011, respectively.

In tandem with approved provisions to occasionally restructure its commissions or establish new or subsidiary ones as may be necessary, the ECOWAS rebranding through the 1993 Revised Treaty also restructured of the original commissions under the 1975 treaty into specialized technical commissions, namely, Transport, Communication and Tourism; Food and Agriculture; Administration and Finance; Human Resources, Information, Social and Cultural Affairs; Industry, Science and Technology and Energy; Trade, Customs, Taxation Statistics, Money and Payments; Environment and Natural Resources; and Political, Judicial and Legal Affairs, Regional Security and Immigration. Further restructuring in July 2013 saw the creation of six new departments, namely, Human Resources Management; Education, Science and Culture; Energy and Mines; Telecommunications and Information Technology; and Industry and Private Sector Promotion with Finance and Administration decoupled to allow for a new portfolio of Administration and Conferences to an incoming Ghana Commissioner.

Overall, the restructuring has also led to the expansion of civic space, leading to enactment of popular protocols, including the ECOWAS Supplementary Protocol on Democracy and Good Governance which has remained the best entry point for democratic consolidation in the subregion. Besides demonstrating a zero tolerance for power obtained or maintained by unconstitutional means, the protocol also pushes for a transition from ECOWAS of states to ECOWAS of citizens—through promotion of democratic ideas that are *in tandem* with constitutional convergence, conduct of credible elections, strengthening of critical institutions, poverty alleviation, rule of law and guarantee of rights for all—including of women, children and youth (Garuba, 2015).

In a collective security sense, the Protocol opens up opportunity to prioritise human security over regime security and its associated devastating impacts of internal conflicts in West Africa. Beyond softer governance issues, the protocol's implementation framework reckons with the fact that the wheel of violence—in ECOWAS member states—usually resonates in deep-seated structural issues that are often beclouded by accelerators and triggers. In the face of threats to good governance and inclusive politics, constitutional and citizenship crises, increasing spiral of intrastate conflicts and trans-border crimes as well as impunity and gross human rights violations, the protocol draws attention to the link between human security (i.e. freedom from fear and needs) and the broader debate about theory and practice of security (Ismail, 2011: 165–182). Because it places people at the centre of security and democratic equation, such a broader conception of security and guarantee of safe environment underscores the inextricable link between democracy and development (Garuba, 2015).

More directly linked to the issue of security is the fact that the medley of destabilizing conflicts that West Africa has experienced since the Liberia civil war precipitated an expansion of the mandate of ECOWAS into security regionalism (Omeje, 2013: 8). The ECOWAS Revised Treaty 1993 offered an opportunity to review and craft a more proactive and responsive approach to regional security complex and conflict resolution. A number of its peacekeeping and conflict management mechanisms, including the Moratorium on the Importation, Exportation and Manufacture of Small Arms (1998) and a new security architecture (2008) anchored on the Mechanism for Conflict Prevention, Management, Resolution and Peacekeeping and Security (1999) with other associated support institutions/instruments. Among such institutions/instruments are the Council of Elders (also known as Council of the Wise) and the Mediation and Security Council (MSC), the Early Warning System (ECOWARN), and the Standby Force (ESF). All helped in reforming ECOWAS support operations and "its institutional and operational structures to meet emerging security challenges" (Omeje, 2013: 10). Figure 9.1 shows the schematic of ECOWAS security architecture, while Figure 9.2 shows the operational structure of the ECOWAS Early Warning and Response Mechanism.

These initiatives have recorded remarkable spillovers, including the landmark roles they play in Africa Union's programming on conflict management and transformation, while the opportunity for co-deployment of troops with the United Nations in Liberia (UNMIL) and Sierra Leone (UNAMSIL) has provided the ECOWAS with invaluable lessons in peace support operations and the transition to a new regime of peacekeeping operations.

Also created by the new treaty was ECOWAS Bank for Investment and Development (EBID) with specialized agencies such as West Africa Health Organisation (WAHO). Joining with the ECOWAS Commission as the Fund for Cooperation, Compensation and Development, the ECOWAS Commission and the EBID are two main institutions of ECOWAS saddled with the responsibility of implementing agreed policies and development programmes in areas of agriculture, environment, natural resource management, telecommunications and transportations among others in member states. Added to the construction of transnational highways already referenced, the West Africa Gas Pipeline (WAGP) linking Warri in Nigeria's Niger Delta, Republic of Benin,

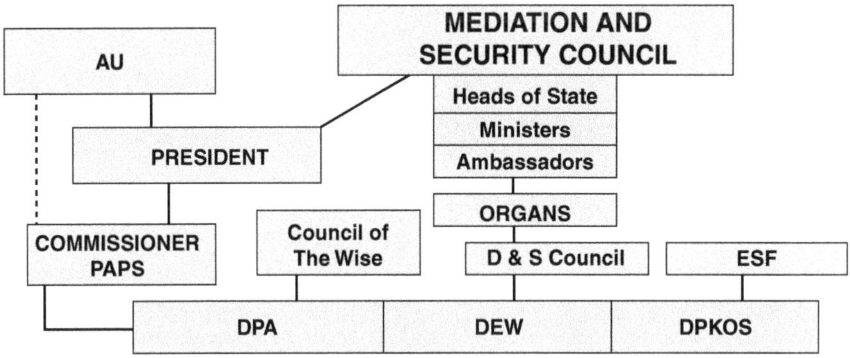

Figure 9.1 ECOWAS hard security architecture

Source: Abdel-fatau Musah (2008). ECOWAS and Institutional Responses to Conflicts: A Case for the Conflict Prevention Framework. Calabar: A presentation at the *Regional Consultation on the Gulf of Guinea* organized by the Centre for Democracy & Development and West Africa Civil Society Forum (WACSOF)

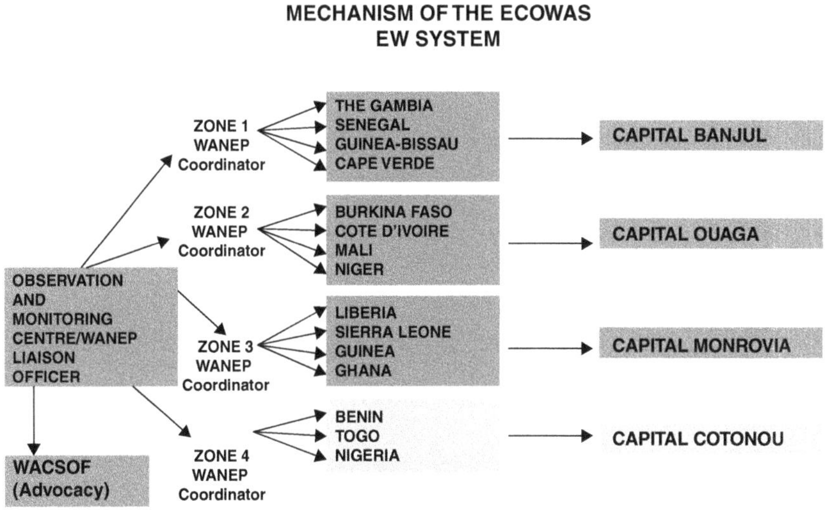

Figure 9.2 Structure of ECOWAS mechanism for early warning and early response

Source: Yoro Kone and Dauda Garuba (2009). Conflict and Institutional Frameworks for Peace Building: Possibilities and Challenges of ECOWAS Early Warning Mechanism. In Jibrin Ibrahim & Oumar Ndongo (Eds.), *Resolving West African Conflicts: Early Warning, Early Response*, Abuja: Centre for Democracy and Development, pp. 5–29

Togo and Ghana is about the biggest visible socio-economic and infrastructural investment in this regard in the ECOWAS region. Estimated at a construction cost of US$700 billion, WAGP has a total pipeline length of 781 kilometres which—beyond facilitating the firing of thermal plants in target countries—is anticipated to facilitate interlinkages of national power grids to the tune of 5,600 kilometres of electricity lines which could give up to 10,000 megawatts (Fayomi & Adeola, 2015: 34).

Notwithstanding this progress, ECOWAS has not functioned without significant challenges. The very first of such challenges is its institutional weaknesses. As a collection of largely fragile, poor and donor-dependent member states, "the regional body is unable to rise above the relatively weak institutions and capabilities" of its member states "to more effectively actualize the goals of economic integration and security regionalism" (Omeje, 2013: 10). The fragility of member states' economies and persistence of non-tariff barriers has weakened intraregional trade intensity and limited their capacity to compete in an increasingly globalizing world. It is for this reason that ECOWAS member states trade more with developed and non-member countries than among themselves. From a total trade averaging US$208.1 billion, ECOWAS exports are "projected at approximately US$137.3 billion, while imports total about US$80.4 billion" (ECOWAS, 2016b), with intraregional trade standing insignificant. Table 9.2 shows poor statistics of intraregional trade flow before and after the inception of ECOWAS; Tables 9.3 and 9.4 show imports and exports of ECOWAS member states as percentage of total imports and exports for 1999–2009 and 2011–2016 respectively; while Table 9.5 shows indicators of trade facilitation among member states. Added to negative picture that the tables paint about intraregional trade is the assertion that that ECOWAS region disburses US$19 for every US$1 on regional imports, "while exporting 80% of total exports in average of raw materials mainly" (ITC, 2016).

In the midst of these unenviable official statistics of intraregional trade, informal intraregional trade among ECOWAS states (mainly food staples such as livestock, maize and millet) is estimated at approximately 75 percent with "considerable room to grow further" (Torres & Seters, 2016: 41). On both formal and informal sides, the largest exporters of food staples in the region are Burkina Faso, Mali and Niger (livestock); Nigeria (cereals and Cassava), while the largest importers are Nigeria, Ghana, Côte d'Ivoire, and Senegal (livestock); Niger, Senegal, and Burkina Faso (maize); and Benin, Ghana, and Niger (sorghum and millet) (Torres & Seters, 2016: 22).

Also, the practice of free movement of persons, goods and services has been casually contravened over the years, due to multiple factors such as absence of a convertible single currency, cross-border parallel trades, infrastructural

Table 9.2 Statistics of intraregional trade flow before and after inception of ECOWAS

Year	*1970*	*1980*	*1990*	*2000*	*2010*	*2014*
Exports	3.0%	10.7%	8.7%	8.3%	9.3%	8.4%
Imports	2.8%	12.8%	12.0%	11.7%	9.5%	9.8%

Source: ITC (2016). International Trade Centre (2016). Facilitating Trade in ECOWAS: Insights from the ITC Business Surveys on Non-Tariff Measures, p. 5

Table 9.3 EOWAS member state exports and imports with the group

	Imports from ECOWAS (as % of total Imports value)						*Exports from ECOWAS (as % of total Exports value)*					
	1999	*2001*	*2003*	*2005*	*2007*	*2009*	*1999*	*2001*	*2003*	*2005*	*2007*	*2009*
1 Benin	11.0	13.7	19.9	26.7	24.9	39.4	13.5	24.0	21.9	22.0	21.3	18.3
2 Burkina Faso	32.2	22.0	87.8	23.8	32.2	25.6	23.8	27.2	44.6	27.6	25.9	25.8
3 Cape Verde	0.1	3.0	0.5	0.4	14.9	1.6	1.4	2.1	8.1	7.2	4.1	1.5
4 Côte d'Ivoire	20.8	24.6	17.5	24.8	28.7	26.1	15.0	20.7	16.2	25.7	5.9	32.8
5 The Gambia	52.1	8.0	11.1	55.1	26.5	19.8	7.3	10.7	8.6	15.7	10.0	13.4
6 Ghana	10.4	7.6	11.6	9.7	32.1	7.8	9.9	15.3	18.6	17.5	10.4	14.1
7 Guinea	1.4	1.6	9.8	27.4	10.1	6.1	8.9	18.5	8.8	25.4	3.3	3.5
8 Guinea-Bissau	...	0.1	0.1	1.5	0.1	...	...	22.9	18.8	53.9	39.2	...
9 Liberia	...	...	...	...	...	...	...	...	...	...	...	...
10 Mali	19.2	13.0	9.1	10.4	9.0	13.2	29.4	33.7	36.4	35.5	46.6	41.2
11 Niger	39.5	45.1	40.8	30.3	31.3	45.8	30.8	34.1	31.5	29.2	23.5	18.8
12 Nigeria	6.5	4.5	4.6	4.0	4.2	8.0	0.5	4.3	2.4	6.1	2.3	3.3
13 Senegal	16.9	17.1	26.5	30.0	37.4	31.9	10.2	19.9	22.8	21.9	17.3	26.2
14 Sierra Leone	33.0	65.3	28.2	11.6	47.4	91.9	26.7	34.4	28.5	33.6	87.4	44.3
15 Togo	16.0	46.2	46.7	53.5	60.0	68.7	19.9	14.2	14.1	13.3	12.2	14.3
ECOWAS	**11.5**	**9.6**	**10.2**	**8.4**	**10.1**	**12.5**	**11.7**	**16.2**	**13.6**	**19.9**	**11.5**	**17.0**

Source: W. K. Olayiwola & O.A. Ola-David, Economic integration, Trade Facilitation and Agricultural Exports Performance in ECOWAS Member Countries (2013). Available on: www.afdb.org/uploads/tx_llafdbpapers/ECONOMIC_INTEGRATION_TRADE_FACILITATION_AND_AGRICULTURAL_EXPORTS_PERFORMANCE_IN_ECOWAS_MEMBER_STATES.pdf

deficits and failure of markets to provide access to new technologies, physical and human capital and information. Even where headways have been made, procedural requirements for registration of importers and products, products' packaging, testing, certification and inspection, as well as other technical measures continue to prove a huge obstacle to non-tariff measures articulated in the ECOWAS regional trade and integration (ITC, 2016). Despite the provisions of Article 59 (1) of the ECOWAS Treaty and a protocol on free movement of persons and goods, there are still instances of violations. Ibeanu (2007: 6) paints a graphic picture of this when he wrote that:

> The story of what West African citizens go through at the hands of border security officials is the same—harassment, extortion, brutality, threats of deportation, and traumatic delays in moving goods across borders, sometime lasting weeks due not countless number of security checkpoints along the border highways, many of them mounted by unauthorised officials. A preliminary study carried out on the Nigerian side of the Nigeria-Benin border by the CLEEN Foundation on September 14, 2004, revealed that a total of 25 security agencies mounted checkpoints and roadblocks within 10 kilometres radius of the border crossing point. Only about 5 of these 'security check points' could be said to be legitimate and necessary for border security. These are the Customs, Immigration, Joint Nigeria-Benin

Table 9.4 Share of intraregional trade in the external trade of ECOWAS member states 2011–2016

Member State/Year	*2011*		*2012*		*2013*		*2014*		*2015*		*2016*		*Avg*
	Exp	*Imp*	*Exp*	*Imp*	*Exp*	*Imp*	*Exp*	*Imp*	*Exp*	*Imp*	*Exp*	*Imp*	
Burkina Faso	7.8	25.6	7.6	22.8	11	22.6	17.6	25	13	18.7	13.9	22.3	17.3
Benin	29.5	20.9	28.8	19.9	26.5	16.3	20.2	11.6	22	15.6	20.9	13.2	20.5
Cape Verde	2.2	1.4	0.4	0.8	1.8	0.8	0.3	1.6	3.8	3.4	1.7	1.8	1.7
Côte d'lvoire	26.4	24.9	29.1	27.3	32	24.6	23.4	23.2	19.7	19.5	25.2	22.6	24.8
Ghana	32.9	9.6	11.4	7.2	8.8	7.8	9.9	3.2	10.5	3.5	10.5	3.4	9.9
The Gambia	86.8	26.6	84.3	33	88.8	29.3	84.7	25.9	77.2	33.4	84	29.6	57
Guinea	7.7	4.5	9.2	2.7	3.4	2.3	25.3	2.8	25	6.6	25.2	6.6	10.1
Guinea-Bissau	10.6	15.3	3	11	3.7	13.2	24.6	11.1	5.3	9.8	6.6	11.4	10.5
Liberia	6.7	21.2	28.7	22.4	17	22	55.1	16.8	60.9	13.2	57.6	13.2	27.9
Mali	15.3	41.8	11.7	46.5	13.2	39.5	10.8	38.3	13.5	34.9	13.5	34.9	26.2
Niger	12	14.5	30.5	18.9	41.7	20.3	40.9	17.7	24.4	13.9	34.5	13.9	23.6
Nigeria	2.8	1.2	3.9	0.4	5.3	4.9	4.4	0.6	6.5	3	5.1	2.8	3.4
Sierra Leone	6.2	24.6	1.2	32.7	6.7	34.7	6.5	44.1	32.9	19	11.4	28.3	20.7
Senegal	37	13.5	36	15.6	38.5	13.7	39.1	11.4	37.8	10.8	38.5	13	25.4
Togo	63.1	8.3	55.2	9.4	59.1	10.8	56.4	10.7	56.3	9.6	57.5	10.4	33.9
External trade of ECOWAS: Share of intracommunity trade in % of external trade of ECOWAS													
Share of intracommunity trade (%)	10	8.8	8	12.2	11.8	13.7	9.8	9.7	13.5	10.7	11.9	11.1	10.9

Source: Fajana, Olufemi (2018). *Accelerating the Implementation of the ECOWAS Trade Libralisation Scheme*. A study on trade integration in ECOWAS sponsored by the Ghana Chambers of Commerce and Industry and the Federation of West Africa Chambers of Commerce and Industry (FWACCI) through funding support by the African Trade Policy Centre (ATPC)

> Anti-Crime Border Patrol, National Drug Law Enforcement Agency and Veterinary Quarantine Service. The remaining 20 are duplications created by law enforcement officials essentially for extortion of motorists and other road users along the ever-busy border route.

Building on the this work, Ugbajah (2016) cited ECOWAS as stating that

> there were a total of 69 checkpoints on the trade route between Lagos (Nigeria) and Abidjan (Côte d'Ivoire) a distance of only 992km; 52 checkpoints between Lome (Togo) and Ouagadougou (Burkina-Faso) a distance of 989km trade route; and 20 checkpoints between Ouagadougou (Burkina-Faso) and Abidjan (Ivory Coast) a distance of just 529km.

The impacts of such checkpoints are reflected in extortions and harassments by security operatives along these trade corridors, and in some cases uncontrolled smuggling by criminals who work discretely with border officials. In February 2008, the present writer was assaulted at the Nigeria-Cotonou border post by Beninois immigration officials for refusing to pay bribe in order to transit

Table 9.5 Some indicators of trade facilitation among ECOWAS states

Countries	*Time required to start a business (number of days)*		*Documents required to exports (number of days)*		*Time to export (number of days)*		*Documents required to import (number of days)*		*Time to import (number of days)*	
	2008	*2014*	*2008*	*2014*	*2008*	*2014*	*2008*	*2014*	*2008*	*2014*
Benin	34	12	8	7	32	25	9	7	37	25
Burkina Faso	16	13	11	10	45	42	13	12	54	49
Cape Verde	52	10	7	7	19	20	7	7	18	20
Côte d'Ivoire	40	7	9	9	23	25	13	13	43	32
The Gambia	27	26	6	6	24	19	6	6	23	19
Ghana	11	14	6	6	19	19	7	7	37	41
Guinea	40	8	7	7	34	36	8	8	32	31
Guinea-Bissau	259	9	6	6	27	25	6	6	24	22
Liberia	32	5	10	10	29	15	12	12	32	29
Mali	25	11	7	6	38	26	12	11	46	34
Niger	19	15	8	6	59	56	10	10	66	61
Nigeria	31	31	9	9	25	3	13	13	42	4
Senegal	9	6	6	6	15	12	6	6	19	14
Sierra Leone	17	12	7	7	29	25	8	8	34	28
Togo	60	10	6	6	24	24	7	7	29	29

Source: Wumi Olayiwola et al. (2015), as cited in Leonard O. Ugbajah, "Status and General Implications of Free Movement of Agro-Produce across West Africa". A presentation at a workshop on Free Movement of Agricultural Commodities across West African Borders, Abuja, August 2016

Cotonou to ECOWAS Summit in Ougadougou, Burkina Faso (*Leadership Newspaper*, 6 February, 2008). To the extent to which it has clogged the wheel of free trade, the ECOWAS Trade Liberalisation Scheme (ETLS) has been critiqued by many private businesses operators who argued that its "operational effectiveness . . . only works on paper and is essentially ineffective" (Deloitte, 2017).

A source also had it that "only about one-third to one-half of intra-ECOWAS trade circulates duty-free, meaning the internal free trade area is still a big concern" (Semedo, 2013: 11), while the Community Levy—a 0.5-percent approved tax on imports from non-ECOWAS member states meant to complement member states' contributions are neglected due to competing national priorities. Similar contradictions have also been identified between Francophone monetary zone (UEMOA) and non-Francophone monetary zone of ECOWAS, regarding their "completion framework policies" derived directly from the differences in English common law and French civil law and practices (Semedo, 2013: 11–12).

Perhaps, the greatest challenge to developmental regionalism, peace and economic transformation envisaged by ECOWAS is located in the gap between regional and national development agendas and what Bossuyt (2016: vi) refers to as "the hugely diverging interests among memberstates." It's only in recent times that much is happening to consciously internalize and incorporate the subregional agendas of ECOWAS into long-term national development plans of its member states. This has not in any radical manner changed the overbearing influence of France on its Francophone member states to the extent that stirs rivalry and absence of consensus among different national leaders and slows the pace of how the regional body functions. The ECOWAS Vision 2020 adopted in 2011 is thus better situated to correct this in that it anticipates a borderless peaceful, prosperous and cohesive West Africa where the citizens are capacitated to access and harness the subregion's potentials and abundant resources for the attainment of sustainable development. This vision of transformation portends useful comparative lessons for the SADC.

Comparative lessons for the SADC

SADC is the ECOWAS version of a regional economic community in Southern Africa by virtue of its membership composition and focus. Both RECs top the records of intratrade of regional and trade groups among the eight AU-recognised RECs in Africa. Table 9.6 shows that SADC leads, while ECOWAS follows closely.

It started as a loose alliance of nine-member-Southern African Development and Coordination Conference (SADCC)[3] in 1980—under the initiative of the Frontline States. Its mandate was to coordinate international community support against member states' economic dependency on white supremacist rule in Southern Africa. Its membership has since increased to sixteen, namely, Angola, Botswana, Comoros, DR Congo, Lesotho, Madagascar, Malawi, Mauritius, Mozambique, Namibia, Seychelles, South Africa, Swaziland, Tanzania, Zambia and Zimbabwe.

Founded originally in 1974 to push for the liberation of Southern Africa countries, the FLS soon dispersed when Namibia and South Africa became liberated as the last bastions of colonialism and white minority rule in the 1990s. After Namibia had joined as the 10th member in 1990 and South Africa was set on its course to holding a multiparty elections that eventually happened in 1994, a decision was taken at the Summit in Windhoek (Namibia) in 1992 to transit SADCC from "a regional functional cooperation concept to a trade-based regional integration model" in the context of member states' realization that "political struggle for liberalization need economic foundation to be successful" (Peters, 2010: 98, 100–101). This also informed the change of its name from SADCC to SADC and an adjustment of its objectives and strategy initially focusing imports substitution to reflect complementary regional and national programmes which include political issues (Fall, Vachon & Winckler, 2014: 22).

Shaped by several historical, political and economic factors, the evolution of SADC derived from a strong bond of cooperation among its members dating to their period of struggle from colonialism and white minority rule under the Frontline States. Figure 9.3 shows the maps of ECOWAS and the SADC.

Table 9.6 Intratrade of regional and trade groups in Africa 2005–2013

RECs	*Measure*	*2005*	*2006*	*2007*	*2008*	*2009*	*2010*	*2011*	*2012*	*2013*
COMESA	US dollars (Millions)	3367.8	4037.7	4731	6862	6703.7	8738.6	9292.1	10866.6	11342.1
	Percentage	5.1	5.1	4.8	5.4	7.1	7.4	9.5	8.1	9.4
EAC	US dollars (Millions)	1128	1012.1	1383.6	1914.4	1755	2086.5	2596.4	3051.9	2755.5
	Percentage	18.5	15.5	17.7	18.9	18.8	18.6	19.7	20.7	19.5
ECCAS	US dollars (Millions)	438.8	554.9	1301.7	1105.3	1119.2	1626.5	1201.4	1352.3	1236.8
	Percentage	0.9	0.9	1.7	1	1.6	1.8	1	1.1	1
ECOWAS	US dollars (Millions)	5978.7	6550.6	7308.1	10241.7	8016.5	9637.1	10417.2	12060.4	13479
	Percentage	9.6	8.4	3.4	9.6	9.7	8.3	6.3	7.8	9.3
IGAD	US dollars (Millions)	980	1029.4	1242.8	1581.7	1496.2	1950.6	2430.6	2336.1	2405.2
	Percentage	9.8	9.1	7.8	7.7	8.7	9.2	**11.8**	14.1	12.6
SADC	US dollars (Millions)	9083.4	10889.2	14510.4	18489.8	16068.5	22813.3	24000.2	29072.5	36104.8
	Percentage	9.7	9.8	10.5	10.8	12.3	12.6	10.8	13.3	16.8
CEN-SAD	US dollars (Millions)	961.3	1050.2	1101.8	1751.4	195.9	1633.2	1693.8	1933.3	21512.2
	Percentage	6.4	6	5.9	6.7	7.5	6.7	6	6.6	7.8
UMA	US dollars (Millions)	116.7	2333.1	2901.6	4569.4	3235.9	3451.5	3639.2	4675.3	5547
	Percentage	1.9	2	2.1	2.5	2.9	2.4	2.7	2.7	3.7

Source: Chinyama, E.J. & Tanoe, D. (2015). Moving Forward on Africa's Regional Integration Agenda: Learning from Best Practices and Efforts. *International Journal of Economics & Management Sciences*, Vol. 5 (2), p. 7

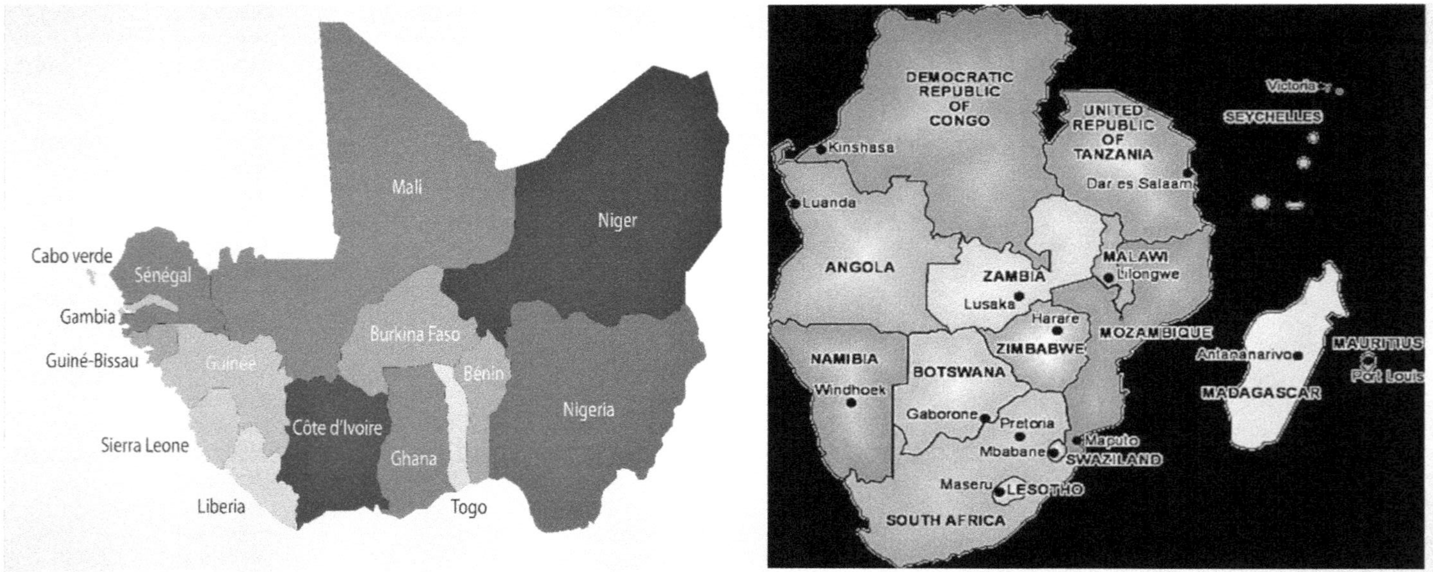

Figure 9.3 Maps of ECOWAS and the SADC

Source: ECOWAS: http://ecpf.ecowas.int/?s=Ecowas+map SADC: www.sadc.int/about-sadc/overview/

What is obvious is that even though the SADC is younger than ECOWAS, its roots are much older in terms of its track-record of political and military history of collaboration against colonialism and white supremacist rule in Southern Africa (Khadiagala, 1994; Sule, 1997). And like ECOWAS, the lifting of the super-power overlay after the demise of the Cold War, the realization of multiparty elections/black majority rule in South Africa, and the shift towards market-centred economic reforms in Southern Africa "ushered the region into a new phase of cooperation" (Essuman-John, 2009: 12) and challenges of internal security. Put differently, the historic factor of common security interest combined with other political, geo-strategic and economic factors to increase regional integration in SADC countries. Under the new regime, the central objectives are "to achieve economic development, peace and security, and growth, alleviate poverty, enhance the standard and quality of life of the peoples of Southern Africa, and support the socially disadvantaged" (SADC, 2012). Table 9.7 shows basic statistics of SADC member states. The figures reveal that South Africa is the largest economy with a GDP of US$349 billion and Angola the second with US$124 billion to rank 2nd and 5th position in Africa, and 33rd and 59th in the world respectively in 2017. Comoros Island, Seychelles and Lesotho are the poorest with GDPs of US$652 million, US$1.48 billion and US$2.76 billion respectively.

The SADC is guided by certain cardinal principles such as sovereign equality of member states; solidarity, peace and security; human rights, democracy and rule of law; equity, balance and mutual benefit; and peaceful settlement of

Table 9.7 SADC country by area (2014), population (2018) and GDP (2017)

Country	*Area (Sq.km)*	*Population*	*Rank (Population)*		*GDP (US$)*	*Rank (GDP)*	
			Africa	*World*		*Africa*	*World*
Angola	1,246,700	30,774,205	12	46	124.209	5	59
Botswana	581,730	2,333,201	42	144	17.168	20	115
Comoros	2,235	832,347	52	163	0.652	53	183
Congo DR	2,344,858	84,004,989	4	16	41.441	12	89
Lesotho	30,355	2,263,010	43	145	2.768	46	164
Madagascar	587,041	26,262,810	15	51	11.463	28	133
Malawi	118,484	19,164,728	20	61	6.206	37	149
Mauritius	2,040	1,268,315	49	158	12.428	27	130
Mozambique	799,380	30,528,673	13	47	12.681	25	127
Namibia	824,292	2,587,801	41	43	12.687	24	126
Seychelles	455	95,235	57	201	1.482	50	174
South Africa	1,219,090	57,398,421	6	25	349.299	2	33
Swaziland	17,364	1,391,385	47	153	4.491	41	157
Tanzania	947,300	59,091,392	5	24	51.725	10	81
Zambia	752,618	17,609,178	22	66	25.504	18	104
Zimbabwe	390,757	16,913,261	23	69	17.491	19	114
TOTAL	**9,864,699**	**352,518,951**			**US$692**		

Source: Compiled from *Statistics Times*. Available at: https://statisticstimes.com

disputes. These principles, as also enshrined in the ECOWAS Treaty, inform the kind of developmental regionalism, peace and economic transformation programmes it initiates and operates in Southern Africa. Structurally, the SADC is organized into three broad components, namely, Secretariat overseen by the Executive Secretary; and Regional Integration, and Finance and Administration each of which is overseen by a Deputy Executive Secretary. The REC functions on eight directorates and eight units. Beyond overall responsibility for the management of the Secretariat, the Executive Secretary oversees the Directorate of Origin, Politics, Defence and Security and a number of units such as Gender, Internal Audit, Macro-economic Convergence Surveillance and Public Relations. The first Deputy Executive Secretary (Regional Integration) oversees five core regional integration-related directorates, namely, Trade, Finance and Investment; Infrastructure and Services; Food, Agriculture and Resources; Social, Human Development and Special Programmes; and Policy, Planning and Resource Mobilisation. The second Deputy Executive Secretary is saddled with the responsibility of overseeing two directorates (Budget and Finance, and Human Resources and Administration) and four units covering Conference Services, Procurement, Legal and Information/Communications Technologies (SADC, 2008). The directorates are supervised by Directors, while the units are led by Senior Officers.

Like ECOWAS, the SADC operates on protocols adopted by member states. There are up to 30 different protocols currently in force in the REC among which are: Trade (1996); Transport, Communications & Meteorology (1996); Shared Watercourses (2000); Corruption (2001); Facilitation of Free Movement of Persons (2005); Energy (2006); Finance and Investment (2006); Gender and Development (2008); Trade in Services (2012); Employment and Labour (2014); and Agreement Amending Annex 1—Cooperation on investment—on the Protocol on Finance and Investment (2016). Beyond being tools aimed at eliminating trade barriers and promoting free movement of persons, goods and services in SADC countries, the protocols also facilitate the achievement of milestones defined in SADC's Regional Indicative Strategy Development Plan (RISDP) which was adopted and launched at the Council of Ministers meeting in Dar es Salaam, Tanzania in August 2003 and in March 2004, respectively.

Within the context of five priority clusters, (namely: trade, industry, finance and investment; infrastructure and services; food, agriculture and natural resources; social and human development and special programmes; and cross-cutting issues), the RISDP sequences SADC realization of Free Trade Area (FTA) in 2008, a custom union in 2010, a common market in 2015, a monetary union in 2016 and an economic union with a single currency in 2018 (Junior, 2015: 10). Except for the FTA which is still facing challenges as a result of overlapping membership with other regional bodies and diversity of economic structures and levels of development, none of the targets was met. Overlapping memberships have prompted situations where member countries of ECOWAS and SADC randomly pick and choose different aspects of the different REC agenda to implement, while caring less for the limited consequences for non-compliance and violations. Also, many bilateral partners and donors have made matters worse by initiating and implementing national programmes that work at cross-purposes with regional integration agenda. However, what appears to be paying off for SADC is its decision to consolidate its multimembership of regional economic communities in a Tripartite Free Trade Area (COMESA-SADC-EAC TFTA) anchored on market integration, infrastructure and Industrial development. The FTA which spans 26 countries of estimated 600 million population with approximately US$1 trillion Gross Domestic Products (Chinyama & Tanoe, 2015: 2) is now perceived as "a guide to overcoming the problem of overlapping membership facing Africa's multiple RECs and the attainment of a continent-wide REC" (Ukaoha & Ukpe, 2013: 1). The estimated growth of combined intra-African trade in the tripartite FTA over a period of 10 years (2004 and 2014) has been put at US$30 billion (Chinyama & Tanoe, 2015: 5). ECOWAS also shares a similar, but narrower collaboration with the Economic Community of Central African States (ECCAS) in the development of a joint programme for combating cross-border livestock disease (Magbagbeola, 2016: 14).

Along the line of SADC's adoption of RISDP in 2003 to push for this regional development and structural transformation, ECOWAS has similarly invested in numerous initiatives that are consisted with productive capacity development and structural transformation over the last decade. Among these are the adoption of West African Common Industrial Policy (2010) aimed at increasing local raw material processing and the subregion's share of global exports and raising share of manufacturing; the development and unveiling of ECOWAS Vision 2020 aimed at creating a "borderless, peaceful prosperous and cohesive region" (ECOWAS, 2010: 2); and the promotion of ECOWAS Strategic Plan for 2011–2015 which prioritises development of energy, transport and information, and communications technology infrastructure (Osakwe, 2015: 2). These ever-widening initiatives have hatched a side variety of strategies and programmes (Bossuyt, 2016: iv, 5) such as the ECOWAS Common Investment Market with a developed Common Investment Code and Policy, ECOBIZ World Market Information System, Inter-Institutional Committee under the ECOWAS Trade Negotiation Capacity Building (TNCB) project, Community Computer Centre (CCC) and the Common External Tariff (CET) that took effect in January 2015 ahead of plan of transforming into a Customs Union. Based on identified priorities of the Comprehensive Africa Agriculture Development Programme (CAADP), ECOWAS has also adopted a policy (ECOWAP) aimed at boosting agricultural productivity and exports, attaining food security and promoting sustainable livelihoods for farmers in member states. While ECOWAS and SADC have continued to explore opportunities to improve their regional integration processes, so much is still required to sustain the implementation of these initiatives' associated action plans. It is in this context that transformative regionalism transcends mere initiatives to promoting productive capacity development and economic transformation (Osakwe, 2015: 11).

Like ECOWAS, SADC is yet to meet its full expectations, despite its seeming commanding heights. The conflicts which started in Lesotho and the DR Congo (former Zaire) in 1994 and 1996 (respectively) were the initial peace and security challenges that SADC had had to deal with immediately after its transformation into a regional body for economic cooperation and integration. The decision by SADC to intervene militarily in the long-drawn crisis that culminated in the attempted coup in Lesotho with a combination of South African Defence Force (SADF) and Botswana Defence Force (BDF) pointed to the shape of things to come the way of the regional body in the area of peace and security (Essuman-Johnson, 2009: 413). Subsequent hostilities in the Great Lakes, the South Sudan rebellion and the Angola civil war only further compounded the situation in DR Congo which had become a failed state at the eruption of conflicts in 1996 to pose the biggest challenge to SADC.

More than what the civil wars in Liberian and Sierra Leone were to ECOWAS, the multicountries' interests in the DRC were too big for the SADC to manage through its structure on Politics, Defence and Security; particularly the "disagreement over whether it should become an integral part of the SADC structure" (Essuman-Johnson, 2009: 414). Similar to the divisions among ECOWAS member states about the legitimacy to intervene in the Liberian crisis in 1990, the eventual agreement within SADC that member states "that felt able to intervene to assist a member state at the request of its government, should do so" (Essuman-Johnson, 2009: 414) came handy for Angola, Namibia and Zimbabwe. Notwithstanding the outcome of the intervention, what was obvious about it was that it was a non-collectivised response by the SADC. If it were, chances are that it would have accompanied that with an implementation engine for the different accords signed by the warring groups in Lusaka (Zambia), Pretoria (South Africa) and Sun City (Kinshasa, DRC). This inadequacy was to deepen the human security and humanitarian crisis in DR Congo for a long time.

Similar to the situation with ECOWAS, peace and security challenges in the SADC region have had their peculiarities requiring different resolution approaches. The push for "quiet diplomacy" by SADC in the Zimbabwean crisis between the ruling ZANU-PF and Movement for Democratic Change in 2008 and the insistence by ECOWAS and its international backers (Africa Union and United Nations) that the will of the people as demonstrated in the Gambian elections in December 2016 must be respected by the then incumbent and loser President Yahya Jammeh also demonstrated the different contexts under which both regional bodies function (Zhangazha, 2017).

On regional economic front, ECOWAS and SADC face the same challenges ranging from absence of complementarity of tradable goods and services to unrealistic targets and expectations. Over time, exaggerated ambitions have interfaced with inadequate investment in standard and quality infrastructure, border post development, customs modernization and private sector involvement in a sense that is incongruous with and a hindrance to trade liberalisation. Member states' under-funding of RECs, coupled with the tendency to hold on strongly to their sovereignties, has negatively impacted the expected link between regional strategies of both bodies and national agendas. This delinking has undermined policy harmonization in the areas of free movement, trade and tourism, border control and customs, energy efficiency, agriculture, youth employment and labour, and healthcare delivery. Such incoherencies are inimical to transformative regionalism.

Also, there has been what seems a deliberate gagging by bigger powers such as Nigeria and South Africa within ECOWAS and SADC around crucial internal conflicts with serious regional implications. Likened to what Bach (2007: 302) calls "a pattern of dominance without power", the Niger Delta crisis and Boko Haram terrorism in Nigeria have lingered outside the radar of ECOWAS for many years, while xenophobic attacks on foreigners in South Africa have also grown unabated under the nose of SADC, despite early warning signs about their potential threats to peace and security in both regions. Meanwhile, the potential danger of xenophobic attacks to peace and security in Southern Africa was long flagged in the Africa Peer Review Mechanism (APRM) report on South Africa. The domineering power asymmetries between Nigeria and its fellow member states in ECOWAS on the one hand, and South Africa and other member countries of SADC on the other hand, have been unduly exploited to flout regulations on trade liberalization (ETLS) and common external tariff (CET). There have also been cases of non-compliance to judgements of Community Court of Justice/Tribunal without strong protest from many member states. Nigeria has not only unilaterally closed its borders with Benin Republic, but has also flouted several ECOWAS Court judgements.

Other critical barriers to regional integration in ECOWAS and the SADC regions have been colonial baggage resulting in rivalry and lack of consensus between Anglophone and Francophone countries and poor commitments by national leaders on account of selfish interests often deceptively packaged and presented as national interests. In particular, the overbearing influence of France on its former colonies that aggregate UEMOA has precipitated duplication of regional policy as much as it has posed a huge restriction and undermined ECOWAS's ability to enforce commitments to regional integration by member states. This near absence of political commitment, beyond undermining the potentials of ECOWAS and the SADC, portends what Bossuyt (2016: vi) construes in the context of ECOWAS as "a selective ability for collective action to address political crises in member states."

Closely associated with these barriers is the language barrier across member states. ECOWAS and the SADC function in three co-official languages, namely, English, French and Portuguese, as enshrined in Article 87 of the ECOWAS Revised Treaty and Article 37 of Chapter 15 of the SADC Treaty as amended in 2001. The policy on language linked directly to the official languages of member states' colonial masters on the presumption that it will help deal with the deleterious challenge of English-French-Portuguese language between UEMOA and non-UEMOA countries as much as the SADC's English-French-Portuguese language barrier among member countries. However, the reality is that such a vertical integration process excludes mass traders who operate from outside the framework of government languages. Thus, despite easing governance at both national and regional levels, the vertical integration depicted by English-French-Portuguese co-official language has enormous implications for intraregional trade and integration.

Beyond language barrier, the diversity of ECOWAS region and its intraregional trade opportunities have not been better exploited to improve market competiveness and regional integration. Indeed, it has been argued that the export and import baskets of SADC region are more diversified than those of the ECOWAS region, even though "the results of analysis of the complementarities of trade structures and . . . the potential for increased intraregional trade in SADC appear less promising", hence it may be "more beneficial for countries to seek to trade against their comparative advantages rather than with it" (Keane, Calì & Kennan, 2010: 16–17).

In the face of a linear model of integration anchored on "a progressive move from free trade area status to a common market, and monetary and economic union", ECOWAS and SADC have for too long focused more on removal of trade barriers to the exclusion of "much deeper issues such as the development of productive capacities and structural transformation" (Osakwe, 2015: 11–14) and the barrier of absence of a single currency as a chief determinant of intraregional trade flows.

Similarly, both ECOWAS and the SADC lag behind in intraregional trade which in the case of the former is dominated by *extractive resources* (oil, iron, bauxite, manganese, gold) and *agriculture* (coffee, cocoa, cotton, rubber, fruits and vegetables), and SADC by oil, agricultural products, electricity and clothing/textiles products. Even though the two RECs parade the best of intraregional trade statistics, they still do not reflect the enormous potentials that they represent. More specifically, official statistics of intraregional trade in both regions in the 2010s oscillated between 10 percent and 13 percent, even as informal transactions facilitated by networks of shared ethnicity, geography and cultural affinity in and around border communities—largely agricultural produce—continued to soar.

Despite claims that Intra-ECOWAS and intra-SADC trades as percentages of total trade have grown at roughly 18 percent ($47.3 billion) and 15 percent ($53 billion) over periods of 2005–2014 and 2004–2014 respectively (ECOWAS, 2016c; Chinyama & Tanoe, 2015: 5), the export figures of both RECs to other regions of the world have continued to ballooned, with Nigeria and South Africa dominating by up to 76 percent and 60 percent respectively. ECOWAS exports to countries of European Union, North American Free Trade Association (NAFTA) and Asia/Oceania account for 23 percent, 24 percent and 16 percent respectively. In ECOWAS region, Nigeria alone accounts for 41 percent of ECOWAS exports, while Ghana trail far behind with 18 percent, and Senegal and Côte d'Ivoire with 10 percent each. According to the same source, Nigeria and Ghana account for 59 percent of ECOWAS imports; the eight UEMOA countries of Benin, Burkina Faso, Côte d'Ivoire, Guinea, Bissau, Mali, Niger, Senegal, and Togo share 36 percent, while the remaining five countries (Cape Verde, The Gambia, Guinea Bissau, Liberia and Sierra Leone) control 5 percent. Likewise, available statistics put SADC total exports at 45 percent to countries of Asian Pacific Economic Cooperation (APEC), 27 percent to the European Union, 3 percent and 15 percent to non-SADC member states of Africa and the rest of world respectively. SADC imports maintained percentages similar to those of exports with Asia-Pacific Economic Cooperation (APEC) and the European Union (EU), while non-SADC member states of Africa and the rest of the world percentages were 15 percent and 13 percent respectively (SADC, n.d.). Notwithstanding these parallels, more recent statistics put Nigeria's records of intra-ECOWAS exports and imports at 87 percent and 41 percent respectively, but laments that the country's trade with other member states is less than 4 percent of its total world trade; contrary to South Africa which accounts for 61 percent SADC's GDP and leads "top performing countries of the REC in trade integration (Fajana, 2018: 10). The slow pace of progress with intraregional trade, in addition to the limited inter-REC trade within Africa, contradicts the very reason for regional integration and the dream the dream of realizing an African free trade area.

Perhaps, one critical challenge that requires serious attention from ECOWAS and SADC in most contemporary sense is the question of Economic Partnership Agreements (EPAs). The EPAs exist as a culmination of almost seven decades development cooperation between European countries under the European Union and countries in African, Caribbean and Pacific regions. The agreements seek the removal of trade barriers (a free trade area) between Europe and ACP countries as applied to Article 24 of the General Agreement on Trade and Tariff (GATT). In the quest for economic growth and integration, the EPAs aim to connect African, Caribbean and Pacific (ACP) states into the global economy without undermining their political choices and development priorities. As laudable as this seems, the reality has been far from it. Across ECOWAS and SADC regions, the EU has gone ahead to negotiate the EPAs with individual countries in violation of the very reasons for regionalism. Nigeria's insistence that the EPAs be negotiated collectively by ECOWAS member states as a bloc was broken, after 13 ECOWAS member states—with the exception of Nigeria and The Gambia—took turns in signing the EPAs. With The Gambia signing the EPA in November 2018, the only country now left is Nigeria. This is in spite of the allusion to the integral place of a unified and efficient regional market in the standing agreements between ECOWAS and the EU, and the latter and SADC-EPA States (Botswana, Lesotho, Mozambique, Namibia, South Africa and Swaziland) that supports member states to collectively negotiate and sign the EPAs as a bloc. Article 3 of the EU-SADC-EPA States Agreement and Article 4 of the EU-ECOWAS/UEMOA Agreement contain the statement that "The Parties recognise that regional integration is an essential part of their partnership and a powerful tool for achieving the objectives of this Agreement and agree to give it their strong support."

Thus, taking on ECOWAS and SADC member countries individually for negotiation and signing of the EPAs upstages, negates and relegates the regional foundations and principles on which both RECs were built. Indeed, it shows why many countries of both regional blocs have become susceptible to EU's arm-twisting as evident in how the EPAs have gone. The insistence that the EPAs be negotiated collectively by ECOWAS member states as a bloc was broken, after 13 ECOWAS member states—with the exception of Nigeria and The Gambia—took turns in signing the EPAs. With The Gambia signing the EPA in 2018, Nigeria is now the only country left out of the EPAs among the entire ECOWAS states. Ghana's Minister of Trade and Industry, Ekwow Spio Garbrah, was particularly quoted as saying that his country decided to sign the interim agreement to grant exporters special privileges, adding that its "fishing industry will collapse if the agreement is not signed" (Pomeyie, 2016). In similar vein, so much expectations have been raised about the potential benefits of EPAs to the economies of SADC countries. In particular, Botswana's cattle, Lesotho's luxury mohair, Mozambique's Cashew, Namibia's fish, South Africa's Rooibos and Swaziland's sugar top the list of the commodities to attract the economies of scale envisaged. Unlike Nigeria's efforts in protecting regional interest (even though unsuccessfully), South Africa has been chided for taking its time in "negotiating EPAs with the EU", instead of broadening the process to include other smaller members of the Southern Africa Customs Union (MapuvaI and Muyengwa-MapuvaII, 2014: 31) who also double as members of SADC.

While unequal economic capacity to withstand long negotiations in the face of dire need for resources to keep afloat may be adduced to the observed 'betrayal' depicted by most member states of ECOWAS and SADC to sign the EPAs individually, funding gaps arising from failing financial obligations have further compounded the situation and pushed both RECs to the edge of perennial quest for freebies. The 11th European Development Fund for 2014–2020 allocated a budget heading of 97 million Euro to ECOWAS region for its 2017 Annual Action Programme covering Peace, security and regional stability and Regional economic integration and support for trade sectors. Similarly, less than 10 percent of regional projects of SADC are estimated to be funded by member countries, while the balance is contributed by International Partners (TRALAC, 2018). This overwhelming reliance/dependence by ECOWAS and SADC on external funding for their programmes has not only made them exist on the goodwill of what Adetula (2004) refers to as "Euro-American capital", it has also compromised the ownership and sustainability of both regional bodies. To the extent to which they constitute a race to the bottom, the EPAs defeat the very reason for which ECOWAS and SADC were conceived and established in the first instance—i.e. collective protection and maximization of benefits that could advance regional economic development. But rather than be in despair, ECOWAS and SADC member states should see EPAs as a common challenge requiring a convergence in comparative experience sharing and collective solutions that can better improve regional integration across RECs in Africa.

Concluding remarks

Regional integration has become the most patronized path for addressing unintended externalities precipitated by the crisis of globalization and facilitating regional development by many countries of the World, especially the developing countries. Its adoption in post-independence West Africa which predated contemporary globalization is reflected in the formation of ECOWAS, and grounded/rooted in a collective developmental state approach to nation building. Anchored on a collective self-motivation to create a single market, ECOWAS survived only to the extent to which it leveraged the cooperation and comparative advantages of its member states to promote intraregional trade. It is in this context that Nigeria's first military ruler, Yakubu Gowon (1984: 21) refers to it as "the most ambitious attempt at regional economic integration to date".

Despite its profound achievements, ECOWAS has experienced enormous barriers in its quest for regional integration. Beyond the fact of its slow-paced processes, its biggest challenges came when its regional integration project was obstructed by post-Cold War conflicts that started in Liberia and later took turns to ravage other countries such as Sierra, Guinea, Guinea-Bissau, Côte d'Ivoire and Mali. This constituted negative circuit breakers, requiring a decisive response. That response came with ambitious and determined efforts facilitated by Nigeria to proffer solutions to conflicts in the subregion through the deployment of ECOMOG peacekeeping forces in Liberia and Sierra Leone, while also continuing with its original mandate of promoting regional economic cooperation and development. The efforts also set the regional body on the course of a restructuring mission that sought to reposition it to more proactively deliver on regional economic cooperation and conflict transformation as well as to expand a civic space aimed at realizing a successful transition from ECOWAS of States to ECOWAS of Citizens. Anchored on the Revised ECOWAS Treaty (1993), the transformational focus of the restructuring shares much similarities with the vision, mission and programmes that SADC currently pushes in Southern Africa region. Established originally by a collection of Frontline States committed to reducing their economic dependence on South Africa, SADC has undergone a radical realignment that has made its primary target (i.e. South Africa) become its *de facto* leader (Adetula, 2004).

ECOWAS and SADC have made landmark achievements on diverse fronts of regional peace and security, political and economic governance, but this has not been without challenges. Prominent among these are inadequate investment in integration infrastructure (particularly transnational transport facilities); poor funding that has forced both RECs to be donor-dependent; baggage of overbearing influence of the French government on its former colonies organized under UEMOA; and impunity and non-conformist behaviours by regional hegemons such as Nigeria in the ECOWAS region and South Africa in the SADC region. Other challenges are a vertical integration language-induced barriers that exclude mass traders who operate outside the framework of government languages; and pretentious focus on removal of trade barriers to the exclusion of much deeper issues of development of production capabilities and structural transformation that are amenable to driving true integration; including the absence of a single currency. Also, there are high concerns about the poor productive capacity of member states of ECOWAS and SADC (majority of which currently trade in competitive products instead of preferred complementary products) and the deleterious consequences of being producers of raw materials and consumers of finished products that they do not determine their prices as depicted in the EPAs. The EPAs remain a "pyrrhic victory" (McDonald, Lande & Matanda, 2013), especially in the context in which they seek to prematurely open African markets to the vagaries of cheaper goods from Europe.

These and many other barriers re-affirms the claim by the United Nations for Economic Commission for Africa (2010) that regionalism has only proliferated in post-independence sub-Saharan Africa without taking intraregional trade to the level projected. Re-echoing Adedeji (2002) that the *raison d'être* for subregional approach to Africa economic integration (as envisaged in the Final Act of Lagos) has been breached, the former Chairperson of AU Commission, Nkosazana Dhlamini-Zuma, remarked that despite their strides and immense potentials, regional economic communities have only recorded minimal successes in promoting economic development and poverty alleviation (Tanyanyiwa & Hakuna, 2014: 109). Referred elsewhere as "regionalisation without region-building", Bach (2016a: 13) argues that the situation denotes "the interplay between regionalism (as a project), regionalization (as a process) and region-building (as an outcome) in Africa". Even at that, it has not diminished the hope that deliberate and sustained efforts in pushing for the implementation of the various policy instruments adopted by both regional bodies would deliver anticipated results, including the realization of continental free trade area (FTA).

Notwithstanding these barriers, ECOWAS and SADC have demonstrated enormous capacity and huge milestones for advancing developmental regionalism, peace and security, and economic transformation in Africa. As part of the way forward for moving both RECs from competitive goods production to complementary regional tradable goods, there is the need to strengthen policy direction, collectivise regional security efforts, align national agendas with regional goal and objectives and invest in the development of standards and quality infrastructures. Also, there should be collaboration and cross-fertilisation across national, regional and existing RECs in the areas of research, peer learning and capacity development. Proactive involvement and empowerment of players outside government—particularly the private sector and civil society—will also help to advance implementation of integration policies at both national and regional levels. Lastly, regional integration in the context of a process that requires significant time, patience and perseverance to mature. As argued by Momodu (2016: 21), it is a marathon and not a Sprint. Except governments and citizens make painstaking efforts to analysis and reckon with the fact that it requires time, patience and perseverance to mature, the tendency would be to dismiss its importance to the growth and development of member states.

Notes

1 Africo-Liberians encompass Liberia's indigenous aboriginal ethnic groups such as Kpale, Loma, Bassa, Krahn, Gio, Madingo and Mano spread across the borders into neighbouring countries.

2 Americo-Liberians are forbearers of slavery who were repatriated from the Americas and got settled in coastal locations in Liberia between 1821 and 1822 until self-rule was granted them in 1847.

3 The nine founding members are Angola, Botswana, Lesotho, Malawi, Mozambique, Swaziland, Tanzania, Zambia and Zimbabwe.

References

Adedeji, A. (1970). Prospects of Regional Economic Co-Operation in West Africa. *The Journal of Modern African Studies*, Vol. 8 (2), July, pp. 213–231.

Adedeji, A. (2002). History and prospects for Regional Integration in Africa, paper presented at The Third Meeting of the African Development Forum, on the theme of 'Defining Priorities for Regional Integration', Addis Ababa, 5 March.

Adebajo, A. (2014). Two Prophets of Regional Integration: Prebisch and Adedeji. In B. Currie-Alder, R. Kanbur, D. M. Malone & R. Medhora (Eds.), *International Development: Ideas, Experience, and Prospects*. Oxford: Oxford Scholarship Online. Available at: https://idl-bnc.idrc.ca/dspace/bitstream/10625/51561/1/IDL-51561.pdf

Adetula, V.A.O. (2004). Regional Integration in Africa: Prospect for Closer Cooperation between West, East and Southern Africa. A paper presented at the meeting of IDASA/FREDSKORPSET Research Exchange Programme: Governance and Democracy, holding at Parktonian Hotel 120 De Korte Street, Braamfontein, Johannesburg, South Africa, May 2–4.

Adetula, V.A.O., Bereketeab, R. & Jaiyebo, O. (2016). *Regional Economic Communities and Peacebuilding in Africa: The Experiences of ECOWAS and IGAD*. NAI Policy Dialogue No 12. Uppsala: Nordic Africa Institute.

Akpomera, E.I. (1994). *International Organisation and Peacekeeping Operations in Africa: A Comparative Study*. Benin City: M.Sc. dissertation in International Relations submitted to the Department of Political Science and Public Administration, University of Benin.

Aning, K. & Atuobi, S. (2012). The Economic Community of West African States and the Responsibility to Protect. In W. A. Knight & F. Egerton (Eds.), *Routledge Handbook of the Responsibility to Protect* (pp. 216–231). London: Routledge.

Bach, D.C. (1999). The Revival of Regional Integration in Africa. In A.I. Asiwaju & D.C. Bach (Eds.), *Transfrontier Regionalism: The Revival of Regional Integration in Africa* (pp. 43–77). Ibadan: Institutfrançais de recherché enAfrique.

Bach, D.C. (2007). Nigeria's "Manifest Destiny" in West Africa: Dominance without Power. *Afrika Spectrum*, Vol. 42 (2), pp. 301–321. Available at: http://nbn-resolving.de/urn:nbn:de:0168-ssoar-356316

Bach, D.C. (2016a). The Diversity of African Regionalisms. *Great Insight*, July–August, pp. 13–15.

Bach, D.C. (2016b). *Regionalism in Africa: Genealogies, Institutions and Trans-State Networks*. Abingdon: Routledge.

Bossuyt, J. (2016). *The Political Economy of Regional Integration in Africa: The Economic Community of West African States (ECOWAS)*. Nairobi: Embassy of Sweden.

Chinyama, E.J. & Tanoe, D. (2015). Moving Forward on Africa's Regional Integration Agenda: Learning from Best Practices and Efforts. *International Journal of Economics & Management Sciences*, Vol. 5 (2), pp. 1–9.

Deloitte (2017). The ECOWAS Trade Liberalisation Scheme: Myth and Reality. *The Guardian* (Lagos), 10 April, p. 47.

Economic Partnership Agreement between the European Union and Its Member States, of the One Part, and the SADC EPA States, of the Other Part (2016). *Official Journal of the European Union*, L.250. Available at: http://trade.ec.europa.eu/doclib/docs/2015/october/tradoc_153915.pdf

Economic Partnership Agreement between the West African States, The Economic Community of West African States (ECOWAS) and the West African Economic and Monetary Union (UEMOA) of the One Part and the European Union and Its Member States of the Other Part (2003). Available at: http://trade.ec.europa.eu/doclib/docs/2015/october/tradoc_153867.pdf

ECOWAS (2010). *ECOWAS Vision 2020: Towards a Democratic and Prosperous Community*. Abuja: ECOWAS.

ECOWAS (2016a). *Basic Information*. Available at: www.ecowas.int/about-ecowas/basic-information/

ECOWAS (2016b). *Doing Business in ECOWAS: Import and Export*. Available at: www.ecowas.int/doing-business-in-ecowas/import-and-export

ECOWAS (2016c). *Trade*. Available at: www.ecowas.int/ecowas-sectors/trade/

ECOWAS Revised Treaty (1993). Abuja: ECOWAS. Available at: www.ecowas.int/wp-content/uploads/2015/01/Revised-treaty.pdf

ECOWAS (1975). Treaty of the Economic Community of the West African States. Concluded at Lagos on 28 May 1975. Available at: http://www.internationaldemocracywatch.org/attachments/351_ecowas%20treaty%20of%201975.pdf

Essien, A.E. (2013). A Record of Regional Integration in West Africa. *Regional Integration Observer*, Vol. 1 (2), pp. 1–5.

Essuman-Johnson, A. (2009). Regional Conflict Resolution Mechanisms: A Comparative Analysis of Two African Security Complexes. *African Journal of Political Science and International Relations*, Vol. 3 (10), pp. 409–422.

Fajana, O. (2018). *Accelerating the Implementation of the ECOWAS Trade Libralisation Scheme*. A study on trade integration in ECOWAS sponsored by the Ghana Chambers of Commerce and Industry and the Federation of West Africa Chambers of Commerce and Industry (FWACCI) through funding support by the African Trade Policy Centre (ATPC).

Fall, F., Vachon, B. & Winckler, C. (2014). Regional Intergration: Comparism Between SADC and ECOWAS. In Seck, D. (Ed.), *Regional Economic Integration in West Africa: Advances in Africa Economic, Social and Political Development*. Cham: Springer International Publishing.

Fayomi, O. & Adeola, G.L. (2015). ECOWAS and Sub-Regional Integration in West Africa: An Appraisal. *Covenant University Journal of Politics and International Affairs*, Vol. 3 (1), pp. 29–40.

Garuba, D. (2015). *Reflecting on the Cycle of Violence in West Africa*. Available at: www.wathi.org/reflecting-on-the-cycle-of-violence-in-west-africa/

Garuba, D.S. (1996). *Predatory Accumulation and the Internationalisation of Post-Cold War Conflicts in Africa*. Benin City: M.Sc. dissertation in International Relations submitted to the Department of Political Science and Public Administration, University of Benin.

Goodridge, R.B. (2006). The Economic Community of West African States. In *Economic Integration of West African Nations: A Synthesis for Sustainable Development. Taipei City:* International MBA dissertation submitted to National Cheng Chi University.

Gowon, Y. (1984). *The Economic Community of West African States: A Study in Political and Economic Integration*. PhD thesis. Coventry, England: University of Warwick.

Ibeanu, O. (2007). *Beyond Declaration: Law Enforcement Officials and ECOWAS Protocols on Free Movement of Persons and Goods in West Africa*. Lagos: CLEEN Foundation.

Ibeanu, O., Garuba, D. & Ibrahim, J. (2009). Breaking the Vicious Cycle of Resource Violence in West Africa. In O. Ibeanu & J. Ibrahim (Eds.), *Beyond Resource Violence: Civil Society and the Challenges of Peacebuilding* (pp. xiii–xxviii). Abuja: Centre for Democracy and Development.

Institute of Peace and Security Studies (2016). *Brexit: Lessons Learnt for Regional Integration in Africa*. Available at: www.ipss-addis.org/new-ipss/news-events/brexit-_lessons_learnt_for_regional_integration_in_africa/

International Trade Centre (2016). *Facilitating Trade in ECOWAS: Insights from the ITC Business Surveys on Non-Tariff Measures*. Discussion paper for the high-level regional roundtable on NTMs in Abidjan, Côte d'Ivoire, June 14–15.

Ismail, O. (2011). ECOWAS and Human Security. In T. Jaye, D. Garuba & S. Amadi (Eds.), ECOWAS and the Dynamics of Conflict and Peacebuilding (pp. 165–182). Dakar: Council for the Development of Social Science Research in Africa.

Jaye, T., Garuba, D. & Amadi, S. (2011). Introduction. In T. Jaye, D. Garuba & S. Amadi (Eds.), *ECOWAS and the Dynamics of Conflict and Peacebuilding* (pp. 1–7). Senegal: Council for the Development of Social Science in Africa.

Junior, M.G. (2015). *Comparison of Regional Communities in Arica: The Case of SADC*. Praia & Bonn: West Africa Institute & Centre for European Integration Studies.

Karaki, K. & Verhaeghe, E. (2017). *Understanding ECOWAS Trade Policy and Trade Facilitation: Advancing Economic Integration one Hurdle at a Time*. Maastricht, Netherlands: European Centre for Development Policy Management.

Keane, J., Calì, M. & Kennan, J. (2010). *Impediments to Intra-Regional Trade in Sub-Saharan Africa*. London: Oversea Development Institute. Available at: www.odi.org/publications/6146-impediments-intra-regional-trade-sub-saharan-africa

Khadiagala, G.M. (1994). *Allies in Adversity: The Frontline States in Southern African Security 1975–1993*. Athens: Ohio University Press.

Kufour, K.O. (2006). *The Institutional Transformation of the Economic Community of West African States*. Aldershot: Ashgate.

Magbagbeola, N.O. (2016). *Foreign Trade and Investment Promotion in West Africa: The Role of ECOWAS*. A Presentation at the Africa-Ireland Economic Forum, Dublin, Republic of Ireland, June 17.

Mangeni, F. (2014). The Political Economy of Integration in Africa: A Case Study of Issues to be Addressed in the COMESA Customs Union. In Ann Mugunga (Ed.), *Key Issues in Regional Integration Volume III* (pp. 1–32). Lusaka: Common Market of Eastern and Southern Africa.

MapuvaI, J. & Muyengwa-MapuvaII, L. (2014). The SADC Regional Bloc: What Challenges and Prospects for Regional Integration? *Law, Democracy and Development*, Vol. 18, pp. 22–35.

McDonald, S., Lande, S. & Matanda, D. (2013). *Why EPAs Undermine Africa's Economic Integration*. Washington, DC: Wilson Center & Manchester Trade. Available at: www.wilsoncenter.org/sites/default/files/EPA%20Article.pdf

Momodu, R. (2016). New AU-RECs Relationship Needed for Integration. *Great Insight*, July/August, pp. 21–23.

Newswatch [Lagos] (1990). p. 16.

Odaudu, S. (2008). Because of N500 I Was Beaten, Handcuffed. *Leadership (Abuja)*, 6 February. Available at: https://allafrica.com/stories/200802060313.html

Olayiwola, W.K. & Ola-David, O.A. (2013). *Economic integration, Trade Facilitation and Agricultural Exports Performance in ECOWAS Member Countries*. A paper prepared for presentation at the 8th African Economic Conference on *Regional Integration in Africa*, Johannesburg, South Africa, October 28–30. Available at: www.afdb.org/uploads/tx_llafdbpapers/economic_integration_trade_facilitation_and_agricultural_exports_performance_in_ecowas_member_states.pdf

Olonisakin, F. (2011). ECOWAS: From Economic Integration to Peace-Building. In T. Jaye, D. Garuba & S. Amadi (Eds.), *ECOWAS and the Dynamics of Conflict and Peacebuilding* (pp. 11–26). Dakar: Council for the Development of Social Science Research in Africa.

Omede, A.J. (2012). The Economic Community of West African State's Peace Agreements and Accord on Liberia: A Retrospective Analysis. *International Journal of Politics and Good Governance*, Vol. 3 (3), pp. 1–21.

Omeje, K. (2013). The Achievements and Challenges of ECOWAS in Security Regionalism in West Africa. *Regional Integration Observer*, Vol. 1 (2), pp. 8–10.

Osakwe, P. N. (2015). *Transformative Regionalism, Trade and the Challenge of Poverty Reduction in Africa*. Trade and Poverty Paper Series No. 1.UNCTAD/WEB/ALDC/2015/1. New York and Geneva: United Nations Conference on Trade and Development.

Peters, W.-C. (2010). *The Quest for an African Economic Community: Regional Integration in Its Role in Achieving African Unity: The Case of SADC*. Frankfurt: Peter Lang GmbH.

Pomeyie, C. (2016). *Ghana to Sign Interim EPA with EU, Footprint to Africa*, July 26. Available at: http://footprint2africa.com/ghana-sign-interim-epa-eu/

SADC (2008). *SADC: Directorates and Units*. Available at: www.sadc.int/sadc-secretariat/directorates/

SADC (2012). *About SADC: Facts and Figures*. Available at: www.sadc.int/about-sadc/overview/sadc-facts-figures/

Semedo, Gervasio (2013). The Record of Trade Liberalisation in the Framework of West Africa Regional Integration Processes. *Regional Integration Observer*, Vol. 1 (2), pp. 11–13.

Sule, A.D. (1997). *The Role of the Frontline States in the Decolonisation of Southern Africa*. Benin City: M.Sc. dissertation in International Relations submitted to the Department of Political Science and Public Administration, University of Benin.

Tanyanyiwa, Vincent Itai1 & Hakuna, Constance (2014). Opportunities for Regional Integration in Africa: The Case of SADC. *Journal Of Humanities and Social Science*, Volume 19 (12), PP 103–115.

Torres, C. & Seters, J. van (2016). *Overview of Trade and Barriers to Trade in West Africa: Insights in Political Economy Dynamics, with Particular Focus on Agricultural and Food Trade*. (Discussion Paper 195). Maastricht: ECDPM

TRALAC (2018). 38th SADC Summit: Promoting infrastructure development and youth empowerment for sustainable development. Available at: https://www.tralac.org/news/article/13350-38th-sadc-summit-promoting-infrastructure-development-and-youth-empowerment-for-sustainable-development.html

Turner, J.W. (1998). *Continent Ablaze: The Insurgency Wars in Africa, 1960 to the Present*. Johannesburg: Jonathan Ball Publishers.

Ugbajah, L.O. (2016). Status and General Implications of Free Movement of Agro-Produce across West Africa. Presentation at Workshop on Free Movement of Agricultural Commodities across West African Borders organized by National Association of Nigeria Traders (NANTS), Abuja, August 18.

Ukaoha, K. & Ukpe, A. (2013). The ECOWAS Trade Liberalisation Scheme: Genesis, Conditions and Appraisal. *ECOWAS Vanguard*, Vol. 2 (3), pp. 1–10.

United Nations Conference on Trade and Development (2013). *Economic Development in Africa 2013: Intra-African Trade: Unlocking Private Sector Dynamism*. Geneva: United Nations.

United Nations Economic Commission for Africa & Economic Community of West African States (2015). *An Assessment of Progress towards Regional Integration in the Economy Community of West African States since Its Inception*. Addis Ababa & Abuja: UNECA & ECOWAS.

United Nations Economic Commission for Africa-UNECA (2010). *Assessing Regional Integration in Africa IV: Enhancing Intra-African Trade*. Addis Ababa: UNECA.

WestAfrica (London) (1991). 1–7 July, p. 1085.

Woolfrey, S. (2013). *Is Developmental Regionalism a Coherent Paradigm for African Integration?* Available at: www.tralac.org/discussions/article/5328-is-developmental-regionalism-a-coherent-paradigm-for-african-integration.html

Zagaris, B. (1978). The Economic Community of West African States (ECOWAS): An Analysis and Prospects. *Case Western Reserve: Journal of International Law*, Vol. 10 (1), pp. 93–122. Available at: https://scholarlycommons.law.case.edu/jil/vol10/iss1/7

Zhangazha, T. (2017). ECOWAS vs. SADC? Comparison Is Good, Context Still Matters. Available at: http://nehandaradio.com/2017/01/25/ecowas-vs-sadc-comparison-good-context-still-matters/

10 Harnessing south-south cooperation

A BRICS perspective on regional developmentalism

Fantu Cheru

Introduction

The global crisis around the turn of the decade has accelerated changes in the global political economy with the "old" trans-Atlantic North in decline and the "new" global South in expansion, especially Asia (Amsden, 2001). The scope and depth of the 2008 global financial crisis and its aftermath has exposed the weak ideological underpinnings of neo-liberal globalization that bestrode the globe with impunity. The emergence of coterie of middle-income developing countries, especially the so-called BRICS, is a significant development and this could lead to exponential rebalancing global power (Bello, 2014). As the 2004 report by the National Intelligence Council (NIC, 2004) rightly pointed out:

> The likely emergence of China and India, as well as others, as new major global players—similar to the advent of a united Germany in the 19th century and a powerful United States in the early 20th century—will transform the geopolitical landscape, with impacts potentially as dramatic as those in the previous two centuries.

There have been two contesting views on the rise of the BRICS. One is marked by considerable enthusiasm about its potential. The shift from bipolarity to multi polarity is expected to usher in a new set of international alignments, potentially marking a definitive break with some of the post-World War II institutions and practice (NIC, 2008a: 31; Gray and Murphy, 2013).

Multi-polarity also implies more room for individual African countries to manoeuvre as the three economic blocs—North America, Europe and Asia—compete fiercely for access to African energy and other raw material resources to fuel their respective economies. In short, it is assumed that multipolarity will enable African and the developing countries to mix-and-match different economic policy instruments to guide the market without having to worry about disciplinary actions by the institutions of the world system, such as the IMF and the World Bank (Bellow, 2014; Desai, 2013). That the G-7 gave way to the G20 in the wake of the 2008 global financial crisis (incorporating the BRICS countries as well as other emerging economies), is taken as a testimony to the growing influence of the emerging powers in global politics.

Others are more sceptical about the transformative potential of the BRICS. Here, the BRICS countries are viewed not so much as major reformers of the current global neo-liberal order but as new members happily included in a still hierarchal world order because they too will play by the basic rules of neo-liberalism (Bond and Garcia, 2015; Vanaik, 2014; Mittelman, 2016). This was illustrated by the behavior and actions of the BRICS during the height of the 2008 global financial crisis. Despite criticizing the reckless economic policies of the United States and the failure of its regulatory institutions to pre-empt the financial meltdown, the BRICS countries went along with the rest of the G-20 to rescue the major financial institutions who were considered "too big to fail" and to double the resources of the International Monetary Fund (IMF) so that it can prevent further financial meltdown.

The aim of this chapter is threefold: (a) to critically examine the potential contribution of the BRICS countries in reforming the current undemocratic system of global governance system and ensure a seat at the table for developing countries; (b) to assess whether the rise of the BRICS can offer African countries the policy space they need in order to experiment with alternative development models; and (c) to examine the extent to which the BRICS countries, individually or collectively, can strengthen regional development and integration in Southern Africa through the financing of regional infrastructure in order to promote intraregional trade and resource-based industrialization.

The genesis of "BRICS" as an economic and political metaphor

The term *BRIC* was first coined by the investment bank Goldman Sachs in 2001, signifying the rising importance of Brazil, Russia, India and China in the world economy (Wilson and Purushothaman, 2003). The "S" in the BRICS was added after South Africa joined the group in 2011 on the invitation of the founding members.

The main importance of the BRICS lies in the fact that it accounts for more than half of the world GDP growth rates over the past 20 years (see Table 10.1). Although growth in the emerging countries have considerably slowed down over the past two years and the future remain uncertain, as a group, the BRICS have been the best performing economies over the past twenty years, thus contributing to significant growth to the world economy. BRICS may account for 42 percent of the world's population, 18 percent of its GDP, 15 percent of world trade and 40 percent of its currency reserves.

It is projected that the combined economies of the BRICs could eclipse the combined economies of the current richest countries in the world by 2050 (Wilson and Purushothaman, 2003). These countries encompass over twenty-five percent of the world's land coverage, forty percent of the world's

Table 10.1 Comparison of projected real GDP growth of BRICS and the G6, 2000–2049

5-yr	*BRICS*				*G6*					
Ave. in %	*Brazil*	*China*	*India*	*Russia*	*France*	*Germ.*	*Italy*	*Japan*	*UK*	*US*
2000–2004	2.4	8.0	5.2	6.0	2.2	1.1	1.8	1.5	2.4	2.5
2005–2009	4.1	7.4	6.1	4.9	1.9	2.1	1.7	0.9	2.2	2.7
2010–2014	4.1	6.1	6.0	3.8	1.7	1.6	1.6	1.0	2.2	2.2
2015–2019	3.8	5.0	5.7	3.4	1.8	1.2	1.5	1.4	1.9	2.1
2020–2024	3.7	4.7	5.7	3.4	1.7	0.7	1.0	1.4	1.5	2.2
2025–2029	3.8	4.1	5.9	3.6	1.6	0.6	0.6	1.0	1.5	2.5
2030–2034	3.9	3.8	6.1	3.1	1.5	1.3	0.5	0.3	1.8	2.7
2035–2039	3.8	3.9	6.1	2.6	1.8	1.7	0.8	0.4	2.0	2.8
2040–2044	3.6	3.6	5.7	2.2	1.7	1.4	1.3	0.8	1.8	2.6
2045–2049	3.4	3.00	5.3	1.9	1.7	1.3	1.5	1.1	1.6	2.6

Source: Goldman Sachs (2007), "The N-11: More than an Acronym", *Global Economics Paper No. 153, compiled from Appendix II*

population and hold a combined GDP (PPP) of 15.43 trillion dollars. On almost every scale, they would be the largest entity on the global stage. China alone is poised to have more impact on the world over the next 20 years than any other country in the world. China surpasses the US earlier (2027 as opposed to 2035), Japan by 2015, and its GDP will be almost double than that of the US by 2050 (Leme, 2006). India's economy could be larger than all but the US and China in 30 years. Russia would overtake Germany, France, Italy and the UK before 2050. This fact makes it clear that the global governance of the world economy would need to change radically in order to incorporate them (Goldman Sachs, 2001).

In addition to their combined economic weight in the global economy, several public and private companies from the BRICS countries are now positioning themselves as leading companies in critical sectors of the world economy. Of the world's top 500 companies by market capitalization, the list included 31 from the BRIC economies, which is a relatively conservative estimation. China alone would warrant more than 30 company if the list were to reflect its share of world GDP. The BRICs also now dominate in the growth of sovereign investment funds as well as in the value of foreign exchange reserves (Goldman Sachs, 2007).

As a result of their phenomenal growth, the BRICs are expected to boost a sizeable middle class with an average earning of over 15,000 dollars per year by 2025—about 200 million people in total. The BRICs economies taken together could be larger than the G-6 (i.e., US, Germany, UK, Japan, France, and Italy) by 2039. Goldman Sachs predicts China and India to be the dominant global suppliers of manufactured goods and services while Brazil and Russia would become similarly dominant as suppliers of raw materials.

Thus, the BRICs have the potential to translate their economic power into political power to challenge the dominance of the G-7 countries in the governance of the global economy and the multilateral system in general. This could

Table 10.2 BRIC in 2050

Gross Domestic Product 2008			*Gross domestic product 2050*		
Rank	*Country*	*GDP in Millions of USD*	*Rank*	*Country*	*GDP in USD Millions*
1	United States	14,264,600	1	CHINA	70,710,000
2	Japan	4,923,761	2	United States	38,514,000
3	CHINA	4,401,614	3	INDIA	37,668,000
4	Germany	3,667,513	4	BRAZIL	11,366,000
5	France	2,865,737	5	Mexico	9,340,000
6	United Kingdom	2,674,085	6	RUSSIA	8,580,000
7	Italy	2,313,893	7	Indonesia	7,010,000
8	RUSSIA	1,676,586	8	Japan	6,677,000
9	Spain	1,611,767	9	United Kingdom	5,133,000
10	BRAZIL	1,572,839	10	Germany	5,024,000
11	Canada	1,510,957	11	Nigeria	4,640,000
12	INDIA	1,209,686	12	France	4,592,000
13	Mexico	1,088,128	13	South Korea	4,083,000
14	Australia	1,010,699	14	Turkey	3,943,000
15	South Korea	947,010	15	Vietnam	3,607,000
16	Netherlands	868,940	16	Canada	3,149,000
17	Turkey	729,443	17	Philippines	3,010,000
18	Poland	525,735	18	Italy	2,950,000
19	Indonesia	511,765	19	Iran	2,663,000
20	Belgium	506,392	20	Egypt	2,602,000
21	Switzerland	492,595	21	Pakistan	2,085,000

Source: compiled from Goldman Sachs report, "The N-11: More than Acronym", Global Economics Report No. 153, March 28, 2007

lead to a rebalancing o the unbalanced rules in global economic governance, benefitting the less powerful developing countries by offering them 'the policy space' they needed to experiment with alternative development strategies that does not subscribe to the dominant neo-liberal approach.

From Yekaterinburg, Russia to Durban, South Africa: the evolution of the BRICS as an economic and political bloc

As earlier noted, although the term BRIC was first coined by Goldman Sachs in 2001, to signify the economic weight of Brazil, Russia, India and China in the world economy, the four countries did not constitute themselves as a political bloc until the inaugural summit meeting held in Yekaterinburg, Russia on June 16, 2009. South Africa only became a member of the grouping in 2011, having been invited by the founding members in December 2010. Subsequently, the group was renamed as BRICS—with the "S" standing for South Africa--to reflect the group's expanding membership.

The single most important topic that has occupied the attention of the leaders of the BRICS countries since the first BRICS summit in 2009 has been the urgent need to reform the current global economic governance architecture,

Table 10.3 Global position of BRICs companies in 2007 FT Global 500

Global Rank 2007	*company*	*Country*	*Market value in Billions of USD*
6	Gazprom	Russia	245.91
9	Industrial and Commercial Bank of China	China	224.79
23	Bank of China	China	165.51
35	China Construction Bank	China	128.53
41	China Life Insurance	China	116.28
52	Petrobras	Brazil	105.88
53	Sinopec	China	104.01
68	Rosneft	Russia	88.50
74	Vale do Rio Doce	Brazil	88.14
95	Lukoil	Russia	73.49
103	Sberbank of Russia	Russia	70.48
131	Unified Energy System	Russia	58.10
152	Surgutneftegas	Russia	51.33
166	Bank of Communications	China	47.07
182	Reliance Industries	India	43.87
187	Oil & Natural Gas	India	43.21
196	Ping An Insurance	China	41.67
205	Bradesco	Brazil	40.85
208	Banco Itaú	Brazil	39.72
239	M M C Norisk Nickel	Russia	35.36
244	Ambev	Brazil	34.73
257	Bharti Airtel	India	33.29
265	China Merchant Bank	China	32.44
313	National Thermal Power	India	28.41
319	Tata Consultancy Services	India	27.72
331	Banco Brasil	Brazil	26.90
345	Infosys Technologies	India	25.83
469	Reliance Communications	India	19.76
475	Mobile Telesystems	Russia	19.61
487	Itaúsa	Russia	19.30
500	Wipro	India	18.69

Source: Financial Times Magazine 30 June/1 July 2007

particularly the governance of the global financial institutions. To accomplish this goal, the BRICS have relied on two pragmatic approaches: (a) *constructive Engagement* of the existing system; and (b) pragmatic but "*counter-hegemonic*" *response* to the present undemocratic world order. Let me briefly talk about each of these strategies.

1. *Reforming the global governance system*

The BRICS actively sought to change the rule of the current global governance system through constructive engagement of the existing system as members of the G-20, the IMF and the World Bank. The 2008 global financial crisis provided an opportunity for the BRICS to press forward on their combined demands for reforming the global financial architecture. As the G-20 scrambled to replenish IMF resources in order to enable the institution to fight the crisis, the BRICS were the only countries that could contribute substantial amounts towards the IMF crisis response fund.

In June 2012, the BRICS pledged $75 billion for boosting the IMF's $430 billion crisis reserve fund, which would substantially enhance its capacity to support the Euro zone. India, Russia and Brazil all contributed $10 billion each, South Africa contributed $2 billion, and China a massive $43 billion. But this was conditional on IMF quota and governance reform.[1] Subsequently, in 2010, the IMF Executive Board, in its "2010 Governance and Quota Reform" endorsed a decision to provide greater representation and quotas to emerging powers in keeping with their larger presence in the global economy. This decision was seen as a historic step towards strengthening the Fund's legitimacy and effectiveness. The IMF Board also endorsed proposals that called for a more representative, all-elected Executive Board. Unfortunately, the decision was blocked by the US congress and the stalemate is likely to continue even with the election of Donald Trump as America's president in 2016.

The proposed reform would have shifted more than 6 percent of quota shares to emerging market and developing countries while protecting the quota share and voting power of the poorest members. The 6 percent quota re-allocation would have come from the over-represented countries, resulting in a major rebalancing of voting power. As a result of these changes, China's voting share was expected to increase from 2.98 percent in 2008 to 6.07 percent, while India's share would have increased from 1.91 percent to 2.63 percent by 2013. Importantly, the share of the US would have declined to 16.49 percent from 17.6 percent, thus preventing the US from using its veto power to stop any major decisions in the IMF (IMF, 2010).

These reform proposals were expected to be in place by 2012. Unfortunately, the United States Congress has effectively blocked any move towards the reform of the governance structure of the IMF. This American intransigence is unlikely to be broken anytime soon. It is clear that the developed countries are unwilling to dismantle a global governance system that has served them well since World War II. Only when we see a breakthrough in Security Council membership and radical shifts in the voting power at the IMF and the World Bank can we truly say that middle-powers have exerted their influence on global governance.

2. *Strengthen intra-BRICS economic cooperation by establishing new financing institutions*

The second strategy of creating alternative institutions to promote intra-BRICS trade and investment is where the BRICS countries have made the most progress. The Contingent Reserve Arrangement (CRA) is the outcome of BRICS response to the 2008 financial crisis, after which they stood as leading lights of world's economic growth. The creation of a "BRICS Bank" is a direct response to the reluctance of developed countries in reforming IMF and World Bank after 2008.

In March 2013, during the BRICS summit in Durban, South Africa, the members countries agreed to create a global financial institution which they intend to rival the IMF and the World Bank. It took another two years before the BRICS Development Bank became a reality. During the 6th BRICS Summit held in Fortaleza Brazil in July 2014, the heads of states signed the document to create new development bank and a reserve currency pool (VI BRICS Summit, 2014). The new BRICS Financial Architecture is composed of three parts:

a. *The BRICS Development Bank*: The authorized capital of the BRICS Development Bank would be $100 billion. Each country will contribute equally to initial subscribed capital of $50 billion. The membership of the Bank would be open to members of the United Nations, who will be able to subscribe to the share of the Bank. However, BRICS members' share in the total paid up capital of the Bank (also their voting share) cannot be less than 55 percent, thus ensuring that the founding members retain control over the BRICS Development Bank at all times.

Each of the partners will have a stake in the functioning of the Bank. The bank's headquarter is in Shanghai. The Bank's regional centre for Africa is in South Africa. The management of the Bank is shared between India, Brazil and Russia. The first president of the Bank is from India. The first Chair of the Board of Governors and the Board of Directors will be appointed by Russia and Brazil.

The BRICS Development Bank began operation on 21 July 2015. The BRICS Development Bank would provide funding for infrastructure and sustainable projects in BRICS and other emerging economies and developing countries. In 2016, the BRICS Bank approved loans worth $811 million for renewable energy projects: $300 million to Brazil; $81 million to China; $250 million to India; and $180 million to South Africa.

b. *The Contingent Reserve Arrangement*: The CRA is a timely initiative by the BRICS to devise their own 'bank of last resort'. The IMF was the only agency that provided this facility, until ASEAS+3 (ASEAN together with Japan, China and South Korea) formed the *Chiang Mai Initiative Multilateralism in 2010*. The CMIM began with a commitment fund of $120 billion, which was later increased to $240 billion in 2012.

The *Contingent Reserve Arrangement* would have an initial pool of $100 billion, with China contributing $41 billion, and India, Brazil and Russia each contributing $18 billion, and South Africa contribution the remaining $5 billion. As regards to accessing the resources, South Africa can draw twice its contribution, while China can draw one-half of its $41 billion contribution. India, Brazil and Russia can draw an amount equivalent to their share.

c. *The Multilateral Cooperation Agreement on Innovation (MCAI)*: The third less talked about instrument, though hardly a challenge to existing structures of global economic governance, was an agreement on intra-BRICS credit provision in local currencies for promoting intra-BRICS trade. The Multilateral Cooperation Agreement on Innovation (MCAI) is an arrangement, within the BRICS Interbank Cooperation Mechanism, between the development banks (e.g., China's Exim Bank and its counterparts) that was formalized in 2010. The MCAI aims at supporting projects that foster investments in technological innovation, especially in infrastructure and sustainable energy, as well as innovation in industry, financial services and agribusiness. Further, it also seeks to expand cooperation between the development banks in the member countries for increasing trade and services as well as intra-BRICS investments, financial services, cooperation in capital markets, treasury transactions, stock exchange investments and the issuance of local currency bonds according to national laws, thus minimizing transaction costs in intra-BRICS economic activities.

Many leftist analysts prematurely celebrated the establishment of the BRICS Development Bank and the Contingent Reserve Arrangement as a sign of the BRICS commitment to challenge the neo-liberal globalization strategy long dominated by the United States and its western allies (Bellow, 2014; Weisbrot, 2014). What these critics miss out is the fact that the key institutions of the world system—the World Bank and the IMF—were the first to embrace these new financial institutions, and many western countries followed since membership in these institutions is open to the UN and other countries. The BRICS countries expressed their intentions by stating that the aim of the BRICS Development Bank and the CRA is not to compete with, but to complement the operations of the existing multilateral and regional financial institutions, such as the World Bank and the Asian Development Bank.

Giants with a clay feet! How solid are the BRICs?

The BRICS, who had once been the bright spark in the global economy, have now become its big headache. Their ability to project themselves as an emerging and alternative power in global politics is constrained by domestic and external factors. With the exception of India, the other BRICS are experiencing deep economic and political crisis, with South Africa growing at 1 percent in 2015 and China at 6.7 percent, lower than the double digit growth of a few years ago. The problem of the BRICS is not only limited to economics. Corruption, internal weaknesses and political dysfunction have raised the risk level.

(a) The domestic dimensions

Despite the potential of the BRICs to become an important mediating force in the global power structure, each of the member countries exhibits a number of economic and political weaknesses (Nussil, 2016). These domestic economic and political problems could undermine the potential for sustained cooperation between them. Economic growth in these newly emerging economies is accompanied by obscene disparities between rich and poor. South Africa and Brazil, besides being the most unequal societies in the world, are the weak links in the BRICS ensemble.

- **Brazil** faces many obstacles. Brazil is experiencing the worst recession since the 1970s. Compared to the other Asian economies, Brazil is much less open to trade; its investment and savings are lower (savings and investment ratios are around 18–19 percent of GDP compared to an investment rate of 36 percent of GDP in China and an Asian average of around 30 percent); and its public and foreign debt are much higher (currently at 58 percent of GDP on a net basis). Moreover, Brazil is sufficiently corrupt and suffers from poor governance (Wilson and Purushothaman, 2003). A literal coup d'état, organized by the old compradorial elite took place which ousted a seating female president through a corrupt impeachment process.
- **South Africa** is also sufficiently corrupt. Bad governance, particularly during the reign of President Jacob Zuma, has assumed an internalized feature of the African National Congress (ANC), which Cyril Ramaphosa, the current president of South Africa is trying to address. As in Brazil, politics in South Africa seem to be interested mostly in leveraging state power to facilitate criminal accumulation. Bad governance has a huge impact on the performance of the economy.
- **Russia**, according to the National Intelligence report 2025, has the potential to be richer, more powerful and more self-assured in 2025 (NIC, 2008a: 31). On the other hand, multiple constraints could limit Russia's ability to achieve its full economic potential. These include a shrinking population; shortfall in energy investments; infrastructure bottlenecks; decaying public health and education sectors; and underdeveloped banking sector. Since the incorporation of Crimea into Russia by Vladimir Putin, the Russian economy is being battered by sanctions and low oil prices.
- **India**, although it faces lingering deficiencies in its domestic infrastructure, energy production, excessive pollution and skilled labour, will continue to register rapid economic growth. Behind the US, China and India are the biggest emitters of greenhouse gases. The pressure on them will grow to take on serious commitments to reduce carbon emissions in a post-2012 emissions control regime (NIC, 2008b: 93). This is likely to put a brake on their growth targets.
- **China**'s growth trajectories can be hampered by mounting social pressures arising from growing income inequality, a fraying social safety net, poor business regulation, hunger for foreign energy, enduring corruption and environmental devastation (NIC, 2008b: 30). Moreover, the continued trade war with the United States is unlikely to be resolved anytime soon as both sides are prepared to impose counter measures. This will likely affect negatively China's growth trajectory.

It is, therefore, important to point out at the outset that African countries should not expect too much from the BRICS as a significant source of development finance. The national context in each of the BRICS is likely to define individual behavior—whether to pursue policies of *'bilateralism'* or cooperative "*trilateralism*", or conventional "multilateralism" towards the African continent.

There is also a growing scepticism about the legitimacy of the members of the BRICS to represent the interests of non-members in their respective regions. These self-appointed regional leaders are viewed with great suspicion by the other countries in their respective regions (Thakur, 2014). For example, Brazil's self-proclaimed leadership of South America is being contested by oil-rich Venezuela and Chile. In Asia, one cannot ignore the competition between India, China and Japan. In the case of South Africa, many African countries are suspicious of South Africa's motives and it's championing of the New Partnership for African Development (NEPAD) and the African Renaissance to promote its leadership status on the continent. Whether South Africa can leverage its membership in the BRICS to convince Brazil, Russia, China and India to invest more in strategic sectors in the SADC region remains to be seen.

(b) Problem of multiple membership and conflicting loyalties

In addition to weak economic and political fundamentals at the domestic level, there are also other issues that divide the BRICs than what unites them. Each member of the BRICS maintains membership in more than two regional and global political organizations. This could lead to conflicting loyalties and undermine the potential for cooperation between them.

Of the five BRICS, only China and Russia are members of the UN Security Council. Brazil, India and South Africa certainly would like to become members of UNSC, but it is unlikely that they would get the support of China and Russia. While Brazil, India and South Africa are members of the India, Brazil, South Africa (IBSA) Dialogue Forum, these same countries are also members of BRICS. On the security front, Russia and China are members of the Shanghai Cooperation Organization while India, with long border conflict with China, maintains only an observer status. On the other hand, all the

Table 10.4 BRICS: conflicting loyalties

	Permanent-5 of UN Security Council	*IBSA*	*G-8*	*G-20*[2]	*Shanghai Cooperation Organization*[3]	*Subscribe to some aspects of neo-liberal globalization*
Russia	X	—	X	X	X	X
China	X	—		X	X	X
Brazil	—	X		X	—	X
India	—	X		X	*XY	X
South Africa	—	X		X	—	X

*Observer member

BRICS are members of the G-20 grouping. On the question of UN Security Council membership, Russia and China, both permanent members, are unlikely to support India's and South Africa's bid to become members of the Security Council (Alden and Vieira, 2005).

The implications of multiple membership and conflicting loyalties to the ability of the BRICS to present a unified position on reforming the global governance architecture becomes even more doubtful in the face of the desire of each member of the BRICS to maintain stronger bilateral relations with the United States for economic and strategic reasons. For example, India's foreign policy has moved away from the moral rhetoric and strong anti-American stance of merely a decade ago (Ganguly, 2003). The US-India Civilian Nuclear Cooperation and India's increasing role in multilateral forms has positioned India differently than a champion of the Third World of the Nehru era. Both China, India and South Africa also conduct annual reviews covering defence and economic issues with the United States through their respective bi-national strategic partnership commissions. These meetings take place in each other's capital every other year. Therefore, in the pecking order of global politics, Africa stands at the bottom of the BRICS foreign policy priorities.

These stronger relations between the BRICS and the United States are clear indications that these countries, despite their anti-imperialist rhetoric, are committed to the ideology of neo-liberal globalization. They are not against the current multilateral arrangement as long they are consulted in writing the rules of the game (Mittelman, 2013; Bond and Garcia, 2015). They are singularly focused on constructing a paradigm of globalization that is favourable to them. *One must, therefore, guard against romanticizing the emergence of powerful bloc that speaks with one voice representing the interest of African countries and developing countries in general.*

Finally, despite presenting themselves as champions of Third World interests, relations between the BRICS and Africa will be increasingly defined with more explicit regard to national interests, encapsulated within a broader foreign and security policy. Bilateralism is not in itself negative, but as it is currently practiced it serves to reinforce existing fragmentation at the expense of more regional integration efforts in Africa. Three of the five BRICS countries--Brazil, China and India—maintain their own respective bilateral engagement platform with Africa: The *India-Africa Forum*, the *China Africa Forum* (FOCAC) and the *Brazil-Africa Forum*. This preference to bilateralism makes it difficult to coordinate the activities of the BRICS countries around an African-owned and African-driven regional development strategy in Southern Africa (Besada and Kindornay, 2013; Bester, 2012).

What has been the real impact of the BRICS on global development?

Despite much optimism, there are clear indications that BRICS lacks the capacity to function as a powerful and innovative new force of resistance in the realm of global politics and governance. These countries are not uniformly united and have not made a conscious decision to challenge the continued dominance of the G7 countries in global governance. They are highly differentiated group with conflicting interests and allegiances. They are engaged in "plurilateral diplomacy" to maximize their own autonomy vis-à-vis the dominant western powers with whom they have stronger economic, political and strategic relationships which they can ill afford to abandon.

Secondly, despite the rhetoric of solidarity and Third World unity, the BRICS are likely to follow their own paths, and perhaps less likely to rally behind every issue of interest to developing countries as a whole. If we take as an example the case of reforming the global trading system in agriculture, Brazil, India and South Africa are rarely on the same page. All three countries have each gone their separate ways and secured bilateral trade deals and walked away from their multilateralism position in trade negotiations. While Brazil has taken an offensive position in the Doha Development Round on issues of agricultural market access (being a member of the Cairns Agricultural Exporting Countries grouping), India has been less flexible since it is a country constituted of poor subsistence farmers who could easily be wiped out by indiscriminate liberalization of agricultural trade regime. South Africa, on the other hand, is somewhere in between, mostly supporting its big farmers who happen to be white.

In short, the emergence of new middle powers in the world economy does not necessarily produce policy space for African countries. Countries such as India, Brazil, China and South Africa flex their muscle not to make the world a better place for poor countries, but *rather to make themselves independent of the constraining environment of the present order* (Vanaik, 2013). These countries are not against neo-liberal globalization. They respect multilateral rules and arrangements, but want to be fully consulted in their design, negotiation and interpretation. As such, their continued and close involvement with the United States and active participation in the existing multilateral system is aimed at constructing a paradigm of globalization favourable to them. It would, therefore, be naive for African countries to assume that the rise of the BRICS will produce the desired 'policy space' from the constraining environment of the current world order (Mittelman, 2013).

Regional development in Southern Africa: what role for the BRICS?

Regional integration has enormous potential for promoting growth and unleashing the development potential of African countries by lifting the binding constraints to growth, such as access to affordable transportation, and by lowering direct and indirect costs of doing business in order to build competitive and more diversified economies (Ramachandran et al., 2009). To date, however, the level of intra-African trade remains low in comparison with intraregional trade in other regions, both developed and developing. Over the period 2004–2006, for example, intra-African exports represented 8.7 percent of the region's total exports. Intra-African imports, on the other hand, represented 9.6 percent of total imports (UNCTAD, 2009; UNECA, 2010). A 2011 report by UNECA identified economic and institutional challenges as the main impediments to intraregional trade in Africa (UNECA/AU, 2012). These include: poor and inadequate infrastructure; bureaucratic and physical hindrances, such as road charges, transit fees and administrative delays at borders and ports; and the absence of subregional credit, insurance, and banking services to finance production and trade (UNECA, 2011).

Among the problems mentioned earlier, poor and inadequate infrastructure is recognized as one of the major impediments to Africa's structural transformation and long term growth (AfDB, 2006; Brixiova et al., 2011). Although there have been a number of initiatives by African governments and donor institutions to narrow Africa's infrastructure gap, mobilizing the necessary finance has remained the greatest challenge. Many African countries are, therefore, increasingly looking to the emerging countries, such as China, to meet their infrastructure financing needs. The real question is the following: What steps must the members of SADC take to entice the BRICS countries, individually or collectively, to invest more in infrastructure in the subregion in order to promote resource-based cluster development and strengthen regional integration?

Promoting regional integration in Southern Africa through resource-based corridor development

Regional integration can be enhanced through the development of regional value chains in agricultural commodities, minerals, and other natural resource products (UNECA, 2015). The Southern Africa region is a fertile ground for promoting regional value chains in natural resources. The subregion is home to six development corridors: Maputo Development Corridor (MDC); Beira Development Corridor; Durban Development Corridor; North-South Corridor; Maputo-Limpopo Corridor; and the Walvis Bay Corridor. All of them are in different stages of development and operation. Each corridor is anchored by large cities such as Lusaka, Harare, Beira, Durban, Johannesburg and Cape Town, and a hierarchy of several secondary cities in each of the member countries (USAID, 2007; Mtegha et al., 2012). When fully operationalized, they will contribute to the development of a dynamic macro-region with enormous economic weight in Africa.

Reviving the Spatial Development Initiative (SDI) in South Africa and SADC

The potential for city cluster development at national and trans-boundary jurisdictions involving two or more countries are huge, but there are few detailed studies on spatial dimensions of urbanization and industrialization that policy makers can rely on to develop comprehensive strategies to promote

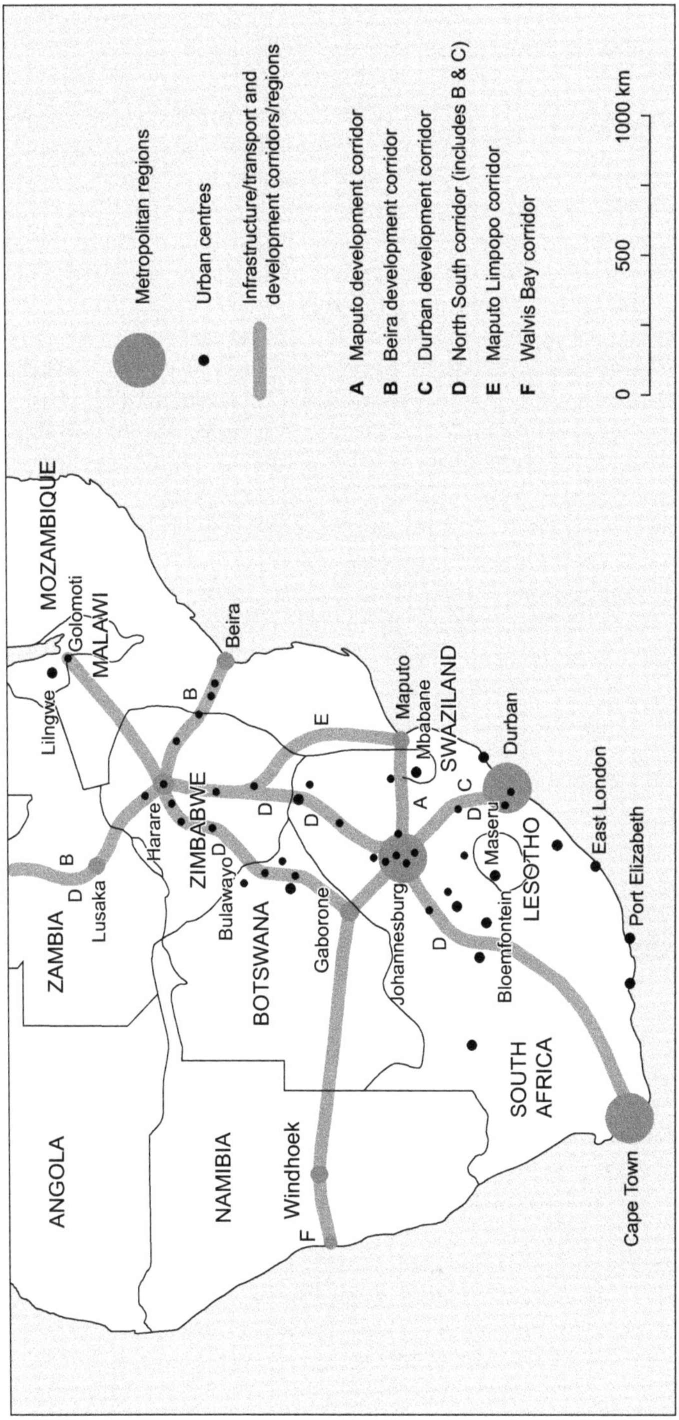

Figure 10.1 Southern Africa development corridors

cluster-based economic development. The one country that has done the most extensive ground-breaking work on spatial dimensions of urbanization and industrialization along the mineral and agricultural value-chains is South Africa.

The Spatial Development Initiative (SDI) is an in-depth review of an example of resource-based industrialization at both the national and interregional levels. It was conceived by the South African government in 1995 (after democratic elections of 1994) as an attempt to improve the functioning of government in targeted regions of the country, particularly in those areas where the greatest potential for resource-based growth existed (Mtegha et al., 2012). The SDI programme was aimed at enhancing the attractiveness for investment through the identification of investment opportunities in resource-based development, providing infrastructure and the removal of a range of policy, legislative and institutional bottlenecks to spur private sector investments (Thomas, 2009). The initiative was later extended to include Botswana, Zimbabwe, Namibia, Malawi, Tanzania, Rwanda, Democratic Republic of the Congo and Angola. The methodology was later expanded to cover the rest of Africa under the New Partnership for Africa's Development (NEPAD), which was termed the NEPAD Spatial Development Programme (SDP).

The SDI methodology is focused on facilitating investment-led growth in a specific geographic location to exploit a particular underutilized resource through the establishment of a network of development corridors and integrated urban regions with the necessary trunk infrastructures (e.g., roads, rail, harbour) for enhanced regional and global connectivity. The approach rests on three pillars: (a) initiating anchor projects (e.g., steel, mining); (b) trunk infrastructure for enhanced connectivity, (c) development of economic potentials in high impact sectors, such as agriculture, forestry, fisheries, and so forth and enhancing resource linkages; and (d) densification of further economic activities by strengthening ancillary and feeder infrastructure to enlarge the corridor's catchments area and beneficiaries downstream, giving contracting possibilities for SMEs and expanding job opportunities to local communities.

Box 10.1 The Maputo Development Corridor (MDC): achievements

The MDC was the first SDI to be implemented at a regional level in Southern Africa. It involved a partnership between the governments of Mozambique and South Africa. The corridor links South Africa's most industrialized regions of Gauteng and Mpumalanga provinces to the Mozambican port of Maputo, and centres on a system of road, rail, border posts, ports and terminal facilities. While the MDC encountered a number of problems on both sides the two countries' borders, by and large, it has been successful on many fronts. It has created a host of industrial and commercial opportunities along the 590 km route from Johannesburg to

Maputo, which is now populated with anchor investments such as steel mills, petrochemical plants, quarries, mines and smelters, sugar cane and forestry plantations. The corridor has facilitated over $5 billion in private sector investments into regional infrastructure development, industrial development and natural resource exploitation and beneficiation within the city-region of Johannesburg and Maputo.

Among the key investments include the N4 Maputo Toll Road; the development of the Pande/Temane gas field in Mozambique; the anchor investment into the Mozal Aluminum Smelter in Maputo Bay; the Beluluane Industrial Park—a 600 hectare free zone industrial park adjacent to the Mozal plant, attracting foreign and local investors into heavy industry and manufacturing. In short, the MDC has acted as an economic catalyst for the provinces within national boundaries through the cross-border flows of South African and other investments, particularly the cities and towns that benefit from the increased interaction.

Source: Bowland & Otto, SAIIA brief, August 2012; Roodt (2008)

To date, however, with the possible exception of the MDC which is judged to be successful on balance, few other cross-border SDIs appear to have made demonstrable progress in Southern Africa (Roodt, 2008; Bowland and Otto, 2012). Among the reasons for failure are: poor political buy-in; lack of capacity in participating countries to effectively develop and manage the process; weak investment climate and poor regulatory environment; and weak domestic private sector incapable of seizing upon opportunities created by foreign investors and participating in investment opportunities.

Simplified resource corridor (SDI) methodology

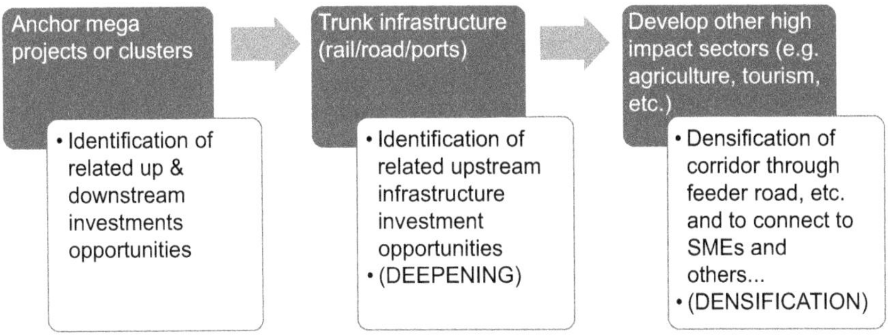

Figure 10.2 SDI methodology

Source: Jourdan (1998)

The "deepening" of resource industries via resource linkages in up-stream and down-stream industrial clusters enhances economic linkages in several ways: (a) fiscal linkages (capturing and efficient deployment of rents for long-term development; (b) knowledge linkages (skills formation, R&D, and enhanced technical capacity; (c) backward linkages (inputs, capital goods, services, etc.); (d) forward linkages (development of intermediate products, manufacturing, logistics and other sectors through beneficiation and value-addition); and (e) spatial linkages (infrastructure and local economic development). In sum, the SDI approach is an objective way to prioritize regional infrastructure projects and anchor investments, stimulate investments into productive capacity, and promote wider development potential through densification strategies and clustering.

This process of geographic consolidation of development initiatives around market-driven business opportunities is referred to as "densification", which means enhancing the development benefits through both backward and forward linkages to improve supply chains, facilitating the ability of SMEs to provide more goods and services locally and linking agricultural or resource development to other investments (Perkins and Robbins, 2011; Jourdan, 1998). Aligning public and private investment around a market-based development plan will amplify the broad benefits for farmers and other entrepreneurs of turning transportation routes into development corridors. Significant investments in roads, railways, processing facilities, warehouses, energy infrastructure and ports would reduce transportation times and costs and stimulate successive rounds of investments, turning the development corridors into engines of regional growth and development.

Securing adequate financing for infrastructure development is only one of challenges among many for corridor-based spatial development initiatives to succeed. There are other a priori conditions, and these include: (a) demonstration of the true economic potential of a given territorial space, such as proven reserve of oil, gas or gold; (b) ability to mobilize private sector participation and demonstration of positive rate of return from such investments; (c) careful and targeted investment on infrastructure to locations where they are likely to have the most advantage, rather than being spread thinly; and (d) get a buy-in from local communities by demonstrating the positive spillover effects of projects to SME's and in terms of job creation.

In summary, the various corridor development initiatives across Southern Africa designed to connect cities and regions within a country and between countries are important building blocks for promoting industrialization and regional economic integration. However, promoting regional integration, involves more than building roads, ports and rail lines. These alone are inadequate to produce agglomeration of economies. But in order to realize these broad objectives, the quality of planning at national, regional and national levels have to be improved significantly; the quality of the labour force has to be improved; and an enabling business environment must exist to attract

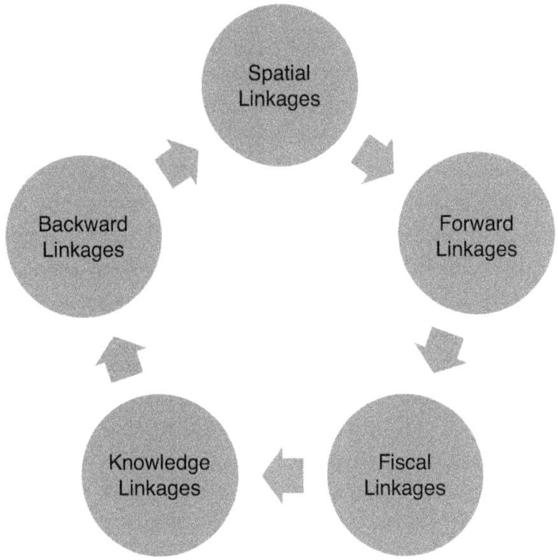

Figure 10.3 Resources-economy linkage potential

Source: Jourdan (1998)

investments (Tiwari, 2002; Roodt, 2008; Thomas, 2009). These enabling conditions are the same ones that are demanded by investors from the BRICS countries before they decide to invest in any African country. SADC member states should never expect any less stringent criteria from the BRICS countries.

Role of external actors in supporting regional development: how different are the BRICS from the traditional donors?

There is a growing debate about the role of external actors in the making and unmaking of regions. They can either become agents of transformation at best or "spoilers" at worst. Given Africa's subordinate role with external partners, it is not always the case that Africa's vision of regional integration might not necessarily be compatible with the interests and visions of the external actors. In recent years, there has been a shift in regionalist visions and ideas in Africa as a result of greater donor influence in the policy-making of African countries. In contrast to "old" and inward-oriented projects of "developmentalist interregionalism" advocated by Raul Prebisch of ECLAC in the 1960s and 1970s, a majority of current African regionalist schemes are liberal and market-oriented as a result of globalization (Söderbaum, 2004). It was in the mid-1980s and the 1990s when "open regionalism" was widely adopted as the theoretical framework that led governments to promote market-led, export-driven regional integration. The boom of "open regionalism" as the defining framework of regional processes clearly coincided with the consolidation of neo-liberal globalization. Both paradigms reinforced each other. From there on, regional schemes were considered building blocks towards establishing a truly global market economy.

A closer integration of the African countries and regions into the global economy is, according to the EU's official rhetoric, seen as the most promising way to increase the continent's trade volume while simultaneously fostering development. Importantly, this strategy is considered to bring about mutual benefits, both for the EU and for the weaker partner regions (European Commission, 2007). As a result, western donor institutions have invested large sums in building the capacities of the main Regional Organizations (ROs) in Africa, especially the African Union (AU) and the regional economic communities (RECs) (Gray, 2011). Other influential donors, such as the World Bank, the US and Germany) give more emphasis to business and civil society actors and so-called "bottom-up" regionalization. A distinctive feature of the wave of new regionalism since the 1990s has been the promotion of Free Trade Agreements (FTAs) and Investment Treaties as key tools to stimulate liberal economic and political reforms.

Most external actors and donor agencies declare that their policies and funding strategies are designed to help African actors build their 'own' regions and regional organizations. However, there is a growing awareness about the fact that donors simply are not neutral financiers and promoters of endogenous or homegrown regional projects. External donors are primarily driven by their own political and economic interests and attempts to enhance external control rather than by strategies to achieve maximum development impact and African ownership (Gray, 2013,2014).

In the case of the BRICS, the approach they take on regional integration is not any different from the model of "open regionalism" practiced by the OECD countries that continue to champion neo-liberal globalization. Given their neo-liberal orientation, the BRICS countries are, therefore, unlikely to support regional integration schemes in Southern Africa that goes against the notion of "open regionalism" and free trade. Moreover, the BRICS will demand the same liberal economic conditions that western governments and corporations consider prerequisites before they can take the decision whether to invest or not in the countries of Southern Africa.

Ownership vs. donorship?

The issues of national and/or regional ownership could also be seen in the light of national vs. regional support. At present African ownership, especially the national ownership, is generally considered limited when it comes to Africa's relations with its external partners (AfDB, 2012; European Commission, 2008; World Bank, 2007; UNDP, 2013). For instance, the evaluation of DFID's Southern Africa Program in 2010 finds that ownership needs to be addressed at both regional and national levels to be effective, and that the cooperation should be based on partnership and mutual accountability (Department for International Development [DFID], 2010). The evaluation of the World Bank's support of multicountry operations comes to a similar conclusion as it recognizes that the WB support to regional partnerships, which often are dominated by donors, have performed less successful than regional projects which have had "a strong country voice" (World Bank, 2007: xvii). As these evaluations point out, ownership is considered closely related to commitment and thus to good performance in the development cooperation.

One should expect the same results with Africa's relations with the new and emerging southern partners. Although the BRICS countries proudly propagate that they do not apply any conditions in their relationship with African partners, they do impose non-policy conditions, such as the purchase of goods and services and in contract negotiations for major construction projects. As the BRICS move into the mainstream of international development cooperation, they have begun to demand the same policy conditions as western private enterprises and creditor institutions since these policy demands are standard practices in the conduct of international trade and investment (Carmody, 2013).

In conclusion, regional cooperation or broader south-south cooperation efforts are meaningless unless they are anchored in strong national plans to promote "autonomous" development. What individual Southern African countries do in regards to FDI, public service provision, agricultural development, social protection, and so forth can help determine to a considerable degree whether these countries develop or not. Although these powers are not always simple or easy to exercise, they have by no means completely disappeared from the national arena. For Southern African countries to gain more from their relationship with the BRICS, they must do their homework right in order to negotiate from a position of strength.

What is to be done to harness the relationship with the BRICS?

The BRICS can be an important source of development finance for the countries of Southern Africa seeking to strengthen regional trade and development. However, before this can happen, the countries of Southern Africa have to put in place the enabling policy conditions that will allow private flows to take place. Money and capital flows where the policy environment is conducive: stable macroeconomic environment; effective government institutions for implementation; respect for property rights; reliability and predictability of the rules of economic engagement; and a commitment by government to arrest corruption.

Although a lot has changed over the past decade, many governments in Southern Africa are far from creating a policy environment conducive to greater intraregional trade and investment. There exist too many unnecessary and bureaucratic barriers to trade within the SADC-COMESA region. Import controls and export licensing, customs hold-ups, restrictive exchange controls, and a complicated system of documentation, customs clearance and visa requirements have been the major impediments to intra-Africa trade, further increasing transaction costs for the private sector. The problem is further compounded by the underdeveloped monetary and banking system, inadequate transport and communication networks, and high transaction costs involved in conducting business because of endemic corruption (Cheru, 1991). Overcoming these policy and institutional problems is a precondition for attracting trade and investment from the BRICS countries, and for building an effective regional economic arrangements.

Moving forward, the following additional measures are needed by the SADC countries:

- *Common regional framework on industrialization*: directing BRICS expansion into areas of national/subregional interest; technology and skills transfers;
- *Regional platform for infrastructure development*: as a basis for mobilizing infrastructure finance from BRICS into co-financing arrangement with the Africa Infrastructure facility and the World Bank;
- *Common regulations on investment*: This might include requirements for local inputs into BRICS ventures; encouraging the creation of backward and forward linkages to existing or newly stimulated local companies;
- *Common framework on trade*: SADC need to pursue regional as opposed to bilateral trade agreements which can lead to a fragmentation of the region and weaken bargaining power.

At the end of the day, whether the BRICS can positively contribute to the development of SADC all depends on African agency and on the capacity of African leaders to negotiate from a stronger and informed platform. The BRICS certainly know what they want from African countries. It is up to SADC member governments to do their homework and strategically engage the BRICS in order to produce a "win-win" development outcome. Failure to do so can only result in what Cheru and Obi (2010) aptly call "colonialism by invitation".

Conclusions

Two perspectives on the BRICS were advanced at the beginning of this chapter: one is marked by considerable optimism about the potential of the BRICS; the other more sceptical about their transformative potential in global and regional development. The conclusions of this chapter concur with the latter view, namely, that the BRICS continue to be too incoherent a bloc to provide effective alternative to the present global order for a number of reasons.

First, there is more that divides the BRICS than what unites them. From multilateral trade reform to climate financing, individual BRICS countries approach each issue from the perspective of national interest and one should not expect them to take unified positions on all issues. Since all of them compete fiercely to have greater access to the African market and other investment opportunities, they are unlikely to create a common pool of resources to finance regional infrastructure that might end up benefiting companies from one BRICS country at the expense of the others (Alden and Vieira, 2005). Instead, each country, with the exception of Russia, will continue to pursue their interests through their respective bilateral engagement platforms, such as FOCAC and IAF. Therefore, a collective BRICS approach to regional development in Southern Africa will be hard to materialize.

Second, South Africa, as a member of the BRICS, is less likely to play a constructive role in the development of Southern Africa. Because of its own sub-imperial ambition in the continent, any support by BRICS to promote infrastructure-based regional development in the subregion will be designed with South Africa's interest as paramount. This will not bode well in a subregion where South Africa's motives are always viewed with great suspicion (Mokoena, 2007).

It is, therefore, reasonable to conclude that the rise of the BRICS in itself does not produce the desired "policy space" for African countries to experiment with alternative regional development strategies unconstrained by the institutions of neo-liberal globalization. The key for African countries in today's world is to try to weave through the parameters set by the world economy and maintain as much independence or "policy space" as possible. While regional integration and south-south cooperation can become important aspects of "strategic integration", they must be complemented with a strong national and continental strategy in order to harness the relationship with the BRICS. Greater continental unity and policy coordination is required to maximize bargaining capacity vis-à-vis these new partners and avoid wars of incentives.

Notes

1 "BRICS Pledges $75 billion to IMF's Bailout Fund", *Business Standard*, 2012. www.business-standard,com/article/international/brics-pledges-75-bn-to-imf-s-bailout-fund-112061900142_html.

2 G-20 was formally established in 1999 and its membership include: Argentina, Australia, BRAZIL, Canada, CHINA, France, Germany, INDIA, Indonesia, Italy, Japan, Mexico, RUSSIA, Saudi Arabia, SOUTH AFRICA, South Korea, Turkey, United Kingdom, United States, European Union. It has no Charter and members are selected randomly, making it an undemocratic institution like the G-8.

3 Shanghai Cooperation Organization is an intergovernmental mutual-security organization founded in 2001. Members: China, Russia, Kazakhstan, Kyrgyzstan, Tajikistan, Uzbekistan

References

AfDB (2006), 'Infrastructure Development and Regional Integration: Getting the Policy Framework Right', concept note paper for the 2006 Annual Meetings, Ouagadougou, Burkina Faso, 16 May.

AfDB (2012), *Fostering Regional Integration in Africa: An Evaluation of the Bank's Multilateral Operations 2000–2010*, Tunis: AfDB.

Alden, Chris and Macro Antonia Vieira (2005), 'The New Diplomacy of the South: South Africa, Brazil, India and Trialeralism', *Third World Quarterly* 26 (7): 1077–1095.

Amsden, Alice H. (2001), *The Rise of 'the Rest': Challenges to the West from the Late-Industrializing Countries*, Oxford: Oxford University Press.

Bellow, Walden (2014), 'The BRICS: Challengers to the Global Status Quo', *Foreign Policy in Focus*, August 29. http://fpif.org/brics-challengers-global-status-quo/.

Besada, Hany and S. Kindornay, eds. (2013), *Multilateral Development Cooperation in a Changing Global Order*, Houndmills, Basingstoke, Hampshire and New York, NY: Palgrave Macmillan.

Bester, Angela (2012), *Results-Based Management in the United Nations Development System: Progress and Challenges*, New York, UN-DESA, for the Quadrennial Comprehensive Policy Review.

Bond, Patrick and Ana Garcia, eds. (2015), *BRICS: An Anti-Capitalist Critique*, London: Pluto Press.

Bowland, Cayley and Lisa Otto (2012), 'Implementing Development Corridors: Lessons from the Maputo Corridor', Policy Briefing 54, SAIIA, Johannesburg.

Brixiova, Z., E. Mutambatsere, C. Ambert and D. Etienne (2011), 'Closing Africa's Infrastructure Gap: Innovative Financing and Risks', *Africa Economic Brief* 1 (2).

Carmody, Padraig (2013), *The Rise of the BRICS in Africa: The Geopolitics of South-South Relations*, London: ZED Books.

Cheru, Fantu (1991), *The Not So Brave New World! Problems and Prospects of Regional Integration in Post-Apartheid Southern Africa*, Bradlow Series, Johannesburg, South African Institute of International Affairs.

Cheru, Fantu and Cyril Obi (2010), *The Rise of China and India in Africa: Challenges, Opportunities and Critical Interventions*, London: ZED Books.

Desai, Radhika (2013), 'The BRICS Are Building a Challenge to Western Economic Supremacy', *The Guardian*, April 2. www.theguardian.com/commentisfree/2013/apr/02/brics-challenge-western-supermacy.

Department for International Development (DFID) (2010), DFID's Southern Africa Country Programme 2004–2009.

European Commission (2007), *Evaluation of the Commission's Support to Southern African Development Community: SADC Regional Level Evaluation*, Brussels: European Commission, p. 3.

European Commission (2008), *Evaluation of the Commission's Support to the region of Eastern and Southern Africa and the Indian Ocean*, Brussels: European Commission.

Ganguly, Sumit (2003), 'India's Foreign Policy Grows Up', *World Policy Journal* 20 (4): 41–47.

Goldman Sachs (2001), 'Building Better Global Economics: BRICs', Global Economic Paper No. 66.

Goldman Sachs (2007), 'Current Answers (and Questions) about BRICS and the N-11', July, Goldman Sachs, New York.

Gray, Julia (2011), 'External Actors and Outside Funding in South-South Regional Trade Agreements', paper presented for the conference on 'The Political Economy of International Organizations.

Gray, Julia (2013), 'Can Foreign Aid Buy Cooperation? External Funding and International Organizational Adaptation', University of Pittsburgh, draft.

Gray, Julia (2014), 'Domestic Capacity and the Implementation Gap in Regional Trade Agreements', *Comparative Political Studies* 47 (1): 55–84.

Gray, Kevin and Craig N. Murphy (2013), 'Rising Powers and the Future of Global Governance', *Third World Quarterly* 34 (2): 183–193.

IMF (2010), *IMF Executive Board Approves Major Overhaul of Quotas and Governance*, Washington, DC: IMF. www.imf.org/external/np/sec/pr/2010/pr10418.htm

Jourdan, Paul (1998), 'Spatial Development Initiative: The Official View', *Development Southern Africa* 15 (5): 717–725.

Leme, Paulo (2006), 'The "B" in BRICS: Unlocking Brazil's Growth Potential', Global Economic Paper No. 150, Goldman Sachs, December 4.

Mittelman, James (2013), 'Global Bricolage: Emerging Market Powers and Polycentric Governance', *Third World Quarterly* 34 (1): 23–37.

Mittelman, James (2016), 'Repositioning in Global Governance: Horizontal and Vertical Shifts amid Pliable Neoliberalism', *Third World Quarterly* 37 (4): 665–681.

Mokoena, Refilwe (2007), 'South-South Cooperation: The Case of IBSA', *South African Journal of International Affairs* 14 (2): 125–145.

Mtegha, Hudson, Paseka Leeuw, S. Naicker and Mapadi Molepo (2012), *Resources Corridors: Experiences, Economics and Engagement: A Typology of Sub-Saharan Africa Corridors*, Johannesburg: University of Witwatersrand, School of Mining and Engineering, Center for Sustainability in Mining Industry.

National Intelligence Council (2004), *Mapping the Global Future*, Report of the National Intelligence Council's 2020 Project, Washington, DC, December.

National Intelligence Council (2008a), *Global Trends 2025: A Transformed World*, Washington, DC: US Government Printer, November, p. 31.

National Intelligence Council (2008b), *Global Trends 2030: Climate Change*, Washington, DC: NIC, p. 93.

Nussil, Suzana (2016), 'The World's Rising Powers are Falling', *Foreign Policy*, July 6.

Perkins, Dave and Glen Robbins (2011). 'The Contribution to Local Enterprise Development of Infrastructure for Commodity Extraction Projects: Tanzania's Central Corridor and Mozambique's Zambezi Valley', Making the Most of Commodities Programme (MMCP), MMCP Discussion Paper No. 9.

Ramachandran, Vijaya, Alan Gelb and Manjur Kedia Shah (2009), *Africa's Private Sector: What's Wrong with the Business Environment and What to Do about It*, Washington, DC: Center for Global Development.

Roodt, Monty (2008), 'The Impact of Regional Integration Infrastructure and Initiatives in Southern Africa Cross-Border Region: The Maputo Development Corridor', *African Sociological Review* 12 (1): 88–102.

Söderbaum, Fredrik (2004), *The Political Economy of Regionalism: The Case of Southern Africa*, Basingstoke: Palgrave Macmillan.

Thakur, Ramesh (2014), 'How Representative Are BRICS?', *Third World Quarterly* 35 (10): 1791–1808.

Thomas, Roslin (2009), *Development Corridors and Spatial Initiatives in Africa*, Johns Hopkins University.

Tiwari, Geetam (2002), *Urban Transport for Growing Cities: High Capacity Bus Systems*, New Delhi: Macmillan India; Roodt, Monty (2008), op.cit.

UNCTAD (2009), *Economic Development in Africa, 2009: Strengthening Regional Integration for Africa's Development*, Geneva: UNCTAD.

UNDP (2013), *Evaluation of the Regional Programme for Africa, 2008–2013*. New York: United Nations Development Programme.

UNECA (2010), *Assessing Regional Integration in Africa IV: Enhancing Intra-Africa Trade*, Addis Ababa: UN Economic Commission for Africa.

UNECA (2011), *Economic Report on Africa 2011: Governing Development in Africa: The Role of the State in Economic Transformation*, Addis Ababa: UN Economic Commission for Africa.

UNECA (2015), *Economic Report on Africa 2015: Industrializing through Trade*, Addis Ababa: Economic Commission for Africa, pp. 101–112.

UNECA/AU (2012), *Status of Integration in Africa: Recent Developments and Initiatives, Difficulties Encountered and Perspectives*. Report prepared for the 4th Joint Annual Meeting of the AU Conference of Ministers of Economy and Finance, and ECA Conference of African Ministers of Finance, Planning and Economic Development (Addis Ababa, 28–29 March 2011), E/ECA/COE/30/10; AU/CAMEF7EXP(VI), 7 February.

USAID (2007), *Maputo Corridor Performance Assessment: A Transport Logistic Diagnostic Tool Study*, Arlington: Nathan Associates Inc.

Vanaik, Achin (2013), 'Capitalist Globalization and the Problem of Stability: Enter the New Quintet and Other Emerging Powers', *Third World Quarterly* 34: 194–213.

Vanaik, Achin (2014), 'Emerging Powers: Rise of the South or a Reconfiguration of Elites?', Shifting Power: Critical Perspectives on Emerging Economies, Transnational Institute.

VI BRICS Summit (2014), 'Six Summit: Fortaleza Declaration and Action Plan', *Ministry of External Affairs of Brazil*, July 15. http://brics6.itamaraty.gov.br/category-english/21-documents/223-six-summit-declaration.

Weisbrot, Mark (2014), 'BRICS' New Financial Institutions Could Undermine US-EU Global Dominance', *Al Jazeera*, July 18.

Wilson, Dominic and Roopa Purushothaman (2003), 'Dreaming with the BRICS: The Path to 2050', Goldman Sachs, Global Economic Paper No. 99, October.

World Bank (2007), *The Development Potential of Regional Programs: An Evaluation of World Bank Support of Multicountry Operations*, p. xvii. Washington, DC: World Bank.

11 Towards sustainable developmental regionalism and peace in Southern Africa

Cyril Obi

Introduction

This chapter examines the challenges of developmental regionalism in Southern Africa. Beyond exploring the conceptual and policy issues facing the region as a "developmental" actor, it explores what developmental regionalism means for conflict prevention, mediation and peacebuilding at the regional level. The basic assumption underpinning the chapter is that developmental regionalism cannot be sustained outside of a fundamental understanding of history, state, politics, economics and society in southern Africa. This is predicated upon a critical perspective to Southern Africa's evolving "hybrid" regionalism both with regard to the nature of intraregional trade and complex transformations taking place within the subregion, and the persistence of vertical economic ties between Africa and the world's economic powers in a rapidly globalizing post-Cold war world (Geda and Seid 2015: 20; Aniche and Ukaegbu 2016: 108–119).

Africa is home to many regional economic communities (RECs), mostly driven by the quest for continental unity and self-sufficiency (Motsamai and Qobo 2012: 145) and the imperatives of accelerated Afro-centric economic growth. While some observers point to the differences in the levels of development between different African RECs, others point to the ways in which some of them overlap, sometimes pursuing contradictory policies. Of particular note, is the observation by Geda and Seid (2015: 22) that "compared to the continent's trade with the outside world, formal intra-Africa trade has remained at a very low level constituting no more that 10 percent of total annual trade of each REC on average in 2013". By contrast they equally note that "over 80% of exports are still destined for markets outside Africa, with the European Union (EU) and the United States of America (USA) accounting for over 50% of this total. The last decade witnessed a shift from these traditional partners to the emerging economies of China, India, and Brazil among others" (cited in Geda and Seid 2015: 22). What this pattern suggests is that while African leaders recognize, and have invested energy into pooling resources and creating RECs, these are yet to lead to the much-expected increased intra-African trade in ways that can benefit human development, peace and security on the continent. It is this observation that partly feeds the impetus to integrate a state-guided developmental ethos into regional integration in Africa. Many scholars and practitioners hope that this will help consolidate the interconnections between African economies and regional actors, and further move the continent towards the socio-economic transformation.

In interrogating the connection between development and regionalism, it is useful to revisit the evolution of regionalism and its links to development over the decades, particularly the shifts in the global discourse from "old/state-led" regionalism of the 1960s and 1970s to its post-1990s form: new/open/market-led, which is more of a neo-liberal response to globalization, and the more recent advocacy for a variant of the old form of regionalism. The emphasis on "new" regionalism appears to focus on the integration of regional into "a liberalized and harmonized single global system of free trade and capital flows, driven by market forces" (Schillinger 2008: 12). This view of "new regionalism" as a strategy of facilitating economic growth and poverty reduction that draws from a largely neo-liberal perspective with its emphasis on liberal democracy and free markets (Doidge 2007) has not gone unchallenged. Some of its critics draw on lessons from the "old" regionalism and comparative perspectives, calling attention to the role(s) that the state, regional economic communities (RECs) and peoples can play in shaping developmental regional integration.

The older version of developmental regionalism referred "to the joint policies of economic cooperation, coordination, and integration among underdeveloped countries designed to accelerate the rate of member states and the geographic region" (Sloan 1971: 142), while the "new" variant is more of a "response to the pressures and incentives associated with economic globalization" (Nesadurai 2003: 237). In this regard,

> deriving from the notion of the developmental state, developmental regionalism encapsulates the developmental state idea of state intervention in markets to promote national development in this case by adopting an approach to regionalism through which to nurture emerging domestic firms to eventually become internationally competitive.
>
> (Nesadurai 2003: 238)

The search for regional pathways to Africa's development is not new and ranges from the regionalist experiments of the pre-independence and post-colonial era, particularly the 1960s and 1970s—the RECS, the 1980 Lagos Plan of Action, and the Abuja Treaty for the African Economic Community—all aimed at African economic self-reliance and development. However, the momentum of the regionalist impetus slowed down momentarily due to the global economic recession and structural adjustment programmes of the 1990s, or was diverted towards addressing intraregional conflicts and challenges to peace and security as pre-conditions for peace, security and development.

However, the "revival" of regionalist discourse and policy advocacy as a strategy of African development gained more traction, partly as a response to globalization and the quest for Afrocentric development in a post-Cold War world. With reference to Africa, specifically southern Africa, there appeared to be a two-track co-existence of both "old" and "new" forms of regionalism. While on the one hand there was a clear move towards greater integration of regional trade and markets, and the consolidation of economic complementarities and comparative advantage as steps towards catalyzing integration of African regions into global markets, there was also a collective state-inspired policy thrust directed towards poverty reduction, domestic industrialization, production and infrastructural development. While we can associate the former with a liberal model or regional integration, the latter reflects more of a developmental and pan-Africanist ethos. Since this chapter focuses more on developmental regionalism, the analysis will focus on the challenges it faces and reflects on how best to address them.

Some of the challenges facing developmental regionalism range from the historical, to the socio-economic and political, including intraregional inequalities, population movements across national borders, and the pre-dominance of vertical transnational and global integration over horizontal and low-levels of intra-African integration (Aniche and Ukaegbu 2016: 109–110). These also include the near-absence of "ripe conditions" for state-guided/market-based, or hybrid developmental regionalism, the less-than-optimal capacity of regional mechanisms and institutions to implement radical steps capable of unleashing the processes and forces of transformation and development in a new globalized context, and consensus-building across the region's developmental states on an agenda of change.

Also relevant are challenges linked to the emergence of new actors, new levels of interaction, competing and conflicting national economic policies/ priorities, inequalities within and between countries, changing domestic demands and priorities, that also affect the momentum that defines the key elements necessary for driving developmental regionalism in the southern African context. These among others may demand new thinking and knowledge, empowering the South African Development Council (SADC) to play a more proactive role in regional transformation, peace and security, addressing disparities between member states, people-to-people integration, exploring ways of empowering regional citizenship to claim collective rights across national borders, and building local productive capacities and economic complementarities across borders. It also includes how RECs such as the SADC can play a pivotal role in renegotiating the terms of regional engagement with the global economic system in ways that promote greater equity in region-global relations, and more benefits for African citizens. Equally important is prioritizing the deepening of the regional development-peace nexus and transforming regional economic integration along creative and productive lines that balance socio-economic growth with redistributive equity and productivity.

In setting about this task, this chapter is divided into five sections. The introduction is followed by a theoretical exploration of developmental regionalism, and its connection with regional peace. In the third section the chapter provides an overview of the main challenges to developmental regionalism in southern Africa. The fourth section seeks to draw the connections between developmental regionalism and sustainable peace in Southern Africa. In the fifth and concluding section, the main arguments are summed up and some recommendations are made for consolidating a people-centered developmental regionalism and peacebuilding in Southern Africa.

Developmental regionalism: a theoretical overview

As noted in the preceding section, the more recent form of regionalism is linked to globalization (Söderbaum and Hettne 2010: 14; Söderbaum 2003: 1–2; Hettne 2015: 543–571). Furthermore, some analysts define regionalization as "the (empirical) process that leads to patterns of cooperation, integration, complementarity and convergence within a particular cross-national geographical space" while providing for some flexibility in "levels of regionness" (Schillinger 2008) in terms of capacity and coherence. This perspective is arguably closer to "old" regionalism.

Schillinger (2008) is of the view that "developmental regionalism encapsulates the idea of state activism and state intervention in markets to promote national development agenda". He associates the "renewed interest in the concept of a developmental regionalism", with the time when the notion of a developmental state "came back to the centre of development-policy debate" (2008: 12). It is important to note however that this approach does not necessarily reject the liberal perspective to regionalism; it only advances the role of a developmental state in it. To cite Schillinger again (2008: 12), "through a more selective and regulatory approach to liberalization, it seeks to harness the potential from intra-regional trade for industrialization and efficiency gains".

Söderbaum and Hettne (2010) on their part refer to developmental regionalism as involving "concerted efforts from a group of countries within a geographical region to enhance the economic complementarity of constituent political units in order to strengthen the total capacity of the regional economy". Ajulu (2008: 32) emphasizes the centrality of the state to the process by arguing that "in the context of developmental regionalism, conditions for success cannot happen on their own, the state has to play a key role". He further asserts that the developmental state "governs the market to achieve certain goals" pointing out that "political intervention is the backbone of the developmental integration model." Without going into the debate on the developmental state and its impact on the vision of developmental regionalism, it stands to reason that it should be seen as a renewed form of regional integration-as-political-project. It is a form of politics that seeks to catalyze collective economic growth through a heterodox approach that gives primacy to a directive role for the state in relation to the market. Such a project will envision the selective integration regions into the emerging global market.

However, in the absence of fully-fledged developmental states, or regional developmental states, it will have to make do with a collective political sense and vision of a common regional economic project that benefits the countries and peoples of a defined geopolitical regional space. As noted elsewhere, this raises questions about the relative size, influence and power of the various actors engaged in the regional project, and how the regional approach can bridge, manage or close the gaps between the wealthier, and less-wealthy members of the region. Also relevant is the persistence of state-centrism, which means that state actors continue to view regionalism through the lens of competing national interests and sovereignties.

The foregoing goes beyond the co-existence of elements of two regionalisms: new/open and developmental, but also touches upon the criteria for examining the ongoing integration project in southern Africa. Is the region facing the challenge of making a choice between one or the other model, or is it more of a case of adopting a process that eclectically combines diverse elements? Is it becoming a "hybrid" of both forms, or is it the more troubling question as to whether the conditions for developmental regionalism have really taken deep roots in the first place? These are questions to be returned to when examining the reality of regional integration in southern Africa since the turn of the 21st century.

Two points are emphasized in relation to the conceptual overview of developmental regionalism in southern Africa. They relate to the co-existence of two models of regionalism—the old and the new, and the primacy given to the role of the developmental state (and governing elites) as a driver of developmental regionalism. The real question therefore lies in reading the trends in Southern Africa, understanding what the emerging hybrid of integration models portend for state-led regional development, implications for peacebuilding in Southern Africa and prospects for the future.

The challenge of developmental regionalism in Southern Africa

The challenge of developmental regionalism arguably presupposes that this approach contains certain elements capable of transforming Southern Africa. In this regard, the chapter's focus will be to address the following questions: Why developmental regionalism now? What is in it for the states and peoples of southern Africa, and by logical extension, Africa? Under what conditions can developmental regionalism be nurtured and sustained?

In addressing these questions, some attention will be paid to two divergent views, those of the optimists that believe that the region is already on track towards realizing the vision of developmental regionalism, and their critics, the not-so-optimistic school of thought that are of the view that developmental regionalism is still more of rhetoric than reality, and that a lot more has to be done if it is to be implemented in the first place, talk less of being nurtured and sustained.

Following the deleterious impact of structural adjustment or market-led economic reform programmes of the 1980s and 1990s, particularly its harsh socio-economic consequences for many African states, more African analysts have sought homegrown alternatives. Of note is the preference for heterodox policies that seek to move away from neo-liberal economic principles or "market fundamentalism" in favour of varying degrees of state guidance or regulation of the market. This alternative discourse also returned the concept of the "developmental state" as a catalyst for economic growth and transformation. In a similar vein, this perspective found expression in state-led developmental regionalism (without completely precluding elements of market-led integration).

In its 2011, Report, the Economic Commission for Africa (ECA), defines a developmental state as those "that have the capacity to deploy its authority credibility and legitimacy in a binding manner to design and implement development policies and programmes for promoting transformation and growth, as well as for expanding human capabilities" (ECA 2011: 7). Applying this definition to Africa, the report asserts that the

> primary goal of the African developmental state is to overcome the continent's inherent development challenges, focusing on high and sustainable economic growth rates through diversification and transformation. The key mechanism is a comprehensive development framework that steers social and economic policies to work in a complementary manner.

If this logic is applied to developmental regionalism, it implies a model of regional integration where states play a key role in designing and implementing policies and programmes to overcome developmental challenges, and transform regional economies for the development of citizens of member states.

However, in spite of its conceptual sophistication and attractiveness, several commentators remain sceptical about whether developmental regionalism is taking place in Southern Africa, or likely to succeed. Reflecting on this point, Schillinger (2008: 13) notes,

> it is still open to debate whether the prerequisites for or ingredients of developmental regionalism (developmental vision, strong and committed leadership, state capacity, meritocracy, the 'ability to mobilize the nation around economic development within the capitalist system', and the willingness to give pool sovereignty among others) exist in southern Africa, or likely to develop any time soon.

The same point is taken up by other scholars, including Ajulu (2008), who cautions that "in the context of developmental regionalism, conditions for success cannot happen on their own, the state has to play a directive role". Still on the same point, Motsamai and Qobo (2014: 354), argue that South Africa, a key factor in the Southern Africa regional integration project, "is far from exhibiting characteristics similar to those that were present in most of the

Asian countries that transformed themselves from economic backwardness to prosperity".

The optimistic perspective

The optimistic school of thought is of the view that African RECs are making progress, albeit in the face of setbacks such as the global economic recession, the inequalities in the international economic system that tend to marginalize the continent and discriminate against the access of its products to global markets, or render them vulnerable to the vagaries of volatile and unfair international pricing.

More often than not, optimists trace the evolution of various pan-African and regional projects of economic integration. In the Southern African case, landmarks such as the Southern African Trade Protocol of 1996, ratified in 2000, the establishment of the Organ on Politics, Defense and Security Cooperation and the Regional Indicative Strategic Plan, the 2011 agreement for the Tripartite Free Trade Area as well as the launching of Vision 2050 complete with plans for a southern African common market, economic and monetary union, have been celebrated as steps in the right direction. In this regard the efforts of member states of the SADC as well as its Secretariat do contain some elements of developmental regionalism.

There is no doubt that some progress has also been achieved at the level of producing a sophisticated regional development framework for southern Africa. It has been noted that, "SADC has seen very substantial growth in regional trade flows since the year 2000 due in part to liberalization and in part to growing incomes in the region alongside urbanization trends" (Arndt and Roberts 2018: 297). However, while observers are keen to point to the immense potential for regional integration as a modality for accelerated development, they also recognize the need for better implementation of collective decisions at the regional level. It should be noted that the optimists are perhaps right on two grounds, that considerable effort is being directed towards developmental regionalism at the level of designing regional mechanisms and norms, and secondly that states have supported the evolution of a framework that is likely to act as an enabling context for advancing the regional project. However, such an optimistic reading has not been without its critics, who are referred to in this chapter as belonging to the not-so-optimistic perspective.

The not-so-optimistic perspective

The not-so-optimistic, school of thought tends to be of the view that in spite of two decades of the SADC Trade Protocol, and the ambitious aspirations contained in the Revised Regional Indicative Strategic Plan (RIDP), including plans for a tripartite COMESA-EAC-SADC FTA, and the Strategic Indicative Plan for the Organ (SIPO), there is little to show in terms of effective implementation of effective steps towards regional integration (Qobo 2007; Mapuva and Muyengwa-Mapuva 2014: 24–25; Soko 2007: 2; Vanheukelom and Bertelsmann-Scott 2016; Nathan 2012, 2013: 201–209). Critics of the Revised RIDP (2015–2020) and SIPO II continue to point to the challenges they face in meeting set targets, the lack of consensus in terms of what to prioritize and how to go about it, and the limitations facing the SADC which contributes to its limited progress towards matching the lofty ambitions of its plans with concrete achievements in the areas of economic integration and peace and security (Kok 2015; Vanheukelom and Bertelsmann-Scott 2016).

Schillinger's (2008: 13) observation, that

> it is still open to debate whether the perquisites for, or ingredients of developmental regionalism (developmental vision, strong and committed leadership, state capacity, meritocracy, the "ability to mobilise the nation around economic development within the capitalist system" and the willingness to give up and pool sovereignty among others exists in Southern Africa, or are likely to develop soon,

remains relevant even today. The non-optimists are of the view southern Africa has not made much progress as its regional institutions and mechanisms are considered to be rather weak, with limited capacity to implement policies and decisions (Bischoff 2012; Ajulu 2008; Soko 2007). They also point to how the regional project is undermined by asymmetrical economic relations with the world's traditional and emerging powers, overlapping memberships of RECs by member states leading to problems of policy coordination and coherence.

Other issues identified as factors working against integration in the region include: low levels of intraregional trade, poor infrastructure, few formal cross-border economic/production complementarities, imbalances between, and uneven levels of economic development among member states, disparities in levels of natural resource endowment and development. The case is sometimes made of how the South African economy which accounts for over 60 percent of intraregional trade and 70 percent or the regions GDP (Mapuva and Muyengwa-Mapuva 2014: 31), dwarfs those of its regional neighbours, and dominates intraregional trade. Some argue that South Africa accounts for 80 percent of Namibia's imports, 90 percent of Botswana's imports, 65 percent of Zambia's imports and about 80 percent of Zimbabwe's imports (Mapuva and Muyengwa-Mapuva 2014; Soko 2007). More recent figures from *Trading Economics* (2018), indicate that the following countries in sub-Saharan Africa accounted for the following share of South Africa's total exports: Botswana—4.7 percent; Namibia—4.4 percent; Mozambique—3.6; and Zambia—2.8 percent. In contrast these countries did not account for any significant exports to South Africa. What the trends suggest is that while regional trade has grown, this has largely been in favour of South Africa and reflects severe intraregional trade imbalances.

It also reflects the earlier view of Mapuva and Muyengwa-Mapuva, that the existence of an economic giant in the region reduces possibilities for tapping into complementarities that are so important to developmental regionalism. Many observers are of the view, that as a pivotal state, South Africa has a key role to play in developmental regionalism in Southern Africa. Although this can be a rather politically sensitive issue, the reality of the country's economic size and trade relations with neighbouring states strongly suggests this is an issue that it has to engage with.

Soko (2007: 2) makes the compelling point that "regional integration in Southern Africa will not succeed unless South Africa, by far the largest and most diversified economy in the region, discharges its responsibilities in accordance with its hegemonic status". It should be noted however, that this position is not entirely oblivious of other considerations including issues such as the possible presence of competing or counter-hegemonic actors, the state of readiness and the politics of the South African state within SACU and SADC. In this regard, Soko identifies three considerations that will influence the conditions under which the South African state can effectively play the role of an anchor for developmental regionalism in Southern Africa. These include 'how South African elites balance the country's regional obligations with domestic pressures, dealing with the legacy of apartheid South Africa's destabilization of the region, and the extent to which the country's leadership is accepted by other regional states'. Given the political challenges confronting South Africa's ruling party, and other factors, including episodes of xenophobic attacks against immigrants from other African countries, it not clear if South African elites are any closer to a consensus on how to balance regional and national interests. This situation poses a particular challenge for people-to-people integration in Southern Africa, which is further compounded by the competing national and regional agendas.

Other issues that come up include the impact of the global economic recession on regional economies, ways in which concerns of national interests and sovereignty slow down or even undermine consensus-building, new emerging transnational threats to regional integration (human trafficking, arms trafficking and illegal migration), and the reality of economic disparities among the 15 member SADC countries which poses a challenge to integration. Also of note, is the critique that has been levelled against the SADC by some observers who note that the organization has not been able to keep up with some of the target dates for the implementation of key plans. Mapuva and Muyengwa-Mapuva (2014: 26), point to certain cases such as the failure to achieve set targets such as the SADC Trade protocol, the establishment of the common market, and regional monetary union. In the same regard, commentators on the peace and security dimension of developmental regionalism are equally critical. Scholars like Van Nieuwkerk and Nathan have argued that southern Africa has not assumed the level of a "security community". Van Nieuwkerk also notes that the building of consensus and capacity needed for tackling challenges to poverty, transnational crimes, illegal migration, governance-related issues and other human insecurities remains potent challenges to developmental regionalism in Southern Africa.

In an earlier study (Maclean 1999: 944), explores the connection between new or "bottom-up" regionalism and peacebuilding in southern Africa, noting among others, that "strengthening capacities of civil societies is a critical step to building sustainable political, economic and social structures" in conflict-affected countries such as Mozambique, South Africa, Angola and the Democratic Republic of the Congo (DRC). It could be argued that while most Southern African countries are in a post-conflict phase, there remains a gap between the agendas of a new regionalism and peacebuilding. Of note in this regard are issues of democratization, human rights, trans-border migration, transitional justice, reconciliation and reconstruction and the re-negotiation of regional "social contract".

The dialectics of developmental regionalism in Southern Africa and the challenge of sustainability

The foregoing clearly illustrates why developmental regionalism has to take centre-stage in southern Africa at this point in time. The simple reason is that experience shows that the way forward lies in a heterodox approach where the states of the region need to reach a consensus on how best to pool their energies and resources to govern and transform the regional development project. What this suggests is that although there is an emerging consensus within the community about what needs to be done, the people and states of the region stand to gain significantly from the benefits that will inevitably flow from removing the hurdles that lie in the path of developmental regionalism. Of note also is the need to think through how to peacefully build upon the developmental politics of states within the regions both within countries and in terms of intraregional cooperation and coordination alongside the corresponding "activist" political will.

In so far as South Africa continues to loom large over the region, there will be challenges linked to its domination of regional trade, and the rapid penetration and expansion of South African capital into neighbouring states. There is also the issue of migration from low-income to more prosperous Southern African states, with South Africa receiving a large number of migrants from neighbouring and other African countries, which in the context of economic contraction has sparked episodes of xenophobic attacks on African foreigners, including citizens of some SADC countries. It has also been noted that "South Africa has experienced greater success in exporting goods to the SADC region than other member states have had in exporting to South Africa. South African still dominates services exports and is by far the largest source of intra-SADC FDI" (Arndt and Roberts 2018: 300). It underlines the point that apart from dominating the regional economy, South Africa occupies a critical place in shaping the agenda of regional integration.

Therefore an agenda of developmental regionalism will have to include the political will to drive deliberate efforts to engineer greater diversity in the economies and markets in the region. It will have to involve the redistribution of economic opportunities in a more equitable way, within and across all SADC member states, develop infrastructure that promote intraregional trade, and bridge existing inequalities, while promoting symbols and activities that uphold common regional values and principles.

Several critical steps need to be taken in relation to new thinking by scholars, civil society activists and policy makers on how to engineer breakthroughs in terms of innovative ideas to reinvigorate local skills and talents necessary for the domestic production of internationally competitive goods and services as one of the important steps towards integrated developmental regionalism. This will both involve research, innovation, capacity building at all levels, continuous dialogue, and sharing information on new findings across the region. It will also be instrumental as states seek buy-in from citizens and various sectors of society as well as economic actors. In a globalized age, SADC member states cannot run away from the reality that ideas drive change. Part of the change will also involve paying more attention to, and shifting resources from norm setting to effective implementation of new regional developmental policies and interventions.

Sustaining developmental regionalism will require fresh ideas/knowledge and the political commitment of effective developmental states, visionary elites and empowered citizens to address the historical and socio-economic and structural factors that fuel crises and instability within member states. Regional and national interests need not compete against each other, rather coherent strategies should be devised for managing them, broaden the concept of sovereignty, recognize, grow and build on complementarities by resolving differences peacefully. These and other issues will benefit from research and knowledge production on areas of critical need accompanied by a political context that feeds innovative thinking and information into the policy design and implementation processes. Also important is the need to renegotiate the place of the region in the global division of labour and renegotiate more favourable terms of trade as well as selective integration into the global market. It should also be noted that developmental regionalism should be driven by democratic developmental states and a mobilized regional citizenry.

Connecting developmental regionalism to developmental regional peace

The notion or the regionalism, peace and security nexus is one that finds resonance in the quest of African countries for collective self-reliance, development, peace and security. The case of regional integration projects such as the Economic Community of West African States (ECOWAS) and the SADC underscore the link between development, peace and security. As Francis (2006: 7) opines,

> the inextricable link between economic regionalism and security integration highlights the fact that it is impossible to achieve economic growth

> and developmental objectives of integration in an environment of wars, armed conflicts and perpetual political instability.

He however goes on to caution against the dominant discourse of the development-security nexus, particularly how this seeks to impose a "liberal peace agenda on the developing world" (Francis 2006: 8). It is therefore important to critically interrogate the inequalities and contradictions embedded in such externally imposed agendas.

Commenting on the linkage between development and security, Maclean (1999: 954–955), notes that in relation to southern Africa, "the new regionalism is inseparable from the new security regime", pointing to "the SADC's new common security organization which includes references to the new security issues of economics, environment and human rights." In this regard, she makes a case for locating peace in the new regionalism-peace nexus.

From this perspective, security regionalism and development though intimately intertwined, should not be taken on face value. While several analysts have conceptually explored the notion of security regionalism or the regionalism-security nexus with regard to Africa (Söderbaum and Tavares 2009: 69–81; Franke 2007: 31–64; Williams 2010: 97–105), and some have explored its importance of its developmental dimension (Francis 2006: 7–20), few if any have explored the structural aspects of its peacebuilding dimension. In this regard, two points need to be seriously considered. These are the ways in which peacebuilding actions strengthen the local, national and regional context of development, and how development provides a socio-economic context for peace and security within a transformational dialectic of regionalism.

The jury is still out on the extent to which regionalism in South Africa has connected to the consolidation of peace and security. While some are of the view that "security and development have been de-linked" (Bischoff 2012: 86–87), others point to certain positive strides in a rather mixed performance record (Dzinesa 2013). Perhaps the most interesting debate over the security and peace performance of the SADC is the one between Laurie Nathan, and Gwinyayi Dzinesa, and Elling Tjønneland, in the *African Security Review* of September 2013, where the latter two scholars challenge what they consider to be the "overly critical book" written by Laurie Nathan on the security performance of the SADC (Nathan 2012).

However, some of Nathan's critique seems to be relevant to a discussion of the possible connections between developmental regionalism, and peace in Southern Africa. Of note, are his observations relating to the three factors underpinning "SADC's poor record of peacemaking and peacebuilding." In his view, these include,

> an absence of common values among member states, which has militated against effective responses to crises and the development of mutual trust and common policies; the reluctance of these states to surrender a degree of sovereignty to multilateral bodies, which is a sine qua non of

regional integration; and the economic and administrative weakness of states, which affects all SADC forums and programmes.

Citing examples of the lack of unity and coherence in terms of regional responses to conflict in the DRC, election-related conflict in Zimbabwe, and Madagascar, Nathan, and other scholars place their fingers on one of the challenges to regional peacebuilding.

Given the region's history of settler colonialism, liberation struggles and the co-existence of democratic and long-running strong man politics, or authoritarian regimes, the issue of forging developmental ethos for regional peace becomes problematic, outside of a paradigmatic shift in the vision of the region's leaders. The observation by Bischoff (2012: 86), remains relevant. In his view, there is a need for a broader, people-cantered approach to security and peace. Furthermore, he observes that in terms of the dominant approach to regional security, "issues of acceptable governance, the fight against poverty and disease, enhancing greater understanding of how with the help of civil society to bring about an inclusive peace, takes second place". While the foregoing critiques may have some merit, the real challenge lies in connecting regional developmental regionalism to developmental regional peacebuilding. One of the important steps is to think through the steps for fully integrating the SADC's peace and security architecture into an ethos of developmental regionalism. This will require much thinking, and dialogue between the various stakeholders in the developmental, social policy, peace and security sectors across all levels of society in SADC member states. A lot of the groundwork for conflict transformation should ideally be rooted in local/grassroots and national structures, before being connected and harmonized at the regional levels. In the final analysis, the regional developmental and peace projects will lie in the hands of "willing stakeholders" guided by the Southern African states, with the organs of the SADC as the implementing agencies.

Conclusion: options and prospects

The challenge of developmental regionalism in Southern Africa is a potent one. However, developmentalism is critical to the transformation of the region, as it will open the door to the harmonization of policies and mechanisms capable of lifting millions of people out of poverty, integrate regional markets, and promote democratic governance, prosperity and peace. The prospects for sustainable developmental regionalism will ultimately depend on the emergence of democratic developmental states in the region. The project of developmentalism is also dependent on the political will of the southern African leadership and governing elites to effectively transform their states along inclusive democratic-developmental lines, address existing gaps and challenges, and collectively pursue the developmental agenda in ways that represent the aspirations of the regions' citizens as the core and object of a developed, democratic and prosperous community.

The SADC will also have to act as a catalyst for harmonizing domestic with regional policies, and should be further capacitated/empowered to fully represent and implement regional policies and decisions. In relation to the ongoing review of the implementation of the Revised RISDP (2015–2020), the persisting challenges in the areas of industrialization, infrastructure, market integration and peace and security, the SADC will need to undertake some rethinking of its strategies, which addressing the persisting dissonance between domestic and regional policies. It may also need to pay greater attention to drawing lessons from other subregions that have achieved greater success in achieving coherence with the African Union's peace and security architecture. The unique position of South Africa in the regional market, particularly in relation to trade imbalances among SADC member states will need to be engaged and strategically renegotiated and restructured to strengthen the foundation for long-term developmental regionalism.

The prospects for developmental regionalism in Southern Africa will be as much an economic as a political and social transformation project. That is if the states in the region become developmental in the sense of (peoples and social sectors) influencing, defining and shaping the equitable and equal development of Southern African countries. If that happens, it will unleash the collective energies and human resources capable of achieving sustainable local, national and globally integrated "regionness". It will have to be a collective project coordinated by an empowered SADC that aligns the domestic political and economic struggles of the people with the developmental aspirations of a new regionalism that is both sustainable and rooted in transformative peace.

References

Ajulu, Rok, "Open versus developmental integration: What options for SADC?," *Revisiting Regionalism in Southern Africa*, Proceedings of the Fourth Southern Africa Forum (SAFT), held in Pretoria, South Africa on 3–4, September 2007, published by the Institute for Global Dialogue and Friedrich Ebert Stiftung, 2008.

Aniche, Ernest Toochi and Victor Emeka Ukaegbu, "Structural dependence, vertical integration and regional economic cooperation in Africa: a study of Southern African Development Community," *African Review*, Vol. 8, Issue 2, 2016.

Arndt, Channing and Simon J. Roberts, "Key issues in regional growth and integration in Southern Africa," *Development Southern Africa*, Vol. 35, No. 3, 2018.

Bischoff, Paul-Henri, "What's been built in twenty years, SADC and Southern Africa's political and regional security culture," *Strategic Review for Southern Africa*, Vol. 34, No. 2, 2012.

Doidge, Mathew, "Joined at the hip: Regionalism and Inter-regionalism," *Journal of European Integration*, Vol. 29, No. 2, 2007.

Dzinesa, Gwinyayi, "A Commentary on Laurie Nathan's Community of Insecurity," *African Security Review*, Vol. 22, No. 3, 2013.

Economic Community of Africa (ECA), *Economic Report on Africa 2011, Governing Development in Africa: The Role of the State in Economic Transformation*, Addis Ababa: ECA, 2011.

Francis, David, "Linking peace, security and development regionalism: Regional economic and security integration in Africa," *Journal of Peacebuilding and Development*, Vol. 2, No. 3, 2006.

Franke, Benedikt, "Competing regionalisms in Africa and the continent's emerging security architecture," *African Studies Quarterly*, Vol. 9, No. 3, 2007.

Geda, Alemayehu and Edris Hussein Seid, "The potential for internal trade and regional integration in Africa," *Journal of African Trade*, Vol. 2, 2015.

Hettne, Bjorn, "Beyond new regionalism," *New Political Economy*, Vol. 10, No. 4, 2015.

Kok, Naomi, 'Post-conflict development: What South Africa can achieve through SADC," *ISS Paper*, Vol. 279, 2015.

Maclean, Sandra, "Peacebuilding and the new regionalism in Southern Africa," *Third World Quarterly*, Vol. 20, No. 5, 1999.

Mapuva, Jephais and Loveness Muyengwa-Mapuva, "The SADC regional bloc: What challenges and prospects for regional integration?" *Law, Democracy and Development*, Vol. 18, 2014.

Motsamai, Dimpho and Mzukisi Qobo, "Regionalism in Africa: Developing crisis and the growing influence of emerging powers," in Lorenzo Fioramonti (ed.), *Regions and Crises: New Challenges for Contemporary Regionalisms*, London: Palgrave-Macmillan, 2012.

Nathan, Laurie, *Community of Insecurity: SADC's Struggle for Peace and Security in Southern Africa*, Farnham: Ashgate, 2012.

Nathan, Laurie, "How should peace and security performance of SADC be evaluated," *African Security Review*, Vol. 22, No. 3, 2013.

Nesadurai, Helen E. S., "Attempting developmental regionalism through Afta: The domestic sources of regional governance," *Third World Quarterly*, Vol. 24, No. 2, 2003.

Schillinger, Hubert, "Introduction," *Revisiting Regionalism in Southern Africa*, Proceedings of the Fourth Southern Africa Forum (SAFT), held in Pretoria, South Africa on 3–4, September 2007, published by the Institute for Global Dialogue and Friedrich Ebert Stiftung, 2008.

Sloan, John, "The strategy of developmental regionalism: Benefits, distribution, obstacles and capabilities," *Journal of Common Market Studies*, Vol. 10, No. 2, 1971.

Söderbaum, Fredrik, "Introduction: Theories of New Regionalism," in Fredrik Söderbaum and Timothy M. Shaw, *Theories of Regionalism*, International Political Economy Series, London: Palgrave Macmillan, 2003.

Soko, Mills, "The political economy of regional integration in Southern Africa," *Notre Europe*, Vol. 23, 2007.

Qobo, Mzukusi, "The challenges of regional integration in Africa: In the context of globalization and the prospects for a United States of Africa," *ISS Paper*, Vol. 145, June 2007.

Qobo, Mzukusi and Dimpho Motsamai, "Developmental state construction and strategic regionalism: The continental reach of South Africa's development finance institutions," *Global Policy*, Vol. 5, September 2014.

Söderbaum, Fredrick and Bjorn Hettne, "Regional security in a global perspective," in Ulf Engel and Joao Gomes Porto (eds.), *Africa's New Peace and Security Architecture: Promoting Norms, Institutionalizing Solutions*, Farnham: Ashgate, 2010.

Söderbaum, Fredrick and Rodrigo Tavares, "Problematizing regional organizations in African security," *African Security*, Vol. 2, No. 2–3, 2009.

Tjønneland, Elling N., "Making sense of the Southern African development community," *African Security Review*, Vol. 22, No. 3, 2013.

Trading Economics, https://tradingeconomics.com/south-africa/exports-by-country (accessed November 11, 2018).

Vanheukelom, Jan and Talitha Bertelsmann-Scott, *The Political Economy of Regional Integration in Africa: The Southern African Development Community (SADC)*, Maastricht: ECDPM, 2016.

Williams, Paul D., "Explaining and understanding security cooperation in Africa," *African Security Review*, Vol. 19, No. 2, 2010.

Index

For Product Safety Concerns and Information please contact our EU representative GPSR@taylorandfrancis.com
Taylor & Francis Verlag GmbH, Kaufingerstraße 24, 80331 München, Germany

www.ingramcontent.com/pod-product-compliance
Ingram Content Group UK Ltd.
Pitfield, Milton Keynes, MK11 3LW, UK
UKHW020148200926
475702UK00016B/2612
* 9 7 8 0 3 6 7 5 1 6 9 8 7 *